*Sources for
Intellectual Foundations
of Modern Education*

Merrill's International Education
Series under the Editorship of Kimball
Wiles, Dean of the College of Educa-
tion, University of Florida.

Sources for
Intellectual Foundations
of Modern Education

Edited by

William E. Drake

University of Texas

CHARLES E. MERRILL BOOKS, INC., Columbus, Ohio

To Arlene—
a dynamic frontier and individualistic spirit

Library of Congress Catalog Card Number: 67-20191

1 2 3 4 5 6 7 8 9 10 / 72 71 70 69 68 67

Printed in the United States of America

Preface

Central to the selected readings in *Sources for Intellectual Foundations of Modern Education* is the idea of integrating the content of the foundations course with the content of the required professional courses in educational psychology, curriculum theory, methods of instruction, and student teaching.

There is increasing pressure across the nation to upgrade the quality of the professional training of teachers. One aspect of that effort lies in the area of the foundations courses. What should be the content of the professional sequence foundation course which is usually required at the senior college level? It is in response to this question that these readings are presented.

While the readings were selected to give added intellectual substance to the basic text, *Intellectual Foundations of Modern Education**, they can be used successfully for other purposes. In either case the emphasis is on those concepts considered fundamental to the development of a coherent and functional professional outlook on the part of the reader. The selections of the first three chapters deal with those concepts held to be basic to any and all present day educational effort; whereas the selections of the other seven chapters treat specialized but equally significant conceptual areas. In the face of the tendency toward more and more specialized subject matter there was never greater need for an imphasis on the inter-disciplinary nature of meaning and value in a free society.

Special acknowledgement is here made to all those students, assistants, and friends who have contributed to the final production of this study. Also, appreciation is extended to those authors and publishers who have granted for the reprinting of their published works.

William E. Drake
University of Texas

---

*William E. Drake (Columbus, Ohio: Charles E. Merrill Books, Inc., 1967).

Building the Habits of a Teacher as a Teacher

Ultimately there are two bases upon which the habits of a teacher as a teacher may be built up. They may be formed under the inspiration and constant criticism of intelligence, applying the best that is available. This is possible only where the would-be teacher has become fairly saturated with his subject-matter, and with his psychological and ethical philosophy of education. Only when such things have become incorporated in mental habit, have become part of the working tendencies of observation, insight, and reflection, will these principles work automatically, unconsciously, and hence promptly and effectively. And this means that practical work should be pursued primarily with reference to its reaction upon the professional pupil in making him a thoughtful and alert student of education, rather than to help him get immediate proficiency. (John Dewey: "The Relation of Theory to Practice in Education," National Society for the Scientific Study of Education, *The Relation of Theory to Practice in the Education of Teachers*, Third Yearbook, Part I (Bloomington, Illinois: Public School Publishing Company, 1904), pages 9-30.

Contents

CHAPTER ONE

MAN AS A SYMBOL CREATING ANIMAL

1.1 EDITORIAL COMMENT

Readings in this chapter were selected to give substance to the concept of man as a symbol creating animal. Each of the contributions has a significance of its own, but in no sense is meant to be a complete treatment.

Rene Dubos in his discussion of "Science and Man's Nature" warns us against the "estrangement of the scientific enterprise from the human condition." As professor at the Rockefeller University he has sought to link the scientific enterprise to humanistic concern, and in doing so has combined both vision and insight in his educational endeavors.

The selection from Charles Darwin's great classic *The Descent of Man* emphasizes the role of language in the development of the human mind as this relationship was visualized during the latter part of the nineteenth century. Here Darwin is reinforcing his basic idea that man is truly a product of an evolutionary process.

Susanne Langer, as an eminent philosopher, tells us why the physical sciences have "overshadowed everything else that human thought produced to rival it," and why there is a need for a new key in the modern philosopher's thought pattern. This new key is to be found in the fact that "our sense-data are primarily symbols" and not of the essence of reality, and that the power of symbolism is our present cue to the next forward step in education, just as the "finality of sense data" was the cue of a former epoch.

Dr. Dobzhansky's article on "Biology, Molecular and Organismic" does much to clarify the issues relating to the present major controversy in the field of biology. The issues raised are of vital significance to the teacher for they lie at the heart of our conception of the nature of man. Why is there a tendency to accept the mechanistic point of view in biology, and if this point of view gains the ascendancy in modern life, what effect will it finally have on the educative process?

1.2   THE SHAPING OF CULTURE*

by Rene Dubos

So general is the belief in the unity of nature, and in the power of the scientific approach, that this method is now applied to most areas of human concern, from the natural sciences to the historical sciences, from the analysis of the human fabric to the appreciation of human arts, naive as it may be to hope that methods developed for the study of inanimate objects can be applied to the much more complex and qualitatively different problems of social human life. But despite their premature character, the attempts to apply the scientific method as used by the natural sciences to problems for which it is not suited are of interest because they reveal a general awareness that we have under cultivation only a small area of the fields which can be exploited by science.

MAN AND HIS FUTURE

A symposium entitled "Man and His Future" was held in London in 1963. Its purpose was to examine the consequences of the fact that "research is creating and promising methods of interference with natural processes which could destroy or could transform every aspect of human life which we value."[4]

The participants in the symposium found it rather easy to discuss the role of science in several current problems, such as: how to feed the billions of hungry people in the world; how to maintain an adequate supply of raw materials and of energy; how to accelerate the process of learning; how to prepare man for space travel. There was a tacit agreement among them that by using the proper scientific approach "almost everything one can imagine possible will in fact be done, if it is thought to be desirable." In contrast, the participants found no basis for common discourse when the discussions turned to the physical, psychological, emotional, cultural, or ethical traits which are desirable for human betterment. Indeed, the sheer diversity of views concerning what constitutes the good life led one of them to conclude that the only possible social policy for science as well as for human institutions was "piecemeal social engineering," that scientists must forego ambitious social plans and dedicate themselves instead to limited goals.

---

*Reprinted from *Daedalus*, 94 (Winter, 1965), pages 223-244, with permission of Dr. Dubos and the American Academy of Arts and Sciences.
[4]G. E. W. Wolstenholme, ed., MAN AND HIS FUTURE, Boston: Little, Brown & Co., 1963.

History shows, however, that human institutions cannot merely drift if they are to survive. Each civilization is characterized by the special kind of problems which it elects to emphasize. Furthermore, all societies operate on certain assumptions, and move toward certain goals. Despite our pathetic attempt at objectivity, we as scientists are in fact highly subjective in the selection of our activities, and we have goals in mind when we plan our work. We make *a priori* decisions concerning the kind of facts worth looking for; we arrange these facts according to certain patterns of thought which we find congenial; and we develop them in such a manner as to promote social purposes which we deem important. The most sweeping assumption in our communities at the present time is that the good life will automatically emerge if we focus our scientific efforts on the production of things and on the manipulation of the body machine, even though a large percentage of scientists probably believe that such an attitude is responsible for incoherence in technological civilization.

One might argue, of course, that incoherence is not objectionable *per se,* that incoherence may even be a symbol of intellectual integrity, and a necessary condition for the evolutionary development of mankind, since no one knows how to formulate either the ultimate truth, or the good life, or even the intermediary goals on the way to these ideals. In practice, however, there are limits to the amount of incoherence that man and his societies can tolerate; the popular success of anti-utopian and antiscientific literature at the present time may indicate that we are approaching the breaking point.

I shall attempt in the following pages to discuss several disturbing aspects of the interplay between man's nature and the environment created by scientific knowledge. First to be considered will be the fact that, while the external environment and the ways of life are being revolutionized by technology, biological man remains fundamentally the same as he was when he emerged from his animal past. Outwardly, man makes adjustments to the new conditions of life; inwardly, however, he has so far failed to make true adaptations to them, and this discrepancy creates physiological and psychological conflicts which threaten to become increasingly traumatic.

Another cause of incoherence in our societies is that modern knowledge, especially scientific knowledge, relates less and less to human experience. In many cases, the technical apparatus of knowledge reaches into aspects of reality which are beyond human grasp. There is a disjunction between scientific knowledge and direct human experience.

Because science and technology are now advancing without the guidance of a well thought out philosophy of natural and social values, they achieve results and produce effects which in many cases no longer correspond to real human needs. Man, through science, has released disruptive forces which he has not yet learned to control. In front of his eyes, these forces are undermining the relationships slowly built through evolutionary processes between nature, the works of reason, and the hidden aspects of man's nature.

H. G. Wells pointed out in A MODERN UTOPIA that ours is an adaptive civilization, incompatible with static social structures. Since we transform the external world through technology, we must also change our societies and ways of life because the maintenance of adaptive fitness is as essential for the survival of institutions as it is for the survival of living things. As presently formulated, however, evolutionary and social concepts give but an inadequate picture of man's relation to his environment. Their inadequacy comes from the fact that human societies and ways of life are rapidly changing while certain fundamental components of man's nature remain essentially unaltered.

Ever since the Neolithic revolution, man has become increasingly proficient in controlling the external world—beasts, forests, floods, climate, and many other natural forces. He has also developed enough knowledge of his own body and behavior to exercise some measure of control over certain obvious aspects of his life. Indeed, his confidence that he can modify and improve not only external nature, but also his own nature, constitutes the rationalistic basis for modern technological civilization. In Western countries, at least, technology has transformed the external world, medicine is learning to manipulate the body and the mind, social institutions are striving to establish universal respect for human dignity. Thus, ways of life are undergoing profound adaptive changes in an attempt to keep *social* man in tune with the rapid changes in the environment which are brought about by technological innovations.

In contrast, many important aspects of man's fundamental nature are not changing at all or change so slowly that they are out of phase with the modern world. Biological evolutionary mechanisms are far too slow to keep pace with social evolution. For example, most functions of the body continue to exhibit diurnal and seasonal cycles, as well perhaps as cycles of other periodicities. Even though the ideal of technology is to create a constant and uniform environment, physiological functions still undergo cyclic changes because they are linked to the cosmic forces under which human evolution took place. When modern life carries the day into the night, maintains the same temperature and food supply throughout the year, and imposes rapid changes of latitude in a jet aircraft, it creates physiological conflicts because man's body machine continues to function according to the cosmic order. Anyone who travels by jet aircraft has a direct perception of the physiological disturbances caused in his body by the change of latitude. The immediate effects of the conflict between the paleolithic constitution of man and the exigencies of modern life can be documented by chemical, physiological and psychological measurements, but little is known of their long range consequences. There is no doubt, however, that many physiological disturbances have their origin in the conflict between the modern environment and the paleolithic ordering of physiological functions.

The so-called fight and flight response constitutes another manifestation of very ancient hidden forces which are still operating in modern man. It consists in a series of physiological and chemical processes which are rapidly mobilized in the body under conditions of threat, and which were certainly useful in the past. When prehistoric man encountered an enemy or a wild beast, a variety of hormonal processes placed his body in readiness either for combat or for running away. Today, the same processes are still set in motion under circumstances which modern man symbolizes as a threat, for example during social conflicts at the office or at a cocktail party. The physiological consequences of the fight and flight response, however, are no longer useful and indeed are probably noxious, since the proprieties of civilized life require the subjugation of the direct, physical response, and thus prevent the expenditure of physical energy.

Many other ancestral mechanisms which persist in modern man must find some outlet, even though they no longer correspond to a necessity of life. Just as a kind of hunting activity remains a need for the house cat even when it is well fed at home, similarly man has retained from his evolutionary past certain needs which no longer have a place in the world he has created, yet which must be satisfied.[5] Ancient civilizations were aware of the profound effects that hidden physiological and psychological forces exert on human behavior and they commonly symbolized these forces by a ferocious bull struggling against reason. In fact, ancient people had developed empirical procedures to let those occult forces manifest themselves under somewhat controlled conditions. As shown by E. R. Dodds in THE GREEKS AND THE IRRATIONAL, the Dionysian celebrations, the Eleusinian mysteries, and many other myths and rituals, served as release mechanisms for fundamental human urges which did not find adequate expression in the rational and classical aspects of Greek life; even Socrates found it wise to participate in the Corybantic

---

[5]An extended discussion of these aspects of human nature which survive from man's paleolithic origins will be found in my book, MAN ADAPTING, New Haven: Yale University Press, 1965.

rites.[6] Many such ancient traditions still persist in the advanced countries of Western culture, even though in a distorted form. In the most modern city, as among the hills of Arcadia three thousand years ago, men and women perceive in springtime that nature is awakening and at work in their bodies, just as it is in the beasts and trees. Carnival is still celebrated when the sap starts running.

Scientific knowledge of the persisting ancestral aspects of man's nature hardly goes beyond a vague awareness of their existence. Limited though it is, this knowledge is nevertheless sufficient to make it clear that medical and social philosophies are based on assumptions which should be re-examined. Some of these assumptions have come to light in their simplest and perhaps crudest forms during discussions of the medical problems posed by the necessity to make man more effective in the technological age, and also to prepare astronauts for life in space capsules.

At the London symposium mentioned above,[7] the participating scientists each had his own formula for modifying man by mechanical prostheses, organ grafting, drug action, or eugenic control. But they hardly concerned themselves with the effects of these alterations on the aspects of man's nature which Dodds grouped under the adjective *irrational*. A similar indifference appears in a recent article by a physician specialized in problems of space medicine. According to him, the sensible solution of these problems is to drastically modify man; the easiest approach being, in his view, to replace certain organs by mechanical parts more efficient for dial reading and better suited to electronic control. Natural, ordinary man could thus be converted into an "optiman"!

Needless to say, the efficiency that biotechnologists aim at fostering in the various forms of "optiman" has little to do with the ancient but still vigorous biological human urges. Commentators in the daily press and in magazines have pointed out in many humorous or scornful articles that some scientists appear to be unaware of these fundamental needs of man's nature. The lay public has pragmatically recognized that man retains from his ancestral past certain needs and drives which, even though scientifically ill-defined, nevertheless cry out for some form of expression.

There are also many tacit assumptions in the belief that the goal of technology, including medicine, should be to provide man with a sheltered environment in which he is protected as completely as possible from traumatic experiences. This assumption is dangerous because of the

---

[6]E. R. DODDS, THE GREEKS AND THE IRRATIONAL, Berkeley: University of California Press, 1951.
[7]Wolstenholme, *op. cit.*

fact that many important traits of man's nature cannot develop normally, or remain in a healthy state, without constant stimulation and challenge.[8] Life at constant temperature through air conditioning, learning made effortless through mechanical aids, avoidance of conflicts through social adjustment, are examples of the means by which modern life eliminates or minimizes physiological or psychological effort, but by the same token causes an atrophy of man's adaptive mechanisms. Thus, while protection from stresses and effort may add to the pleasure or at least comfort of the moment, and while emotional neutrality minimizes social conflicts, the consequences of an excessively sheltered life are certainly unfavorable in the long run. They are even dangerous in that the human jelly fish becomes adjusted to a particular place and time, but loses his ability to readjust as surroundings change.

Scientific Knowledge and Human Experience

In contrast with the arts, science is usually identified with logic and reason. Indeed, a large part of scientific history obviously consists in the progressive unfolding of a logical process; each particular field of science has its own inner logic, which makes one fact derive from another. It is also true, on the other hand, that the growth of science presents many aspects which are essentially independent of logic. At any given period, scientists are profoundly influenced by the assumptions which they accept as a basis for their work, and by the goals which they pursue consciously or more often unconsciously. To a large extent, these assumptions and these goals are those of the social community as a whole.

The most influential assumption of modern science is that the best and indeed the only scientific approach to the study of natural phenomena and of living organisms is to divide them into fragments and to investigate elementary structures and properties in greater and greater detail. While it is repeatedly, and properly, pointed out that this analytical approach has been immensely fruitful in discoveries, there is far too little recognition of the disturbing fact that it has led to the neglect of other fields of science. Although everyone recognizes that the very existence of natural phenomena and of living organisms is the manifestation of the interplay between their constituent parts under the influence of environmental factors, hardly anything is known of the mechanisms through which natural systems function in an integrated manner.

---

[8] Dubos, *op. cit.*

In the course of reductionist analysis, the scientist tends to become so much involved intellectually and emotionally in the elementary fragments of the system, and in the analytical process itself, that he loses interest in the organism or the phenomena which had been his first concern. For example, the student of man who starts from a question singled out because of its relevance to human life is likely to progress seriatim to the organ or function involved, then to the single cell, then to the cellular fragments, then to the molecular groupings or reactions, then to the individual molecules and atoms; and he would happily proceed, if he knew enough, to the elementary particles where matter and energy become indistinguishable. Problems of great interest obviously arise at each step in the disintegration of the original phenomenon. But in practically all cases the phenomenon itself is lost on the way, and the knowledge acquired in the course of its analysis usually throws little light on its determinants and modalities—let alone on the approach to its control. Scientists might find it useful now and then to evaluate their professional activities in the light of Kant's admonition, "To yield to every whim of curiosity, and to allow our passion for inquiry to be restrained by nothing but the limits of our ability, this shows an eagerness of mind not unbecoming to scholarship. But it is wisdom that has the merit of selecting from among the innumerable problems which present themselves, those whose solution is important to mankind."

Loss of interest in phenomena as they occur in Nature is found in practically all fields of science. It would be out of place to discuss here the consequences of this aspect of scientific professionalism for the advancement of knowledge. But it is relevant to the present theme to suggest that therein lies in part the cause of the estrangement of the general public from science. The primary interest of the public is in the phenomena of nature or in the living organisms, whereas the deepest commitment of the professional scientist is to the results of his analytical processes. In consequence, the scientist generally loses his public as he loses sight of the original problem.

Furthermore, whereas science was at first a method to deal with the world of matter and of life as man perceives it through his senses, much of the scientist's knowledge is now acquired through technical and mental processes which operate outside the range of immediate human experience. Etienne Gilson stated in his William James Lectures at Harvard that "Every scientist naturally has the temper and the tastes of a specialist . . . . the natural tendency of science is not towards unity, but towards an ever more complete disintegration." This statement certainly describes a state of affairs which is increasingly prevalent, but it does not, in my opinion, deal with the most important aspect of the problem. A more disturbing aspect of modern science is that the specialist himself commonly loses contact with the aspect of reality which was his primary concern, whether it was matter, life or man.

In his own experience of the physical world, the physicist does not use his specialized knowledge for a richer or more subtle contact with reality; nor is the biologist rendered capable of perceiving the living experience more acutely because he is familiar with intermediate metabolism or x-ray diffraction patterns of contractile fibers. The theoretical physicist apparently finds it difficult to convert the mathematical formulae on which he depends into experiences or thoughts meaningful to his own senses and reason. The general biologist finds no trace of the creativeness of life in the macromolecules he isolates from the cell. The student of consciousness cannot relate the operations of the sense organs or of the nerve impulse to the emotions elicited by a fragrant rose or a romantic sunset.

There has been much talk during recent years of the lack of communication between the humanistic and the scientific aspects of knowledge. In reality, however, this disjunction is not so critical as is often suggested. Each and every one of us can and does learn many facts and concepts pertaining to areas of knowledge totally different from the one in which he is a specialist. The breakdown in communication is complete only when the concepts cannot be related to human experience. The physicist, the biologist, the humanist, and the layman can all find a common ground for discourse if they talk about the matter, life, or man as perceived by the senses, or as apprehended in the form of images, analogies, and responses. But discussions of matter in terms of mathematical symbolism, or of life and man in terms of disintegrated components, cannot be related to any form of direct experience. Specialists must return to the original human basis of their work if they want to converse with mankind.[9]

SCIENCE AND TECHNOLOGY AS INDEPENDENT FORCES

Just as scientific knowledge is becoming alienated from human experience, so are its technological applications becoming increasingly alienated from human needs. Although modern technology appears at

---

[9]Owen Barfield, WORLDS APART, A DIALOGUE OF THE 1960's, London: Faber and Faber, 1963.

first sight but a spectacular extension of what it started out to be in the eighteenth and nineteenth centuries, in reality it is moving toward other goals. This change of focus is contributing to the disjunction between science and mankind.

The natural philosophers and sociologists of the Age of Reason were concerned with a few well-defined problems of obvious importance for the welfare of the human race. Everywhere they saw misery and dis-ease caused by acute shortages of food and of elementary conveniences; they observed that ignorance of the natural forces generates terror, superstitions and often acts of cruelty. The task they set for science was therefore to abolish the threat of scarcity, and to gain enough knowledge to help man face the natural world without fear. These goals were within the range of human experience. By making it possible to reach them, science was truly acting as a servant of mankind.

In contrast, science and the technologies derived from it now often function as forces independent of human goals. In many cases, as we have seen, knowledge creates concepts that man cannot restate in terms of his experience, and increasingly technology creates services and products that man does not really need. All too often, knowledge and technology pursue a course which is not guided by a pre-determined social philosophy. The knowledge of ionizing radiations and of atomic structure was developed by men with the highest ideals who can be regarded as saints of science, yet immense harm has come from their creations. The guilt for this harm cannot be placed on villains with selfish interests or bent on hurting mankind; it results rather from a political and social process which allows science to move blindly in the social arena.

Even though dangers are also inherent in the knowledge concerning automation, synthetic chemicals, or almost any other new technology, surprisingly little is done to evaluate the possible social consequences of these innovations. One dramatic illustration of this negligence is the research budget of the State Department. Science, lavishly endowed by public funds, produced nuclear weapons—the means by which man can now destroy himself. The problem of preventing this catastrophe is primarily the State Department's responsibility. Yet its total budget for policy research studies is negligible. Indeed, there is very little federal support for any kind of scholarly work on the explosive international issues now facing the world. Nor is there much recognition of the fact that the recent advances in medicine have created vast new problems which are essentially social, political, and economic rather than scientific. As E. M. Forster predicted in *The Machine Stops*, technology moves on, but not on our lines; it proceeds, but not to our goals. It is urgent that science and technology be given goals of significance and value to man lest the sorcerer's apprentice be converted from a literary symbol into a terrifying reality.

The Industrial Revolution, with mass production of energy and its rapid injection into all aspects of social life, is everywhere beginning to disrupt the great dynamic processes which have so far maintained the earth in a state compatible with human life. Disruption of the water cycle is speeding water on its way to the sea and increasing its destructive action on land surfaces; denudation of the soil is creating dust bowls all over the earth; pollution of the air and of water is beginning to upset the biological balance and to damage human health. The medical sciences themselves are becoming so effective that they can affect unfavorably the fate of immense numbers of people and of their descendants, often creating new pathological processes as they control old diseases. Their greatest impact, probably, will be not so much on the size of the world population as on its genetic qualities, and on its other qualitative characteristics.

Needless to say, there is nothing fundamentally new in the fact that technology alters the relationship between man and nature. For many thousand years, man has modified his environment by using fire, farming the land, building houses, opening roads, and even controlling his reproduction. The all important difference, however, is that many modern applications of science have nothing to do with human biological needs and aim only at creating new demands, even though these be inimical to health, to happiness, or to the aspirations of mankind. Technology allowed to develop for its own sake often acts as a disruptive force which upsets the precarious relationships upon which civilizations have been built in the past. It creates new environmental conditions to which man finds it difficult to adapt, and which destroy some of the most valuable human attributes.

A process of adaptation is, of course, going on continuously between man and the new world he is creating. As we have seen, however, some important traits which are built into the fabric of man's nature are not likely to be eliminated, or significantly modified, despite all the changes which occur in his societies and ways of life. Even when man becomes an automated and urbane city dweller, his physiological processes remain geared to the daily rotation of the earth around its axis and to its annual rotation around the sun; the paleolithic bull which survives in his inner self still paws the earth whenever a threatening gesture is made on the social scene. The tragic paradox is that science fosters ways of life and manners of response which are often determined by technological expediency, whereas it hardly concerns itself with the fundamental characteristics and needs of man's nature.

While most human beings believe that the proper study of mankind is man, the scientific establishment has not tooled itself for this task. The great scientific institutions are geared for the analytical description of the body machine, which they approach in much the same spirit as they do simple inanimate objects. They pay little heed to the scientific study of man as a functioning entity, exhibiting all the complex responses that living entails. Nor do they pay much attention to the environmental factors which condition the manifestations of human life.

The disjunction between man's nature and the creations of science and technology inevitably manifests itself in social disturbances. In principle, these disturbances are not beyond the scope of scientific study; in practice, however, they have a low order of priority in the world of learning. The study of man as an integrated unit, and of the ecosystems in which he functions, is grossly neglected because it is not in the tradition which has dominated experimental science since the seventeenth century. Such a study would demand an intellectual approach, as well as research techniques and facilities, different from those which are fashionable and professionally profitable in the academic establishment.

Two historical reasons account for the tendency of scientists to neglect the problems posed by the complex situations found in the real world. One is that the simpler problems are more likely to yield clear results and rapid professional advance. The other reason is that until recently the applications of science were direct and on the whole beneficial. Only during the past few decades has science become such a powerful force that any technological intervention affects simultaneously many aspects of human life.

Land conservation, water resources, urban development, the physiological and mental qualities of the human race are but a few among the immense problems created by the impact of scientific technology. It is therefore a moral obligation for the scientific establishment to devote itself in earnest to the study of ecosystems, both those of nature and those created by man. But ecosystems cannot be studied by the use of the oversimplified models which constitute the stock in trade of orthodox experimental science.

The urgency to escape from shackles of the scientific past is particularly apparent when attention turns to man himself. One of the strangest assumptions of present day biology is that knowledge of living man will automatically follow from so-called "fundamental" studies of the elementary structures and reactions of fragments derived from living things.

In reality, a very different kind of knowledge is needed to understand the nature of the cohesive forces which maintain man in an integrated state, physically, psychologically, and socially, and enable him to relate successfully to his environment. Hardly anything is known of man's adaptive potentialities, of the manner in which he responds to the stimuli which impinge on him early in his development and throughout his life, of the long range consequences of these responses not only for himself but for his descendants. There are countless problems ranging from those posed by the earlier sexual maturity of children to those involved in urban planning, which should and could be studied scientifically, yet have hardly any place in the curriculum of universities or research institutes.

SCIENCE FOR MAN

Incoherence implies the breakdown of integrative relationships. One remedial measure is, of course, to establish better understanding and communication within the scientific community itself and between it and the public. But there is no knowledge of how this can be done effectively. At most, it is known that a few scientific books of distinction have been widely read, or at least have had a wide influence and are often quoted. A study of the reason for their success might provide some insight into the determinants of the public response to science, and indirectly into the aspects of science which have human values.

There are good reasons to believe that conceptual views of the world, even if purely theoretical, can have as much general appeal as utilitarian applications, and it is obvious of course that the appeal is even greater when the facts have some relevance to the problems which have always preoccupied mankind, whether these be concerned with the place of man in the cosmos or with his survival and welfare. But in any case, scientific communication demands more than the description of facts or the reporting of news. In science, just as in any other field, man can communicate with man only through the channels of shared experiences, or still better, through mutual hopes.

Because of its emphasis on oversimplified models, the scientific community is betraying the very spirit of its vocation—namely, its professed concern with reality. Nature exists only in the form of complex ecosystems, and these constitute the environment which man perceives, and to which he responds. As human life becomes more dependent on technology, it will become more vulnerable to the slightest miscarriage or unforeseen consequence of innovations, hence the need for studies directed to the problems of interrelationships within complex ecosystems. Science will remain an effective method for the acquisition of knowledge meaningful to man, and consequently for social service only if its orthodox techniques can be supplemented by others which come closer to the human experience of reality, and to a kind of social action designed for fundamental human needs.

The study of natural and man-made ecosystems, as well as of man's responses to environmental forces, has as much intellectual dignity and deserves as much academic support as the study of isolated particles and elementary reactions. Only through a scientific knowledge of man's nature and of the ecosystems in which he functions can technology be usefully and safely woven into the fabric of society. Indeed, a truly human concept of technology might well constitute the force which will make science once more part of the universal human discourse, because technology at its highest level must integrate knowledge of the external world and of man's nature.

Since each particular field of science has its inner logic of growth, the scientific enterprise can long continue to move on its own momentum even though it becomes increasingly indifferent to man. Lacking worthwhile social goals, however, science may soon find itself floundering in a sea of irrelevancies. Eventually, it might even be rejected by ordinary men if they were to decide that its values are irrelevant and dangerous. "It seems to me entirely possible," stated recently a Sigma Xi lecturer, "that our society, which, for whatever motives, has invested not only immense sums of money but large amounts of spiritual faith in what it uninformedly conceives science to be, may become as thoroughly disillusioned and rebellious toward scientific and technological authoritarianism as early societies became rebellious towards regal authoritarianism."

Despite its spectacular successes, science is not yet firmly established in the human mind. Its increasing alienation from the problems which are of deepest concern for mankind might well transform the antiutopian outbursts so characteristic of our time from a literary exercise into an antiscience crusade. In its mildest form, such a crusade will at least continue to clamor for a moratorium on science, under the pretext that knowledge is accumulating faster than it can be digested and therefore is becoming dangerous. In reality, of course, there cannot be any retreat from science. Rather, public apprehension and hostility point to the need for an enlargement of science. Scientists must take more to heart the questions which deeply concern human beings; they must learn to give greater prominence to large human values when formulating their problems and their results. Fortunately, this is probably easier than is commonly believed because, as emphasized earlier, history shows that the broad implications of science can become integrated in the intellectual fabric of modern societies. Human cultures, like organisms and societies, depend for survival on their internal integration, an integration which can be achieved only to the extent that science remains meaningful to the living experience of man.

*Since writing this article I have realized that it may be confusing to use the same word *evolution* for biological, cosmic, cultural and social processes. When the word *evolution* is used by a biologist, it implies well-defined mechanisms—in particular mutation and selection. Needless to say changes of a cosmic, cultural or social order do not occur through such mechanisms, nor do they exhibit the same degree of irreversibility as biological evolution.

¹⁰Hutchinson, *op. cit.*

1.3   MENTAL POWERS

by Charles Darwin

LANGUAGE

This faculty has justly been considered as one of the chief distinctions between man and the lower animals. But man, as a highly competent judge, Archbishop Whately remarks, "is not the only animal that can "make use of language to express what is passing in his mind, and can "understand, more or less, what is so expressed by another."[47] In Paraguay the *Cebus azaræ* when excited utters at least six distinct sounds, which excite in other monkeys similar emotions.[48] The movements of the features and gestures of monkeys are understood by us, and they partly understand ours, as Rengger and others declare. It is a more remarkable fact that the dog, since being domesticated, has learnt to bark[49] in at least four or five distinct tones. Although barking is a new art, no doubt the wild parent-species of the dog expressed their feelings by cries of various kinds. With the domesticated dog we have the bark of eagerness, as in the chase; that of anger, as well as growling; the yelp or howl of despair, as when shut up; the baying at night; the bark of joy, as when starting on a walk with his master; and the very distinct one of demand or supplication, as when wishing for a door or window to be opened. According to Houzeau, who paid particular attention to the subject, the domestic fowl utters at least a dozen significant sounds.[50]

The habitual use of articulate language is, however, peculiar to man; but he uses, in common with the lower animals, inarticulate cries to express his meaning, aided by gestures and the movements of the muscles of the face.[51] This especially holds good with the more simple and vivid feelings, which are but little connected with our higher intelligence. Our cries of pain, fear, surprise, anger, together with their appropriate actions, and the murmur of a mother to her beloved child, are more expressive than any words. That which distinguishes man from the lower animals is not the understanding of articulate sounds, for, as every one

---

*Reprinted from *The Descent of Man* (New York: D. Appleton and Company, 1876), pages 84-96.
[47]Quoted in 'Anthropological Review' 1864, p. 158.
[48]Rengger, ibid. s. 45.
[49]See my 'Variation of Animals and Plants under Domestication,' vol. i. p. 27.
[50]'Facultés Mentales des Animaux,' tom. ii. 1872, p. 346–349.
[51]See a discussion on this subject in Mr. E. B. Tylor's very interesting work, 'Researches into the Early History of Mankind.' 1865, chaps. ii. to iv.

knows, dogs understand many words and sentences. In this respect they are at the same stage of development as infants, between the ages of ten and twelve months, who understand many words and short sentences, but cannot yet utter a single word. It is not the mere articulation which is our distinguishing character, for parrots and other birds possess this power. Nor is it the mere capacity of connecting definite sounds with definite ideas; for it is certain that some parrots, which have been taught to speak, connect unerringly words with things, and persons with events.[52] The lower animals differ from man solely in his almost infinitely larger power of associating together the most diversified sounds and ideas; and this obviously depends on the high development of his mental powers.

As Horne Took, one of the founders of the noble science of philology, observes, language is an art, like brewing or baking; but writing would have been a better simile. It certainly is not a true instinct, for every language has to be learnt. It differs, however, widely from all ordinary arts, for man has an instinctive tendency to speak, as we see in the babble of our young children; whilst no child has an instinctive tendency to brew, bake, or write. Moreover, no philologist now supposes that any language has been deliberately invented; it has been slowly and unconsciously developed by many steps.[53] The sounds uttered by birds offer in several respects the nearest analogy to language, for all the members of the same species utter the same instinctive cries expressive of their emotions; and all the kinds which sing, exert their power instinctively; but the actual song, and even the call notes, are learnt from their parents or foster-parents. These sounds, as Daines Barrington[54] has proved, "are "no more innate than language is in man." The first attempts to sing

---

[52]I have received several detailed accounts of this effect. Admiral Sir J. Sulivan, whom I know to be a careful observer, assures me that an African parrot, long kept in his father's house, invariably called certain persons of the household, as well as visitors, by their names. He said "good morning" to every one at breakfast, and "good night" to each as they left the room at night, and never reversed these salutations. To Sir J. Sulivan's father, he used to add to the "good morning" a short sentence, which was never once repeated after his father's death. He scolded violently a strange dog which came into the room through the open window; and he scolded another parrot (saying "you naughty polly") which had got out of its cage, and was eating apples on the kitchen table. See also, to the same effect, Houzeau on parrots, 'Facultés Mentales,' tom. ii. p. 309. Dr. A. Moschkau informs me that he knew a starling which never made a mistake in saying in German "good morning" to persons arriving, and "good-bye, old fellow," to those departing. I could add several other such cases.

[53]See some good remarks on this head by Prof. Whitney, in his 'Oriental and Linguistic Studies,' 1873, p. 354. He observes that the desire of communication between man is the living force, which, in the development of language, "works "both consciously and unconsciously; consciously as regards the immediate end "to be attained; unconsciously as regards the further consequences of the act."

[54]Hon. Daines Barrington in 'Philosoph. Transactions,' 1773, p. 262. See also Dureau de la Malle, in 'Ann. des. Sc. Nat.' 3rd series, Zoolog. tom. x. p. 119.

"may be compared to the imperfect endeavour in a child to babble." The young males continue practising, or as the bird-catchers say, "record-"ing," for ten or eleven months. Their first essays show hardly a rudiment of the future song; but as they grow older we can perceive what they are aiming at; and at last they are said "to sing their song round." Nestlings which have learnt the song of a distinct species, as with the canary-birds educated in the Tyrol, teach and transmit their new song to their off-spring. The slight natural differences of song in the same species inhabiting different districts may be appositely compared, as Barrington remarks, "to provincial dialects;" and the songs of allied, though distinct species may be compared with the languages of distinct races of man. I have given the foregoing details to shew that an instinctive tendency to acquire an art is not peculiar to man.

With respect to the origin of articulate language, after having read on the one side the highly interesting works of Mr. Hensleigh Wedgwood, the Rev. F. Farrar, and Prof. Schleicher,[55] and the celebrated lectures of Prof. Max Müller on the other side, I cannot doubt that language owes its origin to the imitation and modification of various natural sounds, the voices of other animals, and man's own instinctive cries, aided by signs and gestures. When we treat of sexual selection we shall see that primeval man, or rather some early progenitor of man, probably first used his voice in producing true musical cadences, that is in singing, as do some of the gibbon-apes at the present day; and we may conclude from a widely-spread analogy, that this power would have been especially exerted during the courtship of the sexes,—would have expressed various emotions, such as love, jealousy, triumph,—and would have served as a challenge to rivals. It is, therefore, probable that the imitation of musical cries by articulate sounds may have given rise to words expressive of various complex emotions. The strong tendency in our nearest allies, the monkeys, in microcephalous idiots,[56] and in the barbarous races of mankind, to imitate whatever they hear deserves notice, as bearing on the subject of imitation. Since monkeys certainly understand much that is said to them by man, and when wild, utter signal-cries of danger to their fellows;[57] and since fowls give distinct warnings for danger on the ground, or in the sky from hawks (both, as well as a third cry, intel-

---

[55]'On the Origin of Language,' by H. Wedgwood, 1866. 'Chapters on Language,' by the Rev. F. W. Farrar, 1865. These works are most interesting. See also 'De la Phys. et de l'arole,' par Albert Lemoine, 1865, p. 190. The work on this subject, by the late Prof. Aug. Schleicher, has been translated by Dr. Bikkers into English, under the title of 'Darwinism tested by the Science of Language,' 1869.

[56]Vogt, 'Mémoire sur les Microcéphales,' 1867, p. 169. With respect to savages, I have given some facts in my 'Journal of Researches,' &c., 1845, p. 206.

[57]See clear evidence on this head in the two works so often quoted, by Brehm and Rengger.

ligible to dogs),[58] may not some unusually wise ape-like animal have imitated the growl of a beast of prey, and thus told his fellow-monkeys the nature of the expected danger? This would have been a first step in the formation of a language.

As the voice was used more and more, the vocal organs would have been strengthened and perfected through the principle of the inherited effects of use; and this would have reacted on the power of speech. But the relation between the continued use of language and the development of the brain, has no doubt been far more important. The mental powers in some early progenitor of man must have been more highly developed than in any existing ape, before even the most imperfect form of speech could have come into use; but we may confidently believe that the continued use and advancement of this power would have reacted on the mind itself, by enabling and encouraging it to carry on long trains of thought. A complex train of thought can no more be carried on without the aid of words, whether spoken or silent, than a long calculation without the use of figures or algebra. It appears, also, that even an ordinary train of thought almost requires, or is greatly facilitated by some form of language, for the dumb, deaf, and blind girl, Laura Bridgman, was observed to use her fingers whilst dreaming.[59] Nevertheless, a long succession of vivid and connected ideas may pass through the mind without the aid of any form of language, as we may infer from the movements of dogs during their dreams. We have, also, seen that animals are able to reason to a certain extent, manifestly without the aid of language. The intimate connection between the brain, as it is now developed in us, and the faculty of speech, is well shewn by those curious cases of brain-disease in which speech is specially affected, as when the power to remember substantives is lost, whilst other words can be correctly used, or where substantives of a certain class, or all except the initial letters of substantives and proper names are forgotten.[60] There is no more improbability in the continued use of the mental and vocal organs leading to inherited changes in their structure and functions, than in the case of handwriting, which depends partly on the form of the hand and partly on the disposition of the mind; and hand-writing is certainly inherited.[61]

---

[58]Houzeau gives a very curious account of his observations on this subject in his 'Facultés Mentales des Animaux,' tom. ii., p. 348.

[59]See remarks on this head by Dr. Maudsley, 'The Physiology and Pathology of Mind,' 2nd edit. 1868, p. 199.

[60]Many curious cases have been recorded. See, for instance, Dr. Bateman 'On Aphasia,' 1870, p. 27, 31, 53, 100, &c. Also, 'Inquiries Concerning the Intellectual Powers,' by Dr. Abercrombie, 1838, p. 150.

[61]'The Variation of Animals and Plants under Domestication,' vol. ii. p. 6.

Several writers, more especially Prof. Max Müller,[62] have lately insisted that the use of language implies the power of forming general concepts; and that as no animals are supposed to possess this power, an impossible barrier is formed between them and man.[63] With respect to animals, I have already endeavoured to show that they have this power, at least in a rude and incipient degree. As far as concerns infants of from ten to eleven months old, and deaf-mutes, it seems to me incredible, that they should be able to connect certain sounds with certain general ideas as quickly as they do, unless such ideas were already formed in their minds. The same remark may be extended to the more intelligent animals; as Mr. Leslie Stephen observes,[64] "A dog frames a general "concept of cats or sheep, and knows the corresponding words as well "as a philosopher. And the capacity to understand is as good a proof of "vocal intelligence, though in an inferior degree, as the capacity to "speak."

Why the organs now used for speech should have been originally perfected for this purpose, rather than any other organs, it is not difficult to see. Ants have considerable powers of intercommunication by means of their antennæ, as shewn by Huber, who devotes a whole chapter to their language. We might have used our fingers as efficient instruments, for a person with practice can report to a deaf man every word of a speech rapidly delivered at a public meeting; but the loss of our hands, whilst thus employed, would have been a serious inconvenience. As all the higher mammals possess vocal organs, constructed on the same general plan as ours, and used as a means of communication, it was obviously probable that these same organs would be still further developed if the power of communication had to be improved; and this has been effected

---

[62]Lectures on 'Mr. Darwin's Philosophy of Language,' 1873.
[63]The judgment of a distinguished philologist, such as Prof. Whitney, will have far more weight on this point than anything that I can say. He remarks ('Oriental and Linguistic Studies,' 1873, p. 297), in speaking of Bleek's views: "Because on "the grand scale language is the necessary auxiliary of thought, indispensable to "the development of the power of thinking, to the distinctness and variety and "complexity of cognitions to the full mastery of consciousness; therefore he "would fain make thought absolutely impossible without speech, identifying the "faculty with its instrument. He might just as reasonably assert that the human "hand cannot act without a tool. With such a doctrine to start from, he cannot "stop short of Müller's worst paradoxes, that an infant (*in fans*, not speaking) is "not a human being, and that deaf-mutes do not become possessed of reason "until they learn to twist their fingers into imitation of spoken words." Max Müller gives in italics ('Lectures on Mr. Darwin's Philosophy of Language,' 1873, third lecture) the following aphorism: "There is no thought without words, as "little as there are words without thought." What a strange definition must here be given to the word thought!
[64]'Essays on Free-thinking,' &c., 1873, p. 82.

by the aid of adjoining and well adapted parts, namely the tongue and lips.[65] The fact of the higher apes not using their vocal organs for speech, no doubt depends on their intelligence not having been sufficiently advanced. The possession by them of organs, which with long-continued practice might have been used for speech, although not thus used, is paralleled by the case of many birds which possess organs fitted for singing, though they never sing. Thus, the nightingale and crow have vocal organs similarly constructed, these being used by the former for diversified song, and by the latter only for croaking.[66] If it be asked why apes have not had their intellects developed to the same degree as that of man, general causes only can be assigned in answer, and it is unreasonable to expect anything more definite, considering our ignorance with respect to the successive stages of development through which each creature has passed.

The formation of different languages and of distinct species, and the proofs that both have been developed through a gradual process, are curiously parallel.[67] But we can trace the formation of many words further back than that of species, for we can perceive how they actually arose from the imitation of various sounds. We find in distinct languages striking homologies due to community of descent, and analogies due to a similar process of formation. The manner in which certain letters or sounds change when others change is very like correlated growth. We have in both cases the reduplication of parts, the effects of long-continued use, and so forth. The frequent presence of rudiments, both in languages and in species, is still more remarkable. The letter *m* in the word *am*, means *I;* so that in the expression *I am*, a superfluous and useless rudiment has been retained. In the spelling also of words, letters often remain as the rudiments of ancient forms of pronunciation. Languages, like organic beings, can be classed in groups under groups; and they can be classed either naturally according to descent, or artificially by other characters. Dominant languages and dialects spread widely, and lead to the gradual extinction of other tongues. A language, like a spe-

---

[65]See some good remarks to this effect by Dr. Maudsley, 'The Physiology and Pathology of Mind,' 1868, p. 199.

[66]Macgillivray, 'Hist. of British Birds,' vol. ii. 1839, p. 29. An excellent observer, Mr. Blackwall, remarks that the magpie learns to pronounce single words, and even short sentences, more readily than almost any other British bird; yet, as he adds, after long and closely investigating its habits, he has never known it, in a state of nature, display any unusual capacity for imitation. 'Researches in Zoology,' 1834, p. 158.

[67]See the very interesting parallelism between the development of species and languages, given by Sir C. Lyell in 'The Geolog. Evidences of the Antiquity of Man,' 1863, chap. xxiii.

cies, when once extinct, never, as Sir C. Lyell remarks, reappears. The same language never has two birth-places. Distinct languages may be crossed or blended together.[68] We see variability in every tongue, and new words are continually cropping up; but as there is a limit to the powers of the memory, single words, like whole languages, gradually become extinct. As Max Müller[69] has well remarked:—"A struggle for "life is constantly going on amongst the words and grammatical forms "in each language. The better, the shorter, the easier forms are constantly "gaining the upper hand, and they owe their success to their own inherent "virtue." To these more important causes of the survival of certain words, mere novelty and fashion may be added; for there is in the mind of man a strong love for slight changes in all things. The survival or preservation of certain favoured words in the struggle for existence is natural selection.

The perfectly regular and wonderfully complex construction of the languages of many barbarous nations has often been advanced as a proof, either of the divine origin of these languages, or of the high art and former civilisation of their founders. Thus F. von Schlegel writes: "In those "languages which appear to be at the lowest grade of intellectual culture, "we frequently observe a very high and elaborate degree of art in their "grammatical structure. This is especially the case with the Basque and "the Lapponian, and many of the American languages."[70] But it is assuredly an error to speak of any language as an art, in the sense of its having been elaborately and methodically formed. Philologists now admit that conjugations, declensions, &c., originally existed as distinct words, since joined together; and as such words express the most obvious relations between objects and persons, it is not surprising that they should have been used by the men of most races during the earliest ages. With respect to perfection, the following illustration will best shew how easily we may err; a Crinoid sometimes consists of no less than 150,000 pieces of shell,[71] all arranged with perfect symmetry in radiating lines; but a naturalist does not consider an animal of this kind as more perfect than a bilateral one with comparatively few parts, and with none of these parts alike, excepting on the opposite sides of the body. He justly considers the differentiation and specialisation of organs as the test of perfection. So with languages; the most symmetrical and complex ought not to be ranked above irregular, abbreviated, and bastardised languages,

---

[68]See remarks to this effect by the Rev. F. W. Farrar, in an interesting article, entitled 'Philology and Darwinism' in 'Nature,' March 24th, 1870, p. 528.
[69]'Nature,' Jan. 6th, 1870, p. 257.
[70]Quoted by C. S. Wake, 'Chapters on Man,' 1868, p. 101.
[71]Buckland, 'Bridgewater Treatise,' p. 411.

which have borrowed expressive words and useful forms of construction from various conquering, conquered, or immigrant races.

From these few and imperfect remarks I conclude that the extremely complex and regular construction of many barbarous languages, is no proof that they owe their origin to a special act of creation.[72] Nor, as we have seen, does the faculty of articulate speech in itself offer any insuperable objection to the belief that man has been developed from some lower form.

SENSE OF BEAUTY

This sense has been declared to be peculiar to man. I refer here only to the pleasure given by certain colours, forms, and sounds, and which may fairly be called a sense of the beautiful; with cultivated men such sensations are, however, intimately associated with complex ideas and trains of thought. When we behold a male bird elaborately displaying his graceful plumes or splendid colours before the female, whilst other birds, not thus decorated, make no such display, it is impossible to doubt that she admires the beauty of her male partner. As women everywhere deck themselves with these plumes, the beauty of such ornaments cannot be disputed. As we shall see later, the nests of humming-birds, and the playing passages of bower-birds are tastefully ornamented with gaily-coloured objects; and this shews that they must receive some kind of pleasure from the sight of such things. With the great majority of animals, however, the taste for the beautiful is confined, as far as we can judge, to the attractions of the opposite sex. The sweet strains poured forth by many male birds during the season of love, are certainly admired by the females, of which fact evidence will hereafter be given. If female birds had been incapable of appreciating the beautiful colours, the ornaments, and voices of their male partners, all the labour and anxiety exhibited by the latter in displaying their charms before the females would have been thrown away; and this it is impossible to admit. Why certain bright colours should excite pleasure cannot, I presume, be explained, any more than why certain flavours and scents are agreeable; but habit has something to do with the result, for that which is at first unpleasant to our senses, ultimately becomes pleasant, and habits are inherited. With respect to sounds, Helmholtz has explained to a certain extent on physiological principles, why harmonies and certain cadences are agreeable. But besides this, sounds frequently recurring at irregu-

---

[72]See some good remarks on the simplification of languages, by Sir J. Lubbock, 'Origin of Civilisation,' 1870, p. 278.

lar intervals are highly disagreeable, as every one will admit who has listened at night to the irregular flapping of a rope on board ship. The same principle seems to come into play with vision, as the eye prefers symmetry or figures with some regular recurrence. Patterns of this kind are employed by even the lowest savages as ornaments; and they have been developed through sexual selection for the adornment of some male animals. Whether we can or not give any reason for the pleasure thus derived from vision and hearing, yet man and many of the lower animals are alike pleased by the same colours, graceful shading and forms, and the same sounds.

The taste for the beautiful, at least as far as female beauty is concerned, is not of a special nature in the human mind; for it differs widely in the different races of man, and is not quite the same even in the different nations of the same race. Judging from the hideous ornaments, and the equally hideous music admired by most savages, it might be urged that their æsthetic faculty was not so highly developed as in certain animals, for instance, as in birds. Obviously no animal would be capable of admiring such scenes as the heavens at night, a beautiful landscape, or refined music; but such high tastes are acquired through culture, and depend on complex associations; they are not enjoyed by barbarians or by uneducated persons.

Many of the faculties, which have been of inestimable service to man for his progressive advancement, such as the powers of the imagination, wonder, curiosity, an undefined sense of beauty, a tendency to imitation, and the love of excitement or novelty, could hardly fail to lead to capricious changes of customs and fashions. I have alluded to this point, because a recent writer[73] has oddly fixed on Caprice "as one of the most "remarkable and typical differences between savages and brutes." But not only can we partially understand how it is that man is from various conflicting influences rendered capricious, but that the lower animals are, as we shall hereafter see, likewise capricious in their affections, aversions, and sense of beauty. There is also reason to suspect that they love novelty, for its own sake.

BELIEF IN GOD—RELIGION

There is no evidence that man was aboriginally endowed with the ennobling belief in the existence of an Omnipotent God. On the contrary there is ample evidence, derived not from hasty travellers, but from men who have long resided with savages, that numerous races have existed,

---

[73]'The Spectator,' Dec. 4th, 1869, p. 1430.

and still exist, who have no idea of one or more gods, and who have no words in their languages to express such an idea.[74] The question is of course wholly distinct from that higher one, whether there exists a Creator and Ruler of the universe; and this has been answered in the affirmative by some of the highest intellects that have ever existed.

If, however, we include under the term "religion" the belief in unseen or spiritual agencies, the case is wholly different; for this belief seems to be universal with the less civilised races. Nor is it difficult to comprehend how it arose. As soon as the important faculties of the imagination, wonder, and curiosity, together with some power of reasoning, had become partially developed, man would naturally crave to understand what was passing around him, and would have vaguely speculated on his own existence. As Mr. M'Lennan[75] has remarked, "Some explanation of the "phenomena of life, a man must feign for himself; and to judge from "the universality of it, the simplest hypothesis, and the first to occur to "men, seems to have been that natural phenomena are ascribable to the "presence in animals, plants, and things, and in the forces of nature, of "such spirits prompting to action as men are conscious they themselves "possess." It is also probable, as Mr. Tylor has shewn, that dreams may have first given rise to the notion of spirits; for savages do not readily distinguish between subjective and objective impressions. When a savage dreams, the figures which appear before him are believed to have come from a distance, and to stand over him; or "the soul of the dreamer goes "out on its travels, and comes home with a remembrance of what it has "seen."[76] But until the faculties of imagination, curiosity, reason, &c.,

---

[74]See an excellent article on this subject by the Rev. F. W. Farrar, in the 'Anthropological Review,' Aug. 1864, p. ccxvii. For further facts see Sir J. Lubbock, 'Prehistoric Times,' 2nd edit. 1869, p. 564; and especially the chapters on Religion in his 'Origin of Civilisation,' 1870.
[75]'The Worship of Animals and Plants,' in the 'Fortnightly Review,' Oct. 1, 1869, p. 422.
[76]Tylor, 'Early History of Mankind,' 1865, p. 6. See also the three striking chapters on the Development of Religion, in Lubbock's 'Origin of Civilisation,' 1870. In a like manner Mr. Herbert Spencer, in his ingenious essay in the 'Fortnightly Review' (May 1st, 1870, p. 535), accounts for the earliest forms of religious belief throughout the world, by man being led through dreams, shadows, and other causes, to look at himself as a double essence, corporeal and spiritual. As the spiritual being is supposed to exist after death and to be powerful, it is propitiated by various gifts and ceremonies, and its aid invoked. He then further shews that names or nicknames given from some animal or other object, to the early progenitors or founders of a tribe, are supposed after a long interval to represent the real progenitor of the tribe; and such animal or object is then naturally believed still to exist as a spirit, is held sacred, and worshipped as a god. Nevertheless I cannot but suspect that there is a still earlier and ruder stage, when anything which manifests power or movement is thought to be endowed with some form of life, and with mental faculties analogous to our own.

had been fairly well developed in the mind of man, his dreams would not have led him to believe in spirits, any more than in the case of a dog.

The tendency in savages to imagine that natural objects and agencies are animated by spiritual or living essences, is perhaps illustrated by a little fact which I once noticed: my dog, a full-grown and very sensible animal, was lying on the lawn during a hot and still day; but at a little distance a slight breeze occasionally moved an open parasol, which would have been wholly disregarded by the dog, had any one stood near it. As it was, every time that the parasol slightly moved, the dog growled fiercely and barked. He must, I think, have reasoned to himself in a rapid and unconscious manner, that movement without any apparent cause indicated the presence of some strange living agent, and that no stranger had a right to be on his territory.

The belief in spiritual agencies would easily pass into the belief in the existence of one or more gods. For savages would naturally attribute to spirits the same passions, the same love of vengeance or simplest form of justice, and the same affections which they themselves feel. The Fuegians appear to be in this respect in an intermediate condition, for when the surgeon on board the "Beagle" shot some young ducklings as specimens, York Minster declared in the most solemn manner, "Oh, Mr. "Bynoe, much rain, much snow, blow much;" and this was evidently a retributive punishment for wasting human food. So again he related how, when his brother killed a "wild man," storms long raged, much rain and snow fell. Yet we could never discover that the Fuegians believed in what we should call a God, or practised any religious rites; and Jemmy Button, with justifiable pride, stoutly maintained that there was no devil in his land. This latter assertion is the more remarkable, as with savages the belief in bad spirits is far more common than that in good ones.

The feeling of religious devotion is a highly complex one, consisting of love, complete submission to an exalted and mysterious superior, a strong sense of dependence,[77] fear, reverence, gratitude, hope for the future, and perhaps other elements. No being could experience so complex an emotion until advanced in his intellectual and moral faculties to at least a moderately high level. Nevertheless, we see some distant approach to this state of mind in the deep love of a dog for his master, associated with complete submission, some fear, and perhaps other feelings. The behaviour of a dog when returning to his master after an absence, and, as I may add, of a monkey to his beloved keeper, is widely different from that towards their fellows. In the latter case the transports

---

[77]See an able article on the 'Physical Elements of Religion,' by Mr. L. Owen Pike, in 'Anthropolog. Review,' April, 1870, p. lxiii.

of joy appear to be somewhat less, and the sense of equality is shewn in every action. Professor Braubach goes so far as to maintain that a dog looks on his master as on a god.[78]

The same high mental faculties which first led man to believe in unseen spiritual agencies, then in fetishism, polytheism, and ultimately in monotheism, would infallibly lead him, as long as his reasoning powers remained poorly developed, to various strange superstitions and customs. Many of these are terrible to think of—such as the sacrifice of human beings to a blood-loving god; the trial of innocent persons by the ordeal of poison or fire; witchcraft, &c.—yet it is well occasionally to reflect on these superstitions, for they shew us what an infinite debt of gratitude we owe to the improvement of our reason, to science, and to our accumulated knowledge. As Sir J. Lubbock[79] has well observed, "it is not "too much to say that the horrible dread of unknown evil hangs like a "thick cloud over savage life, and embitters every pleasure." These miserable and indirect consequences of our highest faculties may be compared with the incidental and occasional mistakes of the instincts of the lower animals.

---

[78]'Religion, Moral, &c., der Darwin'schen Art-Lehre,' 1869, s. 53. It is said (Dr. W. Lauder Lindsay, 'Journal of Mental Science,' 1871, p. 43), that Bacon long ago, and the poet Burns, held the same notion.
[79]'Prehistoric Times,' 2nd edit. p. 571. In this work (p. 571) there will be found an excellent account of the many strange and capricious customs of savages.

1.4 THE NEW KEY*

by Susanne Langer

Genuine empiricism is above all a reflection on the validity of sense-knowledge, a speculation on the ways our concepts and beliefs are built up out of the fleeting and disconnected reports our eyes and ears actually make to the mind. Positivism, the scientists' metaphysic, entertains no such doubts, and raises no epistemological problems; its belief in the veracity of sense is implicit and dogmatic. Therefore it is really out of the running with post-Cartesian philosophy. It repudiates the basic problems of epistemology, and creates nothing but elbow-room for laboratory work. The very fact that it rejects *problems*, not answers, shows that the growing physical sciences were geared to an entirely different outlook on reality. They had their own so-called "working notions"; and the strongest of these was the concept of *fact*.

This central concept effected the *rapprochement* between science and empiricism, despite the latter's subjective tendencies. No matter what problems may lurk in vision and hearing, there is something final about the guarantees of sense. Sheer observation is hard to contradict, for sense-data have an inalienable semblance of "fact." And such a court of last appeal, where verdicts are quick and ultimate, was exactly what scientists needed if their vast and complicated work was to go forward. Epistemology might produce intriguing puzzles, but it could never furnish facts for conviction to rest upon. A naive faith in sense-evidence, on the other hand, provided just such terminals to thought. Facts are something we can all observe, identify, and hold in common; in the last resort, seeing is believing. And science, as against philosophy even in that eager and active philosophical age, professed to look exclusively to the visible world for its unquestioned postulates.

The results were astounding enough to lend the new attitude full force. Despite the objections of philosophical thinkers, despite the outcry of moralists and theologians against the "crass materialism" and "sensationalism" of the scientists, physical science grew like Jack's beanstalk, and overshadowed everything else that human thought produced to rival it. A passion for observation displaced the scholarly love of learned dispute, and quickly developed the experimental technique that kept humanity supplied thrice over with facts. Practical applications of the new mechanical knowledge soon popularized and established it

---

*Reprinted from *Philosophy in a New Key* (Cambridge, Massachusetts: 1942), pages 14-25, with permission of the President and Fellows of Harvard College.

beyond the universities. Here the traditional interests of philosophy could not follow it any more; for they had become definitely relegated to that haven of unpopular lore, the schoolroom. No one really cared much about consistency or definition of terms, about precise conceptions, or formal deduction. The senses, long despised and attributed to the interesting but improper domain of the devil, were recognized as man's most valuable servants, and were rescued from their classical disgrace to wait on him in his new venture. They were so efficient that they not only supplied the human mind with an incredible amount of food for thought, but seemed presently to have most of its cognitive business in hand. Knowledge from sensory experience was deemed the only knowledge that carried any affidavit of truth; for truth became identified, for all vigorous modern minds, with empirical fact.

And so, a scientific culture succeeded to the exhausted philosophical vision. An undisputed and uncritical empiricism—not skeptical, but positivistic—became its official metaphysical creed, experiment its avowed method, a vast hoard of "data" its capital, and correct prediction of future occurrences its proof. The programmatic account of this great adventure, beautifully put forth in Bacon's *Novum Organum* was followed only a few centuries later by the complete, triumphant summary of all that was scientifically respectable, in J. S. Mill's *Canons of Induction*—a sort of methodological manifesto.

As the physical world-picture grew and technology advanced, those disciplines which rested squarely on "rational" instead of "empirical" principles were threatened with complete extinction, and were soon denied even the honorable name of science. Logic and metaphysics, aesthetics and ethics, seemed to have seen their day. One by one the various branches of philosophy—natural, mental, social, or religious—set up as autonomous sciences; the natural ones with miraculous success, the humanistic ones with more hope and fanfare than actual achievement. The physical sciences found their stride without much hesitation; psychology and sociology tried hard and seriously to "catch the tune and keep the step," but with mathematical laws they were never really handy. Psychologists have probably spent almost as much time and type avowing their empiricism, their factual premises, their experimental techniques, as recording experiments and making general inductions. They still tell us that their lack of laws and calculable results is due to the fact that psychology is but young. When physics was as old as psychology is now, it was a definite, systematic body of highly general facts, and the possibilities of its future expansion were clearly visible in every line of its natural progress. It could say of itself, like Topsy, "I wasn't made, I growed." But our scientific psychology is *made* in the laboratory, and especially in the methodological forum. A good deal has, indeed, been made; but the synthetic organism still does not grow like a wild plant; its technical triumphs are apt to be discoveries in physiology or chemistry instead of psychological "facts."

Theology, which could not possibly submit to scientific methods, has simply been crowded out of the intellectual arena and gone into retreat in the cloistered libraries of its seminaries. As for logic, once the very model and norm of science, its only salvation seemed to lie in repudiating its most precious stock-in-trade, the "clear and distinct ideas," and professing to argue only from empirical facts to equally factual implications. The logician, once an investor in the greatest enterprise of human thought, found himself reduced to a sort of railroad linesman, charged with the task of keeping the tracks and switches of scientific reasoning clear for sensory reports to make their proper connections. Logic, it seemed, could never have a life of its own; for it had no foundation of facts, except the psychological fact that we do think thus and so, that such-and-such forms of argument lead to correct or incorrect predictions of further experience, and so forth. Logic became a mere reflection on tried and useful methods of fact-finding, and an official warrant for that technically fallacious process of generalizing known as "induction."

Yes, the heyday of science has stifled and killed our rather worn-out philosophical interests, born three and a half centuries ago from that great generative idea, the bifurcation of nature, into an inner and an outer world. To the generations of Comte, Mill, and Spencer, it certainly seemed as though all human knowledge could be cast in the new mold; certainly as though nothing in any other mold could hope to jell. And indeed, nothing much *has* jelled in any other mold; but neither have the non-physical disciplines been able to adopt and thrive on the scientific methods that did such wonders for physics and its obvious derivatives. The truth is that science has not really fructified and activated *all* human thought. If humanity has really passed the philosophical stage of learning, as Comte hopefully declared, and is evolving no more fantastic ideas, then we have certainly left many interesting brain-children stillborn along the way.

But the mind of man is always fertile, ever creating and discarding, like the earth. There is always new life under old decay. Last year's dead leaves hide not merely the seeds, but the full-fledged green plants of this year's spring, ready to bloom almost as soon as they are uncovered. It is the same with the seasons of civilization: under cover of a weary Greco-Roman eclecticism, a baffled cynicism, Christianity grew to its conquering force of conception and its clear interpretation of life; obscured by creed, canon, and curriculum, by learned disputation and demonstration, was born the great ideal of *personal experience*, the "rediscovery of the inner life," as Rudolph Eucken termed it, that was to inspire philosophy from Descartes's day to the end of German idealism. And beneath our rival "isms," our methodologies, conferences, and symposia, of course there is something brewing, too.

No one observed, amid the first passion of empirical fact-finding, that the ancient science of mathematics still went its undisturbed way of pure reason. It fell in so nicely with the needs of scientific thought, it fitted the observed world of fact so neatly, that those who learned and used it never stopped to accuse those who had invented and evolved it of being mere reasoners, and lacking tangible data. Yet the few conscientious empiricists who thought that *factual* bases must be established for mathematics made a notoriously poor job of it. Few mathematicians have really held that numbers were discovered by observation, or even that geometrical relationships are known to us by inductive reasoning from many observed instances. Physicists may think of certain facts in place of constants and variables, but the same constants and variables will serve somewhere else to calculate other facts, and the mathematicians themselves give no set of data their preference. They deal only with items whose sensory qualities are quite irrelevant: their "data" are arbitrary sounds or marks called *symbols*.

Behind these symbols lie the boldest, purest, coolest abstractions mankind has ever made. No schoolman speculating on essences and attributes ever approached anything like the abstractness of algebra. Yet those same scientists who prided themselves on their concrete factual knowledge, who claimed to reject every proof except empirical evidence, never hesitated to accept the demonstrations and calculations, the bodiless, sometimes avowedly "fictitious" entities of the mathematicians. Zero and infinity, square roots of negative numbers, incommensurable lengths and fourth dimensions, all found unquestioned welcome in the laboratory, when the average thoughtful layman, who could still take an invisible soul-substance on faith, doubted their logical respectability.

What is the secret power of mathematics, to win hard-headed empiricists, against their most ardent beliefs, to its purely rational speculations and intangible "facts"? Mathematicians are rarely practical people, or good observers of events. They are apt to be cloistered souls, like philosophers and theologians. Why are their abstractions taken not only seriously, but as indispensable, fundamental facts, by men who observe the stars or experiment with chemical compounds?

The secret lies in the fact that a mathematician does not profess to say anything about the existence, reality, or efficacy of *things* at all. His concern is the possibility of *symbolizing things* and of symbolizing the relations into which they might enter with each other. His "entities" are not "data," but *concepts*. That is why such elements as "imaginary numbers" and "infinite decimals" are tolerated by scientists to whom invisible agents, powers, and "principles" are anathema. Mathematical constructions are only symbols; they have meanings in terms of relationships, not of substance; something in reality answers to them, but they are not supposed to be items in that reality. To the true mathematician, numbers do not "inhere in" denumerable things, nor do circular objects "contain" degrees. Numbers and degrees and all their ilk only *mean* the real properties of real objects. It is entirely at the discretion of the scientist to say, "Let x mean this, let y mean that." All that mathematics determines is that *the x* and y must be related thus and thus. If experience belies the conclusion, then the formula does not express the relation of *this x* and *that y;* then x and y may not mean this thing and that. But no mathematician in his professional capacity will ever tell us that *this is x*, and has therefore such and such properties.

The faith of scientists in the power and truth of mathematics is so implicit that their work has gradually become less and less observation, and more and more calculation. The promiscuous collection and tabulation of data have given way to a process of assigning possible meanings, merely supposed real entities, to mathematical terms, working out the logical results, and then staging certain crucial experiments to check the hypothesis against the actual, empirical results. But the facts which are accepted by virtue of these tests are not actually *observed* at all. With the advance of mathematical technique in physics, the tangible results of experiment have become less and less spectacular; on the other hand, their *significance* has grown in inverse proportion. The men in the laboratory have departed so far from the old forms of experimentation—typified by Galileo's weights and Franklin's kite—that they cannot be said to observe the actual objects of their curiosity at all; instead, they are watching index needles, revolving drums, and sensitive plates. No psychology of "association" of sense-experiences can relate these data to the objects they signify, for in most cases the objects have never been experienced. Observation has become almost entirely indirect; and *readings* take the place of genuine witness. The sense-data on which the propositions of modern science rest are, for the most part, little photographic spots and blurs, or inky curved lines on paper. These data are empirical enough, but of course they are not themselves the phenomena in question; the actual phenomena stand behind them as their supposed causes. Instead of watching the process that interests us, that is to be verified—say, a course of celestial events, or the behavior of such objects as molecules and ether-waves—we really see only the fluctuations of a tiny arrow, the trailing path of a stylus, or the appearance of a speck of light, and *calculate to the "facts" of our science.* What is directly observable is only a sign of the "physical fact"; it requires interpretation to yield scientific propositions. Not simply seeing is believing, but *seeing and calculating, seeing and translating.*

This is bad, of course, for a thoroughgoing empiricism. Sense-data certainly do not make up the whole, or even the major part, of a scientist's material. The events that are given for his inspection could be "faked" in a dozen ways—that is, the same visible events could be made to occur, but with a different significance. We may at any time be wrong about their significance, even where no one is duping us; we may be nature's fools. Yet if we did not attribute an elaborate, purely reasoned, and hypothetical history of causes to the little shivers and wiggles of our apparatus, we really could not record them as momentous results of experiment. The problem of observation is all but eclipsed by the problem of *meaning.* And the triumph of empiricism in science is jeopardized by the surprising truth that *our sense-data are primarily symbols.*

Here, suddenly, it becomes apparent that the age of science has begotten a new philosophical issue, inestimably more profound than its original empiricism: for in all quietness, along purely rational lines, mathematics has developed just as brilliantly and vitally as any experimental technique, and, step by step, has kept abreast of discovery and observation; and all at once, the edifice of human knowledge stands before us, not as a vast collection of sense reports, but as a structure of *facts that are symbols* and *laws that are their meanings.* A new philosophical theme has been set forth to a coming age: an epistemological theme, the comprehension of science. The power of symbolism is its cue, as the finality of sense-data was the cue of a former epoch.

In epistemology—really all that is left of a worn-out philosophical heritage—a new generative idea has dawned. Its power is hardly recognized yet, but if we look as the actual trend of thought—always the surest index to a general prospect—the growing preoccupation with that new theme is quite apparent. One needs only to look at the titles of some philosophical books that have appeared within the last fifteen or twenty years: *The Meaning of Meaning;*[7] *Symbolism and Truth;*[8] *Die Philosophie der symbolischen Formen;*[9] *Language, Truth and Logic;*[10] *Symbol*

---

[7]C. K. Ogden and I. A. Richards (1923).
[8]Ralph Munroe Eaton (1925).
[9]Ernst Cassirer, 3 vols. (1923, 1924, 1929).
[10]A. J. Ayer (1936).

und Existenz der Wissenschaft;[11] *The Logical Syntax of Language;*[12] *Philosophy and Logical Syntax;*[13] *Meaning and Change of Meaning;*[14] *Symbolism: Its Meaning and Effects;*[15] *Foundations of the Theory of Signs;*[16] *Seele als Äusserung;*[17] *La pensée concrète: essai sur le symbolisme intellectuel;*[18] *Zeichen, die Fundamente des Wissens;*[19] and recently, *Language and Reality.*[20] The list is not nearly exhaustive. There are many books whose titles do not betray a preoccupation with semantic, for instance Wittgenstein's *Tractatus Logico-Philosophicus,*[21] or Grudin's *A Primer of Aesthetics.*[22] And were we to take an inventory of articles, even on the symbolism of science alone, we would soon have a formidable bibliography.

But it is not only in philosophy proper that the new keynote has been struck. There are at least two limited and technical fields, which have suddenly been developed beyond all prediction, by the discovery of the all-importance of symbol-using or symbol-reading. They are widely separate fields, and their problems and procedures do not seem to belong together in any way at all: one is modern psychology, the other modern logic.

In the former we are disturbed—thrilled or irritated, according to our temperaments—by the advent of psychoanalysis. In the latter we witness the rise of a new technique known as symbolic logic. The coincidence of these two pursuits seems entirely fortuitous; one stems from medicine and the other from mathematics, and there is nothing whatever on which they would care to compare notes or hold debate. Yet I believe they both embody the same generative idea, which is to preoccupy and inspire our philosophical age: for each in its own fashion has discovered the power of symbolization.

They have different conceptions of symbolism and its functions. Symbolic logic is not "symbolic" in the sense of Freudian psychology, and *The Analysis of Dreams* makes no contribution to logical syntax. The

---

[11]H. Noack, *Symbol und Existenz der Wissenschaft: Untersuchungen zur Grundlegung einer philosophischen Wissenschaftslehre* (1936).
[12]Rudolf Carnap (1935; German ed. 1934).
[13]Rudolf Carnap (1935; German ed. 1934).
[14]Gustav Stern (1931).
[15]A. N. Whitehead (1927).
[16]Charles W. Morris (1938).
[17]Paul Helwig (1936).
[18]A. Spaier (1927).
[19]R Gätschenberger (1932).
[20]Wilbur M. Urban, *Language and Reality; the Philosophy of Language and the Principles of Symbolism* (1939).
[21]Ludwig Wittgenstein (1922).
[22]Louis Grudin (1930).

emphasis on symbolism derives from entirely different interests, in their respective contexts. As yet, the cautious critic may well regard the one as a fantastic experiment of "mental philosophy," and the other as a mere fashion in logic and epistemology.

When we speak of fashions in thought, we are treating philosophy lightly. There is disparagement in the phrases, "a fashionable problem," a fashionable term." Yet it is the most natural and appropriate thing in the world for a new problem or a new terminology to have a vogue that crowds out everything else for a little while. A word that everyone snaps up, or a question that has everybody excited, probably carries a generative idea—the germ of a complete reorientation in metaphysics, or at least the "Open Sesame" of some new positive science. The sudden vogue of such a key-idea is due to the fact that all sensitive and active minds turn at once to exploiting it; we try it in every connection, for every purpose, experiment with possible stretches of its strict meaning, with generalizations and derivatives. When we become familiar with the new idea our expectations do not outrun its actual uses quite so far, and then its unbalanced popularity is over. We settle down to the problems that it has really generated, and these become the characteristic issues of our time.

The rise of technology is the best possible proof that the basic concepts of physical science, which have ruled our thinking for nearly two centuries, are essentially sound. They have begotten knowledge, practice, and systematic understanding; no wonder they have given us a very confident and definite *Weltanschauung*. They have delivered all physical nature into our hands. But strangely enough, the so-called "mental sciences" have gained very little from the great adventure. One attempt after another has failed to apply the concept of causality to logic and aesthetics, or even sociology and psychology. Causes and effects could be found, of course, and could be correlated, tabulated, and studied; but even in psychology, where the study of stimulus and reaction has been carried to elaborate lengths, no true science has resulted. No prospects of really great achievement have opened before us in the laboratory. If we follow the methods of natural science our psychology tends to run into physiology, histology, and genetics; we move further and further away from those problems which we ought to be approaching. That signifies that the generative idea which gave rise to physics and chemistry and all their progeny—technology, medicine, biology—does not contain any vivifying concept for the humanistic sciences. The physicist's scheme, so faithfully emulated by generations of psychologists, epistemologists, and aestheticians, is probably blocking their progress, defeating possible insights by its prejudicial force. The scheme is not false—it is perfectly reasonable —but it is bootless for the study of mental phenomena. It does not engender leading questions and excite a constructive imagination, as it does in physical researches. Instead of a method, it inspires a militant methodology.

Now, in those very regions of human interest where the age of empiricism has caused no revolution, the preoccupation with symbols has come into fashion. It has not sprung directly from any canon of science. It runs at least two distinct and apparently incompatible courses. Yet each course is a river of life in its own field, each fructifies its own harvest; and instead of finding mere contradiction in the wide difference of forms and uses to which this new generative idea is put, I see in it a promise of power and versatility, and a commanding philosophical problem. One conception of symbolism leads to logic, and meets the new problems in theory of knowledge; and so it inspires an evaluation of science and a quest for certainty. The other takes us in the opposite direction—to psychiatry, the study of emotions, religion, fantasy, and everything but knowledge. Yet in both we have a central theme: the *human response*, as a constructive, not a passive thing. Epistemologists and psychologists agree that symbolization is the key to that constructive process, though they may be ready to kill each other over the issue of what a symbol is and how it functions. One studies the structure of science, the other of dreams; each has his own assumptions—that is all they are—regarding the nature of symbolism itself. Assumptions, generative ideas, are what we fight for. Our conclusions we are usually content to demonstrate by peaceable means. Yet the assumptions are philosophically our most interesting stock-in-trade.

In the fundamental notion of symbolization—mystical, practical, or mathematical, it makes no difference—we have the keynote of all humanistic problems. In it lies a new conception of "mentality," that may illumine questions of life and consciousness, instead of obscuring them as traditional "scientific methods" have done. If it is indeed a generative idea, it will beget tangible methods of its own, to free the deadlocked paradoxes of mind and body, reason and impulse, autonomy and law, and will overcome the checkmated arguments of an earlier age by discarding their very idiom and shaping their equivalents in more significant phrase. The philosophical study of symbols is not a technique borrowed from other disciplines, not even from mathematics; it has arisen in the fields that the great advance of learning has left fallow. Perhaps it holds the seed of a new intellectual harvest, to be reaped in the next season of the human understanding.

1.5   BIOLOGY, MOLECULAR AND ORGANISMIC*

by Theodosius Dobzhansky

Indisputably, molecular biology has achieved in our day advances of signal importance. Suffice it to mention the elucidation of the chemistry of heredity, the breaking of the genetic code, studies on protein structure and synthesis, and the unraveling of the sequences of chemical reactions in metabolic processes. All this has brought biology considerably closer than it was a generation ago to understanding the phenomena of life. Although it is equally indisputable that this understanding is nowhere near complete as yet, it is fair to say that we are the living witnesses of a great efflorescence of biological sciences. The modern advance is perhaps comparable in magnitude, although probably not in the depth of the philosophical repercussions, to that which occurred roughly a century ago under the stimulus of Darwin's theory of evolution. Every biologist feels gratified by this advance, and hopes that further research in molecular biology will be pursued with all possible vigor. What is debatable is the situation of the organismic biology *vis-à-vis* its molecular sibling.

Nothing succeeds like success. In molecular biology, one spectacular discovery has followed closely on the heels of another. Molecular biology has become a glamor field. It has attracted many able young students as well as older investigators. Glamor and brilliance generate enthusiasm and optimism; they may also dazzle and blindfold. The notion has gained some currency that the only worthwhile biology is molecular biology. All else is "bird watching" or "butterfly collecting." Bird watching and butterfly collecting are occupations manifestly unworthy of serious scientists! I have heard a man whose official title happens to be Professor of Zoology declare to an assembly of his colleagues that "a good man cannot teach zoology." A good man can teach, of course, only molecular biology.

Such pronunciamentos can be dismissed as merely ridiculous. They are, however, caricatures of opinions entertained by some intelligent and reasonable people, whose views deserve an honest and careful consideration and analysis. Science must cope with new problems that arise and devise new approaches to old problems. Some lines of research become less profitable and less exciting and others more so. The progress in a given field of study may slacken because the approaches used have al-

---

*Reprinted from the *American Zoologist*, Volume 4 with permission of the American Society of Zoologists, Chicago, Illinois.

ready yielded most of what they are capable of yielding. Probably every thoughtful scientist can give examples of research efforts which have bogged down, and of types of inquiry which seem to have run into at least temporarily impassable obstacles. If such researches and inquiries are not abandoned altogether they usually drift into more and more narrow specializations and uninspired repetitiousness. On the other hand, an apparently depleted field may burst into renewed fertility when a new idea or a new technique is invented.

Is it, then, possible that biology other than molecular biology has entered upon a period of doldrums? It is good for any scientist from time to time to re-examine and to re-think his aims, purposes, and approaches. Intellectual laziness has been the undoing of many a capable scientist, who rested on the comforting assumption that what was good a generation ago is good enough today. A line of research is not necessarily good because it is traditional, and it is not necessarily worth pursuing because it has become an ingrown habit. But neither is newness and fashionableness a valid enough reason to choose one's line of work. Let us face the problems squarely and honestly.

Biology is structured rather differently from other natural sciences. Since this is equally true of zoology and botany, I prefer to use here the inclusive word, biology, covering both. A biologist, more than, for example, a physicist or a geologist, is faced with several hierarchically superimposed levels of integration in the objects which he studies. Life presents itself to our view almost always in the form of discrete quanta—individuals. But unlike the atoms of classical physics, individuals are conspicuously divisible, and, unlike the atoms of modern physics, divisible into great numbers and a great variety of component elements, cells. Cells are, in turn, complexly structured and well-integrated entities. They contain chemical substances of numerous, probably thousands of, molecular species. It is, however, a gross error to think of a cell simply as a mixture of chemicals, like a mixture that can be made in a test tube. The chemical components are arranged in cells in series of intricately built organelles. Chromosomes and genes have that extraordinary chemical substance, the DNA, as the key constituent. But the DNA in the chromosome is something more than the DNA in a test tube. A chromosome is an organized body, and its organization is as essential as is its composition.

The supra-individual forms of integration seem less tangible in a spatio-temporal sense than the infra-individual ones, but just as interesting and significant. Mankind is less clearly perceived by our sense organs than an individual man, but it is nevertheless as meaningful a biological entity as it is a cultural entity. The sexual mode of reproduction connects individuals into reproductive communities, Mendelian populations. Mendelian populations are united by reproductive bonds into inclusive reproductive systems—biological species. An isolated individual, especially an individual of a sexual species, is at least as clearly an anomaly as a cell isolated from a multicellular body. With asexual modes of reproduction, the bonds which integrate individuals in Mendelian populations and biological species are absent. Other bonds operate, however, in sexual as well as in asexual organisms. Individuals and species belong to ecological communities and ecosystems. An individual taken out of the system in which it normally occurs is incomplete and it may be inviable.

The hierarchy of levels of biological integration may be represented schematically as the following sequence: molecule, cellular organelle, cell, tissue, organ, individual, Mendelian population, species, community, ecosystem. This sequence is, to be sure, not everywhere rigorously adhered to. There are unicellular or (acellular) as well as multicellular organisms; the sexual and the asexual modes of reproduction impose, as indicated above, different modes of integration. Even the level of an individual is not always unambiguously distinct. Consider a colonial form, such as a siphonophore; an individual of the higher order (colony) is composed of several individuals of the lower order which are incapable of independent existence. Among social insects, the colony becomes an entity for which the designation "supraorganism" has been suggested.

Biologists have studied the manifestations of life at all levels of integration. It would therefore be logically possible to distinguish molecular biology, cell biology, individual biology, population biology, community biology, *etc*. This is neither necessary nor convenient in practice. It is, however, desirable to have a simple dichotomy of molecular and organismic biology, the latter name subsuming studies on all levels above the molecular one.

The designation "organismic" is an appropriate one, notwithstanding the fact that this adjective was utilized by the so-called "holists" for some of their special, and now almost completely forgotten, notions. This should not, I think, make the word forever ineligible for use in a context which renders its different meaning unambiguously clear.

Organismic biology, dealing with biological integration levels above the molecular one, has in recent years been referred to, sometimes pejoratively, as the classical or traditional biology, or as natural history. The opinion forcibly expressed by some molecular biologists is that, to be "modern," or even "scientific," organismic biology must be reduced to molecular biology. All that this means in most cases is that many molecular biologists are so excited about what they are doing that they are unable to see why their organismic colleagues can find excitement in something else.

There are, however, also more rational arguments with which the claims of a supremacy of molecular biology are sometimes supported. One reason is simply the acceptance of the mechanistic hypothesis and rejection of vitalism. Biological phenomena are complex patterns of physicochemical ones; there is nothing in living bodies, no special form of energy or any other agency, that is not potentially analyzable into physicochemical components. More than three centuries ago, Descartes wrote "that I do not accept or desire any other principle in Physics than in Geometry or abstract Mathematics, because all the phenomena of nature may be explained by their means, and sure demonstration can be given of them." Descartes also wrote "that the body of a living man differs from that of a dead man just as does a watch or other automation (*i.e.,* a machine that moves of itself), when it is wound up and contains in itself the corporeal principle of those movements for which it is designed along with all that is requisite for its action, from the same watch or other machine when it is broken and when the principle of its movement ceases to act."

Most present-day biologists accept the Cartesian view of the nature of living bodies. Three centuries of research in biology have yielded abundant evidence in favor of this view. Time and again, processes and phenomena which appeared distinctive of living matter were shown to be compounds of chemical and physical constituents. Driesch was probably the last outstanding biologist to espouse the classical vitalist doctrine. He believed that a special force or energy, which he called by the Aristotelian name "entelechy," was active in living bodies. Vitalism is now not only very much a minority view but, and this is characteristic, its present adherents are loath to admit that they are vitalists. For example, Edmund Sinnott is convinced that the development of the organism is presided upon by a "psyche," but, if I understand him aright, this psyche neither substitutes for, nor enters into any give-and-take with, ordinary physical corporeal processes.

The reason why mechanism has triumphed in biology, and vitalism has faded out of the picture, must be made unequivocally clear. Far from all life processes have been, or for that matter are ever likely to be, exhaustively described in chemical and physical terms. A universal negation is notoriously hard to substantiate; there is no irrefutable proof that some sort of an entelechy may not be lurking somewhere. The point is rather that vitalism has turned out to be unnecessary and unprofitable, while mechanism has vindicated itself as a guide to discovery. For this and for no other reason, the contest of mechanism versus vitalism has been a dead issue in biology for at least half a century. Not even the few surviving vitalists deny that physical and chemical processes occur in living bodies, and more examples would not impress them greatly. To do research for the purpose of invalidating vitalism is at present a height of futility. It is not unlike using heavy artillery to kill mosquitoes.

Reduction of the organismic biology to the molecular level may, however, be urged also on different grounds. This is the proposition that chemistry and physics are sciences more "advanced," more exact, and hence superior to biology. More than a century ago (1830–1842), the positivist philosopher Auguste Comte set up a hierarchy of sciences. In his opinion, the most basic science was mathematics; less basic were, in a descending order, mechanics, astronomy, physics, chemistry, biology, and sociology. The progress of scientific inquiry consists of reducing the description of the phenomena studied by the less basic sciences to the more basic ones. The aim of biology is, then, to describe life in terms first of chemistry, and eventually of physics and mechanics, and thus to dispense with biological concepts and ideas altogether. The greatest conceivable success of biology would be to make itself obsolete and unnecessary.

The Comtian positivism had a powerful influence on the world view of nineteenth century scientists, but its reputation has not fared well among philosophers. Some of the greatest modern works on philosophy of science (*e.g.* Ernest Nagel's THE STRUGGLE OF SCIENCE, 1961) do not mention Comte at all. At present not all scientists know his name either, and fewer still have read any of his works. The belief in the Comtian hierarchy of sciences, and the faith in reduction as the intent of scientific inquiry, nevertheless persist and are seldom questioned among scientists, especially among biologists. The matter is, however, far from simple; it deserves being considered with care and caution.

Nagel defines reduction as "the explanation of a theory or a set of experimental laws established in one area of inquiry, by a theory usually though not invariably formulated for some other domain." Reduction of organismic to molecular biology, and of the latter to chemistry, would be effected if biological laws and theories, such as for example Mendel's laws of the theory of inheritance, were shown to be deducible as consequences of the laws and theories of chemistry, physics, or mechanics.

The reductionism is a more sophisticated notion than the simple, and often a little naive, wish to prove that biological phenomena are not manifestations of some sort of vital force or psyche. It must, however, be understood that, while under some conditions the reduction is useful and enlightening, under others it merely detracts from the research effort better applied elsewhere. This is a question of research strategy, not of some sacred and immutable law of scientific development. To be profitable, the reduction should open up new possibilities of using some powerful theories or concepts of a more advanced, or if you wish, more basic, science. It must help making discoveries in the field of science undergoing reduction, and at that, discoveries which could not otherwise be made or not made as easily. Such advantages have accrued, for example, when thermodynamics was reduced to statistical mechanics. In biology, at least some chapters of physiology are being successfully reduced to biochemistry, chemistry, biophysics, and physics. However, here I must again quote Nagel, whose philosophy is, let this be made clear, quite favorable to reductionism. According to Nagel, "the question whether a given science is reducible to another cannot in the abstract be usefully raised without reference to some particular stage of development of the two disciplines. . . . The possibility should not be ignored that little if any new knowledge or increased power for significant research may actually be gained from reducing one science to another at certain periods of their development, however great may be the potential advantages of such reduction at some later time."

Nagel's analysis has not been made especially with biology in view, but it describes splendidly the present situation of the biological sciences. The progress of biology would not be furthered by frenetic efforts to reduce organismic biology to chemistry or physics. This is not because there is anything in living things that is inherently irreducible. It is rather because a different research strategy is more expedient. Those who urge an immediate absorption of the organismic into molecular biology neglect the simple but basic fact that life has developed several levels of organization. These are levels of increasing complexity, and they are hierarchically superimposed. The elementary phenomena and regularities on each succeeding level are organized patterns of those on the preceding level. Organismic biology can be said to be a study of patterns of molecular phenomena. Such a definition of organismic biology is correct as far as it goes, but it does not go quite far enough. It is a study not only of the molecular patterns but also of patterns of patterns.

Some examples should make the meaning of this clear. A gene, or at least its key constituent, is a double-stranded DNA molecule, or perhaps a part of such a molecule. A chromosome is, however, not a heap of genes, but a configuration of genes arranged in a certain way which proved to be adaptively advantageous in evolution. A cell is not a conglomeration of chromosomes but a supremely orderly contrivance consisting not of chromosomes alone but also of many other organelles. An organ and an individual body are, in turn, not simply piles of cells but beautifully designed and often highly complex machines, in which the cellular components are not only diversified but often have lost their separate identities. Mendelian populations and species of sexually reproducing organisms are not throngs or medleys of individuals; they are reproductive communities of interdependent members. Species are categories of classification, but they are not only that. Evidence is rapidly accumulating to show that the gene pool, the collective genotype of a species, is an organized system of coadapted constituents. Biotic communities or ecosystems are not miscellanies of species which happen to live side by side or in the same general region; they are structured associations of more or less mutually interdependent forms.

A follower of the philosophy of Francis Bacon could perhaps hope that if one accumulates an abundance of accurate chemical and biochemical observations, then all biological phenomena on all integration levels could easily be deduced from these observations. Indeed, we have admitted that what the organismic biology studies are patterns, and patterns of patterns, of chemical and physical processes. In actual fact, the development of biology has followed a quite different path, and really no branch of science has trod the way which Bacon, who was not himself a practicing scientist, imagined it would. In biology, research was and is being carried on simultaneously, and discoveries are being made, on all organismic and molecular levels.

The discoveries in one branch of biology often suggest work to be done, and stimulate discovery in other biological disciplines. It is, however, not at all a general rule that these discoveries are made by simple deduction. It was, for example, biochemistry and spectroscopy that yielded the celebrated Watson-Crick model of the structure of DNA. This represents a very important advance in our understanding of what the genes are and how they work. But the existence of genes was discovered with the aid of the methods of hybridization and of statistical analysis of hybrid progenies, not by chemical methods. Even now, given the entire present-day knowledge of the chemistry of DNA, one could hardly deduce from this knowledge that the genes exist and behave as Gregor Mendel found them behaving in inheritance.

A suggestion has also been made that biologists should exercise a kind of restraint, and leave the problems of organismic biology in abeyance until the time should come when these problems could be reduced to the molecular level. This suggestion has at least the merit of a kind of ruthless logic behind it, but like so many other ruthlessly logical proposals, it is a practical impossibility. It is like the advice, also logically impeccable, that a moratorium ought to be declared on all scientific research, to give time for mankind to absorb the knowledge already available. Both proposals are futile, not to say silly, and for the same reason. Man's intellect will not tolerate such shackles, not even were it convinced that these shackles would be good for it.

To make the situation ironic, some of the same people who would declare a moratorium on organismic biology until such time when it can be reduced to molecular terms, also argue that organismic biology is largely a finished business, worthy neither of much attention nor support. Now, it is true that a method of investigation or a line of research may be productive at one time, and become like a squeezed-out lemon afterwards. However, he is a reckless, rather than a courageous man, who wraps himself in a prophet's mantle. The history of science often deals roughly with fortune-tellers. Consider the discipline of human anatomy. It should have been dead four centuries ago; after Vesalius not many new organs can be found in the human body. Yet we find anatomy prospering and forward-looking. Microscopes have opened vistas which were not accessible to Vesalius. Polymorphisms and variations, normal and pathological, individual and racial, have acquired new meaning in the light of genetics and evolution. Finds of fossil human and prehuman remains create such excitement that some discoveries are reported in the daily press before they are buried in weighty monographs.

What is predictable about most discoveries is that they are unpredictable. If they were predictable, they would be made sooner, but making them would be a less inspiring occupation than it is. We have been discussing the methodology and the strategy of modern biology. No synopsis of major or outstanding problems of either the molecular or the organismic biology will be attempted here. Even if I had the wisdom, or the brashness, needed for such an undertaking, it would require a book, instead of an article. I hope, however, that it is not out of place to venture here a very general characterization of the subject matter of biology, both organismic and molecular.

The world of life can be studied from two points of view—that of its unity and that of its diversity. All living things, from viruses to men, have basic similarities. And yet there is an apparently endless variety of living beings. Knowledge and understanding of both the unity and the diversity are useful to man. I like, however, to stress here not the pragmatic aspect, not the applied biology, but the aesthetic appeal. Both the unity and the diversity of life are fascinating. Some biologists find the unity more inspiring, others are enthralled by the diversity. This is evidently a matter of personal taste, and a classical adage counsels that tastes are not fit subjects for disputation (although this is what most disputations are about). The consequence of the polymorphism of tastes is that there always will be different kinds of biologists and different subdivisions of biology. Some of the subdivisions may be offering more fleshpots than others, and hence will be more popular, especially among those for whom the fleshpots are the prime consideration. Other subdivisions will, however, continue to attract some votaries.

The number of described species of animals is estimated to be not less than one million, and of plants about one-third as many. The total number of existing species of organisms may only be guessed—from two to four million. It is, however, not only the great number of yet undescribed species that gives the lie to the oft-repeated contention that the systematic and descriptive biology have already fulfilled their functions and may be relegated to amateurs and to museum drudges. Species identification and description is an indispensable preliminary, but only a preliminary, to other, and perhaps more exciting and significant inquiry. The ferreting-out of new species belongs to what Ernst Mayr has called the "analytical stage," and what is sometimes referred to also as the "alpha-taxonomy." This is followed by the "synthetic stage," and finally by the study of causes and regularities of the evolutionary process. Birds are the group of animals which is attracting the greatest number of workers relative to its size (*i.e.,* to the number of species in the group); the species of birds are, however, so well explored that the chances of finding a new one are probably smaller than in any other group of animals of comparable size. Ornithologists are interested surely not so much in finding new species as in understanding the old ones. So are many, if not most, other systematists.

Remarkably, even paradoxically, the fundamental unity of all living things makes possible an understanding of their prodigious diversity. Nutrition, respiration, irritability, and reproduction are found everywhere. Some of the enzymes in my body are similar in function to the enzymes in the lowly yeast and bacterial cells. My genes are different sequences of the same four "letters" of the "genetic alphabet" which also compose the genes of a fish or of a corn plant. Genes reproduce themselves generally with an astonishing accuracy; the sequences of the four "letters," the nucleotide bases, are usually identical in hundreds of billions of cells of the bodies of the parents and of their progeny. Occasionally, there occur, however, changes, "misprints," mutations. Self-reproduction plus mutation make possible natural selection. Natural selection makes possible evolution. Evolution is not always, and not necessarily, but sometimes, progressive.

The enterprise of biology rests chiefly on two patterns of explanation. One is the organism-the-machine theory, stated quite clearly by Descartes. The other is the theory of evolution, creditable, despite some predecessors and anticipators, to Charles Darwin. Both mechanistic and evolutionary explanations are pertinent to, and are made use of, in molecular as well as in organismic biology. These explanations are not alternative or competing; they are complementary, without, however, being either deducible from or reducible to each other. It is nevertheless possible to say, as a broad generalization, that the molecular biology is preponderantly Cartesian and the organismic biology is basically Darwinian. I utter this generalization not without misgivings; it should not be misunderstood as creating a dichotomy, for such a dichotomy would be a false one. Both the Cartesian and the Darwinian approaches are essential for understanding the unity and the diversity of life at all levels of integration. Nevertheless, at the lower levels of integration the type of question most frequently asked is "how things are," while at the higher levels an additional question insistently obtrudes on the mind of the investigator—"how things got to be that way."

Perhaps the most significant and gratifying trend during the last two decades or so has been the increasing unification of biology as a field of knowledge. Of course, we are all specialists in some particular line or even technique of research. But now more than ever before one can discern the meaningful relationships between all these specialties and techniques. The spectacular progress in molecular biology has surely acted as a unifying agent. To treat molecular biology instead as a bludgeon with which to destroy, or to reduce to insignificance, the organismic biology is basically to misunderstand the nature of life and the requirement for its study.

I venture another, and perhaps equally reckless, generalization— nothing makes sense in biology except in the light of evolution, *sub specie evolutionis*. If the living world has not arisen from common ancestors by means of an evolutionary process, then the fundamental unity of living things is a hoax and their diversity is a joke. The unity is understandable as a consequence of common descent and of universal necessities imposed by common materials. The diversity is intelligible as the outcome of adaptation of life to different environments, or, if I may use this unfortunately ambiguous and yet indispensable concept, to different ecological niches.

If one could imagine a universe in which the environment would be completely uniform in space and in time, then in such a universe a single kind of living inhabitant could conceivably be all that an evolutionary process might produce. The real universe is certainly not uniform. The living matter has responded to the diversity of physical environments by evolving a diversity of genotypes able to survive and to reproduce in a variety of environments. Organic diversity is necessary because no single genotype can possess a superior adaptedness in all physical environments. This is, if anything, even more true with respect to the biotic environments. The more different organisms inhabit a territory, the greater becomes the variety of ecological niches. In a sense, the growth of the organic diversity is a self-accelerating process.

Although there is again no sharp dichotomy here, the concepts of adaptedness and adaptation occupy a more important position in

organismic than in molecular biology. The existence of several hierarchically superimposed levels of organic integration is in itself understandable only as an adaptation. Living beings survive and reproduce
sometimes in apparently most hostile environments. One can argue that
all environments are hostile, and that death and extinction are probable
events, while survival is improbable. Just how life has managed to overcome this improbability is a problem which many biologists find challenging and fascinating. In my opinion, this problem may well be used
as the framework on which to build the teaching of biology. At least I
found it so, both as a student and as a teacher.

I am, of course, not unaware of dissenting opinions about adaptation.
It has been argued that adaptation is either a tautology (what can survive, survives), or a teleology (a belief that organisms are shaped by or
for a purpose). Such opinions reveal a basic misconception. Darwin has,
once and for all, taken the sting out of teleology. For example, the statement that the hormonal mechanisms in a mammalian female serve the
purpose of reproduction does not imply that these mechanisms were contrived by some kind of entelechy which knew what it wanted to accomplish. Nor does the statement that a wasp seeks a prey in order to
provide food for its offspring mean that the wasp is conscious of the purpose of its activities. Reproduction is accomplished, and the offspring is
fed, by a great many methods other than those used by the mammalian
and by the wasp females.

The meaning of the above statements is really simple and straight-
forward. When certain hormones are produced in the body of a mammalian female, and produced in a certain delicately balanced sequence,
then and only then the chain of events takes place which eventuates in
the birth of a viable infant. The wasp goes through a series of complex
actions, which result in her progeny's feeding and developing, instead of
starving to death or being poisoned by unsuitable food. A logical analysis
of pseudo-teleological statements like the ones above has been made with
great discernment by Nagel in his admirable book THE STRUCTURE OF
SCIENCE. This pseudo-teleological language can be avoided only by
means of ponderous circumlocutions, which are superfluous to a biologist
acquainted with the modern evolutionary thought.

It is a striking and profoundly meaningful fact that organisms are so
constructed, so function, and so behave that they survive and perpetuate
themselves in a certain range of environments frequently enough for
their species to stay in existence for long periods of time. Furthermore, the ranges of the environments propitious for survival and reproduction are widely different for different forms of life. A biologist who
chooses to ignore this widespread adaptedness overlooks a fundamental

and very nearly universal characteristic of all that can be meaningfully studied on every level of biological integration, from the strictly molecular to the highest organismic—the ecosystem level. Even the exceptional failures of the adaptedness, the phenomena of extinction, constitute an obviously meaningful and important subject of study.

Zoologists, and in fact all biologists, should never lose sight of this one highly peculiar, and yet remarkably interesting, animal species—*Homo sapiens*. The worth and utility of biology, and, indeed, of science and of intellectual endeavor as a whole, will perhaps, in the fullness of time, be judged by the contribution they will have made to man's understanding of himself and of his place in the universe. I do not wish this statement to be misconstrued as urging that we jettison our zoology and all strive to become anthropologists or philosophers. By being good biologists, we may make a real contribution to the Science of Man, if not to anthropology in the strict technical sense. It is a hoary fallacy to think that man is nothing but an animal; however, man's nature is in part animal nature, and man's not-so-remote ancestors were full-blown animals. Man's humanity and his animality are not independent or kept in isolated compartments; they are interdependent and connected by reciprocal feedback relationships.

The parts played by the molecular and the organismic biology come out with extraordinary clarity when viewed against the background of the Science of Man. Like that of any other living body, the physiological machinery of the human body is compounded of chemical and physical ingredients. Certain diseases, particularly hereditary ones, are molecular diseases. The elucidation of their etiologies makes some splendid pages in the story of modern biology. Let me cite just one example—that of the sickle-cell anemia. This usually fatal disease is due to homozygosis for a single gene; the heterozygote for this gene and its normal allele is healthy or only mildly anemic. The hemoglobin in the blood of homozygous individuals is chiefly the so-called S hemoglobin; the heterozygote has both S and the normal hemoglobin A. Vernon Ingram and others found that hemoglobin S differs from A in the substitution of just a single amino acid, valine, in place of glutamic acid in the beta chain of the hemoglobin molecule. The mutational change in the gene responsible for the synthesis of the beta chain must have involved the substitution of just a single nucleotide, a single "letter" of the "genetic alphabet." At least fourteen other abnormal hemoglobins, in addition to S, are known to have single amino acids substituted in certain definite positions in the molecule.

Man is, however, an organism, and a highly complex and remarkable one. I suggest to you a single reason, but in itself a sufficient reason, why organismic biology will always occupy a leading place in the enterprise of science. Man seeks to understand himself. The pursuit of self-understanding is a never-ending quest. Darwin's work marked a turning point in the intellectual history of mankind because it showed that mankind was a product of a biological history. The evidence for this is now overwhelmingly convincing, except to a few antievolutionists. But just how and why man's bodily structures, physiological functions, and mental capacities have developed as they did is by no means well understood. The working hypothesis now in vogue is that the process of adaptation to the environment is the main propellant of evolutionary change. Evidence is rapidly accumulating which, in my opinion, substantiates the hypothesis. It remains, however, not only to convince the doubters but, what is more important, to discover just how the challenges of the environment are translated into evolutionary changes.

Man is interested in his future no less than in his past. Evolution is not only a history, it is also an actuality. Of course, *Home sapiens* evolves culturally more rapidly that it evolves biologically. Man must, however, face the problem of adapting his culture to his genes, as well as adapting his genes to his culture. Man is being forced by his culture to take the management and direction of his evolution in his own hands. This is perhaps the greatest challenge which mankind may ever have to face, and this is far too large a problem to be more than mentioned here. It is childish to think that it is solely a biological problem; the entire sum of human knowledge and of human wisdom will be needed. Biology is, however, involved, and this necessarily means both the Cartesian and the Darwinian, the molecular and the organismic biology. Fashions and fads come and go in science as they do in dress and in head gear. The big question remains: What is Man? It remains not because it is hopelessly insoluble but because every generation must solve it in relation to the situation it faces. Biology is here relevant; a solution based only on biology may well be wrong, but, surely, no solution ignoring either the organismic or the molecular biology can be right and reasonable.

REFERENCES

Dobzhansky, Theodosius. HEREDITY AND THE NATURE OF MAN. New York: Harcourt, Brace & World, 1964.
Mayr, Ernst. ANIMAL SPECIES AND EVOLUTION. Cambridge, Mass.: Harvard University Press, 1963.
Nagel, Ernest. THE STRUCTURE OF SCIENCE. New York: Harcourt, Brace & World, 1961.

CHAPTER TWO

ART IN THE WESTERN CULTURE TRADITION

2.1 EDITORIAL COMMENT

The role of art in the educative process is an integral part of man's development as a human being. It's place in the western culture tradition is clearly manifested in the area of ecclesiastical art. In the selections of this chapter we again seek to give substance to the art concept through four selected readings.

Ernest Cassirer's contribution to the development of the idea of man as a symbol creating animal is well recognized in the world of scholarship. In the selection which we present from his writing on the subject of "art" it is quite clear that he views the art role as one way in which man discovers the nature of reality, but the discovery of nature through art is not the same way in which we discover nature through science. In a real sense we can say that they mutually complement and are a part of each other, "depending on one and the same process of abstraction."

The classic example of an art product, directly related to the formal educative process in the tradition of western education, is to be found in Quintilian's *Institutes of Oratory*. Our selection from this great classic is directed to the setting forth of the well established idea that teaching is an art and the setting forth by Quintilian of the reasons.

In the article "Philosophy of Education and the Pseudo-Question" Dr. Maxine Greene, well known for her contributions to modern educational theory, demonstrates that one of the most effective ways of bringing into full view the real meaning of life is through the art form. Reality is revealed to us in multiplex ways and no where is this made more evident than in the bothersome question of "human freedom and responsibility."

Our fourth selection by John Dewey on *Individuality and Experience* clarifies the age old controversy over theory and practice, and indicates the significance of the art role in the educative process. In so doing, Dewey refutes the argument of his critics that he would have students operate without instruction or guidance.

2.2 ART*

by Ernst Cassirer

Like all the other symbolic forms art is not the mere reproduction of a ready-made, given reality. It is one of the ways leading to an objective view of things and of human life. It is not an imitation but a discovery of reality. We do not, however, discover nature through art in the same sense in which the scientist uses the term "nature." Language and science are the two main processes by which we ascertain and determine our concepts of the external world. We must classify our sense perceptions and bring them under general notions and general rules in order to give them an objective meaning. Such classification is the result of a persistent effort toward simplification. The work of art in like manner implies such an act of condensation and concentration. When Aristotle wanted to describe the real difference between poetry and history he insisted upon this process. What a drama gives us, he asserts, is a single action (*mia praxis*) which is a complete whole in itself, with all the organic unity of a living creature; whereas the historian has to deal not with one action but with one period and all that happened therein to one or more persons, however disconnected the several events may have been.[8]

In this respect beauty as well as truth may be described in terms of the same classical formula: they are "a unity in the manifold." But in the two cases there is a difference of stress. Language and science are abbreviations of reality; art is an intensification of reality. Language and science depend upon one and the same process of abstraction; art may be described as a continuous process of concretion. In our scientific description of a given object we begin with a great number of observations which at first sight are only a loose conglomerate of detached facts. But the farther we proceed the more these individual phenomena tend to assume a definite shape and become a systematic whole. What science is searching for is some central features of a given object from which all its particular qualities may be derived. If a chemist knows the atomic number of a certain element he possesses a clue to a full insight into its structure and constitution. From this number he may deduce all the characteristic properties of the element. But art does not admit of this sort of conceptual simplification and deductive generalization. It does not inquire into the qualities or causes of things; it gives us the intuition

---

*Reprinted from *An Essay on Man* (New Haven, Connecticut: Yale University Press, 1944), pages 137-170 with permission of the publisher.
[8]Aristotle, *op. cit.*, 23. 1459ᵃ 17–29. Ed. Bywater, pp. 70–73.

of the form of things. But this too is by no means a mere repetition of something we had before. It is a true and genuine discovery. The artist is just as much a discoverer of the forms of nature as the scientist is a discoverer of facts or natural laws. The great artists of all times have been cognizant of this special task and special gift of art. Leonardo da Vinci spoke of the purpose of painting and sculpture in the words "*saper vedere.*" According to him the painter and sculptor are the great teachers in the realm of the visible world. For the awareness of pure forms of things is by no means an instinctive gift, a gift of nature. We may have met with an object of our ordinary sense experience a thousand times without ever having "seen" its form. We are still at a loss if asked to describe not its physical qualities or effects but its pure visual shape and structure. It is art that fills this gap. Here we live in the realm of pure forms rather than in that of the analysis and scrutiny of sense objects or the study of their effects.

From a merely theoretical point of view we may subscribe to the words of Kant that mathematics is the "pride of human reason." But for this triumph of scientific reason we have to pay a very high price. Science means abstraction, and abstraction is always an impoverishment of reality. The forms of things as they are described in scientific concepts tend more and more to become mere formulae. These formulae are of a surprising simplicity. A single formula, like the Newtonian law of gravitation, seems to comprise and explain the whole structure of our material universe. It would seem as though reality were not only accessible to our scientific abstractions but exhaustible by them. But as soon as we approach the field of art this proves to be an illusion. For the aspects of things are innumerable, and they vary from one moment to another. Any attempt to comprehend them within a simple formula would be in vain. Heraclitus' saying that the sun is new every day is true for the sun of the artist if not for the sun of the scientist. When the scientist describes an object he characterizes it by a set of numbers, by its physical and chemical constants. Art has not only a different aim but a different object. If we say of two artists that they paint "the same" landscape we describe our aesthetic experience very inadequately. From the point of view of art such a pretended sameness is quite illusory. We cannot speak of one and the same thing as the subject matter of both painters. For the artist does not portray or copy a certain empirical object—a landscape with its hills and mountains, its brooks and rivers. What he gives us is the individual and momentary physiognomy of the landscape. He wishes to express the atmosphere of things, the play of light and shadow. A landscape is not "the same" in early twilight, in midday heat, or on a rainy or sunny day. Our aesthetic perception exhibits a much greater variety and belongs to a much more complex order than our ordinary sense perception. In sense perception we are content with apprehending the common and constant features of the objects of our surroundings. Aesthetic experience is incomparably richer. It is pregnant with infinite possibilities which remain unrealized in ordinary sense experience. In the work of the artist these possibilities become actualities; they are brought into the open and take on a definite shape. The revelation of this inexhaustibility of the aspects of things is one of the great privileges and one of the deepest charms of art.

The painter Ludwig Richter relates in his memoirs how once when he was in Tivoli as a young man he and three friends set out to paint the same landscape. They were all firmly resolved not to deviate from nature; they wished to reproduce what they had seen as accurately as possible. Nevertheless the result was four totally different pictures, as different from one another as the personalities of the artists. From this experience the narrator concluded that there is no such thing as objective vision, and that form and color are always apprehended according to individual temperament.[9] Not even the most determined champions of a strict and uncompromising naturalism could overlook or deny this factor. Emile Zola defines the work of art as *"un coin de la nature vu à travers un tempérament."* What is referred to here as temperament is not merely singularity or idiosyncrasy. When absorbed in the intuition of a great work of art we do not feel a separation between the subjective and the objective worlds. We do not live in our plain commonplace reality of physical things, nor do we live wholly within an individual sphere. Beyond these two spheres we detect a new realm, the realm of plastic, musical, poetical forms; and these forms have a real universality. Kant distinguishes sharply between what he calls *"aesthetic* universality" and the "objective validity" which belongs to our logical and scientific judgments.[10] In our aesthetic judgments, he contends, we are not concerned with the object as such but with the pure contemplation of the object. Aesthetic universality means that the predicate of beauty is not restricted to a special individual but extends over the whole field of judging subjects. If the work of art were nothing but the freak and frenzy of an individual artist it would not possess this universal communicability. The imagination of the artist does not arbitrarily invent the forms of things. It shows us these forms in their true shape, making them visible and recognizable. The artist chooses a certain aspect of

---

[9]I take this account from Heinrich Wölfflin's *Principles of Art History.*
[10]In Kant's terminology the former is called *Gemeingültigkeit* whereas the latter is called *Allgemeingültigkeit*—a distinction which is difficult to render in corresponding English terms. For a systematic interpretation of the two terms see H. W. Cassirer, *A Commentary on Kant's "Critique of Judgment"* (London, 1938), pp. 190 ff.

reality, but this process of selection is at the same time a process of objectification. Once we have entered into his perspective we are forced to look on the world with his eyes. It would seem as if we had never before seen the world in this peculiar light. Yet we are convinced that this light is not merely a momentary flash. By virtue of the work of art it has become durable and permanent. Once reality has been disclosed to us in this particular way, we continue to see it in this shape.

A sharp distinction between the objective and the subjective, the representative and the expressive arts is thus difficult to maintain. The Parthenon frieze or a Mass by Bach, Michelangelo's "Sistine Chapel" or a poem of Leopardi, a sonata of Beethoven or a novel of Dostoievski are neither merely representative nor merely expressive. They are symbolic in a new and deeper sense. The works of the great lyrical poets— of Goethe or Hölderlin, of Wordsworth or Shelley—do not give us *disjecti membra poetae*, scattered and incoherent fragments of the poet's life. They are not simply a momentary outburst of passionate feeling; they reveal a deep unity and continuity. The great tragic and comic writers on the other hand—Euripides and Shakespeare, Cervantes and Molière—do not entertain us with detached scenes from the spectacle of life. Taken in themselves these scenes are but fugitive shadows. But suddenly we begin to see behind these shadows and to envisage a new reality. Through his characters and actions the comic and the tragic poet reveals his view of human life as a whole, of its greatness and weakness, its sublimity and its absurdity. "Art," wrote Goethe, "does not undertake to emulate nature in its breadth and depth. It sticks to the surface of natural phenomena; but it has its own depth, its own power; it crystallizes the highest moments of these superficial phenomena by recognizing in them the character of lawfulness, the perfection of harmonious proportion, the summit of beauty, the dignity of significance, the height of passion." [11] This fixation of the "highest moments of phenomena" is neither an imitation of physical things nor a mere overflow of powerful feelings. It is an interpretation of reality—not by concepts but by intuitions; not through the medium of thought but through that of sensuous forms.

From Plato to Tolstoi art has been accused of exciting our emotions and thus of disturbing the order and harmony of our moral life. Poetical imagination, according to Plato, waters our experience of lust and anger, of desire and pain, and makes them grow when they ought to starve with drought. [12] Tolstoi sees in art a source of infection. "Not only

---

[11]Goethe, Notes to a translation of Diderot's "Essai sur la peinture," "Werke," XLV, 260.
[12]Plato, *Republic*, 606D (Jowett trans.).

is infection," he says, "a sign of art, but the degree of infectiousness is also the sole measure of excellence in art." But the flaw in this theory is obvious. Tolstoi suppresses a fundamental moment of art, the moment of form. The aesthetic experience—the experience of contemplation—is a different state of mind from the coolness of our theoretical and the sobriety of our moral judgment. It is filled with the liveliest energies of passion, but passion itself is here transformed both in its nature and in its meaning. Wordsworth defines poetry as "emotion recollected in tranquillity." But the tranquillity we feel in great poetry is not that of recollection. The emotions aroused by the poet do not belong to a remote past. They are "here"—alive and immediate. We are aware of their full strength, but this strength tends in a new direction. It is rather seen than immediately felt. Our passions are no longer dark and impenetrable powers; they become, as it were, transparent. Shakespeare never gives us an aesthetic theory. He does not speculate about the nature of art. Yet in the only passage in which he speaks of the character and function of dramatic art the whole stress is laid upon this point. "The purpose of playing," as Hamlet explains, "both at the first and now, was and is, to hold, as 'twere, the mirror up to nature; to show virtue her own feature, scorn her own image, and the very age and body of the time his form and pressure." But the image of a passion is not the passion itself. The poet who represents a passion does not infect us with this passion. At a Shakespeare play we are not infected with the ambition of Macbeth, with the cruelty of Richard III, or with the jealousy of Othello. We are not at the mercy of these emotions; we look through them; we seem to penetrate into their very nature and essence. In this respect Shakespeare's theory of dramatic art, if he had such a theory, is in complete agreement with the conception of the fine arts of the great painters and sculptors of the Renaissance. He would have subscribed to the words of Leonardo da Vinci that "*saper vedere*" is the highest gift of the artist. The great painters show us the forms of outward things; the great dramatists show us the forms of our inner life. Dramatic art discloses a new breadth and depth of life. It conveys an awareness of human things and human destinies, of human greatness and misery, in comparison to which our ordinary existence appears poor and trivial. All of us feel, vaguely and dimly, the infinite potentialities of life, which silently await the moment when they are to be called forth from dormancy into the clear and intense light of consciousness. It is not the degree of infection but the degree of intensification and illumination which is the measure of the excellence of art.

2.3 INSTITUTES OF ORATORY*

by Marcus Fabius Quintilian

Oratory is manifestly an art, #1-4. Yet some have denied that it
is, and said that its power is wholly from nature, 5-8. Examples
from other arts, 9, 10. Every one that speaks is not an orator, 11-13.
Opinion of Aristotle, 14. Other charges against oratory; that it has
no peculiar subject or matter, and that it sometimes deceives, 15-18.
Refutation of these charges, 19-21. Unfairly objected to it that it
has no proper end, 22-26. Not pernicious because it sometimes
misleads, 27-29. Another objection, that it may be exerted on either
side of a question, and that it contradicts itself; answered, 30-36.
Oratory is sometimes ignorant of the truth of what it asserts; but
the same is the case with other arts and sciences, 36-40. Confirmation of its being an art, 41-43.

1. There would be no end if I should allow myself to expatiate, and
indulge my inclination, on this head. Let us proceed, therefore, to the
question that follows, *whether oratory be an art.*** 2. That it is an art,
every one of those who have given rules about eloquence has been so
far from doubting, that it is shown by the very titles of their books, that
they are written *on the oratorical art;* and Cicero also says, that what
is called *oratory* is *artificial eloquence.* This distinction, it is not only
orators that have claimed for themselves, (since they may be thought,
perhaps, to have given their profession something more than its due,)
but the philosophers, the Stoics, and most of the Peripatetics, agree with
them. 3. For myself, I confess, that I was in some doubt whether I
should look upon this part of the inquiry as necessary to be considered;
for who is so destitute, I will not say of learning, but of the common
understanding of mankind, as to imagine that the work of building, or
weaving, or moulding vessels out of clay, is *an art,* but that oratory,
the greatest and noblest of works, has attained such a height of excellence *without being an art?* Those, indeed, who have maintained the
contrary opinion, I suppose not so much to have believed what they
advanced, as to have been desirous of exercising their powers on a
subject of difficulty, like Polycrates, when he eulogized Busiris and
Clytæmnestra; though he is said also to have written the speech that

*Reprinted from *Institutes of Oratory*, trans. by Rev. John Selby Watson (London:
George Bell and Sons, 1891), pages 151-159.
**Translator's italics throughout.

was delivered against Socrates; nor would that indeed have been inconsistent with his other compositions.[1]

5. Some will have oratory to be a natural talent, though they do not deny that it may be assisted by art. Thus Antonius, in Cicero *de Oratore*,[2] says that oratory is *an effect of observation*, not *an art;* but this is not advanced that we may receive it as true, but that the character of Antonius, an orator who tried to conceal the art that he used, may be supported. 6. But Lysias seems to have really entertained this opinion; for which the argument is, that the ignorant, and barbarians, and slaves, when they speak for themselves, say something that resembles an *exordium*, they *state facts, prove, refute,* and (adopting the form of a *peroration*) *deprecate.* 7. The supporters of this notion also avail themselves of certain quibbles upon words, that *nothing that proceeds from art was before art,* but that mankind have always been able to speak for themselves and against others; that teachers of the art appeared only in later times, and first of all about the age of Tisias and Corax;[3] that oratory was therefore before art, and is consequently not an art. 8. As to the period, indeed, in which the teaching of oratory commenced, I am not anxious to inquire; we find Phœnix, however, in Homer,[4] as an instructor, not only in acting but in speaking, as well as several other orators; we see all the varieties of eloquence in the three generals,[5] and contests in eloquence proposed among the young men,[6] and among the figures on the shield of Achilles[7] are represented both law-suits and pleaders. 9. It would even be sufficient for me to observe, that *everything which art has brought to perfection had its origin in nature,* else, from the number of the arts must be excluded *medicine*, which resulted from the observation of what was beneficial or detrimental to health, and which, as some think, consists wholly in experiments, for somebody had, doubtless, bound up a wound before the dressing of wounds became an art, and had allayed fever by repose and

---

[1]Because in every case he took the wrong side.

[2]I. 20; ii. 7, 8. The word *observatio*, however, as Spalding observes, is not to be found in either of these passages of Cicero.

[3]Corax was a Sicilian, who, about B. C. 470, secured himself great influence at Syracuse by means of his oratorical powers. He is said to have been the earliest writer on rhetoric. Tisias was his pupil. See Cic. Brut. 12; de Orat. i. 20; Quint. iii. 1, 8.

[4]Il. ix. 432.

[5]The *copious* style in the oratory of Nestor; the *simple* in that of Menelaus; and the middle in that of Ulysses. See Aul. Gell. vii.; Clarke ad Il. iii. 213. Capperonier thinks that Phœnix, Ulysses, and Ajax are meant, the speakers in the deputation to Achilles, Iliad ix.

[6]Il. xv. 284: ὁπότε κοῦροι ἐρίσσειαν περὶ μύθων.

[7]Il. xviii. 497-508.

abstinence, not because he saw the reason of such regimen, but because the malady itself drove him to it. 10. Else, too, *architecture* must not be considered an art, for the first generation of men built cottages without *art;* nor *music*, since singing and dancing, to some sort of tune, are practised among all nations. 11. So, if *any kind of speaking whatever* is to be called oratory, I will admit that oratory existed before it was an art; but if every one that speaks is not an orator, and if men in early times did not speak as orators, our reasoners must confess that an orator is formed by art, and did not exist before art. This being admitted, another argument which they use is set aside, namely, that *that has no concern with art which a man who has not learned it can do,* but that men who have not learned oratory can make speeches. 12. To support this argument they observe, that Demades,[8] a waterman, and Aeschines,[9] an actor, were orators; but they are mistaken; for he who has not learned to be an orator cannot properly be called one, and it may be more justly said, that those men learned late in life, than that they never learned at all; though Aeschines, indeed, had some introduction to learning in his youth, as his father was a teacher; nor is it certain that Demades did not learn; and he might, by constant practice in speaking, which is the most efficient mode of learning, have made himself master of all the power of language that he ever possessed. 13. But we may safely say, that he would have been a better speaker if he had learned, for he never ventured to write out his speeches for publication,[10] though we know that he produced considerable effect in delivering them.

14. Aristotle, for the sake of investigation, as is usual with him has conceived, with his peculiar subtlety, certain arguments at variance with my opinion in his Gryllus;[11] but he has also written three books *on the art of rhetoric*, in the first of which he not only admits that it is an art, but allows it a connexion with civil polity, as well as with logic.[12] 15. Critolaus[13] and Athenodorus, of Rhodes, have advanced many arguments on the opposite side. Agnon,[14] by the very title of his book, in

---

[8]Sext. Empir. p. 291. Fabric. Harl. ii. p. 868.

[9]Demosth. pro Cor. p. 307, 314, 329, ed. Reisk.

[10]Cic. Brut. c. 9; Quint, xii, 10, 19.

[11]The work is lost. Gryllus was the son of Xenophon, that was killed at Mantineia. Aristotle seems to have borrowed his name; and he related, according to Diog. Laërt. ii. 58, that many eulogies were written on Gryllus, even for the sake of pleasing his father. The Gryllus of Aristotle is mentioned by Diog. Laërt. v. 22. *Spalding.*

[12]Rhet. i. 2, 1.

[13]Compare ii. 15, 23. On his arguments against oratory, see Sext. Emp. p. 291, 292. *Spalding.*

[14]Of Athenodorus and Agnon nothing certain is known. *Spalding.*

which he avows that he brings an accusation against rhetoric, has deprived himself of all claim to be trusted.[15] As to Epicurus,[16] who shrunk from all learning, I am not at all surprised at him.

16. These reasoners say a great deal, but it is based upon few arguments; I shall therefore reply to the strongest of them in a very few words, that the discussion may not be protracted to an infinite length. 17. Their first argument is with regard to the *subject* or *matter*, "for all arts," they say, "have some *subject*," as is true, "but that oratory has *no peculiar subject*," an assertion which I shall subsequently prove to be false. 18. The next argument is a more false charge, for "no art," they say, "acquiesces in false conclusions, since art cannot be founded but on perception, which is always true; but that oratory adopts false conclusions, and is, consequently, not an art." 19. That oratory sometimes advances what is false instead of what is true, I will admit, but I shall not for that reason acknowledge that the speaker acquiesces in false conclusions, for it is one thing for a matter to appear in a certain light to a person himself, and another for the person to make it appear in that light to others. A general often employs false representations, as did Hannibal, when, being hemmed in by Fabius, he tied faggots to the horns of oxen and set them on fire, and, driving the herd up the opposite hills in the night, presented to the enemy the appearance of a retiring army; but Hannibal merely deceived Fabius; he himself knew very well what the reality was. 20. Theopompus, the Lacedæmonian, when, on changing clothes with his wife, he escaped from prison in the disguise of a woman, came to no false conclusion concerning himself, though he conveyed a false notion to his guards. So the orator, whenever he puts what is false for what is true, knows that it is false, and that he is stating it instead of truth; he adopts, therefore, no false conclusion himself, but merely misleads another. 21. Cicero, when he threw a mist, as he boasts, over the eyes of the judges in the cause of Cluentius, was not himself deprived of sight; nor is a painter, when, by the power of his art, he makes us fancy that some objects stand out in a picture, and others recede, unaware that the objects are all on a flat surface.

22. But they allege also, that "all arts have a certain definite end to which they are directed; but that in oratory there is sometimes no end at all, and, at other times, the end which is professed is not attained." They speak falsely, however, in this respect likewise, for we have already shown, that oratory has an end, and have stated what that end is,

---

[15]The title of his book shows that he is not an impartial judge.
[16]See xii. 2, 24; Cic. de Fin. i. 7.

an end which the true orator will always attain, for he will always *speak well.* 23. The objection might, perhaps, hold good against those who think that the end of oratory is *to persuade,* but my orator and his art, as defined by me, do not depend upon the result; he indeed who speaks directs his efforts towards victory, but when he *has spoken well,* though he may not be victorious, he has attained the full end of his art. 24. So a pilot is desirous to gain the port with his vessel in safety, but if he is carried away from it by a tempest, he will not be the less a pilot, and will repeat the well-known saying, "May I but keep the helm right!"[17] 25. The physician makes the health of the patient his object, but if, through the violence of the disease, the intemperance of the sick person, or any other circumstance, he does not effect his purpose, yet, if he has done everything according to rule, he has not lost sight of the object of medicine. So it is the object of an orator to speak well, for his *art,* as we shall soon show still more clearly, consists in the *act,* and not in the *result.* 26. That other allegation, which is frequently made, must accordingly be false also, that *an art knows when it has attained its end, but that oratory does not know,* for every speaker is aware when he has spoken well.

They also charge oratory with having recourse to vicious means, which no true arts adopt, because it advances what is false, and endeavors to excite the passions. 27. But neither of those means is dishonourable, when it is used from a good motive, and, consequently cannot be vicious. To tell a falsehood is sometimes allowed, even to a wise man;[18] and the orator will be compelled to appeal to the feelings of the judges, if they cannot otherwise be induced to favour the right side. 28. Unenlightened men sit as judges,[19] who must, at times, be deceived, that they may not err in their decisions. If indeed judges were wise men: if assemblies of the people, and every sort of public council, consisted of wise men; if envy, favour, prejudice, and false witnesses, had no influence, there would be very little room for eloquence, which would be employed almost wholly to give pleasure. 29. But as the minds of the hearers waver, and truth is exposed to so many obstructions, the

---

[17] A proverbial expression, from the Greek ὀρθὰν τὰν ναῦν: a portion of a prayer to Neptune: Grant, O Neptune, that I may guide the ship right. *Spalding* refers to Cic. ad Q. Fr. i. 2; Ep. ad Div. xii. 25; Sen. Epist. 85; Aristid. in Rhod. 542 ed. Jebb; Stobæus. p. 577; Isidore, Orig., who gives from Ennius, *Ut clavum rectum teneam, navimcue gubernem*; also Sen. Cons. ad M. Fil. c. 16; Erasmus, Adag. iii. 1, 28.

[18] Cic. Off. ii. 14, 16, 17.

[19] The reader will remember that the *judices* of the Romans were similar to our jurymen, but more numerous. See Adam's Roman Antiquities, or Smith's Dict. of Gr. and Rom. Ant.

orator must use artifice in his efforts, and adopt such means as may promote his purpose, since he who has turned from the right way cannot be brought back to it but by another turning.

30. Some common sarcasms against oratory are drawn from the charge, that orators speak on both sides of a question; hence the remarks, that *"no art contradicts itself*, but that oratory contradicts itself;" that *"no art destroys what it has itself done*, but that this is the case with what oratory does;" that *"it teaches either what we ought to say, or what we ought not to say*, and that, in the one case, it cannot be an art, because it teaches what is not to be said, and, in the other, it cannot be an art, because, when it has taught what is to be said, it teaches also what is directly opposed to it." 31. All these charges, it is evident, are applicable only to that species of oratory which is repudiated by a good man and by virtue herself; since, where the cause is unjust, there true oratory has no place, so that it can hardly happen, even in the most extraordinary case, that a real orator, that is, a good man, will speak on both sides. 32. Yet, since it may happen, in the course of things, that just causes may, at times, lead two wise men to take different sides, (for the Stoics think that wise men may even contend with one another, if reason leads them to do so,[20]) I will make some reply to the objections, and in such a way that they shall be proved to be advanced groundlessly, and directed only against such as allow the name of orator to speakers of bad character. 33. For *oratory does not contradict itself*; one cause is matched against another cause, but not oratory against itself. If two men, who have been taught the same accomplishment, contend with one another, the accomplishment which they have been taught will not, on that account, be proved not to be an art; for, if such were the case, there could be no art in arms, because gladiators, bred under the same master, are often matched together; nor would there be any art in piloting a ship, because, in naval engagements, pilot is often opposed to pilot; nor in generalship, because general contends with general. 34. Nor does oratory *destroy what it has done*, for the orator does not overthrow the argument advanced by himself, nor does oratory overthrow it, because, by those who think that the end of oratory is to persuade, as well as by the two wise men, whom, as I said before, some chance may have opposed to one another, it is probability

---

[20]The Stoics were compelled to hold this opinion, for they said that to govern a state was the business of a wise man, and yet could not venture to affirm that a wise man was to be found in any particular state only. I cannot at this moment, however, find any passage among the ancient authors expressly to that effect. *Spalding.*

that is sought; and if, of two things, one at length appears more probable than the other, the more probable is not opposed to that which
previously appeared probable; for as that which is more white is not
adverse to that which is less white, nor that which is more sweet contrary to that which is less sweet, so neither is that which is more
probable contrary to that which is less probable. 35. Nor does oratory
ever *teach what we ought not to say*, or that which is contrary to what
we ought to say, but that which we ought to say in whatever cause we
may take in hand. 36. And truth, though generally, is not always to be
defended; the public good sometimes requires that a falsehood should
be supported.[21]

In Cicero's second book *De Oratore,*[22] are also advanced the following objections: *that art has place in things which are known, but that
the pleading of an orator depends on opinion, not on knowledge, since
he both addresses himself to those who do not know, and sometimes
says what he himself does not know.* 37. One of these points, whether
the judges have a knowledge of what is addressed to them, has nothing
to do with the art of the orator; to the other, that *art has place in things
which are known,* I must give some answer. Oratory is the art of speaking well, and the orator knows how to speak well. 38. But it is said, he
does not know whether what he says is true; neither do the philosophers,
who say that fire, or water, or the four elements, or indivisible atoms,
are the principles from which all things had their origin,[23] know that
what they say is true; nor do those who calculate the distances of the
stars, and the magnitudes of the sun and the earth, yet every one of
them calls his system an *art;*[24] but if their reasoning has such effect that
they seem not to *imagine,* but, from the force of their demonstrations,
to *know* what they assert, similar reasoning may have a similar effect
in the case of the orator. 39. But, it is further urged, he does not know
whether the cause which he advocates has truth on its side; nor, I
answer, does the physician know whether the patient, who says that he
has the head-ache, really has it, yet he will treat him on the assumption
that his assertion is true, and medicine will surely be allowed to be an
art. Need I add, that oratory does not always purpose to say what is
true, but does always purpose to say what is like truth? but the orator
must know whether what he says is like truth or not. 40. Those who are
unfavourable to oratory add, that pleaders often defend, in certain

---

[21]Compare c. 7, sect. 27, and sect. 27-29 of this chapter.
[22]C. 7. The words are put into the mouth of Antonius.
[23]See the first book of Lucretius.
[24]Or *science,* as we should now term it.

causes, that which they have assailed in others; but this is the fault, not of the art, but of the person.

These are the principal charges that are brought against oratory. There are others of less moment, but drawn from the same sources.

41. But that it is an *art*, may be proved in a very few words; for whether, as Cleanthes maintained, *an art is a power working its effects by a course*, that is *by method*, no man will doubt that there is a certain course and method in oratory; or whether that definition, approved by almost everybody, that *an art consists of perceptions*[25] *consenting and cooperating to some end useful to life*, be adopted also by us, we have already shown that everything to which this definition applies is to be found in oratory. 42. Need I show that it depends on understanding and practice, like other arts? If logic be an art, as is generally admitted, oratory must certainly be an art, as it differs from logic rather in *species* than in *genus*. Nor must we omit to observe that in whatever pursuit one man may act according to a method, and another without regard to that method, that pursuit is an art; and that in whatever pursuit he who has learned succeeds better than he who has not learned, that pursuit is an art.

43. But, in the pursuit of oratory, not only will the learned excel the unlearned, but the more learned will excel the less learned; otherwise there would not be so many rules in it, or so many great men to teach it. This ought to be acknowledged by every one, and especially by me, who allow the attainment of oratory only to the man of virtue.

---

[25]*Perceptionum*. From the Greek κατάληψεις, signifying "things thoroughly comprehended and understood."

2.4 PHILOSOPHY OF EDUCATION AND THE "PSEUDO-QUESTION"*

by Maxine Greene

"It happens that the stage sets collapse. Rising, streetcar, four hours in the office or the factory, meal, streetcar, four hours of work, meal, sleep, and Monday Tuesday Wednesday Thursday Friday and Saturday according to the same rhythm—this part is easily followed most of the time. But one day the 'why' arises and everything begins in that weariness touched with amazement."[1] So Camus describes the sudden perception of the meaningless, the absurd. Somewhat the same mood falls on those who do not think in such terms, but are nonetheless compelled to ask, "Why?" Think of the Chorus in *Oedipus Rex:* "What measure shall I give these generations/ That breathe on the void and are void/ And exist and do not exist?" Think of Hamlet, referring to man: "And yet to me what is this quintessence of dust?" Think of Job: "Is not destruction to the wicked? And a strange punishment to the workers of iniquity? Doth he not see my ways, and count all my steps?" And Ivan Karamasov: "Listen! If all must suffer to pay for the eternal harmony, what have children to do with it, tell me, please?"

Such questions cannot be answered by empirically verifiable statements. The need for answers is so intense, however, that the very wanting generates confusion about meanings; and this confusion tends, as Stevenson says, to "fill the world with fictitious philosophical 'entities'."[2] "Pseudo"—or "limiting"—questions though the above may be, their presence cannot but be felt in the philosophy of education classroom. It seems to me that they have to be confronted and dealt with, if our discipline is to achieve its ends.

We conceive these ends variously, but clarity about language, thought, and meaning is instrumental to the attainment of them all. Successful training in required intellectual competencies involves coping directly with obstacles to rational thinking. Moreover, it involves admitting the variety in man's ways of seeing, the several dimensions of his symbolic universe. We recall what Cassirer describes as the "varied threads which weave the symbolic net, the tangled web of human experience."[3]

---

*Reprinted from *Proceedings of the Sixteenth Annual Meeting of the Philosophy of Education Society* (1960), pages 56-61, with permission of the author and the Philosophy of Education Society.
[1]Albert Camus, *The Myth of Sisyphus*, N. Y.: Knopf, 1955, pp. 12-13.
[2]Charles L. Stevenson, *Ethics and Language*, Yale Univ. Press, 1944, p. 39.
[3]Ernst Cassirer, *An Essay on Man*, Doubleday Anchor, 1953, p. 43.

The symbolisms of myth and art, as well as of science, produce worlds of their own; we reveal reality to ourselves in multiplex ways. Not all that is revealed is "known"; there are, simply, several modes of seeing and thinking, each one carving out an appropriate symbolic form. Only as we take this into account, can we admit the persistence of "empty" questions and unverifiable answers which must, if they are not to interfere with knowing, be distinguished from questions that are empirical and answers that have a claim to "truth."

We may dismiss the desperate questions as meaningless; but even when removed from full awareness, they continue operating stubbornly. Like repressed passions, they may exert more influence on behavior than they would if they were out in the open. When they remain unarticulated, closed to examination, they serve as a continual breeding ground for the fictitious, a refuge from the facts of experience. They cause, in Collingwood's terms, that "corruption of consciousness" accompanying the disowning of experiences by repression.[4] Collingwood suggests, however, that that which is disowned may be dominated if it is recognized; it may be made susceptible to intelligent evaluation.

This judgment may apply to the unanswerable questions mentioned above; and one way of bringing them into the open is through the use of art forms, particularly literature. As John Dewey remarks, the form that is found in art makes "clear what is involved in the organization of space and time prefigured in every course of a developing life experience."[5] A symbolic participation in a literary experience requires the deliberate ordering of emotions, attitudes, and beliefs; the organization of responses relevant to the life transcribed in the book. If we assume that our questions are emotive in character, and that emotive statements point, not to objective referents but to a range of feelings and attitudes, the ordering demanded by literature may be put to fruitful use. The very process of ordering brings what is ordinarily hidden into view; feelings and attitudes are, in a sense, objectified; and distinctions between the emotive and the descriptive can be made.

In *Oedipus Rex*, for example, the troubling question raised is that of human freedom and responsibility. The sin, "though never willed," exacts its penalty; and, when Oedipus assumes responsibility for what he could not help, we ask, "Why?" not only with reference to Oedipus but to all those who seem to know not what they do. The answer comes when the Chorus says: "Let every man in mankind's frailty/ Consider

---

[4]R. G. Collingwood, *The Principles of Art*, Galaxy, Oxford Univ. Press, 1958, p. 217.
[5]John Dewey, *Art as Experience*, Minton, Balch & Co., 1934, p. 24.

his last day; and let none/ Presume on his good fortune until he find/ life, at his death, a memory without pain." Clearly meaningful though these words are, they are meaningful in terms of the psychological reactions of those who read them. No cognitive process is immediately produced by them; but a cognitive process *can* be produced when they are talked about as part of a linguistic statement. The reader may know more about his own attitudes after he has turned away; he may even have experienced pity and terror; but his yearnings for a verifiable answer to the question will no longer, it is to be hoped, obscure whatever inquiry he undertakes into the role of human responsibility in life.

In Camus's *The Plague*, the problem of evil is presented, as it might emerge in the contemporary world. Dr. Rieux, revolting against evil in the symbolic form of a plague, seeks no ultimate explanations. He decides that he can only heal, as "a matter of common decency," and that he must take the universe as he finds it. The work summons up questions regarding justice in the universe and the meaning of suffering; and an ordering of attitudes is required if it is to be "understood." Scorning all fictitious entities, Camus deals with the stance demanded in the midst of life. Our reach may, indeed *will*, exceed our grasp; but we need to distinguish between a longing for cognitive certainties and occasions when, as White puts it, "we use sentences in such a way as to grant us the right to be sure. . . ."[6]

We cannot however, teach our students to make such distinctions simply by rational demonstration. We can demonstrate, say, how language creates philosophical difficulties and receive verbal evidence that what we have taught has made sense; but sometimes we may be too easily assuaged. Our students may use words as substitutes for real confrontation, not only of the fictions they carry with them, but, paradoxically, of the problems involved in understanding linguistic usages.

Preoccupied as we are with linguistic legitimacy and clarity, we tend to forget that the roots of language are in feeling, in action; that men begin to speak when they notice and need to name, when they begin to select, in terms of need and purpose, certain forms out of the flowing, undifferentiated stream of life. Sapir found the roots in "unconsciously evolved symbolisms saturated with emotional quality, which gradually took on a purely referential character as the linked emotion dropped out of the behavior in question."[7] Language, originally expressive of emotion, becomes modified to serve the purposes of thought; but, when

---

[6]Morton White, *Religion Politics and the Higher Learning*, Harvard Univ. Press, 1959, p. 46.
[7]Edward Sapir, "Symbolism," in *Encyclopedia of the Social Sciences*, XIV: 492-5.

it becomes intellectualized, it still maintains much of its original expressiveness.

There is a constant transaction between the emotive and the descriptive in both language and thinking; and we serve the cause of rationality if we keep that in mind, and if we keep in mind as well the influence of metaphor and imagery on conceptions of the real. Richards has explained language in terms of submerged metaphor; and Langer speaks of metaphor as language's law of life. "A metaphor," writes Richards, "is a shift, a carrying over of a word from its normal use to a new use. In a sense metaphor the shift of the word is occasioned and justified by a similarity or analogy between the object it is usually applied to and the new object. In an emotive metaphor, the shift occurs through some similarity between the feelings the new situation and the normal situation arouse."[8] He points out that the same word, in different contexts, may be a sense or an emotive metaphor, and that the two kinds are usually combined in language and thought. Relationships are created by means of metaphors; a "unity in variety" appears as the figure connects what appears to have no kinship at all.

The metaphor thus helps man to order his reality and unify it, even as do mathematical and logical signs. Art forms, functioning with expanded metaphors, become, like science, revelations of reality. Bronowski shows how scientific discoveries and works of art are both explorations of hidden likenesses. In the moment of appreciation, he writes, "we remake nature by the act of discovery, in the poem or in the theorem."[9] Science and art, then, order reality; the difference is that scientific ordering must conform to sense data empirically perceived, while aesthetic ordering is not bound by the requirements of "truth." It *is* the east; but Juliet is *not* the sun. It is meaningful, however, to say she is; and saying it enriches the descriptive meaning of "east," "sun," and "Juliet."

My point is that resources of feeling, imagination, impulse and memory may be utilized in cognition if the emotive, distinguished but not divorced from the descriptive, is allowed to complement literal meanings, if it is ascribed a creative power to help in ordering the world. The metaphor and the image play crucial roles in man's efforts to come in contact with his full reality. It is their pervasive operation that explains the human tendency to make analogies, to construct the universe in terms of what is desired and intimately known. Kant once said that all our thinking about final things is done by way of analogy,—

---

[8] I. A. Richards, *Practical Criticism*, Harvest, Harcourt, Brace & Co., 1929, p. 211.
[9] J. Bronowski, *Science and Human Values*, Julian Messner, Inc., 1956, pp. 30-31.

in terms of the great "as if," which is transformed, time and time again, into belief.

An instance of this is man's tendency to project into the cosmos models of his own social system, a tendency so fundamental that it cannot be invalidated simply by discovering its source in model-building and linguistic confusions. The full emotive meanings of analogies may also be explored, to make possible examination of the attitudes long associated with them; and, again, this may be done with the help of literature. Aeschylus's trilogy, the *Oresteia,* is a symbolic account of the establishment of a moral order in ancient Greece; and a participation in its movement may well make visible the insistent impulse to project the familiar into the unknown. Kindred insights may follow a reading of *The Divine Comedy,* where the afterworld represents a fulfillment of everything prefigured on earth; of Shakespeare's tragedies with their stress on the continuities between the inner life of man, the state, and the universe beyond; of *Moby Dick,* in which the cosmic mystery—neutral or malign—is objectified in the body of a whale. Such experiences may at least reveal the kinds of meanings involved in projection and analogy, may permit their exploration, even as analysis proceeds, to the end that they are not confused with rational "knowing" of the world.

The same is true of myths, which man will forever make; and an understanding, a "domination" of the mythical may advance our purposes too. A myth, in Schorer's words, is "a large, controlling image that gives philosophic meaning to the facts of ordinary life; that is, which has organizing value for experience."[10] The myth, for him, undergirds rational belief; and rational belief, in fact, is an intellectual "formulation" of controlling images which are submerged in abstractions as metaphors are submerged in language. Kluckhohn writes that myths in this sense are universal, even in content. This is explained by the "interaction of a certain kind of biological apparatus in a certain kind of physical world with some inevitables of the human condition . . ."[11] which brings about a regularity in imaginative image-making. Again, it is the "nature" of the human being to order the world in terms of what is known, prized, and feared.

We may know enough, perhaps for the first time, to conceive human responses in this way and to recognize that, after all, there are two kinds of experience available to man: that which can be systematically

---

[10]Mark Schorer, *William Blake: The Politics of Vision,* Vintage Books, 1959, p. 27.
[11]Clyde Kluckhohn "Recurrent Themes in Myth and Mythmaking," *Daedalus,* Spring, 1959, p. 270.

known and that which can be freely and spontaneously apprehended. As teachers, concerned with clarification and with norms, we can assume the potency of questions hopeless of rational solution and endeavor, at least, to bring them to the surface of consciousness, so that the kinds of meanings they invoke may be appreciated for what they are. I am suggesting that the principle of complementarity be applied because of the manifold meanings man discovers in his world; and I am making a plea for the mood of celebration, the mood of aesthetic contemplation, both of which may well be needed to complement the analytic frame of mind.

But, even more than that, I am speaking of the need for confrontation, in the name of freedom of action and thought. To recognize that there are no cognitive certainties, no verifiable answers to our most urgent questions is to begin shaping a new vision of life. Analysis and the clarification of concepts play a necessary critical and therapeutic role, in a sense a negative role. Some of us believe, however, that philosophy is also vision and the synthesis of meanings; and we are concerned with man's conceiving himself in some viable way in relation to the unverifiable, to the inscrutable "whiteness" which will not be denied.

It seems to me that such a vision is a necessity if our discipline is to play any sort of directive or normative role. Camus speaks of rebellion against the "injustice" of a world in which there are no comforting answers, no certainties at all. It is a moderate rebellion of fallible, clear-eyed men standing up to the unknowable, aware that they cannot penetrate the neutrality of the universe or reshape it in the image of their desire. Rebels of this sort are those who see that injustice and the incompatibility of desired goods are part of the web of circumstances in which they and all mankind must live—and that they will be forever questioners, living without guarantees, triumphing, if at all, by social act and rational inquiry and fellowship over inscrutability and fatality and death.

There is no "truth" in the above, but there may be meaning in it, the kind of meaning which students can discover in many areas of modern literature. I would want them to confront their questions by participating in worlds made by Joyce, Mann, Faulkner, Hemingway, and others, to look upon their own responses and come to terms with meanings that are non-cognitive and must be celebrated for what they are. Shaping experience in manifold ways, they may learn to live in the world with a more profound recognition that whatever values are to be must be created, whatever directions there are must be empirically defined.

2.5   INDIVIDUALITY AND EXPERIENCE*

by John Dewey

The interesting report of Dr. Munro[1] on the methods of picture-making employed in the classes of Professor Cizek in Vienna raises a question that has to be dealt with in every branch of instruction. The question develops in two directions, one suggested by his statement that it is impossible to exclude outside influences, and the other by his report that upon the whole the more original constructions are those of younger pupils, that older students seem gradually to lose interest, so that no prominent artist has been produced. The problem thus defined consists in the relation of individuality and its adequate development to the work and responsibilities of the teacher, representing accumulated experience of the past.

Unfortunately, the history of schools not only in art but in all lines shows a swing of the pendulum between extremes, though it must be admitted that the simile of the pendulum is not a good one, for the schools remain, most of them, most of the time, near one extreme, instead of swinging periodically and evenly between the two. Anyway, the two extremes are external imposition and dictation, and "free-expression." Revolt from the costly, nerve-taxing and inadequate results of mechanical control from without creates an enthusiasm for spontaneity and "development from within," as it is often phrased. It is found that children at first are then much happier in their work—anyone who has seen Cizek's class will testify to the wholesome air of cheerfulness, even of joy, which pervades the room—but gradually tend to become listless and finally bored, while there is an absence of cumulative, progressive development of power and of actual achievement in results. Then the pendulum swings back to regulation by the ideas, rules, and orders of someone else, who being maturer, better informed and more experienced is supposed to know what should be done and how to do it.

The metaphor of the pendulum is faulty in another respect. It seems to suggest that the solution lies in finding a mid-point between the two extremes which would be at rest. But what is really wanted is a change in the direction of movement. As a general proposition no one would deny that personal mental growth is furthered in any branch of human

---

*Reprinted from *Art and Education* (Merion, Pennsylvania: The Barnes Foundation Press, 1929), pages 175-183, by permission of The Barnes Foundation which retains the copyright.
[1]See article *Franz Cizek and the Free Expression Method* by Thomas Munro, p. 311.

undertaking by contact with the accumulated and sifted experience of others in that line. No one would seriously propose that all future carpenters should be trained by actually starting with a clean sheet, wiping out everything that the past has discovered about mechanics, about tools and their uses and so on. It would not be thought likely that this knowledge would "cramp their style," limit their individuality, etc. But neither, on the other hand, have carpenters been formed by the methods often used in manual training shops where dinky tasks of a minute and technical nature are set, wholly independent of really making anything, having only specialized skill as their aim. As a rule carpenters are educated in their calling by working with others who have experience and skill, sharing in the simpler portions of the real undertakings, assisting in ways which enable them to observe methods and to see what results they are adapted to accomplish.

Such learning is controlled by two great principles: one is participation in something inherently worth while, or undertaken on its own account; the other is perception of the relation of means to consequences. When these two conditions are met, a third consideration usually follows as a matter of course. Having had an experience of the meaning of certain technical processes and forms of skill there develops an interest in skill and "technique": the meaning of the result is "transferred" to the means of its attainment. Boys interested in base-ball as a game thus submit themselves voluntarily to continued practice in throwing, catching, batting, the separate elements of the game. Or boys, who get interested in the game of marbles, will practice to increase their skill in shooting and hitting. Just imagine, however, what would happen if they set these exercises as tasks in school, with no prior activity in the games and with no sense of what they were about or for, and without any such appeal to the social, or participating, impulses as takes place in games!

If we generalize from such a commonplace case as the education of artisans through their work, we may say that the customs, methods and *working* standards of the calling constitute a "tradition," and that initiation into the tradition is the means by which the powers of learners are released and directed. But we should also have to say that the urge or need of an individual to join in an undertaking is a necessary prerequisite of the tradition's being a factor in his personal growth in power and freedom; and also that he has to *see* on his own behalf and in his own way the relations between means and methods employed and results achieved. Nobody else can see for him, and he can't see just by being "told," although the right kind of telling may guide his seeing and thus help him see what he needs to see. And if he has no impelling de-

sire of his own to become a carpenter, if his interest in being one is perfunctory, if it is not an interest in *being* a carpenter at all, but only in
getting a pecuniary reward by doing jobs, the tradition will never of
course really enter into and integrate with his own powers. It will remain, then, a mere set of mechanical and more or less meaningless rules
that he is obliged to follow if he is to hold his job and draw his pay.

Supposing, again, that our imaginary pupil works for and with a
master carpenter who believes in only one kind of house with a fixed
design, and his aim is not only to teach his apprentice to make just that
one kind of house, but to accept it with all his soul, heart and mind as
the only kind of house that should ever be built, the very type and
standard model of all houses. Then it is easy to see that limitation of
personal powers will surely result, not merely, moreover, limitation of
technical skill, but, what is more important, of his powers of observation, imagination, judgment, and even his emotions, since his appreciations will be warped to conform to the one preferred style. The
imaginary case illustrates what often happens when we pass from the education of artisans to that of artists. As a rule a carpenter has to keep
more or less open; he is exposed to many demands and must be flexible
enough to meet them. He is in no position to set up a final authority
about ends and models and standards, no matter how expert he may be
in methods and means. But an architect in distinction from a builder is
likely to be an "authority"; he can dictate and lay down what is right
and wrong, and thus prescribe certain ends and proscribe others. Here
is a case where tradition is not enhancing and liberating, but is restrictive
and enslaving. If he has pupils, he is a "master" and not an advanced
fellow worker; his students are disciples rather than learners. Tradition
is no longer tradition but a fixed and absolute convention.

In short, the practical difficulty does not reside in any antagonism of
methods and rules and results worked out in past experience to individual desire, capacity and freedom. It lies rather in the hard and narrow
and, we may truly say, uneducated habits and attitudes of teachers who
set up as authorities, as rulers and judges in Israel. As a matter of
course they know that as bare individuals they are not "authorities"
and will not be accepted by others as such. So they clothe themselves
with some tradition as a mantle, and henceforth it is not just "I" who
speaks, but some Lord speaks through me. The teacher then offers himself as the organ of the voice of a whole school, of a *finished* classic
tradition, and arrogates to himself the prestige that comes from what he
is the spokesman for. Suppression of the emotional and intellectual integrity of pupils is the result; their freedom is repressed and the growth
of their own personalities stunted. But it is not because of any opposi-

tion between the wisdom and skill of the past and the individual capacities of learners; the trouble lies in the habits, standards and ideas of the teacher. It is analogous to another case. There is no inherent opposition between theory and practice; the former enlarges, releases and gives significance to the latter; while practice supplies theory with its materials and with the test and check which keeps it sincere and vital. But there is a whole lot of opposition between human beings who set themselves up as practical and those who set themselves up as theorists, an irresolvable conflict because both have put themselves into a wrong position.

This suggests that the proponents of freedom are in a false position as well as the would-be masters and dictators. There is a present tendency in so-called advanced schools of educational thought (by no means confined to art classes like those of Cizek) to say, in effect, let us surround pupils with certain materials, tools, appliances, etc., and then let pupils respond to these things according to their own desires. Above all let us not suggest any end or plan to the students; let us not suggest to them what they shall do, for that is an unwarranted trespass upon their sacred intellectual individuality since the essence of such individuality is to set up ends and aims.

Now such a method is really stupid. For it attempts the impossible, which is always stupid; and it misconceives the conditions of independent thinking. There are a multitude of ways of reacting to surrounding conditions, and without some guidance from experience these reactions are almost sure to be casual, sporadic and ultimately fatiguing, accompanied by nervous strain. Since the teacher has presumably a greater background of experience, there is the same presumption of the right of a teacher to make suggestions as to what to do, as there is on the part of the head carpenter to suggest to apprentices something of what they are to do. Moreover, the theory literally carried out would be obliged to banish all artificial materials, tools and appliances. Being the product of the skill, thought and matured experience of others, they would also, by the theory, "interfere" with personal freedom.

Moreover, when the child proposes or suggests what to do, some consequence to be attained, whence is the suggestion supposed to spring from? There is no spontaneous germination in the mental life. If he does not get the suggestion from the teacher, he gets it from somebody or something in the home or the street or from what some more vigorous fellow pupil is doing. Hence the chances are great of its being a passing and superficial suggestion, without much depth and range—in other words, not specially conducive to the developing of freedom. If the teacher is really a teacher, and not just a master or "authority," he should know enough about his pupils, their needs, experiences, degrees of skill and knowledge, etc., to be able (not to dictate aims and plans) to share in a discussion regarding what is to be done and be as free to make suggestions as anyone else. (The implication that the teacher is the one and only person who has no "individuality" or "freedom" to "express" would be funny if it were not often so sad in its outworkings.) And his contribution, given the conditions stated, will presumably do more to getting something started which will really secure and increase the development of strictly individual capacities than will suggestions springing from uncontrolled haphazard sources.

The point is also worth dwelling upon, that the method of leaving the response entirely to pupils, the teacher supplying, in the language of the day, only the "stimuli," misconceives the nature of thinking. Any so-called "end" or "aim" or "project" which the average immature person can suggest in advance is likely to be highly vague and unformed, a mere outline sketch, not a suggestion of a definite result or consequence but rather a gesture which roughly indicates a field within which activities might be carried on. It hardly represents thought at all: it is a suggestion. The real intellectual shaping of the "end" or purpose comes during and because of the operations subsequently performed. This is as true of the suggestion which proceeds from the teacher as of those which "spontaneously" spring from the pupils, so that the former does not restrict thought. The advantage on the side of the teacher—if he or she has any business to be in that position—is the greater probability that it will be a suggestion which will permit and require thought in the subsequent activity which builds up a clear and organized conception of an end. There is no more fatal flaw in psychology than that which takes the original vague fore-feeling of some consequence to be realized as the equivalent of a *thought* of an end, a true purpose and directive plan. The thought of an end is strictly correlative to perception of means and methods. Only when, and as the latter becomes clear during the serial process of execution does the project and guiding aim and plan become evident and articulated. In the full sense of the word, a person becomes aware of what he wants to do and what he is about only when the work is actually complete.

The adjective "serial" is important in connection with the process of performance or execution. Each step forward, each "means" used, is a partial attainment of an "end." It makes clearer the character of that end, and hence suggests to an observing mind the next step to be taken, or the means and methods to be next employed. Originality and independence of thinking are therefore connected with the intervening process of execution rather than with the source of the initial suggestion.

Indeed, genuinely fruitful and original suggestions are themselves usually the results of experience in the carrying out of undertakings. The "end" is not, in other words, an end or finality in the literal sense, but is in turn the starting point of new desires, aims and plans. By means of the process the mind gets power to make suggestions which are significant. There is now a past experience from which they can spring with an increased probability of their being worth while and articulate.

It goes without saying that a teacher may interfere and impose alien standards and methods during the operation. But as we have previously seen, this is not because of bringing to bear the results of previous experience, but because the habits of the teacher are so narrow and fixed, his imagination and sympathies so limited, his own intellectual horizon so bounded, that he brings them to bear in a wrong way. The fuller and richer the experience of the teacher, the more adequate his own knowledge of "traditions," the more likely is he, given the attitude of participator instead of that of master, to use them in a liberating way.

Freedom or individuality, in short, is not an original possession or gift. It is something to be achieved, to be wrought out. Suggestions as to things which may advantageously be taken, as to skill, as to methods of operation, are indispensable conditions of its achievement. These by the nature of the case must come from a sympathetic and discriminating knowledge of what has been done in the past and how it has been done.

CHAPTER THREE

SCIENCE IN THE WESTERN CULTURE TRADITION

3.1 EDITORIAL COMMENT

Over a period of years, and especially during the past decade, "Science" has come under caustic criticism by philosophers and theologians. It has been held responsible for the materialistic drift of our civilization, and even the possible destruction of the human race. Because of the contributions of the scientific movement to the advancement of the human mind, and its potentialities for the improvement of our educational efforts, it is necessary that teachers get a larger view of the role of science in our culture than is now in evidence. The selections which follow are directed toward this objective.

In his article on "Science and Its Critics," Dr. Harold McCarthy makes a careful analysis of the criticisms of science, points to the dangers involved in negative criticism of the movement, and especially the attempt on the part of some authorities to return to the dogma of the past.

One of the areas of major criticism of the scientific movement is related to the theory of evolution. In his article on "The Influence of Darwinism on Philosophy," John Dewey shows how the changing concept of the nature of man forces us to choose between a reconstruction of our conceptual framework or seek resolution in some transcendent and supernatural religion.

Because the beginnings of the trend toward a science of education are rooted in the thoughts of seventeenth century teachers and scholars, the work of John Amos Comenius has major significance in understanding the background of the movement. In his *The Great Didactic*, Comenius shows how the efforts of the scientist could bring into fuller reality the purposes of his Christian faith.

One of our deepest needs today is a clearer definition of the term "Science." Professor A. Cornelius Benjamin in his article not only points up the nature of the difficulty, but helps us gain new insight into the nature of the scientific process.

3.2   SCIENCE AND ITS CRITICS*

by Harold E. McCarthy

The man whose philosophy of life is based upon the conviction that the scientific method and the scientific outlook can be and must be extended into all realms where understanding is sought is finding himself more and more surrounded by critics. These critics are men who either distrust science completely or who feel that science must be controlled by, directed by, or at least supplemented by non-scientific disciplines, usually revealed religion or dogmatic metaphysics. The scientific temper of mind is not easy to maintain; and where man's security is seriously threatened, even civilized man finds it easy to return to more primitive types of thinking (*e.g.*, magic and supernaturalism, in general), through which a sense of security, if not security itself, may be achieved. Thus it is that the current criticism of science may be, in part, a reflection of the disordered and confused times in which we live. But where the criticisms of science are sincere (whatever forces they may reflect), they can be ignored by the scientific Humanist only at his peril and in the spirit of dogmatism—a spirit which is surely antithetical to the spirit of science.

The following ten criticisms of science have been given expression again and again and in various forms.

1.

Science is narrow and exclusive: it forgets that there are many things (i.e., "intangibles") which cannot be measured with meter sticks, weighed in balances, tested for tensile strength, or otherwise "scientifically" studied.

This general criticism usually rests upon the implicit or explicit identification of science as such with the special methods of the physical sciences, physics in particular. But one who is familiar with several sciences knows that science is not coextensive with physics and that each special science must develop its own empirico-rational procedures with which to deal with the problems that arise in its own particular field of inquiry.

The scientist does not deny, of course, the existence of relative "intangibles"; but he regards such "intangibles" as challenges to the con-

---

*Reprinted from *The Humanist XII*, No. 2, pages 49-55. Published by the American Humanist Association, Yellow Springs, Ohio, 1962. With permission of the publisher.

struction of relevant and reliable techniques of study, not as absolutes which are beyond all controlled, empirical investigation. To suppose that the techniques of physics somehow define science is to forget, for instance, that the biologist (not to mention the psychologist) has invented techniques that enable him to study facts which would remain completely "intangible" relative to the specific techniques of physics.

Properly understood, then, science is neither narrow nor exclusive, although, at any given time, it is limited. Its basic strength lies not in any supposed narrowness, but in the multiplicity of its modes of attack and the ingenuity exhibited in the progressive construction of diverse procedures of empirical investigation.

2.

The method of science is essentially analysis rather than synthesis; but analysis, taken alone, is both incomplete and destructive.

The implied dichotomy of analysis and synthesis is a false dichotomy; analysis and synthesis go hand in hand in science. Neither analysis nor synthesis is an end in itself for science, but both are means to that reliable and organized knowledge which defines understanding and which makes possible effective prediction and control. Analysis may sometimes be an indirect instrument of destruction; but what is destroyed by such analysis is only that which is not sound enough to undergo analytical scrutiny and survive. The notion that nothing can undergo analysis without being found defective is the sort of extreme pessimism that is not even supported by ordinary experience. The demand that some principles—be they religious, moral, political, economic—should be accepted without analysis is simply the demand that some principles should be accepted without scrutiny and without criticism and hence on the basis of mere emotion, blind faith, absolute authority, or political opportunism. Such a demand is not only incompatible with the scientific outlook but, taken in itself, gives absolutely no guidance as to just *what* principles should be thus accepted. The demand, say, that democracy should be accepted on faith can always be countered by the demand that communism should be accepted on faith. Where the method is that of unreason, conflict is inevitable.

3.

Science is essentially reductive: To the eye of the scientist man is nothing but an animal, love is nothing but a chemical reaction, the mystic experience is nothing but the boiling over of sexual energies, etc.

It is true that no scientist would deny that man, biologically considered, is a mammal, that love has a chemical aspect, that the mystic experience may have some psycho-sexual roots. But the careful scientific thinker, well aware of the complexities involved in the simplest phenomena, understands fully that the human being, if he is to be understood at all, must be studied from a wide variety of points of view. To the objective observer, man expresses what he is, not only in his biochemical structure, but also in his activities: in work and play, love and war, crime and judicial judgment, art and science, magic and religion. The comprehensive study and understanding of man involves, therefore, the cooperation of the physicist, chemist, biologist, psychologist, sociologist, historian, semanticist, critical philosopher, and art critic.

Speculative philosophers may occasionally claim that man is nothing but an animal, or nothing but a spirit, or nothing but a reflection of the Absolute Self; but such narrow and essentially "reductive" views are completely foreign to the scientific spirit, properly understood.

4.

Science is self-confessedly tentative in spirit and at no time guarantees that without which human beings cannot live—absolute certainty.

It is true that science guarantees no absolute certainties, its justified conviction being that it is never safe to close the door on the possible results of future investigation and future experience. Moreover, science notes that the claim to certainty, when universalized, is essentially self-destructive; those who claim to possess certainties are always attacked by those who claim contrary and incompatible certainties. Nothing, then, breeds unhealthy skepticism (not to mention impotent conflict) more than free-for-all claims to absolute truth.

As for the claim that life cannot be lived without some absolute certainties, the appropriate answer is that life *has* been lived without absolute certainties. It may be true that some people are unhappy without the illusion of certainty, but it is also true that no human being can live rationally until he has freed himself from illusion.

It should be remembered, finally, that in rejecting claims to absolute certainty, science does not leave us with the alternative of absolute uncertainty. Rather, we are left with scientific assurance, which is identical with the process of *making* sure. Although this process has no absolutely final term, it may have at any given time a tentative and relative termination.

5.

Science is thoroughly materialistic.

The charge of being materialistic is an old charge and in most cases is a rhetorical device for setting up negative attitudes. It is difficult to know precisely what the charge actually amounts to.

If the charge is that science studies, or is capable of studying, only matter in motion, the answer is simple: Contemporary scientists are busily investigating all sorts of processes—physical, chemical, biological, psychological, sociological. Indeed, with the aid of the techniques of psychoanalysis, scientists are now exploring both the conscious and unconscious dimensions and determinants of such "immaterial" entities as personality, motivation, and artistic creativity. Thus the subject matter of science is not limited to matter in motion.

If, on the other hand, the charge is that the moral orientation of science is, or must be, crude and unspiritual, the answer is again simple. For what higher and more spiritual goals could any man have than those involved in and implied by the whole enterprise of pure science—cooperation, understanding, respect, truth, and a life guided by reason? Such a goal as eternal bliss in some heavenly hereafter is almost crudely hedonistic in comparison.

6.

Science is essentially pessimistic; it necessarily involves the rejection of the three fundamental human hopes—free will, immortality, and the existence of God.

First of all let us note that science, as science, makes no categorical denials of this kind. The factuality of free will, immortality, and God is, for science, a problem of relative evidence. Science insists only that where reliable evidence is lacking, or inadequate, the most one can do is to suspend judgment or to acknowledge one's hopes as the *hopes* that they are.

The only alternative is that of becoming a dogmatist whose basic premise is that belief can be rational even in the absence of relevant evidence. Such a premise, however, defines precisely what is meant by irrationality; and when universalized, it underwrites any belief, no matter how quixotic and personal.

The scientific faith, on the other hand, is the faith in the guidance of evidence wherever evidence may lead. Such a faith is positive, and only the inveterate cynic would regard such a faith as pessimistic.

7.

Science rejects man's intuitive faculty with the claim that intuition is irrelevant to knowledge.

Broadly speaking, science rules out no "faculty" which leads to reliable knowledge.

With respect to intuition in particular (and those who distrust reason often appear to discredit reason in the interest of the "higher" faculty of intuition), it is well to remember that science, far from turning its back on intuition, recognizes that some of the most important scientific laws, principles, and concepts have been first hit upon "intuitively." However, it must be added that no intuition is self-validating and therefore every intuition must be regarded as a hypothesis to be tested rather than as a conclusion to be recorded.

Einstein has somewhere stated that out of one hundred intuitive insights, ninety-nine fail to withstand scrutiny. The hundredth intuitive insight, however, may be of crucial importance. We could say, then, to paraphrase Whitehead, that science counsels us to seek intuitions, but to distrust them.

8.

Science gives us relative knowledge only; therefore the absolute knowledge man seeks must come from extra-scientific disciplines.

We must recognize at the outset that scientific knowledge is human knowledge, expressive on the one hand of the structure of nature, expressive on the other hand of the nature of man, his needs, and his socio-cultural environment. If this is what is meant by "relative," then scientific knowledge is profoundly relative.

Though a scientist may understand man's yearning for the absolute, he must also recognize that no one has ever really been able to indicate the procedures whereby a human being may transcend his own faculties and facilities and thus assume a superhuman point of view. One can say that the structure of the eye necessarily limits what the eye itself can see, but it should not be forgotten that the possession of an eye is the condition of seeing anything at all.

The recognition that man is man and not God should, then, operate in all that we, as men, do and think. It is most unfortunate that this recognition has sometimes been interpreted to mean that man is not man but a mouse.

9.

Science is strictly intellectualistic and, in the long run, means the elimination of the aesthetic, moral, and religious aspects of human experience.

It is true that, in accordance with the scientific spirit, the man of scientific faith does seek for a rational morality that is grounded in tested experience rather than in revelation, authority, or mere tradition.

In like manner, a man of scientific faith also seeks a religion that is purified of superstition and an art that is something more than an escape from fear, frustration, or boredom. Although a man of science may, in this way, be critical of certain aspects of traditional art, morality, and religion, he neither advocates nor wishes the elimination of the aesthetic, moral, and religious aspects of human experience.

In this connection one may note that no one has expressed the implications of the scientific outlook more vigorously than John Dewey, and no one has been more keenly and continuously concerned with the refinement and enhancement of the aesthetic, moral, and religious dimensions of human experience.[1]

10.

Science is in the process of destroying all of us.

It must be admitted that scientific knowledge of the world in which we live may be used to destroy the world and everything of value in it, including science itself. But it does not follow that ignorance is bliss or that the failure to think is a blessing in disguise. Scientific knowledge, considered only as knowledge, is neutral. Like a hammer, it can be used constructively or destructively. But most working scientists, when not badgered by politicians and appealed to through their political loyalties, are interested only in the constructive use of scientific knowledge.

We may approve the claim that science must be integrated with other human interests and activities. But the further claim that a revival of traditional religion will supply the requisite integration, giving guidance to the development of science and thus bringing to pass a great era of peace and prosperity, is without rational foundation. The claim, indeed, can best be seen for what it is against the background of the religious wars, inquisitions, persecutions, intolerances, and attacks upon

---

[1]See John Dewey's *A Common Faith* (New Haven, Yale University Press, 1934).

scientists which have been an integral part of the development of Christianity, past and present.

In the last analysis, it is peculiarly shortsighted to make science a scapegoat for our own passions and prejudices, irrationalisms, nationalisms, and lusts for economic power. It is these, and not science, which are in the process of destroying all of us; and these can be coped with only by way of scientific-humanistic reason, not by way of the destruction of science, nor by way of the revival of the theological faith of our militant fathers.

Science, in the last analysis, is something more than method and something more than neutral knowledge. It is a way of life, demanding respect for truth, honesty, and rational evaluation, demanding the profound recognition of human capability, fallibility, and individuality. That science *is* a way of life is testified to by the vigor with which free science has always been attacked by totalitarian regimes, be they communistic, fascistic, or ecclesiastical.

3.3 THE INFLUENCE OF DARWIN ON PHILOSOPHY[*]

by John Dewey

I

That the publication of the "Origin of Species" marked an epoch in the development of the natural sciences is well known to the layman. That the combination of the very words origin and species embodied an intellectual revolt and introduced a new intellectual temper is easily overlooked by the expert. The conceptions that had reigned in the philosophy of nature and knowledge for two thousand years, the conceptions that had become the familiar furniture of the mind, rested on the assumption of the superiority of the fixed and final; they rested upon treating change and origin as signs of defect and unreality. In laying hands upon the sacred ark of absolute permanency, in treating the forms that had been regarded as types of fixity and perfection as originating and passing away, the "Origin of Species" introduced a mode of thinking that in the end was bound to transform the logic of knowledge, and hence the treatment of morals, politics, and religion.

No wonder, then, that the publication of Darwin's book, a half century ago, precipitated a crisis. The true nature of the controversy is easily concealed from us, however, by the theological clamor that attended it. The vivid and popular features of the anti-Darwinian row tended to leave the impression that the issue was between science on one side and theology on the other. Such was not the case—the issue lay primarily within science itself, as Darwin himself early recognized. The theological outcry he discounted from the start, hardly noticing it save as it bore upon the "feelings of his female relatives." But for two decades before final publication he contemplated the possibility of being put down by his scientific peers as a fool or as crazy; and he set, as the measure of his success, the degree in which he should affect three men of science: Lyell in geology, Hooker in botany, and Huxley in zoology.

Religious considerations lent fervor to the controversy, but they did not provoke it. Intellectually, religious emotions are not creative but conservative. They attach themselves readily to the current view of the world and consecrate it. They steep and dye intellectual fabrics in the seething vat of emotions; they do not form their warp and woof. There is not, I think, an instance of any large idea about the world being

[*]Reprinted from *Popular Science Monthly* (July, 1909).

independently generated by religion. Although the ideas that rose up like armed men against Darwinism owed their intensity to religious associations, their origin and meaning are to be sought in science and philosophy, not in religion.

II

Few words in our language foreshorten intellectual history as much as does the word species. The Greeks, in initiating the intellectual life of Europe, were impressed by characteristic traits of the life of plants and animals; so impressed indeed that they made these traits the key to defining nature and to explaining mind and society. And truly, life is so wonderful that a seemingly successful reading of its mystery might well lead men to believe that the key to the secrets of heaven and earth was in their hands. The Greek rendering of this mystery, the Greek formulation of the aim and standard of knowledge, was in the course of time embodied in the word species, and it controlled philosophy for two thousand years. To understand the intellectual face-about expressed in the phrase "Origin of Species," we must, then, understand the long dominant idea against which it is a protest.

Consider how men were impressed by the facts of life. Their eyes fell upon certain things slight in bulk, and frail in structure. To every appearance, these perceived things were inert and passive. Suddenly, under certain circumstances, these things—henceforth known as seeds or eggs or germs—begin to change, to change rapidly in size, form, and qualities. Rapid and extensive changes occur, however, in many things —as when wood is touched by fire. But the changes in the living thing are orderly; they are cumulative; they tend constantly in one direction; they do not, like other changes, destroy or consume, or pass fruitless into wandering flux; they realize and fulfil. Each successive stage, no matter how unlike its predecessor, preserves its net effect and also prepares the way for a fuller activity on the part of its successor. In living beings, changes do not happen as they seem to happen elsewhere, any which way; the earlier changes are regulated in view of later results. This progressive organization does not cease till there is achieved a true final term, a τελὰς, a completed, perfected end. This final form exercises in turn a plenitude of functions, not the least noteworthy of which is production of germs like those from which it took its own origin, germs capable of the same cycle of self-fulfilling activity.

But the whole miraculous tale is not yet told. The same drama is enacted to the same destiny in countless myriads of individuals so sundered in time, so severed in space, that they have no opportunity for mutual consultation and no means of interaction. As an old writer quaintly said, "things of the same kind go through the same formalities" —celebrate, as it were, the same ceremonial rites.

This formal activity which operates throughout a series of changes and holds them to a single course; which subordinates their aimless flux to its own perfect manifestation; which, leaping the boundaries of space and time, keeps individuals distant in space and remote in time to a uniform type of structure and function: this principle seemed to give insight into the very nature of reality itself. To it Aristotle gave the name, εἶδος. This term the scholastics translated as *species*.

The force of this term was deepened by its application to everything in the universe that observes order in flux and manifests constancy through change. From the casual drift of daily weather, through the uneven recurrence of seasons and unequal return of seed time and harvest, up to the majestic sweep of the heavens—the image of eternity in time—and from this to the unchanging pure and contemplative intelligence beyond nature lies one unbroken fulfilment of ends. Nature as a whole is a progressive realization of purpose strictly comparable to the realization of purpose in any single plant or animal.

The conception of εἶδος, species, a fixed form and final cause, was the central principle of knowledge as well as of nature. Upon it rested the logic of science. Change as change is mere flux and lapse; it insults intelligence. Genuinely to know is to grasp a permanent end that realizes itself through changes, holding them thereby within the metes and bounds of fixed truth. Completely to know is to relate all special forms to their one single end and good: pure contemplative intelligence. Since, however, the scene of nature which directly confronts us is in change, nature as directly and practically experienced does not satisfy the conditions of knowledge. Human experience is in flux, and hence the instrumentalities of sense-perception and of inference based upon observation are condemned in advance. Science is compelled to aim at realities lying behind and beyond the processes of nature, and to carry on its search for these realities by means of rational forms transcending ordinary modes of perception and inference.

There are, indeed, but two alternative courses. We must either find the appropriate objects and organs of knowledge in the mutual interactions of changing things; or else, to escape the infection of change, we *must* seek them in some transcendent and supernal region. The human mind, deliberately as it were, exhausted the logic of the changeless, the final, and the transcendent, before it essayed adventure on the pathless wastes of generation and transformation. We dispose all too easily of the efforts of the schoolmen to interpret nature and mind in terms of real essences, hidden forms, and occult faculties, forgetful of the seriousness and dignity of the ideas that lay behind. We dispose of them by laughing at the famous gentleman who accounted for the fact that opium put people to sleep on the ground it had a dormitive faculty. But the doctrine, held in our own day, that knowledge of the plant that yields the poppy consists in referring the peculiarities of an individual to a type, to a universal form, a doctrine so firmly established that any other method of knowing was conceived to be unphilosophical and unscientific, is a survival of precisely the same logic. This identity of conception in the scholastic and anti-Darwinian theory may well suggest greater sympathy for what has become unfamiliar as well as greater humility regarding the further unfamiliarities that history has in store.

Darwin was not, of course, the first to question the classic philosophy of nature and of knowledge. The beginnings of the revolution are in the physical science of the sixteenth and seventeenth centuries. When Galileo said: "It is my opinion that the earth is very noble and admirable by reason of so many and so different alterations and generations which are incessantly made therein," he expressed the changed temper that was coming over the world; the transfer of interest from the permanent to the changing. When Descartes said: "The nature of physical things is much more easily conceived when they are beheld coming gradually into existence, than when they are only considered as produced at once in a finished and perfect state," the modern world became self-conscious of the logic that was henceforth to control it, the logic of which Darwin's "Origin of Species" is the latest scientific achievement. Without the methods of Copernicus, Kepler, Galileo, and their successors in astronomy, physics, and chemistry, Darwin would have been helpless in the organic sciences. But prior to Darwin the impact of the new scientific method upon life, mind, and politics, had been arrested, because between these ideal or moral interests and the inorganic world intervened the kingdom of plants and animals. The gates of the garden of life were barred to the new ideas; and only through this garden was there access to mind and politics. The influence of Darwin upon philosophy resides in his having conquered the phenomena of life for the principle of transition, and thereby freed the new logic for application to mind and morals and life. When he said of species what Galileo had said of the earth, *e pur se muove*, he emancipated, once for all, genetic and experimental ideas as an organon of asking questions and looking for explanations.

III

The exact bearings upon philosophy of the new logical outlook are, of course, as yet, uncertain and inchoate. We live in the twilight of intellectual transition. One must add the rashness of the prophet to the stubbornness of the partizan to venture a systematic exposition of the influence upon philosophy of the Darwinian method. At best, we can but inquire as to its general bearing—the effect upon mental temper and complexion, upon that body of half-conscious, half-instinctive intellectual aversions and preferences which determine, after all, our more deliberate intellectual enterprises. In this vague inquiry there happens to exist as a kind of touchstone a problem of long historic currency that has also been much discussed in Darwinian literature. I refer to the old problem of design *versus* chance, mind *versus* matter, as the causal explanation, first or final, of things.

As we have already seen, the classic notion of species carried with it the idea of purpose. In all living forms, a specific type is present directing the earlier stages of growth to the realization of its own perfection. Since this purposive regulative principle is not visible to the senses, it follows that it must be an ideal or rational force. Since, however, the perfect form is gradually approximated through the sensible changes, it also follows that in and through a sensible realm a rational ideal force is working out its own ultimate manifestation. These inferences were extended to nature: (*a*) She does nothing in vain; but all for an ulterior purpose. (*b*) Within natural sensible events there is therefore contained a spiritual causal force, which as spiritual escapes perception, but is apprehended by an enlightened reason. (*c*) The manifestation of this principle brings about a subordination of matter and sense to its own realization, and this ultimate fulfilment is the goal of nature and of man. The design argument thus operated in two directions. Purposefulness accounted for the intelligibility of nature and the possibility of science, while the absolute or cosmic character of this purposefulness gave sanction and worth to the moral and religious endeavors of man. Science was underpinned and morals authorized by one and the same principle, and their mutual agreement was eternally guaranteed.

This philosophy remained, in spite of sceptical and polemic outbursts, the official and the regnant philosophy of Europe for over two thousand years. The expulsion of fixed first and final causes from astronomy, physics, and chemistry had indeed given the doctrine something of a shock. But, on the other hand, increased acquaintance with the details of plant and animal life operated as a counterbalance and perhaps even strengthened the argument from design. The marvelous adaptations of organisms to their environment, of organs to the organism, of unlike parts of a complex organ—like the eye—to the organ itself; the foreshadowing by lower forms of the higher; the preparation in earlier stages of growth for organs that only later had their functioning—these things were increasingly recognized with the progress of botany, zoology, paleontology, and embryology. Together, they added such prestige to the design argument that by the late eighteenth century it was, as approved by the sciences of organic life, the central point of theistic and idealistic philosophy.

The Darwinian principle of natural selection cut straight under this philosophy. If all organic adaptations are due simply to constant variation and the elimination of those variations which are harmful in the struggle for existence that is brought about by excessive reproduction, there is no call for a prior intelligent causal force to plan and preordain them. Hostile critics charged Darwin with materialism and with making chance the cause of the universe.

Some naturalists, like Asa Gray, favored the Darwinian principle and attempted to reconcile it with design. Gray held to what may be called design on the installment plan. If we conceive the "stream of variations" to be itself intended, we may suppose that each successive variation was designed from the first to be selected. In that case, variation, struggle, and selection simply define the mechanism of "secondary causes" through which the "first cause" acts; and the doctrine of design is none the worse off because we know more of its *modus operandi*.

Darwin could not accept this mediating proposal. He admits or rather he asserts that it is "impossible to conceive this immense and wonderful universe including man with his capacity of looking far backwards and far into futurity as the result of blind chance or necessity."[1] But nevertheless he holds that since variations are in useless as well as useful directions, and since the latter are sifted out simply by the stress of the conditions of struggle for existence, the design argument as applied to living beings is unjustifiable; and its lack of support there deprives it of scientific value as applied to nature in general. If the variations of the pigeon, which under artificial selection give the pouter pigeon, are not preordained for the sake of the breeder, by what logic do we argue that variations resulting in natural species are pre-designed?[2]

IV

So much for some of the more obvious facts of the discussion of design *versus* chance, as causal principles of nature and of life as a whole. We brought up this discussion, you recall, as a crucial instance. What does our touchstone indicate as to the bearing of Darwinian ideas

---

[1]"Life and Letters," Vol. I., p. 282; cf. 285.
[2]"Life and Letters," Vol. II., pp. 146, 170, 245; Vol. I., pp. 283-84. See also the closing portion of his "Variations of Animals and Plants under Domestication."

upon philosophy: In the first place, the new logic outlaws, flanks, dismisses—what you will—one type of problems and substitutes for it another type. Philosophy forswears inquiry after absolute origins and absolute finalities in order to explore specific values and the specific conditions that generate them.

Darwin concluded that the impossibility of assigning the world to chance as a whole and to design in its parts indicated the insolubility of the question. Two radically different reasons, however, may be given as to why a problem is insoluble. One reason is that the problem is too high for intelligence; the other is that the question in its very asking makes assumptions that render the question meaningless. The latter alternative is unerringly pointed to in the celebrated case of design *versus* chance. Once admit that the sole verifiable or fruitful object of knowledge is the particular set of changes that generate the object of study together with the consequences that then flow from it, and no intelligible question can be asked about what, by assumption, lies outside. To assert—as is often asserted—that specific values of particular truth, social bonds and forms of beauty, if they can be shown to be generated by concretely knowable conditions, are meaningless and in vain; to assert that they are justified only when they and their particular causes and effects have all at once been gathered up into some inclusive first cause and some exhaustive final goal, is intellectual atavism. Such argumentation is reversion to the logic that explained the extinction of fire by water through the formal essence of aqueousness and the quenching of thirst by water through the final cause of aqueousness. Whether used in the case of the special event or that of life as a whole, such logic only abstracts some aspect of the existing course of events in order to reduplicate it as a petrified eternal principle by which to explain the very changes of which it is the formalization.

When Henry Sidgwick casually remarked in a letter that as he grew older his interest in what or who made the world was altered into interest in what kind of a world it is anyway, his voicing of a common experience of our own day illustrates also the nature of that intellectual transformation effected by the Darwinian logic. Interest shifts from the wholesale essence back of special changes to the question of how special changes serve and defeat concrete purposes; shifts from an intelligence that shaped things once for all to the particular intelligences which things are even now shaping; shifts from an ultimate goal of good to the direct increments of justice and happiness that intelligent administration of existent conditions may beget and that present carelessness or stupidity will destroy or forego.

In the second place, the classic type of logic inevitably set philosophy upon proving that life *must* have certain qualities and values—no matter how experience presents the matter—because of some remote cause and eventual goal. The duty of wholesale justification inevitably accompanies all thinking that makes the meaning of special occurrences depend upon something that once and for all lies behind them. The habit of derogating from present meanings and uses prevents our looking the facts of experience in the face; it prevents serious acknowledgment of the evils they present and serious concern with the goods they promise but do not as yet fulfil. It turns thought to the business of finding a wholesale transcendent remedy for the one and guarantee for the other. One is reminded of the way many moralists and theologians greeted Herbert Spencer's recognition of an unknowable energy from which welled up the phenomenal physical processes without and the conscious operations within. Merely because Spencer labeled his unknowable energy "God," this faded piece of metaphysical goods was greeted as an important and grateful concession to the reality of the spiritual realm. Were it not for the deep hold of the habit of seeking justification for ideal values in the remote and transcendent, surely this reference of them to an unknowable absolute would be despised in comparison with the demonstrations of experience that knowable energies are daily generating about us precious values.

The displacing of this wholesale type of philosophy will doubtless not arrive by sheer logical disproof, but rather by growing recognition of its futility. Were it a thousand times true that opium produces sleep because of its dormitive energy, yet the inducing of sleep in the tired, and the recovery to waking life of the poisoned, would not be thereby one least step forwarded. And were it a thousand times dialectically demonstrated that life as a whole is regulated by a transcendent principle to a final inclusive goal, none the less truth and error, health and disease, good and evil, hope and fear in the concrete, would remain just what and where they now are. To improve our education, to ameliorate our manners, to advance our politics, we must have recourse to specific conditions of generation.

Finally, the new logic introduces responsibility into the intellectual life. To idealize and rationalize the universe at large is after all a confession of inability to master the courses of things that specifically concern us. As long as mankind suffered from this impotency, it naturally shifted a burden of responsibility that it could not carry over to the more competent shoulders of the transcendent cause. But if insight into specific conditions of value and into specific consequences of ideas is possible, philosophy must in time become a method of locating and interpreting the more serious of the conflicts that occur in life, and a method of projecting ways for dealing with them: a method of moral and political diagnosis and prognosis.

The claim to formulate *a priori* the legislative constitution of the universe is by its nature a claim that may lead to elaborate dialectic developments. But it is also one that removes these very conclusions from subjection to experimental test, for, by definition, these results make no differences in the detailed course of events. But a philosophy that humbles its pretensions to the work of projecting hypotheses for the education and conduct of mind, individual and social, is thereby subjected to test by the way in which the ideas it propounds work out in practice. In having modesty forced upon it, philosophy also acquires responsibility.

Doubtless I seem to have violated the implied promise of my earlier remarks and to have turned both prophet and partizan. But in anticipating the direction of the transformations in philosophy to be wrought by the Darwinian genetic and experimental logic, I do not profess to speak for any save those who yield themselves consciously or unconsciously to this logic. No one can fairly deny that at present there are two effects of the Darwinian mode of thinking. On the one hand, there are many sincere and vital efforts to revise our traditional philosophic conceptions in accordance with its demands. On the other hand, there is as definitely a recrudescence of absolutistic philosophies; an assertion of a type of philosophic knowing distinct from that of the sciences, one which opens to us another kind of reality from that to which the sciences give access; an appeal through experience to something that essentially goes beyond experience. This reaction affects popular creeds and religious movements as well as technical philosophies. The very conquest of the biological sciences by the new ideas has led many to proclaim an explicit and rigid separation of philosophy from science.

Old ideas give way slowly; for they are more than abstract logical forms and categories. They are habits, predispositions, deeply engrained attitudes of aversion and preference. Moreover, the conviction persists— though history shows it to be a hallucination—that all the questions that the human mind has asked are questions that can be answered in terms of the alternatives that the questions themselves present. But in fact intellectual progress usually occurs through sheer abandonment of questions together with both of the alternatives they assume—an abandonment that results from their decreasing vitality and a change of urgent interest. We do not solve them: we get over them. Old questions are solved by disappearing, evaporating, while new questions corresponding to the changed attitude of endeavor and preference take their place. Doubtless the greatest dissolvent in contemporary thought of old questions, the greatest precipitant of new methods, new intentions, new problems, is the one effected by the scientific revolution that found its climax in the "Origin of Species."

3.4 THE UNIVERSAL REQUIREMENTS OF TEACHING AND OF LEARNING*

by John Amos Comenius

1. Exceptionally fine is that comparison made by our Lord Jesus Christ in the gospel, "So is the kingdom of God, as if a man should cast seed upon the earth; and should sleep and rise night and day, and the seed should spring up and grow, he knoweth not how. The earth beareth fruit of herself; first the blade, then the ear, then the full corn in the ear. But when the fruit is ripe, straightway he putteth forth the sickle, because the harvest is come" (Mark iv. 26).

2. The Saviour here shows that it is God who operates in everything, and that nothing remains for man but to receive the seeds of instruction with a devout heart; the processes of growth and of ripening will then continue of themselves, unperceived by him. The duty of the teachers of the young, therefore, is none other than to skilfully scatter the seeds of instruction in their minds, and to carefully water God's plants. Increase and growth will come from above.

3. Is there any who denies that sowing and planting need skill and experience? If an unpractised gardener plant an orchard with young trees, the greater number of them die, and the few that prosper do so rather through chance than through skill. But the trained gardener goes to work carefully, since he is well instructed, where, when, and how to act and what to leave alone, that he may meet with no failure. It is true that even an experienced man meets with failure occasionally (indeed it is scarcely possible for a man to take such careful forethought that no error can arise); but we are now discussing, not the abstract question of circumspection and chance, but the art of doing away with chance by means of circumspection.

4. Hitherto the method of instruction has been so uncertain that scarcely any one would dare to say: "In so many years I will bring this youth to such and such a point; I will educate him in such and such a way." We must therefore see if it be possible to place the art of intellectual discipline on such a firm basis that sure and certain progress may be made.

5. Since this basis can be properly laid only by assimilating the processes of art as much as possible to those of nature (as we have seen in the 15th chapter), we will follow the method of nature, taking as our

---

*Reprinted from *The Great Didactic*, trans. M. W. Keatinge (London: Adam and Charles Black, 1896), pages 263-278.

example a bird hatching out its young; and, if we see with what good results gardeners, painters, and builders follow in the track of nature, we shall have to recognize that the educator of the young should follow in the same path.

6.   If any think this course of action petty or commonplace, let him consider that from that which is of daily occurrence and universal notoriety and which takes place with good results in nature and in the arts (the teaching art excepted), we are seeking to deduce that which is less known and which is necessary for our present purpose. Indeed, if the facts from which we derive the principles that form the basis for our precepts are known, we can entertain hopes that our conclusions will be the more evident.

FIRST PRINCIPLE

7.   *Nature observes a suitable time.*
For example: a bird that wishes to multiply its species, does not set about it in winter, when everything is stiff with cold, nor in summer, when everything is parched and withered by the heat; not yet in autumn, when the vital force of all creatures declines with the sun's declining rays, and a new winter with hostile mien is approaching; but in spring, when the sun brings back life and strength to all. Again, the process consists of several steps. While it is yet cold the bird conceives the eggs and warms them inside its body, where they are protected from the cold; when the air grows warmer it lays them in its nest, but does not hatch them out until the warm season comes, that the tender chicks may grow accustomed to light and warmth by degrees.

8.   *Imitation.*—In the same way the gardener takes care to do nothing out of season. He does not, therefore, plant in the winter (because the sap is then in the roots, preparing to mount and nourish the plant later on); nor in summer (when the sap is already dispersed through the branches); nor in autumn (when the sap is retiring to the roots once more); but in spring, when the moisture is beginning to rise from the roots and the upper part of the plant begins to shoot. Later on, too, it is of great importance to the little tree that the right time be chosen for the various operations that are needful, such as manuring, pruning, and cutting. Even the tree itself has its proper time for putting forth shoots and blossoms, for growing, and for coming to maturity.

In the same manner the careful builder must choose the right time for cutting timber, burning bricks, laying foundations, building, and plastering walls, etc.

9. *Deviation.*—In direct opposition to this principle, a twofold error is committed in schools.

(i) The right time for mental exercise is not chosen.

(ii) The exercises are not properly divided, so that all advance may be made through the several stages needful, without any omission. As long as the boy is still a child he cannot be taught, because the roots of his understanding are still too deep below the surface. As soon as he becomes old, it is too late to teach him, because the intellect and the memory are then failing. In middle age it is difficult, because the forces of the intellect are dissipated over a variety of objects and are not easily concentrated. The season of youth, therefore, must be chosen. Then life and mind are fresh and gathering strength; then everything is vigorous and strikes root deeply.

10. *Rectification.*—We conclude, therefore, that

(i) The education of men should be commenced in the springtime of life, that is to say, in boyhood (for boyhood is the equivalent of spring, youth of summer, manhood of autumn, and old age of winter).

(ii) The morning hours are the most suitable for study (for here again the morning is the equivalent of spring, midday of summer, the evening of autumn, and the night of winter).

(iii) All the subjects that are to be learned should be arranged so as to suit the age of the students, that nothing which is beyond their comprehension be given them to learn.

SECOND PRINCIPLE

11. *Nature prepares the material, before she begins to give it form.*
For example: the bird that wishes to produce a creature similar to itself first conceives the embryo from a drop of its blood; it then prepares the nest in which it is to lay the eggs, but does not begin to hatch them until the chick is formed and moves within the shell.

12. *Imitation.*—In the same way the prudent builder, before he begins to erect a building, collects a quantity of wood, lime, stones, iron, and the other things needful, in order that he may not have to stop the work later on from lack of materials, nor find that its solidity has been impaired. In the same way, the painter who wishes to produce a picture, prepares the canvas, stretches it on a frame, lays the ground on it, mixes his colours, places his brushes so that they may be ready to hand, and then at last commences to paint.

In the same way the gardener, before he commences operations, tries to have the garden, the stocks, the grafts, and the tools in readiness,

that he may not have to fetch the necessary appliances while at work, and so spoil the whole operation.

13. *Deviation.*—Against this principle schools are offenders: firstly, because they take no care to prepare beforehand the mechanical aids such as books, maps, pictures, diagrams, etc., and to have them in readiness for general use, but at the moment that they need this or that, they make experiments, draw, dictate, copy, etc., and when this is done by an unskilled or careless teacher (and their number increases daily), the result is deplorable. It is just as if a physician, whenever he wishes to administer a medicine, had to wander through gardens and forests, and collect and distil herbs and roots, though medicaments to suit every case should be ready to his hand.

14. Secondly, because even in school-books the natural order, that the matter come first and the form follow, is not observed. Everywhere the exact opposite is to be found. The classification of objects is unnaturally made to precede a knowledge of the objects themselves, although it is impossible to classify, before the matter to be classified is there. I will demonstrate this by four examples.

15. (1) Languages are learned in schools before the sciences, since the intellect is detained for some years over the study of languages, and only then allowed to proceed to the sciences, mathematics, physics, etc. And yet things are essential, words only accidental; things are the body, words but the garment; things are the kernel, words the shells and husks. Both should therefore be presented to the intellect at the same time, but particularly the things, since they are as much objects of the understanding as are languages.

16. (2) Even in the study of languages the proper order is reversed, since the students commence, not with some author or with a skilfully-compiled phrase-book, but with the grammar; though the authors (and in their own way the phrase-books) present the material of speech, namely words, while the grammars, on the other hand, only give the form, that is to say, the laws of the formation, order, and combination of words.

17. (3) In the encyclopædic compilations of human knowledge, the arts are always placed first, while the sciences follow after; though the latter teach of the things themselves, the former how to manipulate the things.

18. (4) Finally: it is the abstract rules that are first taught and then illustrated by dragging in a few examples; though it is plain that a light should precede him whom it lights.

19. *Rectification.*—It follows, therefore, that in order to effect a thorough improvement in schools it is necessary:

(i)   That books and the materials necessary for teaching be held in readiness.

(ii)   That the understanding be first instructed in things, and then taught to express them in language.

(iii)   That no language be learned from a grammar, but from suitable authors.

(iv)   That the knowledge of things precede the knowledge of their combinations.

(v)   And that examples come before rules.

THIRD PRINCIPLE

20.   *Nature chooses a fit subject to act upon, or first submits one to a suitable treatment in order to make it fit.*

For example: a bird does not place any object in the nest in which it sits, but an object of such a kind that a chicken can be hatched from it, that is to say, an egg. If a small stone or anything else falls into the nest, it throws it out as useless. But when the process of hatching takes place, it warms the matter contained in the egg, and looks after it until the chicken makes its way out.

21.   *Imitation.*—In the same way the builder cuts down timber, of as good quality as possible, dries it, squares it, and saws it into planks. Then he chooses a spot to build on, clears it, lays a new foundation, or repairs the old one so that he can make use of it.

22.   In the same way, if the canvas or the surface do not suit his colours, the painter tries to make them more suitable, and, by rubbing them and polishing them, fits them for his use.

23.   The gardener too (1) chooses from a fruit-bearing stock a shoot that possesses as much vitality as possible; (2) transplants it to a garden, and places it carefully in the earth; (3) does not burden it with a new graft unless he sees that it has taken root; (4) before he inserts the new graft, removes the former shoot, and even cuts a piece away round the stock in order that none of the sap may perform any function other than that of vivifying the graft.

24.   *Deviation.*—Against this principle the schools are offenders: not because they include the weak of intellect (for in our opinion all the young should be admitted into the schools) but far more because:

(1)   These tender plants are not transplanted into the garden, that is to say, are not entirely entrusted to the schools, so that none, who are to be trained as men, shall be allowed to leave the workshop before their training is complete.

(2)   The attempt is generally made to engraft that noblest graft of knowledge, virtue and piety, too early, before the stock itself has taken

root; that is to say, before the desire to learn has been excited in those who have no natural bent in that direction.

(3) The side-shoots or root-suckers are not removed before the grafting takes place; that is to say, the minds are not freed from all idle tendencies by being habituated to discipline and order.

25. *Rectification.*—It is therefore desirable:

(i) That all who enter schools persevere in their studies.

(ii) That, before any special study is introduced, the minds of the students be prepared and made receptive of it. (See the following chapter, Principle 2.)

(iii) That all obstacles be removed out of the way of schools.

"For it is of no use to give precepts," says Seneca, "unless the obstacles that stand in the way be removed." But of this we will treat in the following chapter.

FOURTH PRINCIPLE

26. *Nature is not confused in its operations, but in its forward progress advances distinctly from one point to another.*

For example: if a bird is being produced, its bones, veins, and nerves are formed at separate and distinct periods; at one time its flesh becomes firm, at another it receives its covering of skin or feathers, and at another it learns how to fly, etc.

27. *Imitation.*—When a builder lays foundations he does not build the walls at the same time, much less does he put on the roof, but does each of these things at the proper time and in the proper place.

28. In the same way a painter does not work at twenty or thirty pictures at once, but occupies himself with one only. For, though he may from time to time put a few touches to some others or give his attention to something else, it is on one picture and one only that he concentrates his energies.

29. In the same way the gardener does not plant several shoots at once, but plants them one after the other, that he may neither confuse himself nor spoil the operation of nature.

30. *Deviation.*—Confusion has arisen in the schools through the endeavour to teach the scholars many things at one time. As, for example, Latin and Greek grammar, perhaps rhetoric and poetic as well, and a multitude of other subjects. For it is notorious that in the classical schools the subject-matter for reading and for composition is changed almost every hour throughout the day. If this be not confusion I should like to know what is. It is just as if a shoemaker wished to make six or seven new shoes at once, and took them up one by one in turn, only to lay them aside in a few minutes; or as if a baker, who wished to place

various kinds of bread in his oven, were to take them out again immediately, removing one kind as he put in another. Who would commit such an act of folly? The shoemaker finishes one shoe before he begins another. The baker places no fresh bread in the oven until that already in it is thoroughly baked.

31. *Rectification.*—Let us imitate these people and take care not to confuse scholars who are learning grammar by teaching them dialectic, or by introducing rhetoric into their studies. We should also put off the study of Greek until Latin is mastered, since it is impossible to concentrate the mind on any one thing, when it has to busy itself with several things at once.

That great man, Joseph Scaliger, was well aware of this. It is related of him that (perhaps on the advice of his father) he never occupied himself with more than one branch of knowledge at once, and concentrated all his energies on that one. It was owing to this that he was able to master not only fourteen languages, but also all the arts and sciences that lie within the province of man. He devoted himself to these one after the other with such success that in each subject his learning excelled that of men who had given their whole lives to it. And those who have tried to follow in his footsteps and imitate his method, have done so with considerable success.

32. Schools, therefore, should be organised in such a manner that the scholar shall be occupied with only one object of study at any given time.

Fifth Principle

33. *In all the operations of nature development is from within.*

For example: in the case of a bird it is not the claws, or the feathers, or the skin that are first formed, but the inner parts; the outer parts are formed later, at the proper season.

34. *Imitation.*—In the same way the gardener does not insert his graft into the outer bark nor into the outside layer of wood, but making an incision right into the pith, places the graft as far in as it will go.

In this way he makes the joint so firm that the sap cannot escape, but is forced right into the shoot, and uses all its strength in vivifying it.

35. So too, a tree, that is nourished by the rain of heaven and the moisture of the earth, assimilates its nutriment, not through its outer bark, but through the pores of its inmost parts. On this account the gardener waters, not the branches, but the roots. Animals also convey their food, not to their outer limbs, but to the stomach, which assimilates it and nourishes the whole body. If, therefore, the educator of the young

give special attention to the roots of knowledge, the understanding, these will soon impart their vitality to the stem, that is, to the memory, and finally blossoms and fruits, that is to say, a facile use of language and practical capacity will be produced.

36. *Deviation.*—It is on this point that those teachers fall into error who, instead of thoroughly explaining the subjects of study to the boys under their charge, give them endless dictations, and make them learn their lessons off by heart. Even those who wish to explain the subject-matter do not know how to do so, that is to say, do not know how to tend the roots or how to engraft the graft of knowledge. Thus they fatigue their pupils, and resemble a man who uses a club or a mallet, instead of a knife, when he wishes to make an incision in a plant.

37. *Rectification.*—It therefore follows

(i) That the scholar should be taught first to understand things, and then to remember them, and that no stress should be laid on the use of speech or pen, till after a training on the first two points.

(ii) That the teacher should know all the methods by which the understanding may be sharpened, and should put them into practice skilfully.

SIXTH PRINCIPLE

38. *Nature, in its formative processes, begins with the universal and ends with the particular.*

For example: a bird is to be produced from an egg. It is not the head, an eye, a feather, or a claw that is first formed, but the following process takes place. The whole egg is warmed; the warmth produces movement, and this movement brings into existence a system of veins, which mark in outline the shape of the whole bird (defining the parts that are to become the head, the wings, the feet, etc.) It is not until this outline is complete that the individual parts are brought to perfection.

39. *Imitation.*—The builder takes this as his model. He first makes a general plan of the building in his head, or on paper, or in wood. Then he lays the foundations, builds the walls, and lays on the roof. It is not until he has done this that he gives his attention to the small details that are necessary to complete a house, such as doors, windows, staircases, etc.; while last of all he adds ornamentation such as paintings, sculptures, and carpets.

40. An artist proceeds in the same way. He does not begin by drawing an ear, an eye, a nose, or a mouth, but first makes a charcoal sketch

of the face or of the whole body. If he be satisfied that this sketch resembles the original, he paints it with light strokes of the brush, still omitting all detail. Then, finally, he puts in the light and shade, and, using a variety of colours, finishes the several parts in detail.

41. The procedure of the sculptor is the same. When he wishes to carve a statue, he takes a block of marble and shapes it roughly. Then he sets to work more carefully and outlines the most important features. Finally, he chisels the individual parts with the greatest accuracy and colours them artistically.

42. In the same way the gardener takes the most simple and universal part of a tree, namely, a shoot. Later on, this can put forth as many branches as it possesses buds.

43. *Deviation.*—From this it follows that it is a mistake to teach the several branches of science in detail before a general outline of the whole realm of knowledge has been placed before the student, and that no one should be instructed in such a way as to become proficient in any one branch of knowledge without thoroughly understanding its relation to all the rest.

44. It follows also that arts, sciences, and languages are badly taught unless a general notion of the elements be first given. I remember well that, when we began to learn dialectic, rhetoric, and metaphysics, we were, at the very beginning, overburdened with long-winded rules, with commentaries and notes on commentaries, with comparisons of authors and with knotty questions. Latin grammar was taught us with all the exceptions and irregularities; Greek grammar with all its dialects, and we, poor wretches, were so confused that we scarcely understood what it was all about.

45. *Rectification.*—The remedy for this want of system is as follows: at the very commencement of their studies, boys should receive instruction in the first principles of general culture, that is to say, the subjects learned should be arranged in such a manner that the studies that come later introduce nothing new, but only expand the elements of knowledge that the boy has already mastered. Just as a tree, even if it live for a hundred years, puts forth no new branches, but only suffers those that already exist to develope and to spread.

(i) Each language, science, or art must be first taught in its most simple elements, that the student may obtain a general idea of it. (ii) His knowledge may next be developed further by placing rules and examples before him. (iii) Then he may be allowed to learn the subject systematically with the exceptions and irregularities; and (iv), last of all, may be given a commentary, though only where it is absolutely necessary. For he who has thoroughly mastered a subject from the beginning will have little need of a commentary, but will soon be in the position to write one himself.

SEVENTH PRINCIPLE

46. *Nature makes no leaps, but proceeds step by step.*

The development of a chicken consists of certain gradual processes which cannot be omitted or deferred, until finally it breaks its shell and comes forth. When this takes place, the mother does not allow the young bird to fly and seek its food (indeed it is unable to do so), but she feeds it herself, and by keeping it warm with her body promotes the growth of its feathers. When the chick's feathers have grown she does not thrust it forth from the nest immediately and make it fly, but teaches it first to move its wings in the nest itself or perching on its edge, then to try to fly outside the nest, though quite near it, by fluttering from branch to branch, then to fly from tree to tree, and later on from hill to hill, till finally it gains sufficient confidence to fly right out in the open. It is easy to see how necessary it is that each of these processes should take place at the right time; that not only the time should be suitable but that the processes should be graduated; and that there should be not graduation merely, but an immutable graduation.

47. *Imitation.*—The builder proceeds in the same manner. He does not begin with the gables or with the walls, but with foundations. When the foundations are laid he does not go on with the roof, but builds the walls. In a word, the order in which the several stages are combined depends on the relation that they mutually bear to one another.

48. The gardener likewise has to adopt the principle of graduation. The wild-stock must be found, dug up, transplanted, pruned, and cut; the graft must be inserted and the joint made firm, etc., and none of these processes can be omitted or taken in a different order but, if these processes are carried out properly and in the right order, it is scarcely possible, in fact it is impossible, for the result to be unsuccessful.

49. *Deviation.*—It is an evident absurdity, therefore, if teachers, for their own sake and that of their pupils, do not graduate the subjects which they teach in such a way that, not only one stage may lead on directly to the next, but also that each shall be completed in a given space of time. For unless goals are set up, means provided for reaching them, and a proper system devised for the use of those means, it is easy for something to be omitted or perverted, and failure is the result.

50. *Rectification.*—It follows therefore

(i)   That all studies should be carefully graduated throughout the various classes, in such a way that those that come first may prepare the way for and throw light on those that come after.

(ii)   That the time should be carefully divided, so that each year, each month, each day, and each hour may have its appointed task.

(iii)   That the division of the time and of the subjects of study should be rigidly adhered to, that nothing may be omitted or perverted.

EIGHTH PRINCIPLE

51.   *If nature commence anything, it does not leave off until the operation is completed.*

If a bird, urged by the impulse of nature, begin to sit on eggs, she does not leave off until she has hatched out the chickens. If she sat on them for a few hours only, the embryo in the egg would become cold and die. Even when the chickens are hatched she does not cease to keep them warm, but continues to do so until they have grown strong, are covered with feathers, and can endure the cold air.

52.   *Imitation.*—The painter also, who has begun a picture, will produce his work best if he finish it without any interruption. For in this case the colours blend better and hold faster.

53.   For this reason it is best to finish the erection of a building without any interruption; otherwise the sun, the wind, and the rain spoil the work, the later additions will not be so firm, and on every side there will be cracks, weak spots, and loose joints.

54.   The gardener too acts with wisdom, for when once he has begun to work at a graft he does not cease until the operation is completed. Since, if the sap dry in the stock or in the graft, owing to a delay in completing the process, the plant is ruined.

55.   *Deviation.*—It is therefore injurious if boys are sent to school for months or years continuously, but are then withdrawn for considerable periods and employed otherwise; equally so if the teacher commence now one subject, now another, and finish nothing satisfactorily; and lastly, it is equally fatal if he do not fix a certain task for each hour, and complete it, so that in each period his pupil can make an unmistakable advance towards the desired goal. Where such a fire is wanting, everything grows cold. Not without reason does the proverb say "Strike while the iron is hot." For if it be allowed to cool it is useless to hammer it, but it must once more be placed in the fire, and thus much time and iron are wasted. Since every time that it is heated, it loses some of its mass.

56.   *Rectification.*—It follows therefore

(i) That he who is sent to school must be kept there until he becomes well informed, virtuous, and pious.

(ii) That the school must be situated in a quiet spot, far from noise and distractions.

(iii) That whatever has to be done, in accordance with the scheme of study, must be done without any shirking.

(iv) That no boys, under any pretext whatever should be allowed to stay away or to play truant.

NINTH PRINCIPLE

57. *Nature carefully avoids obstacles and things likely to cause hurt.*
For example, when a bird is hatching eggs it does not allow a cold wind, much less rain or hail, to reach them. It also drives away snakes, birds of prey, etc.

58. *Imitation.*—In the same way the builder, so far as is possible, keeps dry his wood, bricks, and lime, and does not allow what he has built to be destroyed or to fall down.

59. So, too, the painter protects a newly-painted picture from wind, from violent heat, and from dust, and allows no hand but his own to touch it.

60. The gardener also protects a young plant by a railing or by hurdles, that hares or goats may not gnaw it or root it up.

61. *Deviation.*—It is therefore folly to introduce a student to controversial points when he is just beginning a subject, that is to say, to allow a mind that is mastering something new to assume an attitude of doubt. What is this but to tear up a plant that is just beginning to strike root? (Rightly does Hugo say: "He who starts by investigating doubtful points will never enter into the temple of wisdom.") But this is exactly what takes place if the young are not protected from incorrect, intricate, and badly written books as well as from evil companions.

62. *Rectification.*—Care should therefore be taken

(i) That the scholars receive no books but those suitable for their classes.

(ii) That these books be of such a kind that they can rightly be termed sources of wisdom, virtue, and piety.

(iii) That neither in the school nor in its vicinity the scholars be allowed to mix with bad companions.

63. If all these recommendations are observed, it is scarcely possible that schools should fail to attain their object.

3.5   ON DEFINING "SCIENCE"*

by A. Cornelius Benjamin

It is no easy task to define science. There are at least two reasons for this. In the first place the word has had a long and complicated history. As a result it has taken on a great variety of meanings, often inconsistent with one another. In the second place, and much more important, it has recently become a term of praise; since science is the "best" way of doing things we demand that advertising, detective stories, social planning, and even religion itself be scientific in method and intent. As a consequence the term has become dangerous because of its misleading associations; when anything calls itself "science," beware!

The problem is further complicated by the fact that every definition is, as everyone knows, to a certain extent arbitrary. One can, like Humpty Dumpty, make words mean exactly what he chooses to have them mean. But all of us, no doubt, feel the social pressure of conventional usage. When Eve saw Adam for the first time, as Mark Twain tells us in *Eve's Diary,* she decided to call him a "man." Why? Because he looked like a man. If as members of a social group we are to use the word "science," we ought to apply it to something that *looks* like science.

Two definitions that are in common use seem to confuse rather than clarify the issue. One of these identifies science with something that is commonly called the "scientific spirit." This, in turn, is defined rather vaguely as a way of looking at the world which is characterized by impartiality, freedom from prejudice, and respect for the criteria of truth. The scientist seems to feel to a very high degree his responsibility to the ideal of knowledge, and cautiously avoids temptations to fall into wishful thinking, or to be duped by his senses, or to accept superstitions or unsupported authority as adequate knowledge. Science, then, can be defined as any study that is characterized by objectivity, unemotionality, rigor, and control.

The other definition swings as far in the opposite direction; it identifies science with the quantitative method as applied in laboratory and experimental techniques. This is in accord with the traditional picture of the scientist, who is commonly represented as a white-coated individual surrounded by test tubes, flasks, and intricate mechanical contrivances. Science, according to this conception, first became scientific

*Reprinted from *The Scientific Monthly,* Vol. LXVIII, No. 3 (March, 1949), pages 192-198, with permission of Dr. Benjamin and *Science.*

when it abandoned purely observational techniques and substituted, on the one hand, manipulatory acts that involved setting up situations not normally occurring in nature apart from human intervention, and, on the other, instrumental aids to increase the range of the sense organs and to render measurement operations more precise.

Both these definitions are perfectly satisfactory if one is willing to accept the consequences of their usage. According to the former, of course, much will be science that is not commonly called by this name—philosophy, history, all the social studies, theology, and many authoritarian studies which, at least within the framework of their method, may be pursued with true regard for the principles of objectivity and control. According to the latter, much will not be science that is commonly called by this name—mathematics (which has no laboratory and performs no experiments); astronomy (which, though it uses instrumental aids, has no laboratory and performs no experiments in the strict sense of the word); theoretical mechanics (which is no more experimental than is geometry); and much of biology and psychology (which are highly restricted in their use of quantitative techniques). If one wishes, therefore, to win friends and influence people he has only to adopt the former definition, according to which he will be in a position to call practically everyone scientific, thus distributing honors widely. If, on the other hand, he is not averse to making enemies, he has only to adopt the latter definition, according to which very few of his associates will be entitled to the dignity of the name.

A much happier procedure, presumably, would be to choose a definition somewhat less broad than the former and somewhat less narrow than the latter. We do not gain in the understanding of a term if we define it so that everything falls under it or so that nothing falls under it. I propose, therefore, as a compromise, that science be defined as "the method of verified hypotheses."

Without further discussion and clarification, however, such a definition carries no enlightenment whatever. We define only when we equate notions we do not understand with notions which we do. Consequently, unless we have a fairly clear conception of what is meant by "hypotheses" and by "verification," we have made no advance. In fact, the definition, at least on the surface, does not look too good, for mathematics is concerned neither with hypotheses nor with verification, and there is a long tradition among natural scientists, beginning with Newton's *Hypotheses non fingo,* running through Mach and Pearson, and ending with contemporary positivists, to the effect that science makes most rapid progress when it abandons the search for hypothetical explanations and confines its attention to mere description and classification.

I

The first step in understanding this definition of science is clarifying the general goal of the scientific enterprise. In the most elementary terms possible, the job of science is to discover facts. Usually this is a simple matter. Many facts impose themselves upon us and we cannot avoid them; living, in fact, is merely a matter of adjusting ourselves to these ever-present facts. But the scientist is instilled with the desire to discover more and more facts. In the attempt to satisfy this need he could, by proceeding very inefficiently, simply look about here and there, waiting, like Mr. Micawber, for something to turn up. But he has been provided by nature with a tool that enables him to do the job much more effectively. Through the activity of his mind he is able to make guesses, controlled by the facts he has already discovered, as to the existence of certain specified facts, in certain specified areas, which he is likely to find if he looks further. Thus by using his mind rather than passively listening to nature he is able to save a great deal of time and effort, since he now knows what to look for and where to look. This directed observation is possible by virtue of his capacity, through imagination and inference, to go beyond the facts already observed and formulate, through the use of symbols and other thought constructions, ideas of objects and processes which may not themselves be capable of observation, but are merely hinted at and suggested by the facts already accumulated. Hence we can describe the job of science more accurately by saying that it is concerned with the construction of a system of ideas that is presumed to portray the realm of facts. At any given stage in science, of course, our knowledge does not fit the facts precisely. On the one hand, since there are many facts that have not yet been discovered, knowledge is always less than the facts; but, on the other hand, since we have anticipated what nature is going to reveal, knowledge is always more than the facts. The final goal of science is to make knowledge fit the facts in all its parts and in all its details.

The method of verified hypotheses can be best understood by considering it from the point of view of its three phases or aspects. One is tempted to speak rather of "stages" than "aspects," and this terminology has a certain advantage. But it suggests a temporal order among the phases of the method, which is somewhat misleading. The important thing is the relations of logical dependence among the phases, not the historical order in which they occur.

The first aspect can be called "getting the facts." In the broad sense, however, it includes not only getting the facts but manipulating, classifying, and correlating them, and perhaps even measuring them as well. The two main processes for getting the data are observation (plus intro-spection if one wishes to include certain types of psychology) and inter-preting reports—both human and instrumental. No one, I should suppose, would call into question the need for resting science ultimately upon observed data; it both begins and ends with things that we see, hear, smell, taste, and touch. This does not mean, of course, that all the entities that are talked about by science are observable, but it does mean that any such as are not directly perceivable must be capable of manifesting themselves indirectly in terms of observable phenomena. Reports are another important device for getting data. What is not com-monly recognized is that human reports function in essentially the same way as do instrumental reports. In both cases, we have something that is given through observation (the written or spoken word of another individual, the image on the eyepiece of a microscope), on the basis of which, through a knowledge of the transmitting medium (reliability of the witness, principles of optics), we judge ourselves to be witnessing a natural object (a total eclipse of the sun, the structure of a cell).

Manipulating the data includes all processes—much too numerous even to list—such as combining and isolating, increasing and decreasing in intensity, speeding and slowing, heating, cooling, dissolving, magnet-izing, dissecting, which are designed to produce a state of affairs that would not have occurred if we had not put our fingers into nature. These are the so-called experimental techniques, though we shall see in a moment that experimentation functions in a much more definitive way in another phase of science. Here we are concerned primarily with what are commonly called "experiments for discovery" rather than "experi-ments for proof." These techniques are designed to induce a reluctant nature to yield her secrets; if she will not speak freely we poke and prod her, thus forcing her to respond in unusual ways.

The descriptive processes are many, though for the purposes of this discussion they may be limited to three: classification, correlation, and measurement. Classification involves the activity of grouping similar objects into classes on the basis of common attributes. Correlation, which depends on classification, involves the determination of the fre-quency with which an object lies in two classes at once, or an object of one class is associated with an object of another class. Measurement is the process of representing the qualities of objects by numbers.

The result of the activities of getting the data, manipulating them, and describing them may be called the "descriptive phase" of science. Many insist that this is all there is to science; a science that has correctly classified and measured all available data has completed its job, and there is nothing to be done except await the discovery of further data, which will then have to be described according to the same pattern. But, whatever may be said for this claim, certainly much of what is commonly included in science is not found here. There are no hypotheses or theories. In the strict sense of the words, neither induction nor deduction has been employed; for the laws, if they are to be accurately descriptive of the data, must be statistical correlations and not universal connections, and no deductive anticipations of future data have been made. There is, in fact, no logical structure evident in the body of symbols constituting a purely descriptive science; each symbol describes its fact, and there is no method by which from the knowledge of one fact we could infer knowledge of another. Consequently explanation is totally absent from such a science; it answers the question How? but does not answer the question Why? A diagram of such a science is given in Figure 1.

The need for including in science something more than pure description arises when the scientist, on close inspection of a descriptive science, notes an important fact. Frequently he discovers that among the symbols constituting such a science one of them, *A*, implies another, *B*. This means that if *A* is true, *B* must also be true. Of course, *B* is already known to be true, since it was derived by the direct description of the fact which it represents. But the scientist now knows that if he hadn't happened to discover *B*, he could have anticipated it from his knowledge of *A;* thus he could have known of the existence of a fact before he observed it. From this recognition it is but a step to two other very important conclusions. May it not be possible to find another symbol of his scheme, *C*, which will be found to imply *Q*, which is not now part of his science but must be included since it is logically demanded by *C?* And may it not be possible to devise a symbol, *K*, which is not now part of the science but will imply *A*, which is already part of the scheme? If the answer to these questions is in the affirmative, he has provided himself with very significant techniques for extending his science into the realm of previously undiscovered facts; he can now anticipate, through an activity of mind based on fact, what nature is likely to reveal in areas that are still unexplored.

This aspect of science may be called the "phase of discovery." In actual scientific procedure deductive expansion of a scheme—i.e., expansion by finding further symbols which are implied by symbols in the scheme—is comparatively rare, and the cases in which it occurs are usually trivial. But expansion through induction—i.e., by finding symbols not in the system which imply symbols which are in the system —is a highly significant method. It is, in fact, precisely what is meant

DESCRIPTIVE SCIENCE

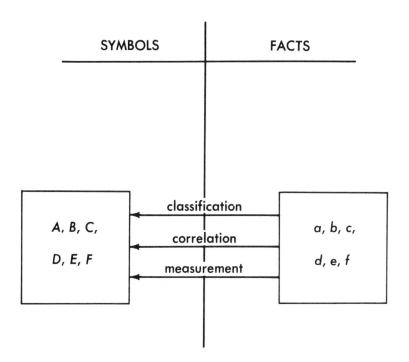

Figure 1

a, b, c, d, e, f ARE FACTS OBTAINED THROUGH DIRECT OBSERVATION, THROUGH REPORTS, AND THROUGH MANIPULATORY OPERATIONS. *A, B, C, D, E, F* ARE DESCRIPTIVE SYMBOLS OBTAINED FROM THESE FACTS BY THE OPERATIONS OF CLASSIFICATION, CORRELATION, AND MEASUREMENT.

by the discovery of hypotheses. The nature of this movement has not yielded to logical analysis. We call it variously "insight," "intuition," "hunch," "illumination"—attempting by all these words to cover the fact that we do not know precisely how it occurs. Deduction is well understood; we know how it operates and we can set up the rules for its validity. But induction is still essentially a mystery. All that we can say about it can be exhausted in a few propositions. It is essential to science. It does occur on numerous occasions. It produces most significant results when preceded by a long and persistent study of facts. Ability to make inductions is distributed very unequally among men.

The most significant defect of induction, however, is that it never gives us truth, but only possibility or, at best, probability. This can be seen from the nature of the implicative relation. If K implies A, then if K is true A must be true. But if A is true we cannot infer from this to the truth of K. K might be false and still imply a true proposition. Since the relation of implication is more commonly expressed in terms of explanation, we can state the same fact by saying that whereas K explains A something other than K might explain A equally well. To be sure, when K occurs to a scientist through an act of illumination or a flash of insight, it usually carries with it a strong feeling of conviction. He feels at the moment that it *must* be true. But later experience usually shows him to have been mistaken, as he quickly learns if he tries to play the races on similar hunches, and as he would readily admit if historians had reported the scientific failures as faithfully as they have preserved the records of scientific successes. The plain fact is that ideas obtained through this act of inspiration, however plausible they may appear at the time, are nothing more than well-founded guesses, and they must be substantiated further before they can be included among the established truths of science. This testing requires the examination of a further phase of science, the phase of verification. Before passing to such considerations, however, mention must be made of another feature of a science that is undergoing the transition from the descriptive to the explanatory stage.

In the search for implicative relations among descriptive symbols the scientist readily sees that these relations do not hold among fuzzy concepts or highly complicated propositions. If, for example, he were to determine the sum of the angles of a triangle by actual measurement, he would find this very rarely to be exactly 180°; in the great majority of cases it would be greater or less than this amount and to varying degrees. Consequently, if geometry were a descriptive science, he would have to express his results statistically, stating, with regard to any class of triangles, how many had the sum equal to 180°, how many were less than this by one second, how many were greater by one second, how many less by two seconds, and so on. It would be extremely difficult, if not impossible, to construct a theory of the triangle in terms of which this could be understood. But it is readily seen that these values fluctuate around 180°, and it requires no great stretch of the imagination to suppose that if the triangles were perfectly drawn the sum would always exactly equal this amount. A simple substitution is then made that immediately brings about this result; the meaning of the word "triangle" is changed to mean "perfect triangle" rather than "actual triangle. The law of triangles then becomes exactly true of perfect triangles, though only approximately true of actual triangles, and can then be explained in terms of the simple definitions and postulates we learned in our high-school geometry.

The frequency with which such notions occur in science, and their importance for a general theory of science, are not generally recognized. Geometry, in the strict sense of the word, is made up wholly of concepts of this kind, with consequences which we shall see later. Physics would find it hard to dispense with perfect gases, ideal levers, frictionless motion, and the like. In the social sciences frequent use is made of such fictions as the completely isolated individual, the ideal State, and the purely economic man. What should be clearly understood in connection with such notions as this is that a science in which they occur has, to this extent, lost its descriptive value. In this elaborating and refining process, which Eddington calls the method of "just like this only more so," we attempt to get away from the complexities and crudities of sense objects in order to replace them by simpler and more precise counterparts. But to the extent to which they are simpler and more precise they are no longer counterparts. The world does not contain perfect levers, ideal gases, economic men, and utopias; when we build science on such notions, therefore, we are no longer talking about the world in which we live. Many who praise the exactness and precision of science fail to realize that only through the use of such fictions and idealizations does science have its mathematical rigor. Applied science fits the world better, but it lacks the neatness and logical structure of idealized science; idealized science has the required coherence, but it loses to a great extent its descriptive value. Einstein has expressed this very well in a statement that is often quoted: "As far as the laws of mathematics refer to reality, they are not certain; and as far as they are certain, they do not refer to reality."

II

Let us now turn to a consideration of the next phase of science—verification. This may be broken up into two subphases. The first involves making predictions on the basis of the assumed hypotheses. This is deductive in character; it begins not with the descriptive symbols, however, but with the hypotheses. The scientist simply asks himself what would have to be true in nature *if* his hypothesis were correct. Such predictions always have the *if . . . then . . .* form, where what follows the *if* is the hypothesis, and what follows the *then* is the anticipated observations, either experimental or nonexperimental. The second of the two phases involves the checking activity. The predicted consequences are compared with the actual facts as disclosed through observation; and the hypothesis is rendered more probable or rejected according as these agree or disagree. In this phase the techniques are the same as those in the descriptive phase—getting and manipulating the data, and classifying, correlating, and measuring them. The direction of the activities is reversed, however: there we were given the data and were concerned with devising symbols; here we are given the symbols and are attempting to verify them in the data. It is in this stage, rather than in the descriptive stage, that experimentation plays its distinctive role.

A science that exhibits all three phases may be called an "explanatory science." This is what is commonly meant by the term when it is employed in ordinary discourse. In a sense, of course, an explanatory science includes a descriptive science, since the former was obtained from the latter by extension through the use of hypotheses and theories. But, as has already been pointed out, this is not quite the case. An explanatory science, by virtue of the use of abstractive and idealizing activities, has lost some of its direct descriptive value. It has lost contact with reality to the extent to which it has achieved a certain logical structure. Whether this involves a net gain for the science itself is debatable; thus we cannot dogmatically assert that an explanatory science is "better" than a descriptive one. But certainly in our recognition of the possibility of such a thing as an explanatory science, we have advanced in our *conception* of science; we now see more clearly what "science" *means*. A diagram of explanatory science is given in Figure 2.

But we are now in a position to realize that the picture is still incomplete. In fairness to mathematics and certain parts of physics, further elaboration of the notion of science is required.

A candid examination of an explanatory science, even one that is highly developed, discloses some significant inadequacies. Rarely is it true that the total body of descriptive symbols can be completely explained in terms of the hypotheses. There are almost certain to be some loose ends, some brute facts, some statements that are descriptively true but cannot be fitted into the scheme. In some cases we may succeed in integrating small groups of the descriptive statements by devising theories that explain them. But these remain islands of order in a sea of disorder. Only rarely can we find a more comprehensive theory that integrates the subgroups with one another just as the simpler theory integrates the statements within the subgroup. All these inadequacies lead us to speculate concerning an ideal state of science in which the logical organization would be perfect and complete. This would pre-

EXPLANATORY SCIENCE
SYMBOLS | FACTS

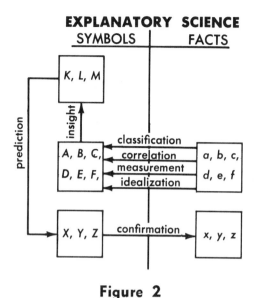

Figure 2

a, b, c, d, e, f ARE FACTS OBTAINED THROUGH DIRECT OBSERVATION, THROUGH REPORTS, AND THROUGH MANIPULATORY OPERATIONS. *A, B, C, D, E, F* ARE DESCRIPTIVE SYMBOLS OBTAINED FROM THESE FACTS BY THE OPERATIONS OF CLASSIFICATION, CORRELATION, MEASUREMENT, AND IDEALIZATION. *K, L, M* ARE HYPOTHESES OR THEORIES OBTAINED FROM THE DESCRIPTIVE SYMBOLS THROUGH INSIGHT (INDUCTION). *X, Y, Z* ARE THE PREDICTED CONSEQUENCES OF THE HYPOTHESES, DERIVED FROM THEM BY DEDUCTION. *x, y, z* ARE THE NEWLY DISCOVERED FACTS WHICH CONFIRM THESE PREDICTED CONSEQUENCES.

sumably be one in which all descriptive statements would be capable of being derived by pure reason from a single theory, this theory itself being so constituted as to be as simple as possible and to involve no internal contradictions. Such an ideal would be achieved in physics, for example, if from a theory of the electron, or some other elementary particle, we could deduce all the phenomena of physics—dynamical, acoustical, electrical, optical, and perhaps even chemical as well.

If, however, we step outside the field of the so-called natural sciences and look about for such a logically complete science, we find one immediately at hand. Geometry (and, in fact, most of mathematics) is precisely such a science. In order to see that this is the case we have only to introduce a substitute terminology. Instead of hypotheses and theories we must speak of axioms, definitions, and postulates, and instead of laws and descriptive statements we must speak of theorems and corollaries. The logical structure is complete, for, at least in a perfect scheme of this type, all theorems and corollaries can be proved in terms of the axioms, definitions, and postulates. But when we consider the abstract character of such a scheme as this, and when we recognize the existence of non-Euclidean geometries, we readily see that the gain in logical cogency has been achieved at the sacrifice of descriptive accuracy. The idealizing activities, which were mentioned earlier, have so dominated the science that it can no longer be said to be about the world at all. The existence of such a science as this shows that the human mind has the capacity for taking at random any group of ideas, actual or fanciful, combining them and deriving their consequences by pure reasoning, and thus constructing a system of underived and derived notions which is internally perfectly consistent, which obeys the rules of logic throughout, but which may convey no information whatever about the world in which we live. Such a science may be called "rational" or "autonomous" and may be represented diagrammatically as in Figure 3.

III

If our analysis of science is correct, each of the sciences should fall roughly into one of these three classes—descriptive, explanatory, or autonomous. Just where it is located will depend on a number of factors —who is doing the classifying, what part of the science is being emphasized, how certain words in the science are to be defined (for example, does "line" mean "something that can be drawn on paper with a pencil" or "length without breadth and thickness"?), the historical stage in which the science is being considered, and so on. Few, however, would deny that autonomous sciences are today well represented by mathematics, rational mechanics, and perhaps other limited areas in physics; explanatory sciences by the rest of the physical sciences and biology; descriptive sciences by the social sciences and psychology, with many, perhaps, preferring to place biology in this class rather than in the class of explanatory sciences. No doubt there is also a *rough* correlation between the development from description through explanation to autonomy, and the actual history of any science. If this correlation were perfect, the autonomous sciences would all be the oldest, and the descriptive sciences the youngest. The fact that geometry was already well developed as a deductive science in the days of the Greeks, and that psychology, which began with the Greeks, is still essentially in its descriptive phase today argues against identifying the logical and the historical developments. No doubt something more than *time* is required

RATIONAL SCIENCE

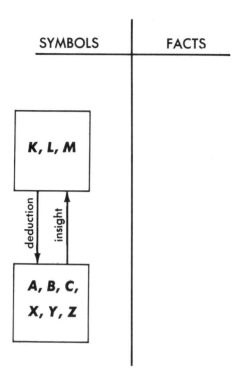

SYMBOLS   FACTS

K, L, M

deduction   insight

A, B, C,
X, Y, Z

Figure 3

K, L, M ARE THE UNDERIVED IDEAS (AXIOMS, POSTULATES, AND UNDE-
FINED TERMS). THE AXIOMS AND POSTULATES ARE ASSUMED TO BE
TRUE, AND THE UNDEFINED TERMS ARE ASSUMED TO BE UNDERSTOOD.
A, B, C, X, Y, Z ARE THE THEOREMS. THEY ARE PROVED TO BE TRUE
BY DEDUCTION THROUGH PURE REASON FROM THE UNDERIVED IDEAS.

for a science to pass from description to autonomy; certainly the character of the subject matter plays a definitive role. It does appear, however, if the above analysis is correct, that a descriptive science remains
in this stage only with difficulty. There is, first, the irresistible desire
on the part of the human mind to ask the question Why? and to attempt
to answer it by engaging in flights of imagination. Second, there is the
recognition of the heuristic value of hypotheses in the discovery of new

data. To this extent the positivist is wrong in insisting that descriptive science represents science at its maturity. Furthermore, once the value of logical structure has been appreciated fully, there is an unrestrainable desire to idealize the subject matter of the science, break its connections with the world, and set it up as a deductive scheme. To this extent the natural scientist should not look with too much scorn on the purely formal character of mathematics.

The type of science that one prefers is, I believe, largely a matter of temperament. The positivist insists on being close to the facts and avoiding speculative notions; the advocate of explanatory science wants to get behind and beneath things to see how they run; the formalist is unhappy in this higgledy-piggledy world and much prefers the neatness of abstract systems.

CHAPTER FOUR

EMPIRICAL
ORIGIN OF IDEAS

4.1   EDITORIAL COMMENT

One of the major differences between classical medieval thought and modern thought lies in the fact that the medieval scholar put his belief before his understanding whereas the modern scholar puts his understanding before his belief. This is easier said than done, however, as Dr. James W. Oliver makes quite clear in his analysis of "The Problem of Epistemology."

The roots of the shift toward a defense of the empirical origin of ideas in modern thought are found in the writings of Francis Bacon and John Locke. We have selected a section from Bacon's *The Advance-*

ment of Learning to clarify our thinking about the relation between authority and knowledge. The major emphasis in John Locke's article, as taken from his *Essay Concerning Human Understanding*, is on the problem of the limits of human knowledge and the relation of these limits to matters of belief, assent, and opinion.

What then are the present day theories of intellectual discipline? In his article on this subject Professor Frederick C. Neff seeks to clarify our thinking on the use of the terms "intellectualism" and "intellectual discipline." What is the nature of a disciplined intellect, especially in relation to empirical inquiry? Since the classical tradition paid little attention to the empirical origin of ideas, it is not difficult to understand why there has been a continuing conflict between those who rely exclusively on the metaphysical tradition and those who seek a reconstruction of our patterns of meaning and value in the light of our new knowledge concerning the nature of the universe, man, and society.

4.2   THE PROBLEM OF EPISTEMOLOGY*

by James W. Oliver

My purpose is to propose that a question which I shall state be taken as the central problem of epistemology. The term 'epistemology' may then be defined so that all and only those discussions which are pertinent to this question will be regarded as epistemological. But I should think it hardly worthwhile to provide an additional and peculiar entry for dictionaries. A more important aim is to encourage philosophers to concentrate on the heart of the matter and to avoid extraneous issues which continue to fill the journals with elaborately profitless discussions.

First I shall state, and comment on, the question which is properly the central problem of epistemology. Then I shall criticize some of the problems which have often been regarded as belonging to this branch of philosophy. Finally I shall answer one possible objection to the position outlined here.

But first I wish to make two comments on what follows. The first is that I am aware that there are unsolved problems connected with what is said below. Thus one needs an account better than any now available as to what a clear literal statement in a natural language is. It may, however, give direction to work on the solution of this problem if it is understood that a purpose for which the solution is wanted is to have something as a basis for discussions in epistemology.

The second comment is that, of all the sentences in the following paragraphs, a number are either normative principles or evaluations. I regard these as involving an element of personal opinion, and as views to be held somewhat tentatively. It would, however, be superfluous to begin all of them with such phrases as 'I think that' or 'In my opinion,' but the absence of such phrases should not suggest the absence of a tentative attitude on the writer's part. I see no reason to avoid using such sentences in philosophical writing; on the contrary, an argument could be offered that philosophical writing must contain them, whatever they may lack in the way of finality.

What is to be taken as the fundamental problem of epistemology is concerned with attitudes of belief toward statements; the crucial question—in a preliminary formulation—is 'What statements should an individual believe?' As one makes a quick survey of the history of philosophy and asks what is the point of philosophical discussions of

*Reprinted from *The Journal of Philosophy*, Volume LVII, No. 9 (April, 1960), pages 297-304, with permission of Professor Oliver and the publisher.

truth, perception, reason, intuition, etc., it seems apparent that the question of belief here formulated has rarely, if ever, been explicitly raised, and yet, a vague awareness that this is the fundamental question seems to have guided, sporadically and inefficiently, discussions in theory of knowledge from Plato down to the present day. Why should one be interested in distinguishing what is true from what is false except as a means of deciding what ought to be believed?

Though it will be desirable to refine the first formulation of the question, it may be emphasized at the start that the problem to be taken as the central one in epistemology is a normative question; anything that would constitute an answer at all will contain the word 'should' or an alternative normative expression. Also, the problem as stated is one in pragmatics. It is concerned with the attitudes of interpreters of a language toward *some* of the sentences in that language. Furthermore, it is intended that this question have the maximum possible neutrality among philosophical systems. I am here attempting to give an issue greater clarity and precision; it is beyond my purpose to offer a solution, even partial, and it would also be inappropriate to formulate the issue so that some one solution is favored. In particular, the formulation gives an advantage to neither empiricism nor rationalism.

The formulation given makes statements the subject matter of epistemology. The term 'statement' is used here in the sense in which it appears in Quine's *Methods of Logic:* statements are sentences in a natural language; each of them is either true or false; not all sentences in a natural language such as English are statements, and, in particular, neither evaluations nor normative principles are statements.

A common alternative to the present view regards propositions as the subject matter of epistemology. Although the notion of proposition has never, to my knowledge, been explicated with anything like the clarity which characterizes the term 'statement', it appears from most accounts that there is a one-to-one correspondence between propositions and the sentences which, as it is usually put, express them. Furthermore, for most assertions *about* statements there seem to be analogous assertions *about* propositions and vice versa. It might appear, then, that taking propositions as the subject matter of epistemology in accordance with a long tradition would be equally as good as the position taken in this paper. There are, however, advantages in formulating the problem in terms of statements. Foremost among these advantages is the possibility of utilizing, wherever appropriate, contemporary researches in logic and semiotic. Also, speaking of statements rather than of propositions seems to make easier the avoidance of confusions of philosophy with psychology. It is preferable, then, to say that our problem is about statements.

As a first step in refining the formulation of the question account should be taken of the obvious point that there are some sentences which are not within the scope of epistemology at all. Whitman says of grass, "it is the handkerchief of the Lord"; the hymnal says "God is love"; and Croce maintains that "art is vision or intuition." These are, apparently, statements, but there is a good reason why an epistemologist should say neither that such sentences ought to be believed nor that they ought not to be believed. The quotation from Whitman is clearly a metaphor; perhaps 'God is love' is also a metaphor, but this is not clear; and the sentence from Croce, even when examined in its context, is not clear enough to permit profitable discussion of its acceptability for belief. Many sentences in ordinary language are, of course, not to be taken literally. Sometimes a literal interpretation of them may be possible; but this sort of "interpretation" is not without its problems, and the epistemologist should be concerned only with the literal result of the process, whatever it may be, and not with the metaphor itself. And while it may be difficult to establish a useful criterion of clarity, surely it should be required that there be some clear meaning for a statement before the question of believing it is considered at all. Hence it is desirable to say that it is only clear literal statements which are to be the concern of the epistemologist, and the problem may be reformulated at this point as 'What clear literal statements should an individual believe?'

A second consideration will result in a further modification of the question. Although Descartes, and the rationalists generally, have advocated views involving only two attitudes of belief—those of complete certainty and complete disbelief—other philosophers—for example, Locke—have noted that people can and do take toward statements a wide range of attitudes or degrees of belief, including the two which interested Descartes, and also including an attitude of no opinion. There is a problem, subordinate to the central one of epistemology, of providing a useful scale of degrees of belief; in general it should try to provide as many degrees as any epistemologist would want, though anyone may use only so many as he finds convenient.

Historically, of course, epistemologists have been interested in different degrees of belief in order to associate them with different kinds of statements, and some comprehensive classification of statements is needed. There is, however, no place in the literature in which one can find a sufficiently complete classification to permit separation, relation, and adequate discussion of all issues of concern to epistemologists.

There are, whether completely satisfactory or not, classifications among analytic, synthetic, and self-contradictory statements; among universal, existential, and singular statements; and among statements in various levels of language. Further distinctions have been made among statements purporting to refer to phenomena, those purporting to refer to physical objects, those purporting to refer to abstract entities, and those purporting to refer to supernatural beings, and, since statements saying what is remembered and those which are predictions may be affected by different epistemological considerations, some classification involving a temporal basis seems called for. A comprehensive cross-classification of statements that will permit one to take into account all the relevant factors discussed in the history of epistemology is a problem preliminary to the solution of the central problem of epistemology. To avoid confusing the normative issue with the selection of a classification, it will, most likely, be desirable to use no normative or evaluative expressions in setting up the kinds of statements for which normative principles are wanted.

What has just been said about degrees of belief and kinds of statements leads to the following modified formulation of the problem:

> What degrees of belief should an individual accord to clear literal statements of various kinds?

Further refinement of the problem is desirable, but we leave our own peculiar view at this point with the observation that the answer to this question will be a set of sentences all of which will be rules or criteria, none of which will be a statement, all of which will be metalinguistic. A simple example might be:

> If 'p' is equivalent to 'q', an individual should accord to 'p' and 'q' the same degree of belief.

Turning now from the special view which I have been advocating, I shall criticize some of the generally recognized problems of epistemology. I take these problems from the excellent article by Ledger Wood in Runes' *Dictionary of Philosophy*. It will be argued, for each of the eight problems mentioned by Professor Wood, either that it is better regarded as not epistemological at all, or that it cannot be profitably discussed until after we have obtained a solution of the proposed central problem of epistemology, or that, when clarified, it is a part of, or identical with, this problem.

The first problem referred to by Professor Wood is "that of the very *possibility of knowledge.* Is genuine knowledge at all attainable?" As formulated, the problem appears to be just as factual in character as the question 'Is salt soluble?' But the formulation only conceals the fundamental question; use of the term "knowledge' here without a definition makes it appear possible to discuss a factual question, whereas this cannot be done until the normative question stated in the first part of this paper is answered. For what can knowledge be but sound belief? And how can a belief be said to be sound except by reference to a set of rules? Max Black has pointed out that a justification of something requires showing it to be consistent with, or deductible from, a standard. And Carnap has argued that a "question of right or wrong must always refer to a system of rules." Just so, the soundness of belief in a statement is a question of conformity with rules for belief. The term 'knowledge', therefore, has no clear meaning until some answer to the fundamental problem of epistemology has been furnished. The question of whether genuine knowledge is possible is not to be discussed until after a set of rules for belief has been provided. And one may doubt that anything worth talking about in this connection will remain after such a set of rules has been provided.

A second problem is that of determining the limits of knowledge. Again, this appears to be a factual question; again, the question has the misleading appearance of being factual only so long as the term 'knowledge' is not recognized as involving a reference to normative principles; again, the question presupposes an answer to the central problem of epistemology; and again, once the central problem is solved nothing of importance remains to be discussed in connection with the limits of knowledge. For providing a set of rules for belief is also determining what the limits of knowledge are.

The third problem mentioned by Professor Wood is that of "the *origin of knowledge.* By what faculty or faculties of mind is knowledge attainable?" One can repeat here the objection to the occurrence of the unanalyzed term 'knowledge'; one can also object to the notion of faculties; but the most important reason for rejecting this question is that discussions of it always or almost always turn out to be inept psychology, or distressing confusions of psychological issues with other questions. My complaint is, of course, an old one; to cite one example, 1937 is the date of the English translation of Carnap's *Logical Syntax of Language,* in which epistemology is criticized as an "inextricable tangle of problems," in which psychological and logical problems are confused. Even when the question being discussed is rather clearly one in psychology—such as Russell's discussion of the origin of the idea corresponding to expressions of negation—all we have is incompetent psychology. The elimination of confusions of philosophical with psychological issues, and the avoidance of unsound work in psychology under the guise of philosophy are two of the purposes of the foregoing normative, metalinguistic formulation of the central problem of epistemology. The question of the origin of knowledge is best regarded as not epistemological at all.

A fourth problem of epistemology is the methodological problem. Though this is not clear, the question presumably has to do with the procedures which *should* be used in the acquisition and elaboration of knowledge. If this *is* the question, it would seem that the principal purpose to be served by advocating deductive, inductive, or other methods is in connection with the problem of the degrees of belief to be accorded to statements arrived at deductively, inductively, or otherwise. Thus, what we have called the central problem of epistemology is comprehensive enough to include the methodological problem, insofar as this problem goes beyond semiotic.

Professor Wood lists as a fifth question that of the *a priori.* "The problem," he says, "is that of isolating the *a priori* or nonempirical elements in knowledge and accounting for them in terms of human reason." Here again, the term 'knowledge' needs definition, and psychological issues should be avoided. But more important is the need to clarify the term '*a priori'*; is this to be taken as a normative or descriptive expression? Are the assertions that there are or are not synthetic *a priori* statements to be regarded as the matters of fact that they appear to be? Defining '*a priori*' as 'that which can be known by reason alone' (*Webster's International*) or "knowledge independent of experience' (Hofstadter's "Basic Philosophy Data Guide") makes use of expressions which, as we have previously seen, conceal the normative problem, and the normative character of the term '*a priori*' is thereby also concealed. A less misleading formulation of the problem of the synthetic *a priori* is: 'Should any synthetic statements be believed regardless of empirical evidence or its absence?' More generally, if the term '*a priori*' is used as a normative expression, the problem of the *a priori* becomes a part of our central problem. An answer to the fundamental problem of epistemology will be, at the same time, an answer to the problem of the *a priori.*

The sixth of Professor Wood's questions in epistemology need not detain us long. This is the "problem of differentiating *the principal kinds of knowledge."* From what has been said previously, it seems clear that, when clarified, this problem becomes part of that proposed in the first part of this paper.

The seventh type of inquiry has to do with *"the structure of the knowledge-situation. . . .* [It attempts] to determine . . . the constitutents of the knowledge situation in their relation to one another." The relations among the elements of perception and the relations of the subjective and objective components of the knowledge situation are examples of these inquiries. It is preferable, however, to reject this problem as having no place in epistemology. One readily understands why philosophers have discussed them, but the discussions are either psychological or metaphysical. If psychological, our earlier comments apply; if metaphysical, we should discard them from epistemology, for establishing our criteria for sound statements should precede our assertions of any clear literal statements that there may be in metaphysics.

Professor Wood says, *"The problem of truth* is perhaps the culmination of epistemological inquiry—in any case it is the problem which brings the inquiry to the threshold of metaphysics." It may have brought many philosophers there, but fortunately we may back off without entering. It is, of course, a commonplace that many different questions have become entangled in discussions of truth, and that the first project in unraveling the issues is the problem of defining the predicate 'is true'. Beyond this the intelligible question is: 'What ought to be believed?', or, more precisely, the central problem of epistemology.

Thus, taking the question formulated in the first part of this paper as the central problem to which epistemologists should direct their attention helps to clarify some traditional issues, and assists in separating epistemological inquiries from those in other fields such as psychology and ontology.

Now let us consider an objection to the view we have been urging. We have steadily insisted on the normative character of epistemology, but there are, of course, many who reject any discussion of normative questions. The verifiability theory of meaning, or, as it is more modestly named by its ablest advocates, the empiricist criterion of meaning, condemns as meaningless any answer to our problem. The logical empiricist will graciously allow that rules for belief may be "rich" in their "non-cognitive import by virtue of their emotive appeal or the moral inspiration they offer." The epistemologist in our sense, then, speaks poetry without realizing it or else he is a preacher without a pulpit.

This is not the place to express one's sympathy with the purposes which it was hoped the empiricist criterion of meaning would serve, nor to analyze the proposal at length. It is sufficient here to note that this criterion either does or does not define the term 'meaningful' or the term 'cognitively meaningful'. If the criterion defines one of these expressions, then it is trivial. If it does not, then it is not clear. For surely if there is one thing that *is* clear, after all the recent discussions of meaning and meaningfulness, it is that these conceptions are not clear, except where some special usage is explicitly indicated. If, then, the criterion is analytic, it is trivial; if it is synthetic, it is obscure.

But, whether the criterion is acceptable or not, it has probably been the center of so much controversy because discussions advocating the criterion have maintained that normative principles are not verifiable and have strongly suggested that they should be discarded as nonsense. We admit, without arguing for these views, that normative principles are different from statements, that only statements can be confirmed, and that no normative principle is either true or false. But from none of these admissions does it follow that discussions in which rules or normative principles are affirmed should be abandoned. Indeed, if they should be, then we cannot say so.

The methods of confirmation and of choice among alternative hypotheses used by scientists or proposed by philosophers of science are, most likely, not to be carried over without modification as a methodology for normative principles. But surely reasons can be given for advocating one set of epistemological rules rather than some alternative. The patterns of inference involved may need further study, but the unsuitability of scientific method should not lead to the conclusion that no method will be suitable.

In conclusion I restate my proposal for the central problem of epistemology: 'What degrees of belief should an individual accord to statements of various kinds?' I have suggested that work in the field will be improved if philosophers concentrate on this question. I also believe that this is one of the great problems which confront all reflective human beings; just as a review of his beliefs led Descartes to doubt and to a need for normative principles governing belief, so a similar review can lead others to a similar need. Perhaps a concentration on their problem will lead to an increased interest in philosophy on the part of educated laymen.

4.3   THE LIMITS OF AUTHORITY*

by *Francis Bacon*

And as for the overmuch credit that hath been given unto authors in sciences, in making them dictators, that their words should stand, and not consuls to give advice; the damage is infinite that sciences have received thereby, as the principal cause that hath kept them low, at a stay, without growth or advancement. For hence it hath comen that in arts mechanical the first deviser comes shortest, and time addeth and perfecteth, but in sciences the first author goeth furthest, and time leeseth and corrupteth. So we see, artillery, sailing, printing, and the like, were grossly managed at the first, and by time accommodated and refined; but contrariwise the philosophies and sciences of Aristotle, Plato, Democritus, Hippocrates, Euclides, Archimedes, of most vigor at the first, and by time degenerate and embased. Whereof the reason is no other but that in the former many wits and industries have contributed in one, and in the latter many wits and industries have been spent about the wit of some one, whom many times they have rather depraved than illustrated. For as water will not ascend higher than the level of the first spring-head from whence it descendeth, so knowledge derived from Aristotle, and exempted from liberty of examination, will not rise again higher than the knowledge of Aristotle. And therefore although the position be good, *A man who is learning must be content to believe what he is told,*[1] yet it must be coupled with this *When he has learned it he must exercise his own judgment and see whether it be worthy of belief;*[2] for disciples do owe unto masters only a temporary belief, and a suspension of their own judgment till they be fully instructed, and not an absolute resignation or perpetual captivity. And therefore to conclude this point, I will say no more but: So let great authors have their due, as time, which is the author of authors, be not deprived of his due, which is, further and further to discover truth. Thus have I gone over these three diseases of learning; besides the which there are some other, rather peccant humors than formed diseases, which nevertheless are not so secret and intrinsic but that they fall under a popular observation and traducement, and therefore are not to be passed over.

The first of these is the extreme affecting of two extremities,—the one antiquity, the other novelty; wherein it seemeth the children of time do

---

*Reprinted from *The Advancement of Learning* (Boston: Ginn and Company, 1904), pages 36-44, 70-74.
[1]*Oportet discentem credere.*
[2]*Oportet edoctum judicare.*

take after the nature and malice of their father. For as he devoureth his children, so one of them seeketh to devour and suppress the other, while antiquity envieth there should be new additions, and novelty cannot be content to add, but it must deface. Surely the advice of the prophet is the true direction in this matter, *Stand ye in the old ways and see which is the good and right way, and walk therein.*[1] Antiquity deserveth that reverence, that men should make a stand thereupon and discover what is the best way; but when the discovery is well taken, then to make progression. And to speak truly, *Antiquity in time is the youth of the world.*[2] These times are the ancient times, when the world is ancient, and not those which we account ancient *by an inverted reckoning,*[3] by a computation backward from ourselves.

Another error, induced by the former, is a distrust that anything should be now to be found out, which the world should have missed and passed over so long time; as if the same objection were to be made to time that Lucian maketh to Jupiter and other the heathen gods, of which he wondereth that they begot so many children in old time and begot none in his time, and asketh whether they were become septuagenary, or whether the law Papia, made against old men's marriages, had restrained them. So it seemeth men doubt lest time is become past children and generation; wherein contrariwise we see commonly the levity and unconstancy of men's judgments, which, till a matter be done, wonder that it can be done, and as soon as it is done wonder again that it was no sooner done; as we see in the expedition of Alexander into Asia, which at first was prejudged as a vast and impossible enterprise, and yet afterwards it pleaseth Livy to make no more of it than this, *It was but taking courage to despise vain apprehensions.*[4] And the same happened to Columbus in the western navigation. But in intellectual matters it is much more common; as may be seen in most of the propositions of Euclid, which till they be demonstrate, they seem strange to our assent; but being demonstrate, our mind accepteth of them by a kind of relation, as the lawyers speak, as if we had known them before.

Another error that hath also some affinity with the former, is a conceit that of former opinions or sects, after variety and examination, the best hath still prevailed and suppressed the rest; so as, if a man should begin the labor of a new search, he were but like to light upon somewhat formerly rejected, and by rejection brought into oblivion;

---

[1]*State super vias antiquas, et videte quænam sit via recta et bona, et ambulate in ea.*
[2]*Antiquitas sæculi juventus mundi.*
[3]*Ordine retrogrado.*
[4]*Nil aliud guam bene ausus vana contemnere.*

as if the multitude, or the wisest for the multitude's sake, were not ready to give passage rather to that which is popular and superficial than to that which is substantial and profound; for the truth is that time seemeth to be of the nature of a river or stream, which carrieth down to us that which is light and blown up, and sinketh and drowneth that which is weighty and solid.

Another error, of a diverse nature from all the former, is the over-early and peremptory reduction of knowledge into arts and methods; from which time, commonly, sciences receive small or no augmentation. But as young men, when they knit and shape perfectly, do seldom grow to a further stature, so knowledge, while it is in aphorisms and observations, it is in growth; but when it once is comprehended in exact methods, it may perchance be further polished and illustrate, and accommodated for use and practice, but it increaseth no more in bulk and substance.

Another error, which doth succeed that which we last mentioned, is that after the distribution of particular arts and sciences, men have abandoned universality, or *the prime philosophy;*[1] which cannot but cease and stop all progression. For no perfect discovery can be made upon a flat or a level; neither is it possible to discover the more remote and deeper parts of any science, if you stand but upon the level of the same science, and ascend not to a higher science.

Another error hath proceeded from too great a reverence, and a kind of adoration, of the mind and understanding of man; by means whereof men have withdrawn themselves too much from the contemplation of nature and the observations of experience, and have tumbled up and down in their own reason and conceits. Upon these intellectualists, which are notwithstanding commonly taken for the most sublime and divine philosophers, Heraclitus gave a just censure, saying, 'Men sought truth in their own little worlds, and not in the great and common world;' for they disdain to spell, and so by degrees to read, in the volume of God's works; and contrariwise by continual meditation and agitation of wit do urge and as it were invocate their own spirits to divine, and give oracles unto them, whereby they are deservedly deluded.

Another error that hath some connexion with this latter is that men have used to infect their meditations, opinions, and doctrines, with some conceits which they have most admired, or some sciences which they have most applied; and given all things else a tincture according to them, utterly untrue and unproper. So hath Plato intermingled his philosophy with theology, and Aristotle with logic, and the second

---

[1]*Philosophia prima.*

school of Plato—Proclus and the rest—with the mathematics. For these were the arts which had a kind of primogeniture with them severally. So have the alchemists made a philosophy out of a few experiments of the furnace; and Gilbertus, our countryman, hath made a philosophy out of the observations of a loadstone. So Cicero, when, reciting the several opinions of the nature of the soul, he found a musician that held the soul was but a harmony, saith pleasantly, *He was faithful to his profession.*[1] But of these conceits Aristotle speaketh seriously and wisely, when he saith, *They who take account of but few things, find it easy to pass judgment.*[2]

Another error is an impatience of doubt, and haste to assertion without due and mature suspension of judgment. For the two ways of contemplation are not unlike the two ways of action commonly spoken of by the ancients: the one plain and smooth in the beginning, and in the end impassable, the other rough and troublesome in the entrance, but after a while fair and even. So it is in contemplation; if a man will begin with certainties, he shall end in doubts, but if he will be content to begin with doubts, he shall end in certainties.

Another error is in the manner of the tradition and delivery of knowledge, which is for the most part magistral and peremptory, and not ingenuous and faithful; in a sort as may be soonest believed, and not easiliest examined. It is true that in compendious treatises for practice that form is not to be disallowed. But in the true handling of knowledge, men ought not to fall either, on the one side, into the vein of Velleius the Epicurean, *who feared nothing so much as the seeming to be in doubt about anything,*[3] nor on the other side into Socrates his ironical doubting of all things; but to propound things sincerely, with more or less asseveration, as they stand in a man's own judgment proved more or less.

Other errors there are in the scope that men propound to themselves, whereunto they bend their endeavors; for whereas the more constant and devote kind of professors of any science ought to propound to themselves to make some additions to their science, they convert their labors to aspire to certain second prizes, as to be a profound interpreter or commenter, to be a sharp champion or defender, to be a methodical compounder or abridger; and so the patrimony of knowledge cometh to be sometimes improved, but seldom augmented.

But the greatest error of all the rest is the mistaking or misplacing of the last or furthest end of knowledge. For men have entered into a

---

[1]*Hic ab arte sua non recessit, etc.*
[2]*Qui respiciunt ad pauca de facili pronunciant.*
[3]*Nil tam metuens, quam ne dubitare aliqua de re videretur.*

desire of learning and knowledge, sometimes upon a natural curiosity and inquisitive appetite; sometimes to entertain their minds with variety and delight; sometimes for ornament and reputation; and sometimes to enable them to victory of wit and contradiction; and most times for lucre and profession; and seldom sincerely to give a true account of their gift of reason, to the benefit and use of men. As if there were sought in knowledge a couch, whereupon to rest a searching and restless spirit; or a terrace, for a wandering and variable mind to walk up and down with a fair prospect; or a tower of state, for a proud mind to raise itself upon; or a fort or commanding ground, for strife and contention; or a shop, for profit or sale; and not a rich storehouse, for the glory of the Creator and the relief of man's estate. But this is that which will indeed dignify and exalt knowledge, if contemplation and action may be more nearly and straitly conjoined and united together than they have been; a conjunction like unto that of the two highest planets, Saturn the planet of rest and contemplation, and Jupiter the planet of civil society and action. Howbeit, I do not mean, when I speak of use and action, that end before-mentioned of the applying of knowledge to lucre and profession, for I am not ignorant how much that diverteth and interrupteth the prosecution and advancement of knowledge; like unto the golden ball thrown before Atalanta, which while she goeth aside and stoopeth to take up, the race is hindered:—

She leaves her course, and lifts the rolling gold.[1]

Neither is my meaning, as was spoken of Socrates, to call philosophy down from heaven to converse upon the earth: that is, to leave natural philosophy aside, and to apply knowledge only to manners and policy. But as both heaven and earth do conspire and contribute to the use and benefit of man, so the end ought to be, from both philosophies to separate and reject vain speculations and whatsoever is empty and void, and to preserve and augment whatsoever is solid and fruitful; that knowledge may not be as a courtesan, for pleasure and vanity only, or as a bond-woman, to acquire and gain to her master's use, but as a spouse, for generation, fruit, and comfort.

Thus have I described and opened, as by a kind of dissection, those peccant humors—the principal of them—which hath not only given impediment to the proficience of learning, but have given also occasion to the traducement thereof; wherein if I have been too plain, it must be remembered, *Faithful are the wounds of a friend, but the kisses of an enemy are deceitful.*[2] This, I think, I have gained, that I ought to be

---

[1] *Declinat cursus, aurumque volubile tollit.*
[2] *Fidelia vulnera amantis, sed dolosa oscula malignantis.*

the better believed in that which I shall say pertaining to commendation, because I have proceeded so freely in that which concerneth censure. And yet I have no purpose to enter into a laudative of learning, or to make a hymn to the Muses, though I am of opinion that it is long since their rites were duly celebrated; but my intent is, without varnish or amplification justly to weigh the dignity of knowledge in the balance with other things, and to take the true value thereof by testimonies and arguments divine and human.

First therefore, let us seek the dignity of knowledge in the arch-type or first platform, which is in the attributes and acts of God, as far as they are revealed to man and may be observed with sobriety; wherein we may not seek it by the name of learning, for all learning is knowledge acquired, and all knowledge in God is original; and therefore we must look for it by another name, that of wisdom or sapience, as the Scriptures call it.

It is so then, that in the work of the creation we see a double emanation of virtue from God: the one referring more properly to power, the other to wisdom; the one expressed in making the subsistence of the matter, and the other in disposing the beauty of the form. This being supposed, it is to be observed that, for anything which appeareth in the history of the creation, the confused mass and matter of heaven and earth was made in a moment; and the order and disposition of that chaos or mass was the work of six days. Such a note of difference it pleased God to put upon the works of power and the works of wisdom. Wherewith concurreth that in the former it is not set down that God said, 'Let there be heaven and earth,' as it is set down of the works following, but actually that God made heaven and earth; the one carrying the style of a manufacture, and the other of a law, decree, or counsel.

. . . .

But yet the commandment of knowledge is yet higher than the commandment over the will; for it is a commandment over the reason, belief, and understanding of man, which is the highest part of the mind, and giveth law to the will itself. For there is no power on earth which setteth up a throne or chair of estate in the spirits and souls of men, and in their cogitations, imaginations, opinions, and beliefs, but knowledge and learning. And therefore we see the detestable and extreme pleasure that arch-heretics and false prophets and impostors are transported with, when they once find in themselves that they have a superiority in the faith and conscience of men; so great, that if they have once tasted of it, it is seldom seen that any torture or persecution can make them relinquish or abandon it. But as this is that which the author of the Revelation calleth the depth or profoundness of Satan, so, by argument of contraries, the just and lawful sovereignty over men's understanding, by force of truth rightly interpreted, is that which approacheth nearest to the similitude of the divine rule.

As for fortune and advancement, the beneficence of learning is not so confined to give fortune only to states and commonwealths, as it doth not likewise give fortune to particular persons. For it was well noted long ago that Homer hath given more men their livings than either Sylla, or Cæsar, or Augustus ever did, notwithstanding their great largesses and donatives and distributions of lands to so many legions. And no doubt it is hard to say whether arms or learning have advanced greater numbers. And in case of sovranty, we see that if arms or descent have carried away the kingdom, yet learning hath carried the priesthood, which ever hath been in some competition with empire.

Again, for the pleasure and delight of knowledge and learning, it far surpasseth all other in nature. For shall the pleasures of the affections so exceed the pleasures of the senses, as much as the obtaining of desire or victory exceedeth a song or a dinner; and must not, of consequence, the pleasures of the intellect or understanding exceed the pleasures of the affections? We see in all other pleasures there is satiety, and after they be used their verdure departeth; which showeth well they be but deceits of pleasure, and not pleasures, and that it was the novelty which pleased, and not the quality. And therefore we see that voluptuous men turn friars, and ambitious princes turn melancholy. But of knowledge there is no satiety, but satisfaction and appetite are perpetually interchangeable; and therefore appeareth to be good in itself simply, without fallacy or accident. Neither is that pleasure of small efficacy and contentment to the mind of man, which the poet Lucretius describeth elegantly:

Pleasant to gaze below, when winds disturb the deep,[1]

'It is a view of delight,' saith he, 'to stand or walk upon the shore side, and to see a ship tossed with tempest upon the sea; or to be in a fortified tower, and to see two battles join upon a plain. But it is a pleasure incomparable, for the mind of man to be settled, landed, and fortified in the certainty of truth, and from thence to descry and behold the errors, perturbations, labors, and wanderings up and down of other men.'

Lastly, leaving the vulgar arguments that by learning man excelleth man in that wherein man excelleth beasts, that by learning man ascend-

---

[1] *Suave mari magno, turbantibus æquora ventis,* etc.

eth to the heavens and their motions, where in body he cannot come, and the like; let us conclude with the dignity and excellency of knowledge and learning in that whereunto man's nature doth most aspire, which is immortality or continuance—for to this tendeth generation, and raising of houses and families; to this tend buildings, foundations, and monuments; to this tendeth the desire of memory, fame, and celebration, and in effect the strength of all other human desires. We see then how far the monuments of wit and learning are more durable than the monuments of power or of the hands. For have not the verses of Homer continued twenty-five hundred years or more without the loss of a syllable or letter, during which time infinite palaces, temples, castles, cities, have been decayed and demolished? It is not possible to have the true pictures or statuaes of Cyrus, Alexander, Cæsar, no, nor of the kings or great personages of much later years; for the originals cannot last, and the copies cannot but leese of the life and truth. But the images of men's wits and knowledges remain in books, exempted from the wrong of time, and capable of perpetual renovation. Neither are they fitly to be called images, because they generate still, and cast their seeds in the minds of others, provoking and causing infinite actions and opinions in succeeding ages. So that if the invention of the ship was thought so noble, which carrieth riches and commodities from place to place, and consociateth the most remote regions in participation of their fruits, how much more are letters to be magnified, which as ships pass through the vast seas of time, and make ages so distant to participate of the wisdom, illuminations, and inventions, the one of the other? Nay further, we see some of the philosophers which were least divine and most immersed in the senses, and denied generally the immortality of the soul, yet came to this point, that whatsoever motions the spirit of man could act and perform without the organs of the body, they thought might remain after death,—which were only those of the understanding, and not of the affection; so immortal and incorruptible a thing did knowledge seem unto them to be. But we, that know by divine revelation that not only the understanding, but the affections purified, not only the spirit, but the body changed, shall be advanced to immortality, do disclaim in these rudiments of the senses. But it must be remembered both in this last point, and so it may likewise be needful in other places, that in probation of the dignity of knowledge or learning I did in the beginning separate divine testimony from human; which method I have pursued, and so handled them both apart.

Nevertheless I do not pretend, and I know it will be impossible for me by any pleading of mine, to reverse the judgment, either of Æsop's cock, that preferred the barley-corn before the gem; or of Midas, that being chosen judge betweep Apollo, president of the Muses, and Pan, god of the flocks, judged for plenty; or of Paris, that judged for beauty and love against wisdom and power; or of Agrippina, *Let him kill his mother so he be emperor*,[1]—that preferred empire with any condition never so detestable; or of Ulysses, *who preferred an old woman to immorality*,[2] being a figure of those which prefer custom and habit before all excellency; or of a number of the like popular judgments. For these things must continue as they have been; but so will that also continue whereupon learning hath ever relied, and which faileth not: *Wisdom is justified of her children.*[3]

---

[1]*Occidat matrem, modo imperet.*
[2]*Qui vetulam prætulit immortalitati.*
[3]*Fustificata est Sapientia a filiis suis.*

4.4 THE GENERAL DESIGN AND PLAN OF THE ESSAY*

by John Locke

Since it is the understanding, that sets man above the rest of sensible beings, and gives him all the advantage and dominion, which he has over them; it is certainly a subject, even for its nobleness, worth our labour to inquire into. The understanding, like the eye, whilst it makes us see and perceive all other things, takes no notice of itself; and it requires art and pains to set it at a distance, and make it its own object. But, whatever be the difficulties that lie in the way of this inquiry; whatever it be, that keeps us so much in the dark to ourselves; sure I am, that all the light we can let in upon our own minds, all the acquaintance we can make with our own understandings, will not only be very pleasant, but bring us great advantage, in directing our thoughts in the search of other things.

This, therefore, being my purpose, to inquire into the original, certainty, and extent of human knowledge; together with the grounds and degrees of belief, opinion, and assent; I shall not at present meddle with the physical consideration of the mind; or trouble myself to examine, wherein its essence consists, or by what motions of our spirits, or alterations of our bodies, we come to have any sensation by our organs, or any ideas in our understandings; and whether those ideas do in their formation, any, or all of them, depend on matter or no. These are speculations, which, however curious and entertaining, I shall decline, as lying out of my way in the design I am now upon. It shall suffice to my present purpose, to consider the discerning faculties of a man, as they are employed about the objects, which they have to do with. And I shall imagine I have not wholly misemployed myself in the thoughts I shall have on this occasion, if, in this historical, plain method, I can give any account of the ways, whereby our understandings come to attain those notions of things we have, and can set down any measures of the certainty of our knowledge, or the grounds of those persuasions, which are to be found amongst men, so various, different, and wholly contradictory; and yet asserted, somewhere or other, with such assurance and confidence, that he that shall take a view of the opinions of mankind, observe their opposition, and at the same time consider the fondness and devotion wherewith they are embraced, the resolution and eagerness

*Reprinted from *Essay Concerning Human Understanding* (Oxford: Clarendon Press, 1894), pages 25-33, 95-100, 121-125, and 139-141.

wherewith they are maintained, may perhaps have reason to suspect, that either there is no such thing as truth at all; or that mankind hath no sufficient means to attain a certain knowledge of it.

It is, therefore, worth while to search out the bounds between opinion and knowledge; and examine by what measures, in things, whereof we have no certain knowledge, we ought to regulate our assent, and moderate our persuasions. In order whereunto, I shall pursue this following method.

First, I shall enquire into the origin of those ideas, notions, or whatever else you please to call them, which a man observes, and is conscious to himself he has in his mind; and the ways, whereby the understanding comes to be furnished with them.[1]

Secondly, I shall endeavour to shew what knowledge the understanding hath by those ideas; and the certainty, evidence, and extent of it.

Thirdly, I shall make some enquiry into the nature and grounds of faith, or opinion; whereby I mean that assent, which we give to any proposition as true, of whose truth yet we have no certain knowledge: and here we shall have occasion to examine the reasons and degrees of assent.

If, by this enquiry into the nature of the understanding, I can discover the powers thereof; how far they reach; to what things they are in any degree proportionate; and where they fail us: I suppose it may be of use to prevail with the busy mind of man, to be more cautious in meddling with things exceeding its comprehension; to stop when it is at the utmost extent of its tether; and to sit down in a quiet ignorance of those things, which, upon examination, are found to be beyond the reach of our capacities. We should not then perhaps be so forward, out of an affectation of an universal knowledge, to raise questions, and perplex ourselves and others with disputes about things, to which our understandings are not suited; and of which we cannot frame in our minds any clear or distinct perceptions, or whereof (as it has perhaps too often happened) we have not any notions at all. If we can find out how far the understanding can extend its view, how far it has faculties to attain certainty, and in what cases it can only judge and guess; we may learn to content ourselves with what is attainable by us in this state.

For, though the comprehension of our understandings comes exceeding short of the vast extent of things; yet we shall have cause enough to magnify the bountiful author of our being, for that proportion and degree of knowledge he has bestowed on us, so far above all the rest of the inhabitants of this our mansion. Men have reason to be well satisfied with

---

[1]For further comments by Locke on the nature of ideas, cf. p. 321.

what God hath thought fit for them, since he hath given them whatsoever is necessary for the conveniences of life, and information of virtue; and has put within the reach of their discovery the comfortable provision for this life, and the way that leads to a better. How short soever their knowledge may come of an universal or perfect comprehension of whatsoever is, it yet secures their great concernments, that they have light enough to lead them to the knowledge of their maker, and the sight of their own duties. Men may find matter sufficient to busy their heads, and employ their hands with variety, delight and satisfaction; if they will not boldly quarrel with their own constitution, and throw away the blessings their hands are filled with, because they are not big enough to grasp every thing. We shall not have much reason to complain of the narrowness of our minds, if we will but employ them about what may be of use to us; for of that they are very capable: and it will be an unpardonable, as well as childish peevishness, if we undervalue the advantages of our knowledge, and neglect to improve it to the ends for which it was given us, because there are some things that are set out of the reach of it. It will be no excuse to an idle and untoward servant, who would not attend his business by candle-light, to plead that he had not broad sun-shine. The candle, that is set up in us, shines bright enough for all our purposes. The discoveries we can make with this, ought to satisfy us; and we shall then use our understandings right, when we entertain all objects in that way and proportion that they are suited to our faculties, and upon those grounds they are capable of being proposed to us, and not peremptorily, or intemperately require demonstration, and demand certainty, where probability only is to be had, and which is sufficient to govern all our concernments. If we will disbelieve every thing, because we certainly cannot know all things; we shall do much-what as wisely as he, who would not use his legs, but sit still and perish, because he had no wings to fly.

When we know our own strength, we shall the better know what to undertake with hopes of success: and when we have well surveyed the powers of our own minds, and made some estimate what we may expect from them, we shall not be inclined either to sit still, and not set our thoughts on work at all, in despair of knowing any thing; or, on the other side, question every thing, and disclaim all knowledge, because some things are not to be understood. It is of great use to the sailor, to know the length of his line, though he cannot with it fathom all the depths of the ocean. It is well he knows, that it is long enough to reach the bottom, at such places as are necessary to direct his voyage, and caution him against running upon shoals that may ruin him. Our business here is not to know all things, but those which concern our conduct.

If we can find out those measures, whereby a rational creature, put in that state in which man is in this world, may, and ought to govern his opinions, and actions depending thereon, we need not to be troubled that some other things escape our knowledge.

This was that which gave the first rise to this essay concerning the understanding. For I thought that the first step towards satisfying several enquiries, the mind of man was very apt to run into, was to take a survey of our own understandings, examine our own powers, and see to what things they were adapted. Till that was done, I suspected we began at the wrong end, and in vain sought for satisfaction in a quiet and sure possession of truths that most concerned us, whilst we let loose our thoughts into the vast ocean of being; as if all that boundless extent were the natural and undoubted possession of our understandings, wherein there was nothing exempt from its decisions, or that escaped its comprehension. Thus men extending their enquiries beyond their capacities, and letting their thoughts wander into those depths, where they can find no sure footing; it is no wonder, that they raise questions, and multiply disputes, which, never coming to any clear resolution, are proper only to continue and increase their doubts, and to confirm them at last in perfect scepticism. Whereas, were the capacities of our understandings well considered, the extent of our knowledge once discovered, and the horizon found, which sets the bounds between the enlightened and dark parts of things, between what is, and what is not comprehensible by us; men would perhaps with less scruple acquiesce in the avowed ignorance of the one, and employ their thoughts and discourse with more advantage and satisfaction in the other.

Thus much I thought necessary to say concerning the occasion of this enquiry into human understanding. But, before I proceed on to what I have thought on this subject, I must here in the entrance beg pardon of my reader for the frequent use of the word "idea," which he will find in the following treatise. It being that term, which, I think, serves best to stand for whatsoever is the object of the understanding when a man thinks; I have used it to express whatever is meant by phantasm, notion, species, or whatever it is which the mind can be employed about in thinking; and I could not avoid frequently using it.

I presume it will be easily granted me, that there are such ideas in men's minds; every one is conscious of them in himself, and men's words and actions will satisfy him that they are in others.

Our first enquiry then shall be, how they come into the mind.

If any idea can be imagined innate, the idea of God may, of all others, for many reasons be thought so; since it is hard to conceive, how there should be innate moral principles, without an innate idea of a Deity:

without a notion of a law-maker, it is impossible to have a notion of a law, and an obligation to observe it. Besides the atheists, taken notice of amongst the ancients, and left branded upon the records of history, hath not navigation discovered, in these later ages, whole nations at the bay of Soladania, in Brazil, in Boranday, and in the Caribbee islands, &c. amongst whom there was to be found no notion of a God, no religion? These are instances of nations where uncultivated nature has been left to itself, without the help of letters, and discipline, and the improvements of arts and sciences. But there are others to be found, who have enjoyed these in a very great measure; who yet, for want of a due application of their thoughts this way, want the idea and knowledge of God. It will, I doubt not, be a surprise to others, as it was to me, to find the Siamites of this number. But for this, let them consult the king of France's late envoy thither, who gives no better account of the Chinese themselves. And if we will not believe La Loubère, the missionaries of China, even the Jesuits themselves, the great encomiasts of the Chinese, do all to a man agree, and will convince us that the sect of the literati, or learned, keeping to the old religion of China, and the ruling party there, are all of them atheists. And perhaps if we should, with attention, mind the lives and discourses of people not so far off, we should have too much reason to fear, that many in more civilised countries have no very strong and clear impressions of a Deity upon their minds; and that the complaints of atheism, made from the pulpit, are not without reason. And though only some profligate wretches own it too bare-facedly now; yet perhaps we should hear more than we do of it from others, did not the fear of the magistrate's sword, or their neighbour's censure, tie up people's tongues: which, were the apprehensions of punishment or shame taken away, would as openly proclaim their atheism, as their lives do.

But had all mankind, every where, a notion of a God (whereof yet history tells us the contrary) it would not from thence follow, that the idea of him was innate. For though no nation were to be found without a name, and some few dark notions of him: yet that would not prove them to be natural impressions on the mind, any more than the names of fire, or the sun, heat, or number, do prove the ideas they stand for to be innate: because the names of those things, and the ideas of them, are so universally received and known amongst mankind. Nor, on the contrary, is the want of such a name, or the absence of such a notion out of men's minds, any argument against the being of a God; any more than it would be a proof that there was no load-stone in the world, because a great part of mankind had neither a notion of any such thing, nor a name for it; or be any show of argument to prove, that there are no distinct and various species of angels, or intelligent beings above us, because we have no ideas of such distinct species, or names for them: for men being furnished with words, by the common language of their own countries, can scarce avoid having some kind of ideas of those things, whose names, those they converse with, have occasion frequently to mention to them. And if they carry with it the notion of excellency, greatness, or something extraordinary: if apprehension and concernment accompany it; if the fear of absolute and irresistible power set it on upon the mind, the idea is likely to sink the deeper, and spread the farther; especially if it be such an idea as is agreeable to the common light of reason, and naturally deducible from every part of our knowledge, as that of a God is. For the visible marks of extraordinary wisdom and power appear so plainly in all the works of the creation, that a rational creature, who will but seriously reflect on them, cannot miss the discovery of a Deity.[1] And the influence that the discovery of such a being must necessarily have on the minds of all, that have but once heard of it, is so great, and carries such a weight of thought and communication with it, that it seems stranger to me, that a whole nation of men should be any where found so brutish, as to want the notion of a God; than that they should be without any notion of numbers, or fire.

The name of God being once mentioned in any part of the world, to express a superior, powerful, wise, invisible being, the suitableness of such a notion to the principles of common reason, and the interest men will always have to mention it often, must necessarily spread it far and wide, and continue it down to all generations; though yet the general reception of this name, and some imperfect and unsteady notions conveyed thereby to the unthinking part of mankind, prove not the idea to be innate; but only that they, who made the discovery, had made a right use of their reason, thought maturely of the causes of things, and traced them to their original; from whom other less considering people having once received so important a notion, it could not easily be lost again.

The Origin of All Our Ideas in Experience

Every man being conscious to himself that he thinks, and that which his mind is applied about, whilst thinking, being the ideas that are there, it is past doubt, that men have in their minds several ideas, such as are those expressed by the words, Whiteness, Hardness, Sweetness, Thinking, Motion, Man, Elephant, Army, Drunkenness, and others. It is in the first place then to be inquired, how he comes by them. I know it is a

---

[1]For Locke's proofs for the existence of God, cf. pp. 258, 340.

received doctrine, that men have native ideas, and original characters, stamped upon their minds, in their very first being. This opinion I have, at large, examined already; and, I suppose, what I have said, in the foregoing book, will be much more easily admitted, when I have shewn, whence the understanding may get all the ideas it has, and by what ways and degrees they may come into the mind; for which I shall appeal to every one's own observation and experience.

Let us then suppose the mind to be, as we say, white paper, void of all characters, without any ideas; how comes it to be furnished? Whence comes it by that vast store which the busy and boundless fancy of man has painted on it, with an almost endless variety? Whence has it all the materials of reason[1] and knowledge? To this I answer, in one word, from experience; in all that our knowledge is founded, and from that it ultimately derives itself. Our observation employed either about external sensible objects, or about the internal operations of our minds, perceived and reflected on by ourselves, is that which supplies our understandings with all the materials of thinking. These two are the fountains of knowledge, from whence all the ideas we have, or can naturally have, do spring.

First, Our senses, conversant about particular sensible objects, do convey into the mind several distinct perceptions of things, according to those various ways wherein those objects do affect them: and thus we come by those ideas we have, of Yellow, White, Heat, Cold, Soft, Hard, Bitter, Sweet, and all those which we call sensible qualities; which when I say the senses convey into the mind, I mean, they from external objects convey into the mind what produces there those perceptions. This great source of most of the ideas we have, depending wholly upon our senses, and derived by them to the understanding, I call *sensation*.

Secondly, The other fountain, from which experience furnisheth the understanding with ideas, is the perception of the operations of our own mind within us, as it is employed about the ideas it has got; which operations, when the soul comes to reflect on and consider, do furnish the understanding with another set of ideas, which could not be had from things without; and such are Perception, Thinking, Doubting, Believing, Reasoning, Knowing, Willing, and all the different actings of our own minds; which we being conscious of and observing in ourselves, do from these receive into our understandings as distinct ideas, as we do from bodies affecting our senses. This source of ideas every man has

---

[1]For the relation between ideas as "the materials of reason" and knowledge as the product which reason makes out of these materials, cf. two groups of selections from Locke's later writings, pp. 322-328.

wholly in himself; and though it be not sense, as having nothing to do with external objects, yet it is very like it, and might properly enough be called internal sense. But as I call the other sensation, so I call this *reflection*, the ideas it affords being such only as the mind gets by reflecting on its own operations within itself. By reflection then, in the following part of this discourse, I would be understood to mean that notice which the mind takes of its own operations, and the manner of them; by reason whereof there come to be ideas of these operations in the understanding. These two, I say, *viz.* external material things, as the objects of sensation; and the operations of our own minds within, as the objects of reflection; are to me the only originals from whence all our ideas take their beginnings. The term operations here I use in a large sense, as comprehending not barely the actions of the mind about its ideas, but some sort of passions arising sometimes from them, such as is the satisfaction or uneasiness arising from any thought.

The understanding seems to me not to have the least glimmering of any ideas, which it doth not receive from one of these two. External objects furnish the mind with the ideas of sensible qualities, which are all those different perceptions they produce in us: and the mind furnishes the understanding with ideas of its own operations.

These, when we have taken a full survey of them and their several modes, combinations, and relations, we shall find to contain all our whole stock of ideas; and that we have nothing in our minds which did not come in one of these two ways. Let any one examine his own thoughts, and thoroughly search into his understanding; and then let him tell me, whether all the original ideas he has there, are any other than of the objects of his senses, or of the operations of his mind, considered as objects of his reflection; and how great a mass of knowledge soever he imagines to be lodged there, he will, upon taking a strict view, see that he has not any idea in his mind, but what one of these two have imprinted; though perhaps, with infinite variety compounded and enlarged by the understanding, as we shall see hereafter.

He that will suffer himself to be informed by observation and experience, and not make his own hypothesis the rule of nature, will find few signs of a soul accustomed to much thinking in a new-born child, and much fewer of any reasoning at all. And yet it is hard to imagine that the rational soul should think so much, and not reason at all. And he that will consider that infants newly come into the world spend the greatest part of their time in sleep, and are seldom awake but when either hunger calls for the teat, or some pain (the most importunate of all sensations), or some other violent impression on the body, forces the mind to perhaps find reason to imagine that a *foetus* in the mother's womb differs not much from the state of a vegetable, but passes the greatest part of its time without perception or thought; doing very little but sleep in a place where it needs not seek for food, and is surrounded with liquor, always equally soft, and near of the same temper; where the eyes have no light, and the ears so shut up are not very susceptible of sounds; and where there is little or no variety, or change of objects, to move the senses.

To ask at what time a man has first any ideas, is to ask when he begins to perceive; having ideas, and perception, being the same thing. I know it is an opinion, that the soul always thinks, and that it has the actual perception of ideas in itself constantly as long as it exists; and that actual thinking is as inseparable from the soul, as actual extension is from the body: which if true, to inquire after the beginning of a man's ideas is the same as to inquire after the beginning of his soul. For by this account soul and its ideas, as body and its extension, will begin to exist both at the same time.

I see no reason therefore to believe, that the soul thinks before the senses have furnished it with ideas to think on; and as those are increased and retained, so it comes, by exercise, to improve its faculty of thinking, in the several parts of it, as well as afterwards, by compounding those ideas, and reflecting on its own operations; it increases its stock, as well as facility, in remembering, imagining, reasoning, and other modes of thinking.

Follow a child from its birth, and observe the alterations that time makes, and you shall find, as the mind by the senses comes more and more to be furnished with ideas, it comes to be more and more awake; thinks more, the more it has matter to think on. After some time it begins to know the objects, which, being most familiar with it, have made lasting impressions. Thus it comes by degrees to know the persons it daily converses with, and distinguish them from strangers; which are instances and effects of its coming to retain and distinguish the ideas the senses convey to it. And so we may observe how the mind, by degrees, improves in these, and advances to the exercise of those other faculties of enlarging, compounding, and abstracting its ideas, and of reasoning about them, and reflecting upon all these; of which I shall have occasion to speak more hereafter.

Thus the first capacity of human intellect is, that the mind is fitted to receive the impressions made on it; either through the senses by outward objects; or by its own operations when it reflects on them. This is the first step a man makes towards the discovery of any thing, and the ground-work whereon to build all those notions which ever he shall have naturally in this world. All those sublime thoughts which tower above the clouds, and reach as high as heaven itself, take their rise and footing here: in all that good extent wherein the mind wanders, in those remote speculations, it may seem to be elevated with, it stirs not one jot beyond those ideas which sense or reflection have offered for its contemplation.

In this part the understanding is merely passive; and whether or no it will have these beginnings, and as it were materials of knowledge, is not in its own power. For the objects of our senses do, many of them, obtrude their particular ideas upon our minds whether we will or no; and the operations of our minds will not let us be without, at least, some obscure notions of them. No man can be wholly ignorant of what he does when he thinks. These simple ideas, when offered to the mind, the understanding can no more refuse to have, nor alter, when they are imprinted, nor blot them out, and make new ones itself, than a mirror can refuse, alter, or obliterate the images or ideas which the objects set before it do therein produce. As the bodies that surround us do diversely affect our organs, the mind is forced to receive the impressions, and cannot avoid the perception of those ideas that are annexed to them.

4.5 SIX THEORIES OF INTELLECTUAL DISCIPLINE*

by Frederick C. Neff

For a variety of reasons the terms "intellectualism" and "intellectual discipline" have fallen gradually into disrepute among a significant number of contemporary educators and philosophers. Because increasing prestige is being attached to what experience validates, those who still conceive of intellect as something apart from experience are finding their position increasingly difficult to maintain. The older notion of mind as a separate entity, operating under its own power, carried with it the implication that it was something sacrosanct and undefiled by mundane affairs. Moreover, the intellect was regarded as the seat of reason, and reason was held to be what most sharply differentiated man from the brutes. Hence, to train the reason was believed to be the ultimate purpose of education, if not the chief end of man.

It has been customary to characterize a disciplined intellect by at least two factors: first, by the possession of a proper fund of knowledge, and, second, by an ability to reason with such knowledge for the purpose of arriving at logical conclusions. So far as it went, there was nothing particularly wrong with such a conception. Certainly, reasoning could scarcely take place if there were no knowledge to reflect upon, and surely knowledge could be of little significance if unutilized by reason. Unfortunately, however, both the content of knowledge and the method of reasoning soon became fixed—in the history of Western thought, at least—in the hands first of Plato and then of Aristotle. The content of knowledge was derived, not from what was meaningful and verifiable in the world about us, but from speculation about eternity, destiny, and other matters remote from everyday affairs. Similarly, methods of reasoning stemmed, not from serviceable modes of inquiry, but from the fixed requirements of formal logic. Resort to systems of classical reasoning was of course consonant with the fact that metaphysical problems could scarcely be attacked by any other than metaphysical means. Knowledge thus came to be regarded as acquaintance with metaphysical truth, while reasoning meant skill in methods of classical logic. This fixed structure of knowledge and reasoning has been perpetuated, with few exceptions, throughout the whole course of Western idealism, eventuating in what has been termed "the genteel tradition" and reaching a culmination in the intricate philosophic system of Hegel.

*Reprinted from *Educational Theory*, Vol. VII, No. 3 (July, 1957), pages 161-171, with permission of Professor Neff and the publisher.

In view of the fact that little importance was then attached to empirical inquiry, it is hardly surprising that Plato should have chosen as the object of knowledge a realm of speculation quite removed from the practical problems of a workaday world. Nor is it likely that Plato would have had either the time or the inclination to philosophize about other realms had not the social hierarchy of his time permitted him to lead the life of an aristocrat, if not that of a philosopher-king. This is not to imply that Plato had nothing to say, or that his insights were inconsequential simply because they were grounded in speculation. We could do worse that to heed the remarks of Plato when he speaks so movingly of the true, the good, and the beautiful. But when he idealizes such concepts to the extent of divorcing them from the world of experience, when he defines them in terms that preclude their translation into modes of human behavior, and when he attaches to them qualities of eternalness, autonomy, and priority over the urgent issues of experiencing man, he strains his lines of communication, despite his captivating eloquence. What Platonic philosophizing did was to cause the content of intellectuality to be defined in terms of knowledge about a so-called "ultimate" reality—a reality that purportedly transcended space, time, and circumstance.

Methods of reasoning about an ultimate reality became understandably limited to what could be called ratiocination, or "speculation about the speculative." At least, such methods could scarcely be considered empirical, inductive, or experimental in the later sense of these terms. And so a system of logic came into being which took as its purpose either to "prove" through nonempirical reasoning what had been born of a priori speculation, or to build quite "logical" hierarchies, often magnificient in their intricacies, upon premises that were as faulty as the undeveloped sciences of their day.

Logic thus came to be crystallized in an "if . . . then" kind of reasoning, a modification of the Aristotelian syllogism. "If" the gods are infallible, "then" their authority ought not to be criticized; "if" diseases are caused by evil spirits, "then" the way to cure them is to drive out the evil spirits; "if", according to Hegel, only wholes are knowable, "then" nothing can ever be really known. In this kind of reasoning, logic consisted almost entirely in the internal consistency of an argument. It was not so much the method that was faulty as the framework of unexamined premises in which the method operated. Much importance was attached to the "then" clause (the conclusion), while the "if" clause (the premise) was more axiomatic than critical. Although such early methods have been largely superseded by more critical modes in inquiry, nevertheless, the conclusions of earlier thinkers have become a quasi-sacrosanct body of "truth," almost ineradicably embedded in the stockpile of Western culture. "This illustrates an important truth," says Bertrand Russell, "namely, that the worse your logic, the more interesting the consequences to which it gives rise."[1]

The foregoing conceptions of mentality and reasoning have their own peculiar disciplines, just as intellect and logic defined in other terms require an altered understanding of discipline. Whether the intellect is to be trained from without in terms of externally imposed authority or whether it is to be shaped from within by means of self-imposed strictures, the fact remains that discipline of some kind is involved whenever thinking takes place. Indeed, as Havelock Ellis has said, "Life itself must always be a discipline; it is so dangerous that only by submitting to some sort of discipline can we become equipped to live in any true sense at all." To be disciplined in the act of doing something means to be trained—either coercively or voluntarily—to make certain choices and to reject others; it means likewise to assume obligation both for the outcomes of whatever is chosen and for the outcomes of whatever is rejected. A person who is disciplined in respect to obeying commands will put aside inclinations to disobey; likewise, an individual trained in the art of clear thinking will reject whatever he considers unsound or illogical. Intellectual discipline may then be defined as the *rigorous employment of a particular method of reasoning and a strict adherence to the conclusions it yields.* It now becomes appropriate to examine some conceptions of intellectual discipline that have been most influential in shaping our educational and cultural values.

First, intellectual discipline may be understood as a *rigorous acquisition of funded knowledge as an intrinsic and final end.* Foremost among those subscribing to this position are the philosophic and literary classicists, to whom knowledge itself represents power. The gearing of knowing to some further purpose is held to be a desecration of the idea that knowledge is its own sublime end. Mind is conceived as very much like a muscle—the more it is exercised, the more efficient and limber it becomes. Development of ability in abstract reasoning and in dealing with general propositions is emphasized, while cultivation of proficiency in professional and vocational skills is not to be viewed as a proper domain of education.

A second conception of intellectual discipline is that it consists in *a rigorous mastery of the rules of formal logic as a means for the resolution of problems.* Among adherents of this point of view are the scho-

---

[1]Bertrand Russell, *A History of Western Philosophy* (New York: Simon and Schuster, 1945), p. 746.

lastics, Aristotelians, and formal logicians. At the heart of this method of reasoning was the syllogism, which usually began with an authoritative or generally accepted premise, under which was placed a specific statement, and which then proceeded to a logical conclusion. This method was employed to advantage by medieval schoolmen, whose concern was to perpetuate orthodox canons of belief and to discourage the emergence of revolutionary or heretical views.

A third conception of intellectual discipline is that it involves *a rigorous following of intuitive bents, "hunches," or insights.* Subscribing to this notion of education are the subjective idealists and the intuitionists. Such an approach is almost the antithesis of objective analysis, for it is neither objective nor analytical. It follow the spirit of Pascal's remark that "the heart has reasons of its own which the head can never understand." A similar sentiment was voiced by Emerson when he wrote, "Nothing is at last sacred but the integrity of your own mind. Absolve you to yourself and you shall have the suffrage of the world."

A fourth conception of intellectual discipline is in terms of *a rigorous search for truth in a transcendental realm.* Included in this category are the transcendentalists, objective idealists, and metaphysical realists. Whereas the intuitionist believed that we should look inward and examine our own bosoms, so to speak, the transcendentalist would have us look outward to a metaphysical world of spiritual fixity. Both make a studied attempt to circumvent experience. Liston Pope, a contemporary transcendentalist, holds that ". . . there must be objective references beyond human desires or social relations, in order to validate the goodness of one's preference or to establish binding standards of moral obligation.[2]

. . . .

In the fifth place, intellectual discipline may be thought of as *a rigorous adherence to the proposition that knowledge derives from an objective observation of descriptively delineable phenomena.* Among those so oriented are the operationalists, physical realists, and logical positivists (or logical empiricists, as they frequently prefer to be called). The intention here is to attain the highest degree of strictly scientific objectivity possible. In the thinking of Herbert Feigl,

> It has become imperative to abandon the dogmatic, other-worldly, supernaturalistic, tender-minded, rationalistic, parochial preconceptions and to replace them by critical, worldly, naturalistic, fact-

---

[2]Liston Pope, "Social Contexts of Personality," *Moral Principles of Action*, ed. R.N. Anshen (New York: Harper & Row, Publishers, 1952), pp. 140-146.

minded, empirical, experimental, and universally applicable ways of thinking.[3]

. . . .

A sixth and final understanding of intellectual discipline is in terms of *a rigorous inquiry into past and present experience for the purpose of intelligently directing the course of future experience.* Here are included the pragmatists, the instrumentalists, and the experimentalists. Intellect in the pragmatic outlook is neither reified nor degraded but is viewed as one of the most significant products in the evolutionary development of man. The gradual emergence of consciousness and conceptualization, along with the appearance and growth of language, provided the raw material upon which thinking is predicated. The intellect of man is regarded, not as artificial or non-natural, but as one among many activities which it is of the nature of man to engage in.

. . . .

The whole point of the foregoing discussion would be lost if we failed to recognize that each of these theories of intellectual discipline represents a value system, and that the values to which we subscribe have a way of influencing our educational and cultural destinies. This is particularly true of our present era, wherein the older sanctions are gradually disappearing and newer values are but seen through a glass darkly. It has become commonplace to characterize our present era as an age of anxiety. It is an age of anxiety because it is a time of flux and transition, and an unstable equilibrium is difficult to maintain. The transition we are experiencing is not quite understood, which makes the problem of deciding which way to go exceedingly complex. For most of us transition simply means change, and change is regarded as a necessary condition of progress. Moreover, we tend to identify change almost exclusively with material advancement. We think immediately of the strides we have made in mass media of communication and transportation, and as evidence we summon to mind the radio, television, and the three-dimensional movie; or new depths of submarine exploration, flights into the stratosphere, and ultrasonic travel.

What is not so commonplace is a grasp of the precise nature of the changes that are taking place, together with a recognized need for some

---

[3]Herbert Feigl, "Aims of Education for Our Age of Science: Reflections of a Logical Empiricist," in National Society for the Study of Education, Fifty-fourth Yearbook, Part I: *Modern Philosophies and Education*, ed. J.S. Brubacher (Chicago: University of Chicago Press, 1955), pp. 305-341.

rather careful reflection before charting our prospective course. This is another way of saying that the transitional character of our time goes deeper than the rather obvious changes in the physical scene—higher-powered automobiles, taller buildings, improved standards of health, and the like. It is bound, sooner or later, to raise the questions of choice between competing sets of value. To put it differently, evidences of material progress are basically surface indications of an increasingly experimental outlook, the import of which is that progress consists in progressively gaining control over social situations for purposes of human betterment. In opposition to this view is the contention that the status quo ought not to be disturbed and that man's role should be that of conforming to some set of fixed principles, which have been variously defined as classical, revealed, transcendental, cosmic, or otherwise absolute and inviolable. From the latter standpoint, those who would invade the established order of things, if not rank heretics, are at least persons whom we should "keep an eye on," and those who would presume to match their wits against nature had better "watch their step."

Science has made such startling advances in respect to man's ability to manipulate natural forces—in medicine and psychiatry, in nuclear fission and astrophysics—that those accustomed to viewing human destiny as foreordained and not to be tampered with are dismayed to find their moorings being loosened on all sides. Today we stand at a crossroads—educationally, morally, socially. For better or for worse, the older sanctions are being seriously challenged, and it is becoming increasingly evident that we must move either forward or backward.

The absolute or traditional point of view demands stress on conformity and uniformity, the pragmatic or progressive on inventiveness and creativity; the former implies adjustment to things "as they are," the latter involves reconstruction and improvement of conditions in terms of what is possible. The former reminds us of our perennially imperfect state and at the same time holds before us a vision of perfection; the latter reminds us of our virtually limitless powers for betterment and bids us construct goals that are attainable. The former perpetuates the dichotomy between the cultural and the practical, while the latter holds that the practical can be cultural and that the cultural can be practical.

CHAPTER FIVE

ROMANTIC
NATURALISM IN
MODERN EDUCATION

5.1 EDITORIAL COMMENT

In order to illustrate the essence of romantic naturalism we have chosen to use a well known selection from one of America's greatest beloved poets, Walt Whitman. Here in the "Song of the Open Road" Whitman identifies his being with a universal love of mother nature.

Above all things Jean Jacques Rousseau was not a scientist, but he was a very sensitive, intuitive, creative artist, and no where is this more dramatically portrayed than in his educational classic *Emile*. If we view this study as a work of great art it is not difficult to grasp the significance of his message. No one has had a greater influence on modern progressive education than did Rousseau.

Johann Pestalozzi was not a philosopher but he was a great teacher, and much of his success as well as his failures was no doubt due to his romantic naturalistic tendencies. Here in this selection he clearly identified man, and thus child nature, with the course of nature. The article stands in striking contrast to the supernaturalistic dogma of his day.

Thomas Paine, as a moving spirit in both the American Revolution and the French Revolution, is well known to students of American history. It is interesting to contrast the freedom loving spirit exemplified in the "Declaration of the Rights of Man and of Citizens" with the terror of the French Revolution. It may well tell us something about the race problems of our day as well as about the contributions of Thomas Paine.

5.2 SONG OF THE OPEN ROAD[*]

by Walt Whitman

Afoot and light-hearted I take to the open road,
Healthy, free, the world before me,
The long brown path before me leading wherever I choose.

Henceforth I ask not good-fortune, I myself am good-fortune,
Henceforth I whimper no more, postpone no more, need nothing,
Done with indoor complaints, libraries, querulous criticisms,
Strong and content I travel the open road.

The earth, that is sufficient,
I do not want the constellations any nearer,
I know they are very well where they are,
I know they suffice for those who belong to them.

(Still here I carry my old delicious burdens,
I carry them, men and women, I carry them with me wherever
    I go,
I swear it is impossible for me to get rid of them,
I am fill'd with them, and I will fill them in return.)

You road I enter upon and look around, I believe you are not all
    that is here,
I believe that much unseen is also here.

Here the profound lesson of reception, nor preference nor denial,
The black with his woolly head, the felon, the diseas'd, the il-
    literate person, are not denied;
The birth, the hasting after the physician, the beggar's tramp,
    the drunkard's stagger, the laughing party of mechanics,

The escaped youth, the rich person's carriage, the fop, the eloping
    couple,
The early market-man, the hearse, the moving of furniture into
    the town, the return back from the town,

---

*Reprinted from Walt Whitman, *Leaves of Grass* (London: D. Bogue, 1881),
Selections.

They pass, I also pass, any thing passes, none can be interdicted,
None but are accepted, none but shall be dear to me.

You air that serves me with breath to speak!
You objects that call from diffusion my meanings and give them
    shape!
You light that wraps me and all things in delicate equable
    showers!
You paths worn in the irregular hollows by the roadsides!
I believe you are latent with unseen existences, you are so dear
    to me.

You flagg'd walks of the cities! you strong curbs at the edges!
You ferries! you planks and posts of wharves! you timber-lined
    sides! you distant ships!
You rows of houses! you window-pierc'd façades! you roofs!
You porches and entrances! you copings and iron guards!
You windows whose transparent shells might expose so much!
You doors and ascending steps! you arches!
You gray stones of interminable pavements! you trodden cross-
    ings!
From all that has touch'd you I believe you have imparted to
    yourselves, and now would impart the same secretly to me,
From the living and the dead you have peopled your impassive
    surfaces, and the spirits thereof would be evident and ami-
    cable with me.

5.3 EMILE[*]

by Jean Jacques Rousseau

God makes all things good; man meddles with them and they become evil. He forces one soil to yield the products of another, one tree to bear another's fruit. He confuses and confounds time, place, and natural conditions. He mutilates his dog, his horse, and his slave. He destroys and defaces all things; he loves all that is deformed and monstrous; he will have nothing as nature made it, not even man himself, who must learn his paces like a saddle-horse, and be shaped to his master's taste like the trees in his garden.

Yet things would be worse without this education, and mankind cannot be made by halves. Under existing conditions a man left to himself from birth would be more of a monster than the rest. Prejudice, authority, necessity, example, all the social conditions into which we are plunged, would stifle nature in him and put nothing in her place. She would be like a sapling chance sown in the midst of the highway, bent hither and thither and soon crushed by the passers-by.

Tender, anxious mother,[1] I appeal to you. You can remove this young tree from the highway and shield it from the crushing force of social conventions. Tend and water it ere it dies. One day its fruit will reward

---

*Reprinted from Jean Jacques Rousseau, *Emile*, trans. Barbara Foxley (London: J. M. Dent and Sons, Ltd., 1911), Selections.

[1] The earliest education is most important and it undoubtedly is woman's work. If the author of nature had meant to assign it to men he would have given them milk to feed the child. Address your treatises on education to the women, for not only are they able to watch over it more closely than men, not only is their influence always predominant in education, its success concerns them more nearly, for most widows are at the mercy of their children, who show them very plainly whether their education was good or bad. The laws, always more concerned about property than about people, since their object is not virtue but peace, the laws give too little authority to the mother. Yet her position is more certain than that of the father, her duties are less trying; the right ordering of the family depends more upon her, and she is usually fonder of her children. There are occasions when a son may be excused for lack of respect for his father, but if a child could be so unnatural as to fail in respect for the mother who bore him and nursed him at her breast, who for so many years devoted herself to his care, such a monstrous wretch should be smothered at once as unworthy to live. You say mothers spoil their children, and no doubt that is wrong, but it is worse to deprave them as you do. The mother wants her child to be happy now. She is right, and if her method is wrong, she must be taught a better. Ambition, avarice, tyranny, the mistaken foresight of fathers, their neglect, their harshness, are a hundredfold more harmful to the child than the blind affection of the mother. Moreover, I must explain what I mean by a mother and that explanation follows.

your care. From the outset raise a wall round your child's soul; another may sketch the plan, you alone should carry it into execution.

Plants are fashioned by cultivation, man by education. If a man were born tall and strong, his size and strength would be of no good to him till he had learnt to use them; they would even harm him by preventing others from coming to his aid;[2] left to himself he would die of want before he knew his needs. We lament the helplessness of infancy; we fail to perceive that the race would have perished had not man begun by being a child.

We are born weak, we need strength; helpless, we need aid; foolish, we need reason. All that we lack at birth, all that we need when we come to man's estate, is the gift of education.

This education comes to us from nature, from men, or from things. The inner growth of our organs and faculties is the education of nature, the use we learn to make of this growth is the education of men, what we gain by our experience of our surroundings is the education of things.

Thus, we are each taught by three masters. If their teaching conflicts, the scholar is ill-educated and will never be at peace with himself; if their teaching agrees, he goes straight to his goal, he lives at peace with himself, he is well-educated.

Now of these three factors in education nature is wholly beyond our control, things are only partly in our power; the education of men is the only one controlled by us; and even here our power is largely illusory, for who can hope to direct every word and deed of all with whom the child has to do.

Viewed as an art, the success of education is almost impossible, since the essential conditions of success are beyond our control. Our efforts may bring us within sight of the goal, but fortune must favour us if we are to reach it.

What is this goal? As we have just shown, it is the goal of nature. Since all three modes of education must work together, the two that we can control must follow the lead of that which is beyond our control. Perhaps this word Nature has too vague a meaning. Let us try to define it.

Nature, we are told, is merely habit. What does that mean? Are there not habits formed under compulsion, habits which never stifle nature? Such, for example, are the habits of plants trained horizontally. The plant keeps its artificial shape, but the sap has not changed its course,

---

[2]Like them in externals, but without speech and without the ideas which are expressed by speech, he would be unable to make his wants known, while there would be nothing in his appearance to suggest that he needed their help.

and any new growth the plant may make will be vertical. It is the same with a man's disposition; while the conditions remain the same, habits, even the least natural of them, hold good; but change the conditions, habits vanish, nature reasserts herself. Education itself is but habit, for are there not people who forget or lose their education and others who keep it? Whence comes this difference? If the term nature is to be restricted to habits comfortable to nature we need say no more.

We are born sensitive and from our birth onwards we are affected in various ways by our environment. As soon as we become conscious of our sensations we tend to seek or shun the things that cause them, at first because they are pleasant or unpleasant, then because they suit us or not, and at last because of judgments formed by means of the ideas of happiness and goodness which reason gives us. These tendencies gain strength and permanence with the growth of reason, but hindered by our habits they are more or less warped by our prejudices. Before this change they are what I call Nature within us.

Everything should therefore be brought into harmony with these natural tendencies, and that might well be if our three modes of education merely differed from one another; but what can be done when they conflict, when instead of training man for himself you try to train him for others? Harmony becomes impossible. Forced to combat either nature or society, you must make your choice between the man and the citizen, you cannot train both.

The smaller social group, firmly united in itself and dwelling apart from others, tends to withdraw itself from the larger society. Every patriot hates foreigners; they are only men, and nothing to him.[3] This defect is inevitable, but of little importance. The great thing is to be kind to our neighbours. Among strangers the Spartan was selfish, grasping, and unjust, but unselfishness, justice, and harmony ruled his home life. Distrust those cosmopolitans who search out remote duties in their books and neglect those that lie nearest. Such philosophers will love the Tartars to avoid loving their neighbour.

The natural man lives for himself; he is the unit, the whole, dependent only on himself and on his like. The citizen is but the numerator of a fraction, whose value depends on its denominator; his value depends upon the whole, that is, on the community. Good social institutions are those best fitted to make a man unnatural, to exchange his independence for dependence, to merge the unit in the group, so that he no

---

[3]Thus the wars of republics are more cruel than those of monarchies. But if the wars of kings are less cruel, their peace is terrible; better be their foe than their subject.

longer regards himself as one, but as a part of the whole, and is only conscious of the common life. A citizen of Rome was neither Caius nor Lucius, he was a Roman; he ever loved his country better than his life. The captive Regulus professed himself a Carthaginian; as a foreigner he refused to take his seat in the Senate except at his master's bidding. He scorned the attempt to save his life. He had his will, and returned in triumph to a cruel death. There is no great likeness between Regulus and the men of our own day.

The Spartan Pedaretes presented himself for admission to the council of the Three Hundred and was rejected; he went away rejoicing that there were three hundred Spartans better than himself. I suppose he was in earnest; there is no reason to doubt it. That was a citizen.

A Spartan mother had five sons in the army. A Helot arrived; trembling she asked his news. "Your five sons are slain." "Vile slave, was that what I asked thee?" "We have won the victory." She hastened to the temple to render thanks to the gods. That was a citizen.

He who would preserve the supremacy of natural feelings in social life knows not what he asks. Ever at war with himself, hesitating between his wishes and his duties, he will be neither a man nor a citizen. He will be of no use to himself nor to others. He will be a man of our day, a Frenchman, an Englishman, one of the great middle class.

To be something, to be himself, and always at one with himself, a man must act as he speaks, must know what course he ought to take, and must follow that course with vigour and persistence. When I meet this miracle it will be time enough to decide whether he is a man or a citizen, or how he contrives to be both.

Two conflicting types of educational systems spring from these conflicting aims. One is public and common to many, the other private and domestic.

If you wish to know what is meant by public education, read Plato's *Republic*. Those who merely judge books by their titles take this for a treatise on politics, but it is the finest treatise on education ever written.

In popular estimation the Platonic Institute stands for all that is fanciful and unreal. For my own part I should have thought the system of Lycurgus far more impractical had he merely committed it to writing. Plato only sought to purge man's heart; Lycurgus turned it from its natural course.

The public institute does not and cannot exist, for there is neither country nor patriot. The very words should be struck out of our language. The reason does not concern us at present, so that though I know it I refrain from stating it.

I do not consider our ridiculous colleges[4] as public institutes, nor do I include under this head a fashionable education, for this education facing two ways at once achieves nothing. It is only fit to turn out hypocrites, always professing to live for others, while thinking of themselves alone. These professions, however, deceive no one, for every one has his share in them; they are so much labour wasted.

Our inner conflicts are caused by these contradictions. Drawn this way by nature and that way by man, compelled to yield to both forces, we make a compromise and reach neither goal. We go through life, struggling and hesitating, and die before we have found peace, useless alike to ourselves and to others.

There remains the education of the home or of nature; but how will a man live with others if he is educated for himself alone? If the two-fold aims could be resolved into one by removing the man's self-contradictions, one great obstacle to his happiness would be gone. To judge of this you must see the man full-grown; you must have noted his inclinations, watched his progress, followed his steps; in a word you must really know a natural man. When you have read this work, I think you will have made some progress in this inquiry.

What must be done to train this exceptional man! We can do much, but the chief thing is to prevent anything being done. To sail against the wind we merely follow one tack and another; to keep our position in a stormy sea we must cast anchor. Beware, young pilot, lest your boat slip its cable or drag its anchor before you know it.

In the social order where each has his own place a man must be educated for it. If such a one leave his own station he is fit for nothing else. His education is only useful when fate agrees with his parents' choice; if not, education harms the scholar, if only by the prejudices it has created. In Egypt, where the son was compelled to adopt his father's calling, education had at least a settled aim; where social grades remain fixed, but the men who form them are constantly changing, no one knows whether he is not harming his son by educating him for his own class.

In the natural order men are all equal and their common calling is that of manhood, so that a well-educated man cannot fail to do well

---

[4]There are teachers dear to me in many schools and especially in the University of Paris, men for whom I have a great respect, men whom I believe to be quite capable of instructing young people, if they were not compelled to follow the established custom. I exhort one of them to publish the scheme of reform which he has thought out. Perhaps people would at length seek to cure the evil if they realised that there was a remedy.

in that calling and those related to it. It matters little to me whether my pupil is intended for the army, the church, or the law. Before his parents chose a calling for him nature called him to be a man. Life is the trade I would teach him. When he leaves me, I grant you, he will be neither a magistrate, a soldier, nor a priest; he will be a man. All that becomes a man he will learn as quickly as another. In vain will fate change his station, he will always be in his right place. *"Occupavi te, fortuna, atque cepi; omnes-que aditus tuos interclusi, ut ad me aspirare non posses."* The real object of our study is man and his environment. To my mind those of us who can best endure the good and evil of life are the best educated; hence it follows that true education consists less in precept than in practice. We begin to learn when we begin to live; our education begins with ourselves, our first teacher is our nurse. The ancients used the word "Education" in a different sense, it meant "Nurture." *"Educit obstetrix,"* says Varro. *"Educat nutrix, instituit pædagogus, docet magister."* Thus, education, discipline, and instruction are three things as different in their purpose as the dame, the usher, and the teacher. But these distinctions are undesirable and the child should only follow one guide.

We must therefore look at the general rather than the particular, and consider our scholar as man in the abstract, man exposed to all the changes and chances of mortal life. If men were born attached to the soil or our country, if one season lasted all the year round, if every man's fortune were so firmly grasped that he could never lose it, then the established method of education would have certain advantages; the child brought up to his own calling would never leave it, he could never have to face the difficulties of any other condition. But when we consider the fleeting nature of human affairs, the restless and uneasy spirit of our times, when every generation overturns the work of its predecessor, can we conceive a more senseless plan than to educate a child as if he would never leave his room, as if he would always have his servants about him? If the wretched creature takes a single step up or down he is lost. This is not teaching him to bear pain; it is training him to feel it.

People think only of preserving their child's life; this is not enough, he must be taught to preserve his own life when he is a man, to bear the buffets of fortune, to brave wealth and poverty, to live at need among the snows of Iceland or on the scorching rocks of Malta. In vain you guard against death; he must needs die; and even if you do not kill him with your precautions, they are mistaken. Teach him to live rather than to avoid death: life is not breath, but action, the use of our senses, our mind, our faculties, every part of ourselves which makes us conscious of our being. Life consists less in length of days than in the keen sense of living. A man may be buried at a hundred and may never have lived at all. He would have fared better had he died young.

Our wisdom is slavish prejudice, our customs consist in control, constraint, compulsion. Civilised man is born and dies a slave. The infant is bound up in swaddling clothes, the corpse is nailed down in his coffin. All his life long man is imprisoned by our institutions.

I am told that many midwives profess to improve the shape of the infant's head by rubbing, and they are allowed to do it. Our heads are not good enough as God made them, they must be moulded outside by the nurse and inside by the philosopher. The Caribs are better off than we are. "The child has hardly left the mother's womb, it has hardly begun to move and stretch its limbs, when it is deprived of its freedom. It is wrapped in swaddling bands, laid down with its head fixed, its legs stretched out, and its arms by its sides; it is wound round with linen and bandages of all sorts so that it cannot move. It is fortunate if it has room to breathe, and it is laid on its side so that water which should flow from its mouth can escape, for it is not free to turn its head on one side for this purpose." . . .

FROM BOOK II

Society has enfeebled man, not merely by robbing him of the right to his own strength, but still more by making his strength insufficient for his needs. This is why his desires increase in proportion to his weakness; and this is why the child is weaker than the man. If a man is strong and a child is weak it is not because the strength of the one is absolutely greater than the strength of the other, but because the one can naturally provide for himself and the other cannot. Thus the man will have more desires and the child more caprices, a word which means, I take it, desires which are not true needs, desires which can only be satisfied with the help of others.

I have already given the reason for this state of weakness. Parental affection is nature's provision against it; but parental affection may be carried to excess, it may be wanting, or it may be ill applied. Parents who live under our ordinary social conditions bring their child into these conditions too soon. By increasing his needs they do not relieve his weakness; they rather increase it. They further increase it by demanding of him what nature does not demand, by subjecting to their will what little strength he has to further his own wishes, by making slaves of themselves or of him instead of recognising that mutual dependence which should result from his weakness or their affection.

The wise man can keep his own place; but the child who does not know what his place is, is unable to keep it. There are a thousand ways out of it, and it is the business of those who have charge of the child to keep him in his place, and this is no easy task. He should be neither beast nor man, but a child. He must feel his weakness, but not suffer through it; he must be dependent, but he must not obey; he must ask, not command. He is only subject to others because of his needs, and because they see better than he what he really needs, what may help or hinder his existence. No one, not even his father, has the right to bid the child do what is of no use to him.

When our natural tendencies have not been interfered with by human prejudice and human institutions, the happiness alike of children and of men consists in the enjoyment of their liberty. But the child's liberty is restricted by his lack of strength. He who does as he likes is happy provided he is self-sufficing; it is so with the man who is living in a state of nature. He who does what he likes is not happy if his desires exceed his strength; it is so with a child in like conditions. Even in a state of nature children only enjoy an imperfect liberty, like that enjoyed by men in social life. Each of us, unable to dispense with the help of others, becomes so far weak and wretched. We were meant to be men, laws and customs thrust us back into infancy. The rich and great, the very kings themselves are but children; they see that we are ready to relieve their misery; this makes them childishly vain, and they are quite proud of the care bestowed on them, a care which they would never get if they were grown men.

These are weighty considerations, and they provide a solution for all the conflicting problems of our social system. There are two kinds of dependence: dependence on things, which is the work of nature; and dependence on men, which is the work of society. Dependence on things, being non-moral does no injury to liberty and begets no vices; dependence on men, being out of order,[5] gives rise to every kind of vice, and through this master and slave become mutually depraved. If there is any cure for this social evil, it is to be found in the substitution of law for the individual; in arming the general will with a real strength beyond the power of any individual will. If the laws of nations, like the laws of nature, could never be broken by any human power, dependence on men would become dependence on things, all the advantages of a state of nature would be combined with all the advantages of social life

---

[5]In my *Principles of Political Law* it is proved that no private will can be ordered in the social system.

so far have been child's play, now they are of the greatest importance. This period when education is usually finished is just the time to begin; but to explain this new plan properly, let us take up our story where we left it.

Our passions are the chief means of self-preservation; to try to destroy them is therefore as absurd as it is useless; this would be to overcome nature, to reshape God's handiwork. If God bade man annihilate the passions he has given him, God would bid him be and not be; He would contradict himself. He has never given such a foolish commandment, there is nothing like it written on the heart of man, and what God will have a man do. He does not leave to the words of another man, He speaks Himself; His words are written in the secret heart.

Now I consider those who would prevent the birth of the passions almost as foolish as those who would destroy them, and those who think this has been my object hitherto are greatly mistaken.

But should we reason rightly, if from the fact that passions are natural to man, we inferred that all the passions we feel in ourselves and behold in others are natural? Their source, indeed, is natural; but they have been swollen by a thousand other streams; they are a great river which is constantly growing, one in which we can scarcely find a single drop of the original stream. Our natural passions are few in number; they are the means to freedom, they tend to self-preservation. All those which enslave and destroy us have another source; nature does not bestow them on us; we seize on them in her despite.

The origin of our passions, the root and spring of all the rest, the only one which is born with man, which never leaves him as long as he lives, is self-love; this passion is primitive, instinctive, it precedes all the rest, which are in a sense only modifications of it. In this sense, if you like, they are all natural. But most of these modifications are the result of external influences, without which they would never occur, and such modifications, far from being advantageous to us, are harmful. They change the original purpose and work against its end; then it is that man finds himself outside nature and at strife with himself.

BOOK V

We have reached the last act of youth's drama; we are approaching its closing scene.

It is not good that man should be alone. Emile is now a man, and we must give him his promised helpmeet. That helpmeet is Sophy. Where is her dwelling-place, where shall she be found? We must know beforehand what she is, and then we can decide where to look for her. And when she is found, our task is not ended. "Since our young gentleman," says Locke, "is about to marry, it is time to leave him with his mistress." And with these words he ends his book. As I have not the honour of educating "A young gentleman," I shall take care not to follow his example.

SOPHY, OR WOMAN

Sophy should be as truly a woman as Emile is a man, *i.e.*, she must possess all those characters of her sex which are required to enable her to play her part in the physical and moral order. Let us inquire to begin with in what respects her sex differs from our own.

But for her sex, a woman is a man; she has the same organs, the same needs, the same faculties. The machine is the same in its construction; its parts, its working, and its appearance are similar. Regard it as you will the difference is only in degree.

Yet where sex is concerned man and woman are unlike; each is the complement of the other; the difficulty in comparing them lies in our inability to decide, in either case, what is a matter of sex, and what is not. General differences present themselves to the comparative anatomist and even to the superficial observer; they seem not to be a matter of sex; yet they are really sex differences, though the connection eludes our observation. How far such differences may extend we cannot tell; all we know for certain is that where man and woman are alike we have to do with the characteristics of the species; where they are unlike, we have to do with the characteristics of sex. Considered from these two standpoints, we find so many instances of likeness and unlikeness that it is perhaps one of the greatest of marvels how nature has contrived to make two beings so like and yet so different.

These resemblances and differences must have an influence on the moral nature; this inference is obvious, and it is confirmed by experience; it shows the vanity of the disputes as to the superiority or the equality of the sexes; as if each sex, pursuing the path marked out for it by nature, were not more perfect in that very divergence than if it more closely resembled the other. A perfect man and a perfect woman should no more be alike in mind than in face, and perfection admits of neither less nor more.

In the union of the sexes each alike contributes to the common end, but in different ways. From this diversity springs the first difference which may be observed between man and woman in their moral relations. The man should be strong and active; the woman should be weak and passive; the one must have both the power and the will; it is enough that the other should offer little resistance.

When this principle is admitted, it follows that woman is specially made for man's delight. If man in his turn ought to be pleasing in her eyes, the necessity is less urgent, his virtue is in his strength, he pleases because he is strong. I grant you this is not the law of love, but it is the law of nature, which is older than love itself.

If woman is made to please and to be in subjection to man, she ought to make herself pleasing in his eyes and not provoke him to anger; her strength is in her charms, by their means she should compel him to discover and use his strength. The surest way of arousing this strength is to make it necessary by resistance. Thus pride comes to the help of desire and each exults in the other's victory. This is the origin of attack and defence, of the boldness of one sex and the timidity of the other, and even of the shame and modesty with which nature has armed the weak for the conquest of the strong.

Who can possibly suppose that nature has prescribed the same advances to the one sex as to the other, or that the first to feel desire should be the first to show it? What strange depravity of judgment! The consequences of the act being so different for the two sexes, is it natural that they should enter upon it with equal boldness? How can any one fail to see that when the share of each is so unequal, if the one were not controlled by modesty as the other is controlled by nature, the result would be the destruction of both, and the human race would perish through the very means ordained for its continuance?

Women so easily stir a man's senses and fan the ashes of a dying passion, that if philosophy ever succeeded in introducing this custom into any unlucky country, especially if it were a warm country where more women are born than men, the men, tyrannised over by the women, would at last become their victims, and would be dragged to their death without the least chance of escape.

Female animals are without this sense of shame, but what of that? Are their desires as boundless as those of women, which are curbed by this shame? The desires of the animals are the result of necessity, and when the need is satisfied, the desire ceases; they no longer make a feint of repulsing the male, they do it in earnest. Their seasons of complaisance are short and soon over. Impulse and restraint are alike the work of nature. But what would take the place of this negative instinct in women if you rob them of their modesty? . . .

If you would inspire young people with a love of good conduct avoid saying, "Be good;" make it their interest to be good; make them feel the value of goodness and they will love it. It is not enough to show this effect in the distant future, show it now, in the relations of the present, in the character of their lovers. Describe a good man, a man of worth, teach them to recognise him when they see him, to love him for their own sake; convince them that such a man alone can make them happy as friend, wife, or mistress. Let reason lead the way to virtue; make them feel that the empire of their sex and all the advantages derived from it depend not merely on the right conduct, the morality, of women, but also on that of men; that they have little hold over the vile and base, and that the lover is incapable of serving his mistress unless he can do homage to virtue. You may then be sure that when you describe the manners of our age you will inspire them with a genuine disgust; when you show them men of fashion they will despise them; you will give them a distaste for their maxims, an aversion to their sentiments, and a scorn for their empty gallantry; you will arouse a nobler ambition, to reign over great and strong souls, the ambition of the Spartan women to rule over men. A bold, shameless, intriguing woman, who can only attract her lovers by coquetry and retain them by her favours, wins a servile obedience in common things; in weighty and important matters she has no influence over them. But the woman who is both virtuous, wise, and charming, she who, in a word, combines love and esteem, can send them at her bidding to the end of the world, to war, to glory, and to death at her behest. This is a fine kingdom and worth the winning.

This is the spirit in which Sophy has been educated, she has been trained carefully rather than strictly, and her taste has been followed rather than thwarted. Let us say just a word about her person, according to the description I have given to Emile and the picture he himself has formed of the wife in whom he hopes to find happiness.

I cannot repeat too often that I am not dealing with prodigies. Emile is no prodigy, neither is Sophy. He is a man and she is a woman; this is all they have to boast of. In the present confusion between the sexes it is almost a miracle to belong to one's own sex.

Sophy is well born and she has a good disposition; she is very warm-hearted, and this warmth of heart sometimes makes her imagination run away with her. Her mind is keen rather than accurate, her temper is pleasant but variable, her person pleasing though nothing out of the common, her countenance bespeaks a soul and it speaks true; you may meet her with indifference, but you will not leave her without emotion. Others possess good qualities which she lacks; others possess her good qualities in a higher degree, but in no one are these qualities better blended to form a happy disposition. She knows how to make the best of her very faults, and if she were more perfect she would be less pleasing.

Sophy is not beautiful; but in her presence men forget the fairer women, and the latter are dissatisfied with themselves. At first sight she is hardly pretty; but the more we see her the prettier she is; she wins where so many lose, and what she wins she keeps. Her eyes might be finer, her mouth more beautiful, her stature more imposing; but no one could have a more graceful figure, a finer complexion, a whiter hand, a daintier foot, a sweeter look, and a more expressive countenance. She does not dazzle; she arouses interest; she delights us, we know not why.

Sophy is fond of dress, and she knows how to dress; her mother has no other maid; she has taste enough to dress herself well; but she hates rich clothes; her own are always simple but elegant. She does not like showy but becoming things. She does not know what colours are fashionable, but she makes no mistake about those that suit her. No girl seems more simply dressed, but no one could take more pains over her toilet; no article is selected at random, and yet there is no trace of artificiality. Her dress is very modest in appearance and very coquettish in reality; she does not display her charms, she conceals them, but in such a way as to enhance them. When you see her you say, "That is a good modest girl," but while you are with her, you cannot take your eyes or your thoughts off her, and one might say that this very simple adornment is only put on to be removed bit by bit by the imagination.

Sophy has natural gifts; she is aware of them, and they have not been neglected; but never having had a chance of much training she is content to use her pretty voice to sing tastefully and truly; her little feet step lightly, easily, and gracefully, she can always make an easy graceful courtesy. She has had no singing master but her father, no dancing mistress but her mother; a neighbouring organist has given her a few lessons in playing accompaniments on the spinet, and she has improved herself by practice. At first she only wished to show off her hand on the dark keys; then she discovered that the thin clear tone of the spinet made her voice sound sweeter; little by little she recognised the charms of harmony; as she grew older she at last began to enjoy the charms of expression, to love music for its own sake. But she has taste rather than talent; she cannot read a simple air from notes.

Needlework is what Sophy likes best; and the feminine arts have been taught her most carefully, even those you would not expect, such as cutting out and dressmaking. There is nothing she cannot do with her needle, and nothing that she does not take a delight in doing; but lacemaking is her favourite occupation, because there is nothing which requires such a pleasing attitude, nothing which calls for such grace and dexterity of finger. She has also studied all the details of housekeeping; she understands cooking and cleaning; she knows the prices of food, and also how to choose it; she can keep accounts accurately, she is her mother's housekeeper. Some day she will be the mother of a family;

by managing her father's house she is preparing to manage her own; she can take the place of any of the servants and she is always ready to do so. You cannot give orders unless you can do the work yourself; that is why her mother sets her to do it. Sophy does not think of that; her first duty is to be a good daughter, and that is all she thinks about for the present. Her one idea is to help her mother and relieve her of some of her anxieties. However, she does not like them all equally well. For instance, she likes dainty food, but she does not like cooking; the details of cookery offend her, and things are never clean enough for her. She is extremely sensitive in this respect and carries her sensitiveness to a fault; she would let the whole dinner boil over into the fire rather than soil her cuffs. She has always disliked inspecting the kitchen-garden for the same reason. The soil is dirty, and as soon as she sees the manure heap she fancies there is a disagreeable smell.

This defect is the result of her mother's teaching. According to her, cleanliness is one of the most necessary of a woman's duties, a special duty, of the highest importance and a duty imposed by nature. Nothing could be more revolting than a dirty woman, and a husband who tires of her is not to blame. She insisted so strongly on this duty when Sophy was little, she required such absolute cleanliness in her person, clothing, room, work, and toilet, that use has become habit, till it absorbs one half of her time and controls the other; so that she thinks less of how to do a thing than of how to do it without getting dirty.

Yet this has not degenerated into mere affectation and softness; there is none of the over refinement of luxury. Nothing but clean water enters her room; she knows no perfumes but the scent of flowers, and her husband will never find anything sweeter than her breath. In conclusion, the attention she pays to the outside does not blind her to the fact that time and strength are meant for greater tasks; either she does not know or she despises that exaggerated cleanliness of body which degrades the soul. Sophy is more than clean, she is pure.

I said that Sophy was fond of good things. She was so by nature; but she became temperate by habit and now she is temperate by virtue. Little girls are not to be controlled, as little boys are, to some extent, through their greediness. This tendency may have ill effects on women and it is too dangerous to be left unchecked. When Sophy was little, she did not always return empty handed if she was sent to her mother's cupboard, and she was not quite to be trusted with sweets and sugar-almonds. Her mother caught her, took them from her, punished her, and made her go without her dinner. At last she managed to persuade her that sweets were bad for the teeth, and that over-eating spoiled the figure. Thus Sophy overcame her faults; and when she grew older other tastes distracted her from this low kind of self-indulgence. With awakening feeling greediness ceases to be the ruling passion, both with men and women. Sophy has preserved her feminine tastes; she likes milk and sweets; she likes pastry and made-dishes, but not much meat. She has never tasted wine or spirits; moreover, she eats sparingly; women, who do not work so hard as men, have less waste to repair. In all things she likes what is good, and knows how to appreciate it; but she can also put up with what is not so good, or can go without it.

Sophy's mind is pleasing but not brilliant, and thorough but not deep; it is the sort of mind which calls for no remark, as she never seems cleverer or stupider than oneself. When people talk to her they always find what she says attractive, though it may not be highly ornamental according to modern ideas of an educated woman; her mind has been formed not only by reading, but by conversation with her father and mother, by her own reflections, and by her own observations in the little world in which she has lived. Sophy is naturally merry; as a child she was even giddy; but her mother cured her of her silly ways, little by little, lest too sudden a change should make her self-conscious. Thus she became modest and retiring while still a child, and now that she is a child no longer, she finds it easier to continue this conduct than it would have been to acquire it without knowing why. It is amusing to see her occasionally return to her old ways and indulge in childish mirth and then suddenly check herself, with silent lips, downcast eyes, and rosy blushes; neither child nor woman, she may well partake of both.

Sophy is too sensitive to be always good humoured, but too gentle to let this be really disagreeable to other people; it is only herself who suffers. If you say anything that hurts her she does not sulk, but her heart swells; she tries to run away and cry. In the midst of her tears, at a word from her father or mother she returns at once laughing and playing, secretly wiping her eyes and trying to stifle her sobs.

Yet she has her whims; if her temper is too much indulged it degenerates into rebellion, and then she forgets herself. But give her time to come round and her way of making you forget her wrong-doing is almost a virtue. If you punish her she is gentle and submissive, and you see that she is more ashamed of the fault than the punishment. If you say nothing, she never fails to make amends, and she does it so frankly and so readily that you cannot be angry with her. She would kiss the ground before the lowest servant and would make no fuss about it; and as soon as she is forgiven, you can see by her delight and her caresses that a load is taken off her heart. In a word, she endures patiently the wrong-doing of others, and she is eager to atone for her own. This amiability is natural to her sex when unspoiled. Woman is made to submit to man and to endure even injustice at his hands. You will never bring young lads to this; their feelings rise in revolt against injustice; nature has not fitted them to put up with it.

> "Gravem
> Pelidæ stomachum cedere nescii."
> Horace, lib. i. ode vi.

Sophy's religion is reasonable and simple, with few doctrines and fewer observances; or rather as she knows no course of conduct but the right her whole life is devoted to the service of God and to doing good. In all her parents' teaching of religion she has been trained to a reverent submission; they have often said, "My little girl, this is too hard for you; your husband will teach you when you are grown up." Instead of long sermons about piety, they have been content to preach by their example, and this example is engraved on her heart.

Sophy loves virtue; this love has come to be her ruling passion; she loves virtue because there is nothing fairer in itself, she loves it because it is a woman's glory and because a virtuous woman is little lower than the angels; she loves virtue as the only road to real happiness, because she sees nothing but poverty, neglect, unhappiness, shame, and disgrace in the life of a bad woman; she loves virtue because it is dear to her revered father and to her tender and worthy mother; they are not content to be happy in their own virtue, they desire hers; and she finds her chief happiness in the hope of making them happy. All these feelings inspire an enthusiasm which stirs her heart and keeps all its budding passions in subjection to this noble enthusiasm. Sophy will be chaste and good till her dying day; she has vowed it in her secret heart, and not before she knew how hard it would be to keep her vow; she made this vow at a time when she would have revoked it had she been the slave of her senses.

5.4 INQUIRIES INTO THE COURSE OF NATURE IN THE DEVELOPMENT OF THE HUMAN SPECIES*

by Johann Pestalozzi

It is the inevitable doom of light appearing in a world of darkness, after giving the first evidence of its existence, to be enveloped for a time in impenetrable mists, raised up against it, in desperate self-defence, by the light-abhorring elements to which its radiant influence speaks as a message of destruction. Thus against the rising sun the fogs are gathering thicker and thicker, until he dispel them by the strength of his noonday beam; and thus against the Eternal Light, ever since the heavenly hosts celebrated his descent on earth, sin has been, and still is, gathering its blackest clouds, and will continue to do so till that overwhelming day when, in final triumph over all darkness, his glory shall be made manifest. This great and awful truth, equally attested by the evidence of every new day, and by the mystery of ages, finds its confirmation in the experience of every individual; and in proportion as we see the effulgence of light divine beaming in the human eye, in the same measure deep, we may conclude, has been the darkness through whose horrors the mind has penetrated to the bright regions of faith, love, and hope. Such a nightly passage was the period of Pestalozzi's life, which elapsed between his first unsuccessful experiment at Neuhof, and his renewed and more prosperous exertions for the cause of education at Stanz and Burgdorf. The former was a mere indication of those truths which, to bring into full consciousness within himself, and to realize in the world, the hand of Supreme Wisdom fitted him by affliction and disappointment of every kind. Of the deep gloom by which his soul was oppressed at that time, he has left a striking monument behind him in his "Inquiries into the Course of Nature in the Development of the Human Species," a work which, as it appears *prima facie* to contradict his other writings, preceding as well as succeeding, can be understood in the connexion which it has with them, only, when considered as expressive of the tumult which the misanthropic suggestions of experience raised up in his soul against the oracles of faith and love so loudly declared in his bosom. To analyse its contents, to place its truths out of the false light in which they appear, into the light of verity in which they ought to stand, to trace its errors to their fountainhead, and to correct them, would be an undertaking

*Reprinted from Johann Pestalozzi, *Henry Pestalozzi and His Plan of Education* (London: E. Biber, 1831), pages 148-157.

far beyond the design of the present pages, involving a depth of meta-physical research, and an extent of volume, which would not easily be endured; but to extract a few of the most characteristic passages will be of great avail in illustrating the tortuous march of Pestalozzi's genius.

The questions which he proposes to himself at the onset are the following:

"What am I? What is the human species?

"What have I done? What is the human species doing?

"I want to know what the course of my life, such as it has been, has made of me? and I want to know what the course of life, such as it has been, has made of the human species?

"I want to know on what ground my volition and my opinions rest, and must rest, under the circumstances in which I am placed?

"I want to know on what ground the volition of the human species and its opinions rest, and must rest, under the circumstances in which it is placed?"

As a preliminary to their solution, he gives this compendious outline of the "march of civilization:"

"By the helplessness of his animal condition man is brought to knowledge.

"Knowledge leads to acquisition, acquisition to possession.

"Possession leads to the formation of society.

"Society leads to power and honour.

"Power and honour lead to the relation of ruler and subject.

"The relation of ruler and subject lead to the distinction of nobles and commons, and to the crown.

"All these relations call for a state of law.

"The state of law calls for civil liberty.

"The want of law entails tyranny and slavery; that is to say, a state of things in which men constitute a society without the intervention of laws for their improvement, and the maintenance of mutual obligations.

"Following the course of nature in another direction, I find in myself a certain benevolence, by which acquisition, honour, property, and power, ennoble my mind, whilst without it, all these privileges of my social condition only tend to degrade me more deeply.

"Tracing his benevolence to its source, I find it to be essentially of sensual, animal origin; but I find likewise within myself a power, which will ennoble its very root, and benevolence so ennobled I call love. But there is a danger still, of love being lost in my longing for self-gratification; I feel desolate as an orphan, and I seek to rise beyond the power of imagination, beyond the limits of all research and knowledge that is possible here below; to the fountainhead of my existence, to derive from thence help against the desolation of my being, against all the ills and weaknesses of my nature."

The social compact is, in his opinion, nothing more or less than a truce entered into by the animal propensities of all parties, which would otherwise be at constant war with one another:

"Let the social constitution be ever so well whited a wall, and let the animal dispositions of power wear ever so admirably the mark of humanity, man never will truly and freely submit to an arrangement, which gives to any one the right to visit by flaying, the aberrations of his animal tendencies. The relation of man to man, in the social state is merely animal. As a mass, as a people, man submits himself not to the powers of the state in his moral capacity; in entering society, there is nothing he contemplates less than the service of God and the love due to his neighbour. He enters society with a view to gratify himself, and to enjoy all those things which, to a sensual and animal being, are the indispensable conditions of satisfaction and happiness.

"The social law is, therefore, not in any wise a moral law, but a mere modification of the animal law.

"Meanwhile, power is deeply interested in my moral condition, that my animal tendencies may never come in conflict with its own propensities. This is the reason why all over the earth it endeavours to represent the social relation as a moral tie, at least on one side. But the disposition of power to represent itself as morally related to the people, does not alter the position in which it really stands to them; and if the persons in power, stimulated by their immoral tendencies, encourage the delusion for their own ends, with a view to cover their civil lawlessness, and their social injustice, they do nothing else but what the wolf and the fox also would do, if they could, with a view to inspire the sheep and the hen with unbounded confidence. Nevertheless, the hen does well to sleep on trees at night, and the sheep to keep to the shepherd, in spite of all that the wolf may say."

Such a view of the social compact should not be too harshly condemned, so long as there is truth in the following definition of honour:

"The savage who cuts into his skin as into a piece of board, daubs himself with dirty colours, and pierces his nose and ears, that he may suspend in them something glittering, exerts himself, with all this, much less, and gives himself less pain, than a European does for the same purpose.

"The Otaheitian toilette, and the European, are not essentially different, nor is the 'order of the bone' of the South Sea islander any way inferior to the various orders in our part of the globe.

"Throughout the whole world, the wish of distinction induces the animal man, to esteem the tail of his coat, or a ring in his nose, higher than himself, and to slay his brother for gin, beads, and ribbons, provided there be any one willing and able to pay such a price for murder."

Nothing, however, can more fully exemplify the view which pervades the whole work, than the picture which it gives of man:

"I see him in his cave, the prey of every power in nature, in equal danger from the tooth of the stronger, and the venom of the weaker brute; the sun dries up the fountain from which he drinks, the rain fills his cavern with mire; streams undermine the dike which protects his dwelling, or the sands of the desert cover his habitation; burning winds deprive him of his sight, the exhalations of the morass stop his breath; and if, for three successive days, he be unable to obtain a fish or a rat, he must die.

"Yet under all climates does he preserve his existence, and overcomes the ills of earth.

"Inexpressibly improvident, he sleeps whenever his wants are satisfied; and whenever he has nothing to fear, he suns himself, or he follows after the prey.

"His hands are ever stained with the blood of his brother; like a tyger he defends his den, and raves against his own species; he claims the ends of the earth as his own, and perpetrates whatever he chooses under the sun.

"He knows of no law and of no Lord; his will is his only law, and of sin he asks: 'What is it?'

"But much as it charms him, the bloodstained freedom of earth, he is unable to endure it; he falls asleep under the sunny palm-tree; in plenty a gnat stings him to death, and in want his own wrath consumes him.

"In whatever condition he be, he longs for a better law than that of his club.

"In whatever condition he be, he grows weary of waging never-ceasing war against his species, and he seeks union with those whose murderer he was.

"But under the icy pole, scorn and fear allow him not to venture upon peace: his heart, cold as the earth, freezes within his bosom; while, under the glowing beams of the opposite climate, his brain is consumed in a fiery rage under the injuries and miseries which he endures, and he refrains from the step which would humanize him.

"Even under the mildest climate he is afraid of his own species; he flees before the man that dwells beyond the mountains, and yet again he slays the stranger before whose people he trembles.

"Nevertheless, it is under this climate that he first stretches out the hand of peace to his brother.

"The harmonious feeling of animal satisfaction tranquillizes his spirit, while in other climates, where nature exhausts his strength, and abandons him to manifold ills, his disposition grows restless and savage.

"But where nature leads him gently by the hand, he leaves his cave with a timid, rather than a savage step. He finds a stone that is too heavy, a branch that is too high for him; he feels that, if another man were with him, he might lift the stone, he might reach the branch; he sees another man near, and a feeling rushes through him, as of hunger and mighty thirst; he is compelled to approach his brother, and in his eye there beams a look such as never beamed in it before; it is the thought, we can help one another; the eye of his brother responds to his look, their bosoms heave, they feel as they never felt before; their hands are joined, they lift the stone, they reach the branch; a new smile of joy appears on their countenances; they perceive what their united efforts can accomplish.

"They enjoy their knowledge; with their knowledge their power increases, and their enjoyment with their power; the signs of union between them are multiplied, and their voice breaks forth into language.

"They speak.

"Now it is done. As the sea by the rocky shore, so is the bloodstained liberty of earth arrested by the word of man.

"For it was waste and desolate, before the breath of his mouth, the word of his lips went over the earth.

"It is by the breath of his mouth that man builds up his world, and himself.

"As long as he was dumb, he was a brute, he speaks, and he has become man.

"Ignorance and suspicion, want and fear, now lose the terrible sway which they exercised over him, and their tyrant law is abolished.

"In his word man now acknowledges the basis of his rights and of his duties.

"He has renounced the bloodstained liberty of his nature for himself, and for his whole species.

"By his word he has become man, subject to the law which is in him, and which he has now given to himself.

"Therefore does he value his word so high; he wishes it to live for ever; he engraves it on tables of stone and of brass, and bards sing in lofty strains the law which he has given to himself, and which he claims as his own.

"How, then? Was the liberty of my nature bloodstained before it knew any law? and was I a brute before I spoke? Is it true that ignorance and suspicion preceded love, confidence, and knowledge, as the thorn and the thistle precede the goodly fruits of the ground, and that the fell sway of bestiality contaminated the earth, before justice and faithfulness offered for her sacrifices of atonement?

"Is it not true, then, that man lived, at first, peaceably on the earth, that he divided it without violence, without injustice, without blood? Is it not true, that the distinction of mine and thine arose from his feelings of justice and equity?

"Is it true, on the contrary, that man divided the earth before he united on it; that he invaded, before he possessed; transgressed, before he laboured; destroyed, before he produced; oppressed, before he cherished; murdered, before he conversed; that the breath of his mouth breathed treason, before there was a word formed on his tongue to declare a law?

"I was corrupt in bestiality, before I became civilized and human; the period of my animal innocence passed away as a moment; my brutal corruption broke in upon me suddenly, and lasted long; and it was only when I was bowed down under the wretchedness of its effects, that I submitted my neck to the yoke of society.

"It is done, however, and all the clay of the earth has now its lord; touch it not, if it be not thine own; the fowl in the air, and the fish in the water has its lord; though thou be thirsty, roll not the stone from a well which is not thine own; though thou be hungry, tear no fruit from a tree, no ear from a haum which is not thine own, nor dare to kill the game that crosses thy way.

"They will hang thee for it. Shudder not: thou thyself hast submitted to this law; the earth would have remained a wilderness, and an abode of wild beasts, and man would have been the most helpless of brutes, if thou hadst not submitted.

"But thou hast submitted, and thy cave is changed into a house; thy house separates thee from the earth, and ties thee to property, and property constitutes thee a member of society. Thy cares are extended over the objects of thy love, the helpmates of thy labours; they reach beyond the grave, for thy son shall be thine heir, thy brother shall defend thy widow, and thy friend provide for thy infant. What then hast thou lost?

"A thousand means and ways are offered to thee, for turning to account that which has remained unemployed, by exertion, order, and knowledge, under the protection of that law which thou hast imposed upon thyself.

"On boundless tracts, plants without name or number grow in luxuriant freedom; thou destroyest them all, and sowest goodly wheat on the boundless tracts.

"Thou cuttest down the glory of the mountains, and plantest the shrub of thy choice on the sunny hills.

"Thou heapest up thine own species, as winds and waves gather the floating sands. Men dwell together like herrings in a bay, or like ants on a puny hill. Nations are locked in by one bolt; in the morning the gate opens, and a world is poured out over the earth.

"Thou sayest to the deep: 'Touch no longer the sands which were thine of old. Thou plantest the watery reed on dry heaths, and in the depth of morasses the flame-coloured madder. Thou measurest the orbs of the stars, and in a thousand years mistakest not an hour of the shadows in the heavens.

"One man cultivates a tract in which hundreds might live, while another subsists on hardly more ground than his corpse will cover.

"This man, by one word, can cause the productions of distant climes to suceed each other, like the fruits of adjoining gardens.

"The stroke of a pen is suspended, and thousands tremble for their lives; for on one hand depends the bread of them all.

"Man is a mighty miracle in the chaotic night of unsearchable nature.

"Ever variable, he undermines his happiness by appeals to the law, and the law again by appeals to chance. Miserable and lawless, he bears the burden of an exhausted existence. On the scaffold here bleeds a woman greater and nobler than the generation in which she lived; in exile there a beggar feels exalted above his king, who shut his ear against him, and banished him from his presence.

"A degraded wretch cherishes in his soul contempt of mankind, and hardens himself in his errors; he provokes the slanderer to reproach him yet more: while the scorn of his pride debases him in his nature, and makes true the calumnies of his detractor.

"Here a delicate woman atones on her knees for a word of offence, which escaped from her lips, and her eyes dare not meet the man whom the most sacred of ties cannot bind; an adorable wife serves in dark obscurity the vile caprices of a husband, whose malignant sneers are unable to disturb the calm composure of her lips. What is all this?

"Nations forgive the crimes of a man, who has extinguished the feelings of humanity in their hearts, who devotes their sons to death, and their daughters to dishonour, who abandoned their cities and villages to plunder, who converted their houses into heaps of stones, their gardens into wastes, and the whole land into a wilderness.

"There nations, like tame bullocks, follow an infant that leads them by a slender thread, and spill their blood for every caprice of the child or of his nurse. Here they are suffocated, like flies under the air pump, by the empty vanity of power; and there again they are drowned in the abundance of their wealth, like bees in overflowing honey. A man turns insane, and speaks nonsense, such as was never heard before, and nations prostrate themselves before him, build altars, and learn piety, order, obedience, and humanity, in the worship of a calf, or of the devil. Legions of knaves lurk in the temples of justice like greedy cats before the holes of mice, and for whole centuries my species is contented to be consumed by them.

"How then shall I find the clue by which I may enter this labyrinth of misery and well-being, of wisdom and folly, of madness and high elevation of mind?

"Even while he dwells in his cave, there is no equality between man and man; under the roof, behind the brick wall and the bolt, the inequality increases; and, when hundreds and thousands are gathered together, he is compelled, in spite of himself, to say to the strong, 'Be thou my shield;' and to the cunning, 'Be thou my guide;' and to the rich, 'Be thou my preserver.'

"This is the origin of power, deeply founded in our nature, and indispensably connected with the development of our species; like the stream which distributes moisture and blessing, when dikes and locks confine it within its due bounds, but when it overflows its borders, and breaks through its limits, lays the country waste; so power is sacred only, when those that hold it, keep faithfully within the bounds assigned to them by the rights of their species.

"It is not power that causes the corruption of our species, but the person in whose hand the power is, or he who criminally misleads that person. When man cannot rise to the divine virtue of fidelity, when his word is like a reel shaken by the wind, when the possession of power raises him no higher, nor renders him more faithful than the man against whose weakness he has to defend himself, then he destroys with the strength of his arm the rights of mankind, and fattens the earth which he renders desolate, with the blood of those against whom he has violated his own word, and the laws of everlasting justice.

"But even in the struggle of lies and injustice our species is developed and rises to the feeling of every dignity, and to the possession of every power, that is implanted in human nature.

"Be not troubled, then, while thou hast to sustain the warfare of truth and justice; tremble not when lies conquer; but the more thou seest the brutality of thy species obtain against truth and justice, the more study thou its corruption: and if thou shouldst be ensnared by the bonds of lawlessness, as the fly by the spider's web, learn to die, that thou mayest remain faithful to thyself, and to thy species.

"It is done, alas; the earth is desecrated by the homage paid to profane power by exalted brutality.

"The insane faithlessness of power has stirred up the feelings of self-defence in the corrupt multitude; and the furious people aim the knife at its guilty throat.

"All the bonds are torn asunder by which power was formerly preserved in a sense of its obligations, under continual temptations to defection and treason.

"Incalculable is the misery of our superannuated continent. An eternal and unchangeable law turns the balance of mortal existence for ever on the side of animal energies and tendencies; and he who combines with them the advantages of power will ever say to the weaker part of his species: ye are made for my sake! And he plays on their crowded ranks as on the wires of the dulcimer. What is it to him whether the wires break or not, they are only wires; as many as there are men in the land, so many are his wires; as many as break, he throws away, and draws new ones across his damaged instrument; for are they not mere wires?

"Alas they are men! but they grow up in the inexpressible degradation of a lawless servitude like the claws on the paws of a bear; they know not what is the design of the growling animal that rests on them; but they are always ready to assail the entrails of any one against whom he may growl.

"Alas they are men! and the degradation of this servitude reduces them again to the state in which they were, before they called power into existence, and said to the strong man: Be thou our shield and our king.

"When once power has become unfaithful, and has learnt to palliate the sin of treason by cold unmeaning language, then the law of humanity is departed from the earth.

"It then says to the weak of our species: This is my law which thou shalt obey. I will sell thee to the kingly nation, which gives me money for thy life and for thy death; beat the drum, and hail the kingly nation that pays so much for human life. Hail the noble race which learns of kings the price of humankind. Hail it with shouts of gratitude, for it directs its golden streams into the bosoms of men-selling rulers, that they, being secured on their thrones, may henceforth offer our species for sale to the men-purchasing island; that our continent may remain what it is, an old rotten structure, daily menacing a complete ruin, lawless, divided, unassisted, and unassistable; and that no nation on the earth may become as this kingly nation, domineering over the seas, and directing the countries as with leading-strings. It is done! the earth is desecrated by the homage paid to profane power by exalted brutality.

"If thou find a gem that glitters in the sun, thy tyrant speaks: Thou and thy children shall dwell in eternal night; all your lives you shall seek beneath the earth for brilliant gems.

"In the depth of the earth, in the horrid darkness of noxious vapours, the injured mother forgets the sun, and the light of day, which she is no longer permitted to behold; she praises the lord who sends her bread in the abodes of darkness; she thanks him in the foul air which she breathes, for every strengthening draught; she presses the dying heir of her wretched existence, whose features she scarcely can discern, to her bosom, with heartfelt delight; she dutifully rejoices at every gem which she finds, and sends it up to her ruler, who beholds the sun, and enjoys all the pleasures of day.

"Is she not an angel in the vaults of night? but is our species such an angel?

"Enthralled by a power which acknowledges no law against itself, man sinks back into all the helplessness and obtuseness of his natural corruption; and the general spread of Sansculotism leads to the dissolution of the social ties.

"Before this comes to pass, kings grow hardened on their thones like the ancient oak; deep horror hovers round their crowns; they stand isolated like barren rocks surrounded by bottomless precipices; celibatarian monks, and misanthropic bachelors, become the last pillars of the state, till they too begin to give way; and then in the desolation of anarchy, which wanton lawlessness has brought on, nations sink into dissolution as corpses in their graves."

That a man whose imagination was dwelling on images like this, whose eye was turned away from the bright prospects of faith, and exclusively directed to the horrors by which our species has contaminated the earth, should writhe under the keen feeling of human degradation, in which he felt himself involved, is no more than might be expected; and accordingly we find Pestalozzi, at the close of the volume which presents human nature under so gloomy an aspect, giving the following portrait of himself:

"Thousands pass away, as nature gave them birth, in the corruption of sensual gratification, and they seek no more.

"Tens of thousands are overwhelmed by the burdens of craft and trade; by the weight of the hammer, the ell, or the crown, and they seek no more.

"But I know a man who did seek more; the joy of simplicity dwelt in his heart, and he had faith in mankind such as few men have; his soul was made for friendship, love was his element, and fidelity his strongest tie.

"But he was not made by this world, nor for it; and wherever he was placed in it, he was found unfit.

"And the world that found him thus, asked not whether it was his fault or the fault of another: but it bruised him with an iron hammer, as the bricklayers break an old brick to fill up crevices.

"But though bruised, he yet trusted in mankind more than in himself; and he proposed to himself a great purpose, which to attain he suffered agonies, and learned lessons such as few mortals had learnt before him. "He could not, nor would he become generally useful; but for his purpose he was more useful than most men are for theirs; and he expected justice at the hands of mankind, whom he still loved with an innocent love. But he found none. Those that erected themselves into his judges without further examination confirmed the former sentence, that he was generally and absolutely useless.

"This was the grain of sand which decided the doubtful balance of his wretched destinies.

"He is no more; thou wouldst know him no more; all that remains of him are the decayed remnants of his destroyed existence.

"He fell, as a fruit that falls before it is ripe, whose blossom has been nipped by the northern gale, or whose core is eaten out by the gnawing worm.

"Stranger that passest by; refuse not a tear of sympathy; even in falling this fruit turned itself towards the stem, on the branches of which it lingered through the summer, and it whispered to the tree, 'Verily, even in my death will I nourish they roots.'

"Stranger, that passest by, spare the perishing fruit, and allow the dust of its corruption to nourish the roots of the tree, on whose branches it lived, sickened, and died."

5.5 DECLARATION OF THE RIGHTS OF MAN AND OF CITIZENS*

by the National Assembly of France

The representatives of the people of France, formed into a National Assembly, considering that ignorance, neglect, or contempt of human rights, are the sole causes of public misfortunes and corruptions of government, have resolved to set forth in a solemn declaration, these natural, imprescriptible, and unalienable rights: that this declaration, being constantly present to the minds of the members of the body social, they may be ever kept attentive to their rights and their duties: that the acts of the legislative and executive powers of government, being capable of being every moment compared with the end of political institutions, may be more respected: and also, that the future claims of the citizens, being directed by simple and incontestible principles, may always tend to the maintenance of the Constitution, and the general happiness.

"For these reasons the National Assembly doth recognize and declare, in the presence of the Supreme Being, and with the hope of His blessing and favor, the following *sacred* rights of men and of citizens:

"I. *Men are born, and always continue, free, and equal in respect of their rights. Civil distinctions, therefore, can be founded only on public utility.*

"II. *The end of all political associations, is, the preservation of the natural and imprescriptible rights of man; and these rights are liberty, property, security, and resistance of oppression.*

"III. *The nation is essentially the source of all sovereignty; nor can any* INDIVIDUAL, *or* ANY BODY OF MEN, *be entitled to any authority which is not expressly derived from it.*

"IV. Political liberty consists in the power of doing whatever does not injure another. The exercise of the natural rights of every man has no other limits than those which are necessary to secure to every *other* man the free exercise of the same rights; and these limits are determinable only by the law.

"V. The law ought to prohibit only actions hurtful to society. What is not prohibited by the law, should not be hindered; nor should any one be compelled to that which the law does not require.

---

*Reprinted from Thomas Paine, *Rights of Man* (London: J. S. Jordess, 1791).

"VI. The law is an expression of the will of the community. All citizens have a right to concur, either personally, or by their representatives, in its formation. It should be the same to all, whether it protects or punishes; and *all being equal in its sight, are equally eligible to all honors, places, and employments, according to their different abilities, without any other distinction than that created by their virtues and talents.*

"VII. No man should be accused, arrested, or held in confinement, except in cases determined by the law, and according to the forms which it has prescribed. All who promote, solicit, execute, or cause to be executed, arbitrary orders, ought to be punished; and every citizen called upon or apprehended by virtue of the law, ought immediately to obey, and renders himself culpable by resistance.

"VIII. The law ought to impose no other penalties but such as are absolutely and evidently necessary: and no one ought to be punished, but in virtue of a law promulgated before the offense, and legally applied.

"IX. Every man being presumed innocent till he has been convicted, whenever his detention becomes indispensable, all rigor to him, more than is necessary to secure his person, ought to be provided against by the law.

"X. No man ought to be molested on account of his opinions, not even on account of his *religious* opinions, provided his avowal of them does not disturb the public order established by the law.

"XI. The unrestrained communication of thoughts and opinions being one of the most precious rights of man, every citizen may speak, write, and publish freely, provided he is responsible for the abuse of this liberty in cases determined by the law.

"XII. A public force being necessary to give security to the rights of men and of citizens, that force is instituted for the benefit of the community, and not for the particular benefit of the persons with whom it is intrusted.

"XIII. A common contribution being necessary for the support of the public force, and for defraying the other expenses of government, it ought to be divided equally among the members of the community, according to their abilities.

"XIV. Every citizen has a right, either by himself or his representative, to a free voice in determining the necessity of public contributions, the appropriation of them, and their amount, mode of assessment, and duration.

"XV. Every community has a right to demand of all its agents, an account of their conduct.

"XVI. Every community in which a separation of powers and a security of rights is not provided for, wants a constitution.

"XVII. The rights to property being inviolable and sacred, no one ought to be deprived of it, except in cases of evident public necessity, legally ascertained, and on condition of a previous just indemnity."

CHAPTER SIX

SCIENTIFIC
INDIVIDUALISM AND
EDUCATION

6.1   EDITORIAL COMMENT

One of the most neglected areas in the professional education of teachers
lies in the field of economics. Not only do teachers know little about
communism, but, also, they know little about the philosophy underlying
the free enterprise system. It is to a partial correction of this deficiency
that the readings of this chapter are presented.

The key figure in the background of thought underlying capitalistic
economic theory is Adam Smith. The enclosed selection, taken from his

An Inquiry Into the Nature and Causes of the Wealth of Nations, deals with his concept of the role of labor in the economic enterprise especially with reference to the accumulation of wealth.

The educational counterpart to the work of Smith is found in Herbert Spencer's "What Knowledge is of Most Worth?" No other one book had more influence on the development of secondary education in the United States during the nineteenth century, and no other writer expressed more clearly the role of science in the development of our free economy.

The problem presented by the development of the free enterprise system was not only one of economic goods but of human relations. Here we are confronted with the real issue concerning the utility of knowledge. No one has given us a deeper insight into the nature of this problem than John Stuart Mill. His essay on the subject which we are reprinting here was first delivered at the Mutual Improvement Society in England in 1823.

Our sternest and most perspicacious critic of the American capitalistic system of the nineteenth century was, in all probability, Thorstein Veblen. While he never developed a formal or systematic philosophy of education he did express keen insight into some of the deepest rooted problems in the American economy, some of which continue to haunt us today. One of the most basic of these problems is pointed to in our selection which is taken from his *The Theory of the Leisure Class*.

6.2 OF THE ACCUMULATION OF CAPITAL OR OF PRODUCTIVE AND UNPRODUCTIVE LABOR*

by Adam Smith

There is one sort of labour which adds to the value of the subject upon which it is bestowed: there is another which has no such effect. The former, as it produces a value, may be called productive; the latter, unproductive[1] labour. Thus the labour of a manufacturer adds, generally, to the value of the materials which he works upon, that of his own maintenance, and of his master's profit. The labour of a menial servant, on the contrary, adds to the value of nothing. Though the manufacturer has his wages advanced to him by his master, he, in reality, costs him no expence, the value of those wages being generally restored, together with a profit, in the improved value of the subject upon which his labour is bestowed. But the maintenance of a menial servant never is restored. A man grows rich by employing a multitude of manufacturers: he grows poor, by maintaining a multitude of menial servants.[2] The labour of the latter, however, has its value, and deserves its reward as well as that of the former. But the labour of the manufacturer fixes and realizes itself in some particular subject or vendible commodity, which lasts for some time at least after that labour is past. It is, as it were, a certain quantity of labour stocked and stored up to be employed, if necessary, upon some other occasion. That subject, or what is the same thing, the price of that subject, can afterwards, if necessary, put into motion a quantity of labour equal to that which had originally produced it. The labour of the menial servant, on the contrary, does not fix or realize itself in any particular subject or vendible commodity. His services generally perish in the very instant of their performance, and seldom leave any trace or value behind them, for which an equal quantity of service could afterwards be procured.

---

*Reprinted from Adam Smith, *An Inquiry Into the Nature and Causes of the Wealth of Nations* (London: Methuen and Company, Ltd., 1904), Chapter III.

[1]Some French authors of great learning and ingenuity have used those words in a different sense. In the last chapter of the fourth book I shall endeavour to show that their sense is an improper one.

[2]In the argument which follows in the text the fact is overlooked that this is only true when the manufacturers are employed to produce commodities for sale and when the menial servants are employed merely for the comfort of the employer. A man may and often does grow poor by employing people to make "particular subjects or vendible commodities" for his own consumption, and an innkeeper may and often does grow rich by employing menial servants.

The labour of some of the most respectable orders in the society is, like that of menial servants, unproductive of any value, and does not fix or realize itself in any permanent subject, or vendible commodity, which endures after that labour is past, and for which an equal quantity of labour could afterwards be procured. The sovereign, for example, with all the officers both of justice and war who serve under him, the whole army and navy, are unproductive labourers. They are the servants of the public, and are maintained by a part of the annual produce of the industry of other people. Their service, how honourable, how useful,[3] or how necessary so-ever, produces nothing for which an equal quantity of service can afterwards be procured. The protection, security, and defence of the commonwealth, the effect of their labour this year, will not purchase its protection, security, and defence for the year to come. In the same class must be ranked, some both of the gravest and most important, and some of the most frivolous professions: churchmen, lawyers, physicians, men of letters of all kinds; players, buffoons, musicians, opera-singers, opera-dancers, &c. The labour of the meanest of these has a certain value, regulated by the very same principles which regulate that of every other sort of labour; and that of the noblest and most useful, produces nothing which could afterwards purchase or procure an equal quantity of labour. Like the declamation of the actor, the harangue of the orator, or the tune of the musician, the work of all of them perishes in the very instant of its production.

Both productive and unproductive labourers, and those who do not labour at all, are all equally maintained by the annual produce of the land and labour of the country. This produce, how great so-ever, can never be infinite, but must have certain limits. According, therefore, as a smaller or greater proportion of it is in any one year employed in maintaining unproductive hands, the more in the one case and the less in the other will remain for the productive, and the next year's produce will be greater or smaller accordingly; the whole annual produce, if we except the spontaneous productions of the earth, being the effect of productive labour.

Though the whole annual produce of the land and labour of every country, is, no doubt, ultimately destined for supplying the consumption of its inhabitants, and for procuring a revenue to them; yet when it first comes either from the ground, or from the hands of the productive labourers, it naturally divides itself into two parts. One of them, and frequently the largest, is, in the first place, destined for replacing a cap-

---

[3]But in the "Introduction and Plan of the Work," "useful" is coupled with "productive," and used as equivalent to it.

ital, or for renewing the provisions, materials, and finished work, which had been withdrawn from a capital; the other for constituting a revenue either to the owner of this capital, as the profit of his stock; or to some other person, as the rent of his land. Thus, of the produce of land, one part replaces the capital of the farmer; the other pays his profit and the rent of the landlord; and thus constitutes a revenue both to the owner of this capital, as the profits of his stock; and to some other person, as the rent of his land. Of the produce of a great manufactory, in the same manner, one part, and that always the largest, replaces the capital of the undertaker of the work; the other pays his profit, and thus constitutes a revenue to the owner of this capital.[4]

That part of the annual produce of the land and labour of any country which replaces a capital, never is immediately employed to maintain any but productive hands. It pays the wages of productive labour only. That which is immediately destined for constituting a revenue either as profit or as rent, may maintain indifferently either productive or unproductive hands.

Whatever part of his stock a man employs as a capital, he always expects is to be replaced to him with a profit. He employs it, therefore, in maintaining productive hands only; and after having served in the function of a capital to him, it constitutes a revenue to them. Whenever he employs any part of it in maintaining unproductive hands of any kind, that part is, from that moment, withdrawn from his capital, and placed in his stock reserved for immediate consumption.

Unproductive labourers, and those who do not labour at all, are all maintained by revenue; either, first, by that part of the annual produce which is originally destined for constituting a revenue to some particular persons, either as the rent of land or as the profits of stock; or, secondly, by that part which, though originally destined for replacing a capital and for maintaining productive labourers only, yet when it comes into their hands, whatever part of it is over and above their necessary subsistence, may be employed in maintaining indifferently either productive or unproductive hands. Thus, not only the great landlord or the rich merchant, but even the common workman, if his wages are considerable, may maintain a menial servant; or he may sometimes go to a play or a puppet-show, and so contribute his share towards maintaining one set of unproductive labourers; or he may pay some taxes, and thus help to maintain another set, more honourable and useful, indeed, but equally

---

[4]It must be observed that in this paragraph produce is not used in the ordinary economic sense of income or net produce, but as including all products, *e.g.*, the oil used in weaving machinery as well as the cloth.

unproductive. No part of the annual produce, however, which had been originally destined to replace a capital, is ever directed towards maintaining unproductive hands, till after it has put into motion its full complement of productive labour, or all that it could put into motion in the way in which it was employed. The workman must have earned his wages by work done, before he can employ any part of them in this manner. That part too is generally but a small one. It is his spare revenue only, of which productive labourers have seldom a great deal. They generally have some, however; and in the payment of taxes the greatness of their number may compensate, in some measure, the smallness of their contribution. The rent of land and the profits of stock are every-where, therefore, the principal sources from which unproductive hands derive their subsistence. These are the two sorts of revenue of which the owners have generally most to spare. They might both maintain indifferently either productive or unproductive hands. They seem, however, to have some predilection for the latter. The expence of a great lord feeds generally more idle than industrious people. The rich merchant, though with his capital he maintains industrious people only, yet by his expence, that is, by employment of his revenue, he feeds commonly the very same sort as the great lord.

The proportion, therefore, between the productive and unproductive hands, depends very much in every country upon the proportion between that part of the annual produce, which, as soon as it comes either from the ground or from the hands of the productive labourers, is destined for replacing a capital, and that which is destined for constituting a revenue, either as rent, or as profit. This proportion is very different in rich from what it is in poor countries.

Thus, at present, in the opulent countries of Europe, a very large, frequently the largest portion of the produce of the land, is destined for replacing the capital of the rich and independent farmer; the other for paying his profits, and the rent of the landlord. But anciently, during the prevalency of the feudal government, a very small portion of the produce was sufficient to replace the capital employed in cultivation. It consisted commonly in a few wretched cattle, maintained altogether by the spontaneous produce of uncultivated land, and which might, therefore, be considered as a part of that spontaneous produce. It generally too belonged to the landlord, and was by him advanced to the occupiers of the land. All the rest of the produce properly belonged to him too, either as rent for his land, or as profit upon this paultry capital. The occupiers of land were generally bondmen, whose persons and effects were equally his property. Those who were not bondmen were tenants at will, and though the rent which they paid was often nominally little more than a quit-rent, it really amounted to the whole produce of the land. Their lord could at all times command their labour in peace, and their service in war. Though they lived at a distance from his house, they were equally dependent upon him as his retainers who lived in it. But the whole produce of the land undoubtedly belongs to him, who can dispose of the labour and service of all those whom it maintains. In the present state of Europe, the share of the landlord seldom exceeds a third, sometimes not a fourth part of the whole produce of the land. The rent of land, however, in all the improved parts of the country, has been tripled and quadrupled since those ancient times; and this third or fourth part of the annual produce is, it seems, three or four times greater than the whole had been before. In the progress of improvement, rent, though it increases in proportion to the extent, diminishes in proportion to the produce of the land.

In the opulent countries of Europe, great capitals are at present employed in trade and manufactures. In the ancient state, the little trade that was stirring, and the few homely and coarse manufactures that were carried on, required but very small capitals. These, however, must have yielded very large profits. The rate of interest was no-where less than ten per cent. and their profits must have been sufficient to afford this great interest. At present the rate of interest, in the improved parts of Europe, is no-where higher than six per cent. and in some of the most improved it is so low as four, three, and two per cent. Though that part of the revenue of the inhabitants which is derived from the profits of stock is always much greater in rich than in poor countries, it is because the stock is much greater: in proportion to the stock the profits are generally much less.[5]

That part of the annual produce, therefore, which, as soon as it comes either from the ground, or from the hands of the productive labourers, is destined for replacing a capital, is not only much greater in rich than in poor countries, but bears a much greater proportion to that which is immediately destined for constituting a revenue either as rent or as profit. The funds destined for the maintenance of productive labour, are not only much greater in the former than in the latter, but bear a much greater proportion to those which, though they may be employed to maintain either productive or unproductive hands, have generally a predilection for the latter.

The proportion between those different funds necessarily determines in every country the general character of the inhabitants as to industry or idleness. We are more industrious than our forefathers; because in the

---

[5]The question first propounded whether profits form a larger proportion of the produce, is wholly lost sight of. With a stock larger in proportion to the produce, a lower rate of profit may give a larger proportion of the produce.

present times the funds destined for the maintenance of industry, are much greater in proportion to those which are likely to be employed in the maintenance of idleness, than they were two or three centuries ago. Our ancestors were idle for want of a sufficient encouragement to industry. It is better, says the proverb, to play for nothing, than to work for nothing. In mercantile and manufacturing towns, where the inferior ranks of people are chiefly maintained by the employment of capital, they are in general industrious, sober, and thriving; as in many English, and in most Dutch towns. In those towns which are principally supported by the constant or occasional residence of a court, and in which the inferior ranks of people are chiefly maintained by the spending of revenue, they are in general idle, dissolute, and poor; as at Rome, Versailles, Compiegne, and Fontainbleau. If you expect Rouen and Bourdeaux, there is little trade or industry in any of the parliament towns of France;[6] and the inferior ranks of people, being chiefly maintained by the expence of the members of the courts of justice, and of those who come to plead before them, are in general idle and poor. The great trade of Rouen and Bourdeaux seems to be altogether the effect of their situation. Rouen is necessarily the entrepôt of almost all the goods which are brought either from foreign countries, or from the maritime provinces of France, for the consumption of the great city of Paris. Bourdeaux is in the same manner the entrepôt of the wines which grow upon the banks of the Garonne, and of the rivers which run into it, one of the richest wine countries in the world, and which seems to produce the wine fittest for exportation, or best suited to the taste of foreign nations. Such advantageous situations necessarily attract a great capital by the great employment which they afford it; and the employment of this capital is the cause of the industry of those two cities. In the other parliament towns of France, very little more capital seems to be employed than what is necessary for supplying their own consumption; that is, little more than the smallest capital which can be employed in them. The same thing may be said of Paris, Madrid, and Vienna. Of those three cities, Paris is by far the most industrious: but Paris itself is the principal market of all the manufactures established at Paris, and its own consumption is the principal object of all the trade which it carries on. London, Lisbon, and Copenhagen, are, perhaps, the only three cities in Europe, which are both the constant residence of a court, and can at the same time be considered as trading cities, or as cities which trade not only for their own consumption, but for that of other cities and

---

[6]*Viz.*, Paris, Toulouse, Grenoble, Bordeaux, Dijon, Rouen, Aix, Rennes, Pau, Metz, Besançon and Douai.—*Encyclopédie*, tom. xii., 1765, *s.v.* Parlement.

countries. The situation of all the three is extremely advantageous, and naturally fits them to be the entrepôts of a great part of the goods destined for the consumption of distant places. In a city where a great revenue is spent, to employ with advantage a capital for any other purpose than for supplying the consumption of that city, is probably more difficult than in one in which the inferior ranks of people have no other maintenance but what they derive from the employment of such a capital. The idleness of the greater part of the people who are maintained by the expence of revenue, corrupts, it is probable, the industry of those who ought to be maintained by the employment of capital, and renders it less advantageous to employ a capital there than in other places. There was little trade or industry in Edinburgh before the union. When the Scotch parliament was no longer to be assembled in it, when it ceased to be the necessary residence of the principal nobility and gentry of Scotland, it became a city of some trade and industry. It still continues, however, to be the residence of the principal courts of justice in Scotland, of the boards of customs and excise, &c. A considerable revenue, therefore, still continues to be spent in it. In trade and industry it is much inferior to Glasgow, of which the inhabitants are chiefly maintained by the employment of capital.[7] The inhabitants of a large village, it has sometimes been observed, after having made considerable progress in manufactures, have become idle and poor, in consequence of a great lord's having taken up his residence in their neighbourhood.

The proportion between capital and revenue, therefore, seems everywhere to regulate the proportion between industry and idleness. Wherever capital predominates, industry prevails: wherever revenue, idleness. Every increase or diminution of capital, therefore, naturally tends to increase or diminish the real quantity of industry, the number of productive hands, and consequently the exchangeable value of the annual produce of the land and labour of the country, the real wealth and revenue of all its inhabitants.

Capitals are increased by parsimony, and diminished by prodigality and misconduct.

Whatever a person saves from his revenue he adds to his capital, and either employs it himself in maintaining an additional number of productive hands, or enables some other person to do so, by lending it to him for an interest, that is, for a share of the profits. As the capital of an

---

[7]In *Lectures*, pp. 154-156, the idleness of Edinburgh and such like places compared with Glasgow is attributed simply to the want of independence in the inhabitants. The introduction of revenue and capital is the fruit of study of the physiocratic doctrines.

individual can be increased only by what he saves from his annual revenue or his annual gains, so the capital of a society, which is the same with that of all the individuals who compose it, can be increased only in the same manner.

Parsimony, and not industry, is the immediate cause of the increase of capital. Industry, indeed, provides the subject which parsimony accumulates. But whatever industry might acquire, if parsimony did not save and store up, the capital would never be the greater.

Parsimony, by increasing the fund which is destined for the maintenance of productive hands, tends to increase the number of those hands whose labour adds to the value of the subject upon which it is bestowed. It tends therefore to increase the exchangeable value of the annual produce of the land and labour of the country. It puts into motion and additional quantity of industry, which gives an additional value to the annual produce.

What is annually saved is as regularly consumed as what is annually spent, and nearly in the same time too;[8] but it is consumed by a different set of people. That portion of his revenue which a rich man annually spends, is in most cases consumed by idle guests, and menial servants, who leave nothing behind them in return for their consumption. That portion which he annually saves, as for the sake of the profit it is immediately employed as a capital, is consumed in the same manner, and nearly in the same time too, but by a different set of people, by labourers, manufacturers, and artificers, who re-produce with a profit the value of their annual consumption. His revenue, we shall suppose, is paid him in money. Had he spent the whole, the food, clothing, and lodging, which the whole could have purchased, would have been distributed among the former set of people. By saving a part of it, as that part is for the sake of the profit immediately employed as a capital either by himself or by some other person, the food, clothing, and lodging, which may be purchased with it, are necessarily reserved for the latter. The consumption is the same, but the consumers are different.

By what a frugal man annually saves, he not only affords maintenance to an additional number of productive hands, for that or the ensuing year, but, like the founder of a public workhouse, he establishes as it were a perpetual fund for the maintenance of an equal number in all times to come. The perpetual allotment and destination of this fund, indeed, is not always guarded by any positive law, by any trust-right

---

[8]This paradox is arrived at through a confusion between the remuneration of the labourers who produce the additions to the capital and the additions themselves. What is really saved is the additions to the capital, and these are not consumed.

or deed of mortmain. It is always guarded, however, by a very powerful principle, the plain and evident interest of every individual to whom any share of it shall ever belong. No part of it can ever afterwards be employed to maintain any but productive hands, without an evident loss to the person who thus perverts it from its proper destination.

The prodigal perverts it in this manner. By not confining his expence within his income, he encroaches upon his capital. Like him who perverts the revenues of some pious foundation to profane purposes, he pays the wages of idleness with those funds which the frugality of his fore-fathers had, as it were, consecrated to the maintenance of industry. By diminishing the funds destined for the employment of productive labour, he necessarily diminishes, so far as it[9] depends upon him, the quantity of that labour which adds a value to the subject upon which it is bestowed, and, consequently, the value of the annual produce of the land and labour of the whole country, the real wealth and revenue of its inhabitants. If the prodigality of some was not compensated by the frugality of others, the conduct of every prodigal, by feeding the idle with the bread of the industrious, tends not only to beggar himself, but to impoverish his country.

Though the expence of the prodigal should be altogether in home-made, and no part of it in foreign commodities, its effect upon the productive funds of the society would still be the same. Every year there would still be a certain quantity of food and clothing, which ought to have maintained productive, employed in maintaining unproductive hands. Every year, therefore, there would still be some diminution in what would otherwise have been the value of the annual produce of the land and labour of the country.

This expence, it may be said indeed, not being in foreign goods, and not occasioning any exportation of gold and silver, the same quantity of money would remain in the country as before. But if the quantity of food and clothing, which were thus consumed by unproductive, had been distributed among productive hands, they would have re-produced, together with a profit, the full value of their consumption. The same quantity of money would in this case equally have remained in the country, and there would besides have been a reproduction of an equal value of consumable goods. There would have been two values instead of one.

The same quantity of money, besides, cannot long remain in any country in which the value of the annual produce diminishes. The sole use of money is to circulate consumable goods. By means of it, provi-

---

9Ed. 1 does not contain "it."

sions, materials, and finished work, are bought and sold, and distributed to their proper consumers. The quantity of money, therefore, which can be annually employed in any country, must be determined by the value of the consumable goods annually circulated within it. These must consist either in the immediate produce of the land and labour of the country itself, or in something which had been purchased with some part of that produce. Their value, therefore, must diminish as the value of that produce diminishes, and along with it the quantity of money which can be employed in circulating them. But the money which by this annual diminution of produce is annually thrown out of domestic circulation, will not be allowed to lie idle. The interest of whoever possesses it, requires that it should be employed. But having no employment at home, it will, in spite of all laws and prohibitions, be sent abroad, and employed in purchasing consumable goods which may be of some use at home. Its annual exportation will in this manner continue for some time to add something to the annual consumption of the country beyond the value of its own annual produce. What in the days of its prosperity had been saved from that annual produce, and employed in purchasing gold and silver, will contribute for some little time to support its consumption in adversity. The exportation of gold and silver is, in this case, not the cause, but the effect of its declension, and may even, for some little time, alleviate the misery of that declension.

The quantity of money, on the contrary, must in every country naturally increase as the value of the annual produce increases. The value of the consumable goods annually circulated within the society being greater, will require a greater quantity of money to circulate them. A part of the increased produce, therefore, will naturally be employed in purchasing, wherever it is to be had, the additional quantity of gold and silver necessary for circulating the rest. The increase of those metals will in this case be the effect, not the cause, of the public prosperity. Gold and silver are purchased every-where in the same manner. The food, clothing, and lodging, the revenue and maintenance of all those whose labour or stock is employed in bringing them from the mine to the market, is the price paid for them in Peru as well as in England. The country which has this price to pay, will never be long without the quantity of those metals which it has occasion for; and no country will ever long retain a quantity which it has no occasion for.

Whatever, therefore, we may imagine the real wealth and revenue of a country to consist in, whether in the value of the annual produce of its land and labour, as plain reason seems to dictate; or in the quantity of the precious metals which circulate within it, as vulgar prejudices suppose; in either view of the matter, every prodigal appears to be a public enemy, and every frugal man a public benefactor.

The effects of misconduct are often the same as those of prodigality. Every injudicious and unsuccessful project in agriculture, mines, fisheries, trade, or manufactures, tends in the same manner to diminish the funds destined for the maintenance of productive labour. In every such project, though the capital is consumed by productive hands only, yet, as by the injudicious manner in which they are employed, they do not reproduce the full value of their consumption, there must always be some diminution in what would otherwise have been the productive funds of the society.

It can seldom happen, indeed, that the circumstances of a great nation can be much affected either by the prodigality or misconduct of individuals; the profusion or imprudence of some, being always more than compensated by the frugality and good conduct of others.

6.3   WHAT KNOWLEDGE IS OF MOST WORTH?*

by Herbert Spencer

One advantage claimed for that devotion to language-learning which forms so prominent a feature in the ordinary *curriculum*, is, that the memory is thereby strengthened. And it is apparently assumed that this is an advantage peculiar to the study of words. But the truth is, that the sciences afford far wider fields for the exercise of memory. It is no slight task to remember all the facts ascertained respecting our solar system; much more to remember all that is known concerning the structure of our galaxy. The new compounds which chemistry daily accumulates, are so numerous that few, save professors, know the names of them all; and to recollect the atomic constitutions and affinities of all these compounds, is scarcely possible without making chemistry the occupation of life. In the enormous mass of phenomena presented by the Earth's crust, and in the still more enormous mass of phenomena presented by the fossils it contains, there is matter which it takes the geological student years of application to master. In each leading division of physics—sound, heat, light, electricity—the facts are numerous enough to alarm any one proposing to learn them all. And when we pass to the organic sciences, the effort of memory required becomes still greater. In human anatomy alone, the quantity of detail is so great, that the young surgeon has commonly to get it up half-a-dozen times before he can permanently retain it. The number of species of plants which botanists distinguish, amounts to some 320,000; while the varied forms of animal life with which the zoologist deals, are estimated at some two millions. So vast is the accumulation of facts which men of science have before them, that only by dividing and subdividing their labours can they deal with it. To a complete knowledge of his own division, each adds but a general knowledge of the rest. Surely, then, science, cultivated even to a very moderate extent, affords adequate exercise for memory. To say the very least, it involves quite as good a training for this faculty as language does.

But now mark that while for the training of mere memory, science is as good as, if not better than, language; it has an immense superiority in the kind of memory it cultivates. In the acquirement of a language, the connexions of ideas to be established in the mind correspond to

*Reprinted from Herbert Spencer, *Education: Intellectual, Moral, and Physical* (New York: D. Appleton and Company, 1897), pages 85-96.

facts that are in great measure accidental; whereas, in the acquirement of science, the connexions of ideas to be established in the mind correspond to facts that are mostly necessary. It is true that the relations of words to their meaning is in one sense natural, and that the genesis of these relations may be traced back a certain distance; though very rarely to the beginning; (to which let us add the remark that the laws of this genesis form a branch of mental science—the science of philology.) But since it will not be contended that in the acquisition of languages, as ordinarily carried on, these natural relations between words and their meanings are habitually traced, and the laws regulating them explained; it must be admitted that they are commonly learned as fortuitous relations. On the other hand, the relations which science presents are causal relations; and, when properly taught, are understood as such. Instead of being practically accidental, they are necessary; and as such, give exercise to the reasoning faculties. While language familiarizes with non-rational relations, science familiarizes with rational relations. While the one exercises memory only, the other exercises both memory and understanding.

Observe next that a great superiority of science over language as a means of discipline, is, that it cultivates the judgment. As, in a lecture on mental education delivered at the Royal Institution, Professor Faraday well remarks, the most common intellectual fault is deficiency of judgment. He contends that "society, speaking generally, is not only ignorant as respects education of the judgment, but it is also ignorant of its ignorance." And the cause to which he ascribes this state is want of scientific culture. The truth of his conclusion is obvious. Correct judgment with regard to all surrounding things, events, and consequences, becomes possible only through knowledge of the way in which surrounding phenomena depend on each other. No extent of acquaintance with the meanings of words, can give the power of forming correct inferences respecting causes and effects. The constant habit of drawing conclusions from data, and then of verifying those conclusions by observation and experiment, can alone give the power of judging correctly. And that it necessitates this habit is one of the immense advantages of science.

Not only, however, for intellectual discipline is science the best; but also for *moral* discipline. The learning of languages tends, if anything, further to increase the already undue respect for authority. Such and such are the meanings of these words, says the teacher or the dictionary. So and so is the rule in this case, says the grammar. By the pupil these dicta are received as unquestionable. His constant attitude of mind is that of submission to dogmatic teaching. And a necessary result is a tendency to accept without inquiry whatever is established. Quite opposite is the attitude of mind generated by the cultivation of science. By science, constant appeal is made to individual reason. Its truths are not accepted upon authority alone; but all are at liberty to test them—nay, in many cases, the pupil is required to think out his own conclusions. Every step in a scientific investigation is submitted to his judgment. He is not asked to admit it without seeing it to be true. And the trust in his own powers thus produced, is further increased by the constancy with which Nature justifies his conclusions when they are correctly drawn. From all which there flows that independence which is a most valuable element in character. Nor is this the only moral benefit bequeathed by scientific culture. When carried on, as it should always be, as much as possible under the form of independent research, it exercises perseverance and sincerity. As says Professor Tyndall of inductive inquiry, "it requires patient industry, and an humble and conscientious acceptance of what Nature reveals. The first condition of success is an honest receptivity and a willingness to abandon all preconceived notions, however cherished, if they be found to contradict the truth. Believe me, a self-renunciation which has something noble in it, and of which the world never hears, is often enacted in the private experience of the true votary of science."

Lastly we have to assert—and the assertion will, we doubt not, cause extreme surprise—that the discipline of science is superior to that of our ordinary education, because of the *religious* culture that it gives. Of course we do not here use the words scientific and religious in their ordinary limited acceptations; but in their widest and highest acceptations. Doubtless, to the superstitions that pass under the name of religion, science is antagonistic; but not to the essential religion which these superstitions merely hide. Doubtless, too, in much of the science that is current, there is a pervading spirit of irreligion; but not in that true science which has passed beyond the superficial into the profound.

"True science and true religion," says Professor Huxley at the close of a recent course of lectures, "are twin-sisters, and the separation of either from the other is sure to prove the death of both. Science prospers exactly in proportion as it is religious; and religion flourishes in exact proportion to the scientific depth and firmness of its basis. The great deeds of philosophers have been less the fruit of their intellect than of the direction of that intellect by an eminently religious tone of mind. Truth has yielded herself rather to their patience, their love, their single-heartedness, and their self-denial, than to their logical acumen."

So far from science being irreligious, as many think, it is the neglect of science that is irreligious—it is the refusal to study the surrounding creation that is irreligious. Take a humble simile. Suppose a writer were daily saluted with praises couched in superlative language. Suppose the wisdom, the grandeur, the beauty of his works, were the constant topics of the eulogies addressed to him. Suppose those who unceasingly uttered these eulogies on his works were content with looking at the outsides of them; and had never opened them, much less tried to understand them. What value should we put upon their praises? What should we think of their sincerity? Yet, comparing small things to great, such is the conduct of mankind in general, in reference to the Universe and its Cause. Nay, it is worse. Not only do they pass by without study, these things which they daily proclaim to be so wonderful; but very frequently they condemn as mere triflers those who give time to the observation of Nature—they actually scorn those who show any active interest in these marvels. We repeat, then, that not science, but the neglect of science, is irreligious. Devotion to science, is a tacit worship—a tacit recognition of worth in the things studied; and by implication in their Cause. It is not a mere lip-homage, but a homage expressed in actions—not a mere professed respect, but a respect proved by the sacrifice of time, thought, and labour.

Nor is it thus only that true science is essentially religious. It is religious, too, inasmuch as it generates a profound respect for, and an implicit faith in, those uniform laws which underline all things. By accumulated experiences the man of science acquires a thorough belief in the unchanging relations of phenomena—in the invariable connexion of cause and consequence—in the necessity of good or evil results. Instead of the rewards and punishments of traditional belief, which men vaguely hope they may gain, or escape, spite of their disobedience; he finds that there are rewards and punishments in the ordained constitution of things, and that the evil results of disobedience are inevitable. He sees that the laws to which we must submit are not only inexorable but beneficent. He sees that in virtue of these laws, the process of things is ever towards a greater perfection and a higher happiness. Hence he is led constantly to insist on these laws, and is indignant when men disregard them. And thus does he, by asserting the eternal principles of things and the necessity of conforming to them, prove himself intrinsically religious.

To all which add the further religious aspect of science, that it alone can give us true conceptions of ourselves and our relation to the mysteries of existence. At the same time that it shows us all which can be known, it shows us the limits beyond which we can know nothing. Not by dogmatic assertion does it teach the impossibility of comprehending the ultimate cause of things; but it leads us clearly to recognise this impossibility by bringing us in every direction to boundaries we cannot cross. It realizes to us in a way which nothing else can, the littleness of human intelligence in the face of that which transcends human intelligence. While towards the traditions and authorities of men its attitude may be proud, before the impenetrable veil which hides the Absolute its attitude is humble—a true pride and a true humility. Only the sincere man of science (and by this title we do not mean the mere calculator of distances, or analyser of compounds, or labeller of species; but him who through lower truths seeks higher, and eventually the highest)—only the genuine man of science, we say, can truly know how utterly beyond, not only human knowledge, but human conception, is the Universal Power of which Nature, and Life, and Thought are manifestations.

We conclude, then, that for discipline, as well as for guidance, science is of chiefest value. In all its effects, learning the meanings of things, is better than learning the meanings of words. Whether for intellectual, moral, or religious training, the study of surrounding phenomena is immensely superior to the study of grammars and lexicons.

Thus to the question with which we set out—What knowledge is of most worth?—the uniform reply is—Science. This is the verdict on all the counts. For direct self-preservation, or the maintenance of life and health, the all-important knowledge is—Science. For that indirect self-preservation which we call gaining a livelihood, the knowledge of greatest value is—Science. For the due discharge of parental functions, the proper guidance is to be found only in—Science. For that interpretation of national life, past and present, without which the citizen cannot rightly regulate his conduct, the indispensable key is—Science. Alike for the most perfect production and highest enjoyment of art in all its forms, the needful preparation is still—Science. And for purposes of discipline—intellectual, moral, religious—the most efficient study is, once more—Science. The question which at first seemed so perplexed, has become, in the course of our inquiry, comparatively simple. We have not to estimate the degrees of importance of different orders of human activity, and different studies as severally fitting us for them; since we find that the study of Science, in its most comprehensive meaning, is the best preparation for all these orders of activity. We have not to decide between the claims of knowledge of great though conventional value, and knowledge of less though intrinsic value; seeing that the knowledge which we find to be of most value in all other respects, is intrinsically most valuable: its worth is not dependent upon opinion, but is as fixed as is the relation of man to the surrounding world.

Necessary and eternal as are its truths, all Science concerns all mankind for all time. Equally at present, and in the remotest future, must it be of incalculable importance for the regulation of their conduct, that men should understand the science of life, physical, mental, and social; and that they should understand all other science as a key to the science of life.

And yet the knowledge which is of such transcendent value is that which, in our age of boasted education, receives the least attention. While this which we call civilization could never have arisen had it not been for science; science forms scarcely an appreciable element in what men consider civilized training. Though to the progress of science we owe it, that millions find support where once there was food only for thousands; yet of these millions but a few thousands pay any respect to that which has made their existence possible. Though this increasing knowledge of the properties and relations of things has not only enabled wandering tribes to grow into populous nations, but has given to the countless members of those populous nations comforts and pleasures which their few naked ancestors never even conceived, or could have believed, yet is this kind of knowledge only now receiving a grudging recognition in our highest educational institutions. To the slowly growing acquaintance with the uniform co-existences and sequences of phenomena—to the establishment of invariable laws, we owe our emancipation from the grossest superstitions. But for science we should be still worshipping fetishes; or, with hetacombs of victims, propitiating diabolical deities. And yet this science, which, in place of the most degrading conceptions of things, has given us some insight into the grandeurs of creation, is written against in our theologies and frowned upon from our pulpits.

Paraphrasing an Eastern fable, we may say that in the family of knowledges, Science is the household drudge, who, in obscurity, hides unrecognised perfections. To her has been committed all the work; by her skill, intelligence, and devotion, have all the conveniences and gratifications been obtained; and while ceaselessly occupied ministering to the rest, she has been kept in the background, that her haughty sisters might flaunt their fripperies in the eyes of the world. The parallel holds yet further. For we are fast coming to the *dénouement*, when the positions will be changed; and while these haughty sisters sink into merited neglect, Science, proclaimed as highest alike in worth and beauty, will reign supreme.

6.4 THE UTILITY OF KNOWLEDGE*

by *John Stuart Mill*

The beneficial effects produced upon the human mind and upon the structure of society by the revival of science and by the cessation of feudal darkness have been so obvious that there is scarcely room for the smallest discussion. No one, I apprehend, would insult the understanding of this Society by reviving the ascetic sophistry of the fanatic Rousseau by maintaining that what are called the comforts and conveniences of life are in fact neither comforts nor conveniences, and add not the smallest particle to human happiness; that the progress of civilization is in fact the progress of barbarism, and that the Hurons and the Iroquois are the happiest and the most enlightened of mankind. Were such a reasoner to arise I should ask him by what authority he claims to know better than A, B, and C what constitutes the happiness of A, B, and C. I should maintain that what all men have uniformly considered as comforts and conveniences cannot be otherwise than comforts and conveniences, and I should require him who considers knowledge as standing in the way of happiness to go and legislate for those savages upon whose blissful state of ignorance he would have an opportunity of trying his skill without those obstacles which he finds in the knowledge of this comparatively enlightened country.

Such doctrines are scarcely worthy of a serious reply, but as the refutation may be made remarkably pointed and concise, it may be better to give it. In reasoning on these general questions a want of precision in the use of language is the principal engine of sophistry. Here the confusion lies in the word *knowledge*, a word so vague and indefinite as to be an easy instrument in the hands of *mala fide* arguers, being capable of signifying just as much or as little as they please. It is not this kind of knowledge which is of such extensive importance. The only useful knowledge is that which teaches us how to seek what is good and avoid what is evil; in short, how to increase the sum of human happiness. This is the great end: it may be well or ill pursued, but to say that knowledge can be an enemy to happiness is to say that men will enjoy less happiness, when they know how to seek it, than when they do not. This reasoning is on a par with that of any one who should refuse when asked to point out the road to York, saying that his inquirer would have a much better

*Reprinted from John Stuart Mill, *Autobiography* (London: Oxford University Press, 1924) pages 266-274, with permission of the publisher.

216

chance of reaching York without direction than with it. It is impossible then to suppose that any one should get up in this Society and maintain that knowledge in the abstract is mischievous. Arguments may indeed be directed against much of what passes current under the name of knowledge to show that it is not really knowledge but prejudice, and is therefore not favourable but unfavourable to happiness. But this is one of those cases where the reason of the exception proves the truth of the general rule. It is precisely because knowledge is useful that prejudice is mischievous.

The question, simple in itself, is in some degree confused by the manner in which it is worded, and which, with deference to the worthy proposer, might, I conceive, have been made more clearly expressive of his meaning. If asked whether the revival of letters has tended to promote happiness I know what to say, and by what arguments to support it; but if I am asked whether it tends to refine or to corrupt manners I confess myself at a stand. The three words, manners, corrupt, and refine, are to me in the sense here bestowed upon them equally enigmatical. If by refinement of manners is meant that ceremonious politeness in intercourse between the higher orders, and that assiduous gallantry towards the fair sex which were the distinguishing characteristics of the old feudal aristocracy, then I should say that manners had not gained but lost by the revival of letters: but far from lamenting I should rejoice in the change, as I do in everything which turns the attention of mankind from the frivolous details of a petty and ceremonious trifling to the concerns which interest their real and substantial welfare. But if the intention of the proposer was to inquire into the effect of increased civilization in promoting genuine morality, then although on a general view of the question all will probably agree with me that this effect has been highly beneficial, it will be no loss of time to examine in detail from how dreadful a state of misery the human race has been elevated by knowledge into a state where they have at least the hope, the speedy hope, of establishing a better state of things.

The revival of art and science has contributed to promote morality in two ways: by the increase of wealth and by the diffusion of information. The discoveries in chemical and mechanical philosophy—should I not rather say the creation of these branches of knowledge?—has enabled the human race to provide themselves abundantly at little expense of labour with those necessaries and comforts which formerly they either could not procure at all, or if at all, only in a very small amount and with very great labour. This increase of wealth must have contributed greatly to the improvement of morality. I would not be understood as affirming that the rich are more moral than the poor. As far as general reasoning and my own particular experience can lead me I should rather adopt the contrary conclusion. But when the augmentation of wealth is not, by being confined in the hands of a few, reduced to be but one expedient more for the oppression of the many; when, I say, instead of being exclusively devoted to the enjoyment of a few, the increase of wealth is generally and equally diffused throughout the whole community; then by conferring upon the working classes the inestimable benefit of leisure, it forces them to seek society, it forces them to seek education. Each working man becomes himself better qualified to distinguish right from wrong, while each knows that he is under the constant surveillance of hundreds and thousands equally instructed with himself. Thus does the improvement of the physical sciences, by increasing and diffusing wealth, indirectly tend to promote morality.

But the evils which man is doomed to suffer from the hands of nature are nothing when compared to those which man frequently suffers from man. Communities have been known to flourish in spots which Nature seems to have selected for the sepulchre of the universe; but there is no country, however favoured by nature, which superstition and misgovernment do not suffice to ruin. Let us therefore take a general view of the situation of our ancestors with respect to these two main points, religion and government.

And first as to their government: he must be an adept in the art of rendering mankind miserable who could devise anything more destructive of all happiness. It was not here the common vice of a rude government, where each man has not yet learned to trust his neighbour, and where no one will as yet renounce the privilege of protecting himself. These are imperfect governments, for they afford imperfect securities for happiness, but they are not in every sense as execrable as the feudal system. Imagine a tribe with a government such as that to which I have alluded spreading itself by conquest over a large portion of the globe, and reducing the native population to the state of domestic cattle! Each chief absolute master of thousands of human beings, and himself acknowledging no regular government, but striving to retain his pristine independency! Not only is no one secure from the arbitrary will of a master; even that master cannot afford him protection against other despots and slaves! It has frequently been made a question whether despotism or anarchy is worst; but this is not the question here, for the feudal system united the evils of both. The laws were openly and flagrantly violated, and the violations remained unpunished. Judge of the security which the administration of justice could afford when the trial by battle was the best expedient which could be devised to ensure the purity of judicature, and where it was usual for the party who was cast in a lawsuit to challenge his judge to mortal combat.

The religion of our ancestors is next to be considered, and here I shall begin by laying down a principle of which the ordinary reasoners on these subjects have usually lost sight. It is not indeed extremely recondite, for it is no other than this, that priests are men. They are usually considered as partaking of that perfect goodness and wisdom which they verbally attribute to the Great Master whom they profess to serve, although the actions and precepts which they ascribe to Him partake but too often of a contrary character.

From the principle that priests are men I draw the inference that in those cases which very frequently occur, and in which their individual interest is opposed to the interest of mankind, they will act as other men would act in similar circumstances; they would pursue their own interest to the detriment of mankind. Now if all men agree to believe whatever they say, they have a decided interest in making them believe everything which is likely to make them venerate and worship their spiritual guides; and if true opinions on the subject of religion are not of a nature calculated to inspire the requisite degree of veneration, it would be unfair to expect that these irresponsible directors of the public mind should confine themselves strictly to what is true; and we might indeed predict with tolerable certainty that they would not fail to intermingle much of what is utterly false, the more so as they may do this without the slightest insincerity. There is no fact better ascertained than the facility with which men are persuaded to believe what they wish. It is only necessary that there should be some one, who may be either a knave or a madman, to start a falsehood; if it is unfavourable to the clergy he will be hunted down as a heretic, but if it is favourable to them it will not be long before he finds many sincere disciples among the clergy themselves, who of course propagate it among the laity. It is in this way that the Catholic priesthood added to their religion the profitable doctrine of purgatory and masses for the dead, the crime-promoting doctrine of indulgences, and above all the terrific engines of auricular confession and absolution, the concentration of which, and particularly of the former, in the hands of the clergy, make it astonishing that mankind should ever have emancipated themselves from the terrific sway of priests and their coadjutors, aristocracies and kings. If at this day we rarely hear of murders perpetrated in the name of religion, still more rarely of those terrible persecutions which once disgraced every nation in Europe, we owe this to the revival of letters and the consequent diffusion of knowledge.

Such a government and such a religion as our ancestors had the happiness to enjoy afford us in some degree the means of appreciating that ancestorial[1] wisdom which is even now held up to us as a model for imitation. In the nineteenth century we are not infrequently called upon to pursue the course which was followed by those sages, our ancestors, in the eleventh and twelfth. But this appeal from the age of civilization to the age of barbarism is made, we may observe, by those and by those alone who now, as then, would wish to see the great mass of mankind subject to the despotic sway of nobles, priests, and kings. But although it is in one respect true that the aristocracy of wealth and rank has given place to the democracy of intellect, I would not insinuate that the evils of feudal despotism and superstition are altogether eradicated even from this enlightened country. Knowledge has done much, but it has not yet done all. We are still subject to a constitution which is at best a shattered fragment of the feudal system; we are still subject to a priesthood who do whatever is yet in their power to excite a spirit of religious intolerance and to support the domination of a despotic aristocracy. We cannot therefore be surprised that those who are interested in misgovernment should raise a cry against the diffusion of knowledge on the ground that it renders the people dissatisfied with their institutions. When despotism and superstition were in their greatest vigour the same cry was raised, and for the same reason. Knowledge has triumphed. It has worked the downfall of much that is mischievous. It is in vain to suppose that it will pass by and spare any institution the existence of which is pernicious to mankind.

---

[1]*Sic.*

6.5 THE THEORY OF THE LEISURE CLASS*

by Thorstein Veblen

During the recent past some tangible changes have taken place in the scope of college and university teaching. These changes have in the main consisted in a partial displacement of the humanities—those branches of learning which are conceived to make for the traditional "culture," character, tastes, and ideals—by those more matter-of-fact branches which make for civic and industrial efficiency. To put the same thing in other words, those branches of knowledge which make for efficiency (ultimately productive efficiency) have gradually been gaining ground against those branches which make for a heightened consumption or a lowered industrial efficiency and for a type of character suited to the régime of status. In this adaptation of the scheme of instruction the higher schools have commonly been found on the conservative side, each step which they have taken in advance has been to some extent of the nature of a concession. The sciences have been intruded into the scholar's discipline from without, not to say from below. It is noticeable that the humanities which have so reluctantly yielded ground to the sciences are pretty uniformly adapted to shape the character of the student in accordance with a traditional self-centred scheme of consumption; a scheme of contemplation and enjoyment of the true, the beautiful, and the good, according to a conventional standard of propriety and excellence, the salient feature of which is leisure—*otium cum dignitate*. In language veiled by their own habituation to the archaic, decorous point of view, the spokesmen of the humanities have insisted upon the ideal embodied in the maxim, *fruges consumere nati*. This attitude should occasion no surprise in the case of schools which are shaped by and rest upon a leisure-class culture.

The professed grounds on which it has been sought, as far as might be, to maintain the received standards and methods of culture intact are likewise characteristic of the archaic temperament and of the leisure-class theory of life. The enjoyment and the bent derived from habitual contemplation of the life, ideals, speculations, and methods of consuming time and goods, in vogue among the leisure class of classical antiquity, for instance, is felt to be "higher," "nobler," "worthier," than what results in these respects from a like familiarity with the everyday life and the knowledge and aspirations of commonplace humanity in a

---

*Reprinted from Thorstein Veblen, *The Theory of the Leisure Class* (New York: The Macmillan Company, 1899), pages 390-400.

modern community. That learning the content of which is an unmitigated knowledge of latter-day men and things is by comparison "lower," "base," "ignoble,"—one even hears the epithet "sub-human" applied to this matter-of-fact knowledge of mankind and of everyday life.

This contention of the leisure-class spokesmen of the humanities seems to be substantially sound. In point of substantial fact, the gratification and the culture, or the spiritual attitude or habit of mind, resulting from an habitual contemplation of the anthropomorphism, clannishness, and leisurely self-complacency of the gentleman of an early day, or from a familiarity with the animistic superstitions and the exuberant truculence of the Homeric heroes, for instance, is, æsthetically considered, more legitimate than the corresponding results derived from a matter-of-fact knowledge of things and a contemplation of latter-day civic or workmanlike efficiency. There can be but little question that the first-named habits have the advantage in respect of æsthetic or honorific value, and therefore in respect of the "worth" which is made the basis of award in the comparison. The content of the canons of taste, and more particularly of the canons of honour, is in the nature of things a resultant of the past life and circumstances of the race, transmitted to the later generation by inheritance or by tradition; and the fact that the protracted dominance of a predatory, leisure-class scheme of life has profoundly shaped the habit of mind and the point of view of the race in the past, is a sufficient basis for an æsthetically legitimate dominance of such a scheme of life in very much of what concerns matters of taste in the present. For the purpose in hand, canons of taste are race habits, acquired through a more or less protracted habituation to the approval or disapproval of the kind of things upon which a favourable or unfavourable judgment of taste is passed. Other things being equal, the longer and more unbroken the habituation, the more legitimate is the canon of taste in question. All this seems to be even truer of judgments regarding worth or honour than of judgments of taste generally.

But whatever may be the æsthetic legitimacy of the derogatory judgment passed on the newer learning by the spokesmen of the humanities, and however substantial may be the merits of the contention that the classic lore is worthier and results in a more truly human culture and character, it does not concern the question in hand. The question in hand is as to how far these branches of learning, and the point of view for which they stand in the educational system, help or hinder an efficient collective life under modern industrial circumstances,—how far they further a more facile adaptation to the economic situation of to-day. The question is an economic, not an æsthetic one; and the leisure-class standards of learning which find expression in the deprecatory attitude of the higher schools towards matter-of-fact knowledge are, for the present purpose, to be valued from this point of view only. For this purpose the use of such epithets as "noble," "base," "higher," "lower," etc., is significant only as showing the animus and the point of view of the disputants; whether they contend for the worthiness of the new or of the old. All these epithets are honorific or humilific terms; that is to say, they are terms of invidious comparison, which in the last analysis fall under the category of the reputable or the disreputable; that is, they belong within the range of ideas that characterises the scheme of life of the régime of status; that is, they are in substance an expression of sportsmanship—of the predatory and animistic habit of mind; that is, they indicate an archaic point of view and theory of life, which may fit the predatory stage of culture and of economic organisation from which they have sprung, but which are, from the point of view of economic efficiency in the broader sense, disserviceable anachronisms.

The classics, and their position of prerogative in the scheme of education to which the higher seminaries of learning cling with such a fond predilection, serve to shape the intellectual attitude and lower the economic efficiency of the new learned generation. They do this not only by holding up an archaic ideal of manhood, but also by the discrimination which they inculcate with respect to the reputable and the disreputable in knowledge. This result is accomplished in two ways: (1) by inspiring an habitual aversion to what is merely useful, as contrasted with what is merely honorific in learning, and so shaping the tastes of the novice that he comes in good faith to find gratification of his tastes solely, or almost solely, in such exercise of the intellect as normally results in no industrial or social gain; and (2) by consuming the learner's time and effort in acquiring knowledge which is of no use, except in so far as this learning has by convention become incorporated into the sum of learning required of the scholar, and has thereby affected the terminology and diction employed in the useful branches of knowledge. Except for this terminological difficulty—which is itself a consequence of the vogue of the classics in the past—a knowledge of the ancient languages, for instance, would have no practical bearing for any scientist or any scholar not engaged on work primarily of a linguistic character. Of course all this has nothing to say as to the cultural value of the classics, nor is there any intention to disparage the discipline of the classics or the bent which their study gives to the student. That bent seems to be of an economically disserviceable kind, but this fact—somewhat notorious indeed—need disturb no one who has the good fortune to find comfort and strength in the classical lore. The fact that classical learning acts to derange the learner's workmanlike aptitudes should fall lightly upon the apprehension of those who hold workmanship of small account in comparison with the cultivation of decorous ideals:

> Iam fides et pax et honos pudorque
> Priscus et neglecta redire virtus
> Audet.

Owing to the circumstance that this knowledge has become part of the elementary requirements in our system of education, the ability to use and to understand certain of the dead languages of southern Europe is not only gratifying to the person who finds occasion to parade his accomplishments in this respect, but the evidence of such knowledge serves at the same time to recommend any savant to his audience, both lay and learned. It is currently expected that a certain number of years shall have been spent in acquiring this substantially useless information, and its absence creates a presumption of hasty and precarious learning, as well as of a vulgar practicality that is equally obnoxious to the conventional standards of sound scholarship and intellectual force.

The case is analogous to what happens in the purchase of any article of consumption by a purchaser who is not an expert judge of materials or of workmanship. He makes his estimate of the value of the article chiefly on the ground of the apparent expensiveness of the finish of those decorative parts and features which have no immediate relation to the intrinsic usefulness of the article; the presumption being that some sort of ill-defined proportion subsists between the substantial value of the article and the expense of adornment added in order to sell it. The presumption that there can ordinarily be no sound scholarship where a knowledge of the classics and humanities is wanting leads to a conspicuous waste of time and labour on the part of the general body of students in acquiring such knowledge. The conventional insistence on a modicum of conspicuous waste as an incident of all reputable scholarship has affected our canons of taste and of serviceability in matters of scholarship in much the same way as the same principle has influenced our judgment of the serviceability of manufactured goods.

It is true, since conspicuous consumption has gained more and more on conspicuous leisure as a means of repute, the acquisition of the dead languages is no longer so imperative a requirement as it once was, and its talismanic virtue as a voucher of scholarship has suffered a concomitant impairment. But while this is true, it is also true that the classics have scarcely lost in absolute value as a voucher of scholastic respectability, since for this purpose it is only necessary that the scholar should be able to put in evidence some learning which is conventionally recognised as evidence of wasted time; and the classics lend themselves with great facility to this use. Indeed, there can be little doubt that it is their utility as evidence of wasted time and effort, and hence of the pecuniary strength necessary in order to afford this waste, that has secured to the classics their position of prerogative in the scheme of the higher learning, and has led to their being esteemed the most honorific of all learning. They serve the decorative ends of leisure-class learning better than any other body of knowledge, and hence they are an effective means of reputability.

In this respect the classics have until lately had scarcely a rival. They still have no dangerous rival on the continent of Europe, but lately, since college athletics have won their way into a recognised standing as an accredited field of scholarly accomplishment, this latter branch of learning—if athletics may be freely classed as learning—has become a rival of the classics for the primacy in leisure-class education in American and English schools. Athletics have an obvious advantage over the classics for the purpose of leisure-class learning, since success as an athlete presumes, not only a waste of time, but also a waste of money, as well as the possession of certain highly unindustrial archaic traits of character and temperament. In the German universities the place of athletics and Greek-letter fraternities, as a leisure-class scholarly occupation, has in some measure been supplied by a skilled and graded inebriety and a perfunctory duelling.

The leisure class and its standards of virtue—archaism and waste— can scarcely have been concerned in the introduction of the classics into the scheme of the higher learning; but the tenacious retention of the classics by the higher schools, and the high degree of reputability which still attaches to them, are no doubt due to their conforming so closely to the requirements of archaism and waste.

"Classic" always carries this connotation of wasteful and archaic, whether it is used to denote the dead languages or the obsolete or obsolescent forms of thought and diction in the living language, or to denote other items of scholarly activity or apparatus to which it is applied with less aptness. So the archaic idiom of the English language is spoken of as "classic" English. Its use is imperative in all speaking and writing upon serious topics, and a facile use of it lends dignity to even the most commonplace and trivial string of talk. The newest form of English diction is of course never written; the sense of that leisure-class propriety which requires archaism in speech is present even in the most illiterate or sensational writers in sufficient force to prevent such a lapse. On the other hand, the highest and most conventionalised style of archaic diction is—quite characteristically—properly employed only in communications between an anthropomorphic divinity and his subjects.

Midway between these extremes lies the everyday speech of leisure-class conversation and literature.

Elegant diction, whether in writing or speaking, is an effective means of reputability. It is of moment to know with some precision what is the degree of archaism conventionally required in speaking on any given topic. Usage differs appreciably from the pulpit to the market-place; the latter, as might be expected, admits the use of relatively new and effective words and turns of expression, even by fastidious persons. A discriminate avoidance of neologisms is honorific, not only because it argues that time has been wasted in acquiring the obsolescent habit of speech, but also as showing that the speaker has from infancy habitually associated with persons who have been familiar with the obsolescent idiom. It thereby goes to show his leisure-class antecedents. Great purity of speech is presumptive evidence of several successive lives spent in other than vulgarly useful occupations; although its evidence is by no means entirely conclusive to this point.

As felicitous an instance of futile classicism as can well be found, outside of the Far East, is the conventional spelling of the English language. A breach of the proprieties in spelling is extremely annoying and will discredit any writer in the eyes of all persons who are possessed of a developed sense of the true and beautiful. English orthography satisfies all the requirements of the canons of reputability under the law of conspicuous waste. It is archaic, cumbrous, and ineffective; its acquisition consumes much time and effort; failure to acquire it is easy of detection. Therefore it is the first and readiest test of reputability in learning, and conformity to its ritual is indispensable to a blameless scholastic life.

On this head of purity of speech, as at other points where a conventional usage rests on the canons of archaism and waste, the spokesmen for the usage instinctively take an apologetic attitude. It is contended, in substance, that a punctilious use of ancient and accredited locutions will serve to convey thought more adequately and more precisely than would the straight forward use of the latest form of spoken English; whereas it is notorious that the ideas of to-day are effectively expressed in the slang of to-day. Classic speech has the honorific virtue of dignity; it commands attention and respect as being the accredited method of communication under the leisure-class scheme of life, because it carries a pointed suggestion of the industrial exemption of the speaker. The advantage of the accredited locutions lies in their reputability; they are reputable because they are cumbrous and out of date, and therefore argue waste of time and exemption from the use and the need of direct and forcible speech.

CHAPTER SEVEN

SOCIAL REALITY
AND EDUCATION

7.1 EDITORIAL COMMENT

The selections of this chapter represent an attempt to focus the attention of prospective teachers on problems concerning the nature of social reality. In this respect the traditional separation of philosophy and history is beginning to give way to a way of looking at the significance of each in relation to the educative process. This is especially true when we are concerned with the role of values and their place in the order of things.

In his essay on "History and the Contemporary" Dr. Herbart Jones demonstrates how our lack of a knowledge of history (not merely the facts but our ignorance of causal relations) is contributing to our inability to intelligently cope with the human problems which are growing out of our industrialized, urbanized, and technological society. Our lack of a sense of social imagination seems to be a major contributing factor to our inability to create the social instruments necessary for a resolution of crucial issues such as growing problems of crime, population explosion, race relations, and jingoistic nationalism.

No selection of readings on the problem of social reality would be adequate without some recongition of the contribution of Karl Marx. The very fact that more than half of the world's population is now under communist rule is an indication of his influence. The selection presented stands in striking contrast to the work of Adam Smith.

Herbart's *The Science of Education* was the first of the significant attempts to develop a science of method. It stands in striking contrast to the later works, such as those of E. L. Thorndike, which are identified with the science of biology. Our selection for this collection of readings is Chapter II of the study and deals primarily with the individuality of the pupil.

Auguste Comte was one of the first of the modern scholars to develop a social philosophy based on an analysis of historical continuity and change. It was his conviction that metaphysical philosophy sanctioned egotism and that theology subordinated the real life of man to an imaginary one. What he sought was the true source of morality and this he was convinced he had found in his work. Our brief selection is a justification for the positive approach to an understanding of the nature of man.

7.2 HISTORY AND THE CONTEMPORARY*

by Howard Mumford Jones

. . . I believe our present over-emphasis upon contemporary values in our schools and colleges, an emphasis underlined by worry and deepened by demand for scientific training, requires some sort of correction, that the source of this correction lies in history, and that if we are to maintain a balanced national life, we must fuse the needs of technology and the needs of culture. I am the more persuaded of this truth for three further reasons.

The first arises not merely from the lack of any settled hostility towards the humanities among scientists, but also from a positive thirst for richer and better knowledge of these branches of learning. Doubtless there are scientists who regard humane learning, including history, as proper only to one's leisure time. Before we condemn this view, let us recall that for Schiller aesthetic activity was the highest expression of the instinct for play; and I read only recently an editorial in a scientific journal arguing that to the trained scientist the humanities offer no greater challenge than is offered by a novel. These vagaries are not, however, characteristic of thoughtful scientific men who, especially in the moral confusion created by the use of the atom bomb, deeply feel that humanity is more than the sum of its computing machines. Thus, the Massachusetts Institute of Technology carries a vigorous program in the humanities through its four undergraduate years, and it is not unique in doing so.

In the second place, the successful application of technological devices to business and industry has created an embarrassing amount of leisure time, so much, indeed, that national gatherings like the Corning Conference and books sponsored by the Russell Sage Foundation have devoted themselves to the difficult question of its use. One of the ironies of history is that whereas to the generation of William Morris, when the work day was usually ten hours long, leisure loomed afar on the horizon like an earthly paradise, today, when labor is talking about the thirty-hour week, the disposal of the other 138 hours has become a national problem. We cannot spend all our waking time staring at television, going to spectator sports, or speeding over the countryside shut up in metal containers moving at 70 miles an hour past the billboards. The

*Reprinted from *Teachers College Record*, Volume 64, No. 8 (May, 1963), pages 631-636, with permission of the copyright owners, the Regents of the University of Wisconsin; from Howard Mumford Jones, *History and the Contemporary*, 1964, The University of Wisconsin Press.

hucksters would, of course, like to monopolize our vacant hours, but a civilization mainly conditioned by advertising arouses so little enthusiasm even among the advertisers that the novel of unhappiness on Madison Avenue has become a standard subspecies of American fiction.

EDUCATION'S TASK

The third reason rises out of our immense responsibility as guard and guide of the Western world, a position that alternately annoys and gratifies both our allies and our enemies. Our opponents, particularly Russia, have a special theory of history, certified by Karl Marx as the one true faith; our allies have each their own history, American ignorance of which gets us into continual hot water, and the so-called uncommited nations, to our immense astonishment, develop interpretations of history that do not include the American century, at least in our terms. In a situation thus complex, it behooves us to move carefully, but it likewise appears that the apparent opposition between history and the contemporary weakens or disappears and that history is one of the most powerful forces in modern times. What, then, is to be done?

The task before education is not easy. In the first place, the problem is not solved by merely requiring more courses in history. To add to the present mandatory instruction more courses in, say, the history of Asia or of Latin America or of Africa would merely clutter up a curriculum already crowded. The problem is not quantitative.

In the second place, even in the conventional course, one is brought up short by the quality of the textbooks now in use. From the point of view of literature, there are, I suggest, three categories of style: good style, bad style, and textbooks. Few history books escape from the third category. I have read, or read in, a good many of them, and in my memory they fade with few exceptions into a common, an indistinguishable grey. Scientific textbooks should, of course, be well written; but provided they are clear, we make no other major demand upon most of them. But history is a part of literature; the great historians from Herodotus to Henry Adams have been distinguished stylists, and the classics in the field are products not merely of accurate research but of imaginative vision, of profound commitment to humanity, of a keen sense of the tragic and the comic, of concern for the religious, philosophical, or moral meaning of human development. Our textbooks turn their backs upon these qualities. One does not expect all the members of the American Historical Association to write like Gibbon, Macaulay, Michelet, or Carl Becker, but is it not true that most textbooks in history are written, not only by professors, but also by the three grey fears—the fear of the young, the fear of pressure groups, and the fear of the teacher? These phantoms preside in all the offices of all the textbook houses. The book must appeal to the young; the book must not offend the susceptibilities, moral or patriotic, of the John Birch Society or the DAR or the White Citizens Council or somebody else; the book must not be beyond the comprehension of the teacher. One wonders in comparison how *Hamlet*, the vocabulary of which is difficult, the meaning of which is obscure, and the themes of which include both incest and an incitement to political assassination, ever gets itself taught in school or college.

PERMANENCE AND CHANGE

The national culture would certainly be improved by better textbooks, but what would benefit us even more is a wider diffusion, a wiser understanding of the historical point of view. Doubtless the uses of history are caught between two platitudes, each of them simplicistic: one, the doctrine that every age remakes the past in its own image; the other, the doctrine that the wisdom of our ancestors was greater than is ours. As Professor Fritz Stern of Columbia has shown in a fascinating anthology, *The Varieties of History*, modern theorists of the subject from Voltaire to Toynbee have tried to establish—between the extremes, as it were— some governing philosophy of the historical process. These efforts are important, but perhaps too complicated for general influence.

Nevertheless, whether under the doctrine that we are the heirs of all the ages in the foremost files of time, or under the doctrine that the United States is the last, best hope of man, we may ponder the importance to education of two simple, yet powerful, truths. One is that the intellectual and aesthetic fashions of no age endure forever so that there is no reason to suppose that the intellectual and aesthetic fashions now regnant in criticism and scholarship are any more absolute than those of the Romantic Movement, or of the Enlightenment, or of the Middle Ages. The second is that the republic was created and shaped during its formative decades by certain philosophic generalizations that held true in their own time, and that, despite irrational psychology, may yet hold in some sense today.

What do I mean by these comments? Regarding the first one, I suggest it takes no great amount of reading in journals of scholarship and organs of criticism to discover that present fashion tends to divide all artists, but particularly writers, whether in past or present time, into the sheep and the goats. The sheep on the whole think well of man;

the goats, with rarer wisdom, interpret him as a tragic blunder. An example from American letters will illustrate the point.

At the opening of the present century, there was little doubt that Ralph Waldo Emerson was a leading American mind, and, unfortunately, very few persons paid any attention to a man named Herman Melville. At present, though it is not true that Emerson is in eclipse—his tough and resilient idealism can never be quite eclipsed—he is undoubtedly outshone by the more baleful star of the author of *Moby Dick* and *Billy Budd*, who had, it seems, a tragic sense that Emerson had not. I have no desire to debate the question whether Emerson or Melville is the greater writer, for I do not conceive of literary studies as involving the award of prizes to First Boy, Second Boy, and Third Boy, and I cheerfully grant it was shameful so long to neglect the powerful and irregular genius of Melville. But when we concentrate, as in our schools we tend to concentrate, upon the sense of evil in Melville—or, for that matter, in anybody else from Beowulf to Mr. Salinger—we not only forswear balance, but we give up history, which reminds us that there are other respectable ways of interpreting humanity. It is not only Sophocles who saw life steadily and saw it whole. The "Inferno" of Dante doubtless has its immediate, melodramatic appeal, but the *Divine Comedy* ends on a great C-major chord: *L'amore chi muove il sole e l'altre stelle*. It is not necessary to be a Catholic to understand that the human race is more than its frustrations. The same serene note appears in Goethe, who was no Christian, and in Marcus Aurelius, who was certainly a pagan. The primary duty of the humanist is not to follow fashion or to heap up historical lore, but is to consider fashion critically in the light of historical learning, and, achieving a responsible philosophy, to teach such wisdom as he can. I believe this duty falls equally upon those who teach in the public schools and those who teach in college and university.

VALUES IN CONFLICT

As for the great philosophical generalizations that lie at the base of our constitutional system, we live in an era susceptible to the Jeffersonian emotions but incapable of accepting the philosophy of Jefferson's age. We are emotionally committed to something called liberty, to a belief in the dignity of the individual and to the right of oppressed peoples to be themselves, but we are bewildered when we attempt to justify our beliefs. We teach the triumph of rational inquiry in courses in physics and mathematics, and we teach a basic distrust of reason in much of our theology, our philosophy, and our art. It is apparently idle to point out that Sigmund Freud was a man of great historical culture whose thinking was strongly influenced by the Bible, by Goethe and by Darwin, and that, far from seeking to destroy the rational basis of culture, he was, he thought, enriching and fortifying the long Western tradition. The enormous vogue of non-rationalist theories of human nature is characteristic of literature in our time—in dramatic contrast to scientists confidently employing the tools of rationality and optimistically exploring outer space and distant planets while the arts proclaim the fatuousness of mankind and the possible extinction of the race. Does not this curious opposition of values in our educational and artistic outlook represent the worship of one of those idols of the theatre against which Bacon warned us long ago? "During periods of crisis," wrote Ortega y Gasset, "positions which are false or feigned are very common. Entire generations falsify themselves to themselves; that is to say, they wrap themselves up in artistic styles, in doctrines, in political movements which . . . fill the lack of genuine convictions." Surely, however, the historical meaning of democratic culture does not culminate in this wedding of opposites, this conjunction of a calculating machine and a psychoanalyst's couch!

THE GREATEST NEED

I hold therefore that one of the overriding intellectual necessities in American education is the need for a richer, finer, more widely diffused and philosophical approach to democratic culture in historical terms. Even if this were not desirable in itself, it is forced upon us by our opponents, the Russians and the Chinese, who have a philosophy and a philosophic interpretation of the historical process. Merely to declare their philosophy wrongheaded and their history fallacious gets us no-where, either at home with our own people, or with our friends and allies, or with the so-called uncommitted nations. As a young Russian exchange student said in my house recently: "I came here to study history. The professors spend a lot of time attacking Marxism, in which I believe, but they do not seem to know how to put any philosophy in its place."

I do not say that there must be an official philosophy of history unanimously agreed on. I say only that a thoughtful consideration of the historic process that has brought the United States into being and long sustained it is basic to education in this republic. I do not think that doctrine should be established by the Congress of the United States or by patriotic groups or by school boards or by the American Historical Association. I say only that we have too long neglected the truth latent in the great figure of speech with which Daniel Webster opened his "Second Reply to Hayne," when he said that after the mariner had been long tossed about by the storm, he will be wise if he takes a new observation of the stars to determine what his course has been and whither he is bound.

The Peace Corps, traveling exhibitions of art screened by the State Department, sending American theatrical companies around the world to produce *Porgy and Bess*, putting American music on the air, giving American news broadcasts over Radio Free Europe, the establishment of information centers in foreign capitals, the sending of Fulbright scholars and Fulbright lecturers to universities in foreign lands—these are very good things in their way; but they remain what they essentially are, instruments of propaganda—sometimes good, sometimes indifferent, sometimes, in their unexpected results, disastrous. They do not differ from the propaganda instruments of other nations. But a totality of statement, a totality of belief about the moral meaning of history and the relation of American culture to that interpretation—this is what I fail to find in our American educational patterns.

I repeat—and I cannot repeat too often—that I do not want either superpatriotism or superpropaganda. What I want is a refusal to interpret the story of man in terms of contemporary anxiety only, and a belief that during the 40 centuries that look down upon us from the Pyramids, in Napoleon's phrase, human life has struggled toward dignity and value. To master this kind of interpretation takes, I grant you, a maturity we have not achieved in our schools and in our universities. But if, in Archibald MacLeish's words, America was promises, our allies, our enemies, and our hesitant and neutral enighbors have some right to know and an inevitable interest in learning how the promissory notes were paid and in what coinage.

TOWARD PHILOSOPHY

That the United States shall understand itself in philosophical terms mediating between the eighteenth-century values into which it was born and a twentieth-century denial of many of these values—this is a demanding task. To ask that the Americans, or a significant fraction of them holding key positions in education, industry, and government, shall likewise try to comprehend the development and sensitivities of the rest of the world—this, indeed, looks like an impossible assignment. I admit the difficulty, but I insist upon the necessity of the burden, which scholarship has nobly begun to bear. To translate this knowledge as we gain it into some sort of viable philosophy is, along with our support of science, the great educational problem of our day. It can be done only through enlightened scholarship. I, for one, have grown weary of historical relativism cynically misread. I hold that the imperative task of scholarship is not, God knows, to be didactic and commonplace, but rather to lead young men and women, boys and girls, to understand that history is something they cannot escape and so to inform and infect other parts of their education with this knowledge that they come to understand that a responsible culture is more than vocationalism, social adjustment, getting your lessons, and a general sense of frustration. Macaulay's great picture of the New Zealander standing on the ruins of London bridge and contemplating the lost glories of the British empire has great fascination, but I should like to juxtapose against it a passage from a document we helped to frame in 1944 and 1945:

> Determined to save succeeding generations from the scourge of war, which twice in our lifetime has brought untold sorrow to mankind, and
>
> To reaffirm faith in fundamental human rights, in the dignity and worth of the human person, in the equal rights of men and women, and of nations large and small, and
>
> To establish conditions under which justice and respect for the obligations arising from treaties and other sources of international law can be maintained, and
>
> To promote social progress and better standards of life in larger freedom, and for these ends
>
> To practice tolerance and live together in peace with one another as good neighbors, and
>
> To unite our strength to maintain international peace and security, and
>
> To secure, by the acceptance of principles and the institution of methods, that armed force shall not be used, save in the common interest, and
>
> To employ international machinery for the promotion of the economic and social advancement of all peoples,

the signatories "resolve to combine our efforts to accomplish these aims."

Such is the opening of the charter of the United Nations. The statement concerns the ultimate purpose of the historical process interpreted for humane and humanitarian ends. If this be not the purpose and meaning of history, why do we study it at all?

7.3 A CONTRIBUTION TO THE CRITIQUE OF POLITICAL ECONOMY*

by Karl Marx

I examine the system of bourgeois political economy in the following order: *capital, landed property, wage labour; the state, foreign trade, world market.* Under the first three headings, I investigate the economic conditions of life of the three great classes into which modern bourgeois society is divided; the interconnection of the three other headings is obvious at a glance. The first section of the first book, which deals with capital, consists of the following chapters: 1. Commodities; 2. Money or simple circulation; 3. Capital in general. The two first chapters form the content of the present part. The total material lies before me in the form of monographs, which were written at periods widely separated from one another, for self-clarification not for publication, and their elaboration in connected form according to the above plan will be dependent on external circumstances.

I am omitting a general introduction which I had projected because on closer reflection any anticipation of results yet to be proved appears to me to be disturbing, and the reader who desires to follow me must be resolved to ascend from the particular to the general. A few indications of the course of my own politico-economic studies may, on the other hand, appear not out of place.

My speciality was that of law, which, however, I only pursued as a subordinate subject along with philosophy and history. In the year 1842-43, as editor of the *Rheinische Zeitung*, for the first time I experienced the embarrassment of having to take part in speaking on so-called material interests. The proceedings of the Rhenish Landtag on thefts of wood and parcelling of landed property, the official polemic which Herr von Schaper, then *Oberpräsident* of the Rhine Province, opened against the *Rheinische Zeitung* on the conditions of the Moselle peasantry, and finally debates on free trade and protective tariffs gave the first incentive to my occupation with economic questions. On the other hand, at that time when the good will "to go further" frequently outweighed specialised knowledge, a weak, philosophically tinged echo of French socialism and communism made itself audible in the *Rheinische Zeitung*. I declared myself against this bungling, but frankly confessed at the same time in a controversy with the *Allgemeine Augsburger*

*Reprinted from Karl Marx, *Selected Works*, Volume I, Ed. V. Adoratsky (New York: International Publishers, 1933), pages 354-359.

Zeitung that my previous studies did not permit me to venture for myself any judgment on the content of the French tendencies. Instead, I eagerly seized on the illusion of the managers of the *Rheinische Zeitung*, who thought that by a weaker attitude on the part of the paper they could secure a remission of the death sentence passed upon it, in order to withdraw from the public stage into the study.

The first work which I undertook for a solution of the doubts which assailed me was a critical review of the Hegelian philosophy of law, a work the introduction to which appeared in 1844 in the *Deutsch-Französische Jahrbücher*, published in Paris. My investigation led to the result that legal relations such as forms of state are to be grasped neither from themselves nor from the so-called general development of the human mind, but rather have their roots in the material conditions of life, the sum total of which Hegel, in accordance with the procedure of the Englishmen and Frenchmen of the eighteenth century, combines under the name of "civil society," but that the anatomy of civil society is to be sought in political economy. The investigation of the latter, which I began in Paris, I continued in Brussels, whither I had emigrated in consequence of an expulsion order of M. Guizot. The general result at which I arrived and which, once won, served as a guiding thread for my studies, can be briefly formulated as follows: In the social production which men carry on they enter into definite relations that are indispensable and independent of their will; these relations of production correspond to a definite stage of development of their material forces of production. The sum total of these relations of production consitutes the economic structure of society—the real foundation, on which rises a legal and political superstructure and to which correspond definite forms of social consciousness. The mode of production in material life determines the social, political and intellectual life processes in general. It is not the consciousness of men that determines their being, but, on the contrary, their social being that determines their consciousness. At a certain stage of their development, the material forces of production in society come in conflict with the existing relations of production, or—what is but a legal expression for the same thing—with the property relations within which they have been at work before. From forms of development of the forces of production these relations turn into their fetters. Then begins an epoch of social revolution. With the change of the economic foundation the entire immense superstructure is more or less rapidly transformed. In considering such transformations a distinction should always be made between the material transformation of the economic conditions of production which can be determined with the precision of natural science, and the legal, political, religious, æsthetic or philosophic—in short, ideological forms in which men become conscious of this conflict and fight it out. Just as our opinion of an individual is not based on what he things of himself, so can we not judge of such a period of transformation by its own consciousness; on the contrary this consciousness must be explained rather from the contradictions of material life, from the existing conflict between the social forces of production and the relations of production. No social order ever disappears before all the productive forces for which there is room in it have been developed; and new higher relations of production never appear before the material conditions of their existence have matured in the womb of the old society itself. Therefore, mankind always sets itself only such tasks as it can solve; since, looking at the matter more closely, we will always find that the task itself arises only when the material conditions necessary for its solution already exist or are at least in the process of formation. In broad outlines we can designate the Asiatic, the ancient, the feudal, and the modern bourgeois modes of production as so many epochs in the progress of the economic formation of society. The bourgeois relations of production are the last antagonistic form of the social process of production—antagonistic not in the sense of individual antagonism, but of one arising from the social conditions of life of the individuals; at the same time the productive forces developing in the womb of bourgeois society create the material conditions for the solution of that antagonism. This social formation constitutes, therefore, the closing chapter of the prehistoric stage of human society.

Frederick Engels, with whom, since the appearance of his brilliant sketches on the criticism of the economic categories (in the *Deutsch-Französische Jahrbücher*), I maintained a constant exchange of ideas by correspondence, had by another road (compare his *The Condition of the Working Class in England*) arrived with me at the same result, and when in the spring of 1845 he also settled in Brussels, we resolved to work out together the opposition of our view to the ideological view of German philosophy, in fact to settle accounts with our previous philosophical conscience. The resolve was carried out in the form of a criticism of post-Hegelian philosophy. The manuscript, two large octavo volumes, had long reached its place of publication in Westphalia when we received the news that altered circumstances did not allow of its being printed. We abandoned the manuscript to the gnawing criticism of the mice all the more willingly since we had achieved our main purpose—to clear our own minds. Of the scattered works in which we placed our views before the public, now from one aspect and now from another, I will mention only the *Manifesto of the Communist Party*, jointly written by Engels and myself, and *Discours sur le libre échange* [*Discourse on Free Trade*] published by me. The decisive points of our view were first scientifically, although only polemically, indicated in my work published in 1847 and directed against Proudhon: *Misère de la Philosophie* [*The Poverty of Philosophy*], *etc*. A dissertation written in German on *Wage Labour*, in which I put together my lectures on this subject delivered in the Brussels *Deutscher Arbeiterverein* [German Labour Union], was interrupted while being printed by the February Revolution and my consequent forced removal from Belgium.

The editing of the *Neue Rheinische Zeitung* in 1848 and 1849, and the subsequent events, interrupted my economic studies which could only be resumed in the year 1850 in London. The enormous material for the history of political economy which is accumulated in the British Museum, the favourable vantage point afforded by London for the observation of bourgeois society, and finally the new stage of development into which the latter appeared to have entered with the discovery of gold in Australia and California, determined me to begin afresh from the very beginning and to work through the new material critically. These studies led partly of themselves into apparently quite remote subjects on which I had to dwell for a shorter or longer period. Especially, however, was the time at my disposal limited by the imperative necessity of earning my living. My contributions, during eight years now, to the first English-American newspaper, the *New York Tribune*, compelled an extraordinary scattering of my studies, since I only occupied myself with newspaper correspondence proper in exceptional cases. However, articles on striking economic events in England and on the Continent constituted so considerable a part of my contributions that I was compelled to make myself familiar with practical details which lie outside the sphere of the actual science of political economy.

This sketch of the course of my studies in the sphere of political economy is intended only to show that my views, however they may be judged and however little they may coincide with the interested prejudices of the ruling classes, are the result of conscientious investigation lasting many years. But at the entrance to science, as at the entrance to hell, the demand must be posted:

> *Qui si convien lasciare ogni sospetto*
> *Ogni viltà convien che qui sia morta*[1]

---

[1]Here all mistrust must be abandoned
And here must perish every craven thought.

7.4 EDUCATION PROPER*

by Johann Friedrich Herbart

The art of arousing a child's mind from its repose—of securing its trust and love in order to constrain and excite it at pleasure, and to plunge it into the whirl of later years before its time, would be the most hateful of all bad arts, if it had not an aim to attain, which can justify such means even in the eyes of those whose reproof is most to be feared. "You will be thankful for it some day," says the teacher to the weeping boy, and truly it is only this hope that justifies the tears wrung from him. Let him be careful that, in overweening confidence, he does not too frequently have recourse to such severe measures. Not all that is well meant is thankfully received, and there is a weak spot in the class of that teacher, who, with perverted zeal, considers that as good which his pupils only experience as evil. Hence the warning—do not educate too much; refrain from all avoidable application of that power by which the teacher bends his pupils this way and that, dominates their dispositions, and destroys their cheerfulness. For thus, the subsequent happy recollection of childhood will also be destroyed, and that frank gratitude which is a teacher's only true thanks.

Is it then better not to educate at all? to confine ourselves to government, and limit even this to what is absolutely necessary? If every one were candid, many would agree to this. The praise already given to England would be repeated; and if once it became a question of praising, excuses would be found for the lack of government, which allows so much license to young gentlemen of position in that happy island. But let us put aside all disputes. The sole question for us is, *can we know beforehand the aims of the future man, a knowledge for which he will one day thank us, instead of having had to find and follow them by himself alone?* If so, no further foundation is needed—we *love* the children, and in them, the men; love does not love doubts any more than it cares to wait for the categorical imperative.[1]

---

*Reprinted from Johann Friedrich Herbart, *The Science of Education* (Boston: D. C. Heath and Company, Publishers, 1896).

[1]By the "categorical imperative" Kant means the moral law, so far as, independent of the external world and of every other command and consideration, it commands, and with its *Thou shalt* claims unlimited, unconditional, obedience. Instead of beginning with this absolute "shall," Herbart demanded that moral teaching should exhibit the highest point of view of willing and action, the determining judgments regarding the Good and Bad, the moral aims of internal and external activity—and while doing so himself, he arrived at his doctrine of ideas (Herbart's *Pädagogische Schriften, Anmerkung von Karl Richter*, 80).

I. Is the Aim of Education Single or Manifold?

The effort to attain scientific unity often misleads the thinker to artificially force into connection with each other, and deduce from each
other, things only lying side by side, and in themselves many and distinct.
People are even carried away into committing the mistake of inferring
unity of things from unity of knowledge, and of postulating the former
with the latter. Such a misconception does not affect the science of education; so much the more does the need exist of being able to grasp in
one conception the whole idea of a work like that of education, so
immeasurably manifold, and yet so intimately connected in all its parts.
For from such a conception proceeds unity of plan and *concentrated
power*. Looking then at the results which educational research must show,
in order to be completely serviceable, we are driven to presuppose and
require for that unity, which the result cannot dispense with, a corresponding unity in the principle from which it may be anticipated. The
question, therefore, is twofold[2]—firstly, if such a principle of unity exists,
whether the method of constructing a science on the basis of *one* conception is known. Secondly, if such a principle offers itself here, whether it
contains by implication the *entire science*. Thirdly, whether *this* construction of the science, and this view which it affords, is the only one, or
whether there be others which, although suitable in a less degree, are
still natural, and which, therefore, cannot be excluded. I have in a
treatise,[1] which is appended to the second edition of my *A B C of Observation* (*A B C der Anschauung*) treated the highest aim of education
—morality—according to this method which there seemed necessary.
I must beg my readers with all due respect to compare carefully that
work—yes, even the whole of it—with the present one; or, at least, to
avoid repetition, I must presume they have done so. To understand that
treatise properly it is before all things necessary to observe the manner
in which moral culture is related to the other parts of culture, that is to
say, how it (moral culture) presupposes them as conditions from which
alone it can with certainty be developed. Unprejudiced persons will I
hope, easily see that the problem of moral education is not separable
from education as a whole, but that it stands in a necessary, far-reaching
connection with the remaining problems of education. But the treatise

---

[2]The contradiction between "the *twofold* question" and the enumeration of *three*
points immediately after, is found also in Herbart's works collected by Hartenstein,
who had the written remains of the philosopher at his disposal for reference. The
oversight was therefore Herbart's own.
[1]*The Æsthetic Revelation of The World.*

itself shows that this connection does not affect all parts of education in such a degree that we have reason to foster those parts only in so far as they stand in this connection. Other aspects of the direct worth of general education, which we are not justified in sacrificing, come now to the front. I therefore believe that the mode of consideration which places morality at the head is certainly the most important, but not the only and comprehensive, standpoint of education. It must be added that if the examination which is begun in that treatise were to be prosecuted, it would lead straight through a complete system of philosophy. But education has no time to make holiday now, till philosophical questions are once for all cleared up. Rather is it to be desired that pedagogy shall be kept as free as possible from philosophical doubts. For all these reasons, I here take a course which will be easier and less misleading for the reader, and which touches more directly upon all parts of the science, but which is disadvantageous for the final thinking out and co-ordination of the whole to the extent that some residue of isolated considerations remain, and something is lacking to the perfect unity of the manifold. So much then for those who feel themselves called upon to sit in judgment on, or better still, to erect a science of education out of their own means.

It is impossible, from the nature of the case, that unity in the aim of education can follow; simply, because everything must proceed from the single thought, namely, *that the teacher must represent the future man in the boy, consequently the aims which the pupil will as an adult place before himself in the future must be the present care of the teacher; he must prepare beforehand an inward facility for attaining them.* He ought not to stunt the activity of the future man; consequently he ought not to confine it to single points, and just as little weaken it by too much diversity. He ought to allow nothing to be lost, either in *Intension* or *Extension*, which his pupil might afterwards demand back from him. However great or little these difficulties may be, so much is clear— *since human aims are manifold, the teacher's cares must be manifold also.*

It is not however, here contended that the multiplicities of education cannot easily be classified under one or a few main formal conceptions;[1] on the contrary, the kingdom of the pupil's future aims at once divides itself for us into the province of *merely possible aims* which he might perhaps take up at one time or other and pursue in greater or less degree as he wishes—and into the entirely distinct province of the

---

[1]*Note by Herbart.*—"I must, from scientific considerations, here observe that I do not give the name of Principle to those Concepts and Propositions to which we can only subordinate a manifold which does not follow from them by strict necessity."

necessary aims which he would never pardon himself for having neglected. In one word, the aim of education is sub-divided according to the aims of *choice*—not of the teacher, nor of the boy, but of the future man, and the aims of *morality*. These two main headings are at once clear to every one who bears in mind the most generally recognised of the fundamental principles of ethics.

II. MANY-SIDEDNESS OF INTEREST— STRENGTH OF MORAL CHARACTER.

(1) How can the teacher assume for himself beforehand the merely *possible* future aims of the pupil?

The objective of these aims as matter of mere choice has absolutely no interest for the teacher. Only the Will of the future man himself, and consequently the sum of the claims which he, in, and with, this Will, will make on himself, is the object of the teacher's *goodwill*; while the power, the initiative inclination, the activity which the future man will have wherewith to meet these claims on himself, form for the teacher matter for consideration and judgment in accordance with the idea of *perfection*.[1] Thus it is not a certain number of separate aims that hover before us now (for these we could not beforehand thoroughly know), but chiefly the *activity* of the growing man—the totality of his inward unconditioned vitality and susceptibility. The greater this totality—*the fuller, more expanded, and harmonious*—the greater is the perfection, and the greater the promise of the realisation of our good will.

Only the flower must not burst its calyx—the fulness must not become weakness through being too long scattered in many directions. Human society has long found division of labour to be necessary, that every one may make what he attempts perfect. But the more limited, the more sub-divided that which is to be accomplished, the more manifold is that which each receives from all the rest. Since, then, intellectual receptivity rests on affinity of mind, and this again on similar activities of mind, it follows that in the higher realm of true humanity, labour ought not to be divided up to the point where each man is ignorant of his neighbour's work. Every man must have a love for all activities, each must be a virtuoso in one. But the particular virtuosoship is a matter of choice; on the contrary, the manifold receptivity which can only grow out of manifold beginnings of one's own individual efforts, is a matter of education. Therefore we call the first part of the educational aim— *many-sidedness of interest*, which must be distinguished from its exag-

---

[1]See translators' Introduction, p. 28. Herbart refers here to two of his five practical ideas.

geration—dabbling in many things. And since no one object of will, nor its individual direction, interests us more than any other, we add to this, lest weakness may offend us by appearing by the side of strength, the predicate—*proportionate* many-sidedness. We shall thus get at the meaning of the common expression, "harmonious cultivation of all the powers," in connexion with which the question arises, what is meant by multiplicity of powers of soul? and also what is signified by the harmony of various powers? [1]

(2) How is the teacher to assume for himself the *necessary* aims of the pupil?

Since morality has its place singly and only in the individual's will, founded on right insight, it follows of itself, first and foremost, that the work of moral education is not by any means to develop a certain external mode of action, but rather insight together with corresponding volition in the mind of the pupil.

I leave untouched the metaphysical difficulties connected with this development. He who understands how to educate, forgets them; he who cannot free himself from them, needs metaphysics *before* a science of education, and the outcome of his speculations will prove to him whether the idea of education is, or is not, a possible one for him.

I look at life, and find very many upon whom morality is a stunted growth, very few with whom it is the principle of life itself. Most men possess a character independent of goodness, and a plan of life formed only according to their own inclination; they do the good when convenient, and gladly avoid the evil, when the better leads to the same goal. Moral principles are wearisome to them, because for them nothing follows from those principles, except now and again a limitation of their course of thought—indeed everything adverse to this limitation is welcome to them. The young poacher has their sympathy, if he sins with some boldness, and they pardon at the bottom of their heart everything which is neither ridiculous nor malicious. If it be the object of moral education to lead the pupil into the ranks of these, we have an easy task; we need only take care that he grows up, without being teased or insulted, in the consciousness of his power, and receives certain principles

---

[1] "The interest which a human being feels directly (used as adverb of mode, not of time) is the source of his life. To open many such sources, and to cause them to flow forth plenteously and unchecked, is the art of strengthening human life, and at the same time of fostering love of one's kind. If each of these interests is as varied as the achievements of many individuals taken together, then the latter are united in one bond by a happy necessity. On the contrary, when each individual cares only for *his* own business or avocation, and all besides is but means to this end, society is a machine, and each member of it keeps his life warm at a single spark, which may be extinguished, and then nothing remains but dismal coldness, satiety, and disgust."—*Aphor. zur Pädagogik.*

of honour, which are easily impressed, because they treat of honour not as a wearisome acquisition, but as a possession which nature makes a present of, and which must be protected and put in force on certain occasions according to conventional forms. But who will warrant us that the future man will not himself search out the good, to make it the object of his willing, the aim of his life, the standard of his self-criticism? Who will protect us against the severe judgment which will then overtake us? How will it be, if he calls us to account, because we presumed to anticipate the chance, which yet, perhaps, might have brought about better opportunities of genuine elevation of spirit, and would certainly not have caused the delusion that education for him is already a thing accomplished. There are instances of the kind; and it is never safe to set up as business manager for another if we have no mind to do the work well. No one at any rate would like to lie under so severe a condemnation from a man of strict moral sense, as he would who has arrogated to himself an influence over any one which might have made him worse.

Therefore that the ideas of the right and good in all their clearness and purity may become the essential objects of the will, that the innermost intrinsic contents of the character—the very heart of the personality—shall determine itself according to these ideas, putting back all arbitrary impulses—this and nothing less is the aim of moral culture. And although I may not be entirely understood, when for brevity's sake I speak of the ideas of the good and right, still, it is well for us that morality has at last thrown aside those half measures, to which it formerly at times condescended under the guise of the doctrine of happiness. My fundamental thought is thus so far clear.

III.   THE INDIVIDUALITY OF THE PUPILS AS POINT OF INCIDENCE.

The teacher aims at the universal; the pupil, however, is an individual human being.

Without compounding the soul out of all kinds of forces, and without constructing the brain out of organs[1] positively useful and able to relieve the mind of a part of its work, we must accept those experiences undisputed, and in their entirety, in harmony with which, the spirit, according to the physical form in which it is embodied, finds in its functions sundry difficulties, and their conversely relative facilities.

---

[1]Herbart jests here about the science of phrenology, founded by Gall, and applied by Leune to Pedagogy in his *Entwickelung der Gall'schen Theorie*, 1803.

But however much we may be challenged to test the flexibility of such natures by experiment, and in no way out of respect for their superiority to attempt to excuse our own inertness, we see already that the purest and best presentation of humanity shows us at the same time a particular man. Yes, and we feel that the individuality *must* come to the surface, if the example of the race is not to appear insignificant by the side of the race itself, and fade away as indifferent. And, finally, we know how beneficial it is for mankind, that different men should resolve upon and prepare for different work. Moreover the individuality of the youth reveals itself more and more under the teacher's efforts, and fortunate is he (the teacher) if that individuality in no way combats his efforts, or, by giving them a crooked direction, causes something different to be developed, which neither teacher nor pupil would desire. The latter fate almost always befals those who have had no experience in dealing with men, and therefore are ignorant of the way in which to treat in the boy, the already existent man. Out of all this there results a negative rule in relation to the aim of education, which is as important as it is difficult to observe, *i.e.* to leave the individuality untouched as far as possible. To do this, it is absolutely necessary that the teacher should discriminate his own peculiarities; he should carefully observe the occasions when his own wishes and his pupil's actions do not agree, and there is no intrinsic preference either for the one or the other. In such cases, his own wishes must at once give way, their expression must be suppressed whenever possible. Undiscerning parents may drill their sons and daughters according to their tastes—they may lay all kinds of varnish on the unpolished wood, which in years of independence will be roughly rubbed off, but not without pain and injury. The true teacher, if he cannot prevent all this, will at least not participate in it. His own structure, for which he always finds a wide and clear space in the child's soul, claims his whole attention. He will be careful how he undertakes matters for which he will earn no thanks; he cheerfully leaves undiminished to the individuality the only glory of which it is capable, namely, to be sharply defined and recognisable even to conspicuousness; he makes it a point of honour that the clear impression of person, family, birth, and nationality may be seen undefaced in the man submitted to his will.

IV. On the Need of Combining the
Aims previously distinguished.

We cannot develop our view of the aim of education *from* one point, without shutting our eyes to the manifold requirements which lie in the nature of the case, for we must at least bring back *to* one point what is to be the aim of a single plan. For where otherwise would our work begin, and where end? How can we save it from the urgent claims made upon it every moment by widely diverse views? Can any teacher have taught thoughtfully without being daily convinced of the deep need of singleness of aim? Can any one think of teaching without being panic-stricken at the mass of varied anxieties and problems which present themselves?

Is *individuality* consistent with *many-sidedness?* Can the former be preserved, while the latter is cultivated? Individuality is angular; many-sidedness is even, smooth, rounded, for agreeably to our demand it ought to be proportionately cultivated. Individuality is defined and circumscribed; many-sided interest, on the contrary, presses outwards in all directions. It must sacrifice itself while individuality remains quiescent or is thrust back; the one must move about in all directions, while the other remains calm in itself, to rush forth impetuously when the time comes.

In what relation does individuality stand to character? They appear either to harmonize with, or directly to exclude each other. For it is by his *character* that one recognizes a man; but by his *moral* character that one ought to recognize him. The less moral individual is not cognizable through morality, but on the contrary by many other individual traits, and just these as it appears make up his character.

Yes, the worst difficulty of all lies between the two chief parts of the educational aim itself. How will many-sidedness allow itself to be confined within the narrow bounds of morality, and how will the stern simplicity of moral humility bear clothing in the gay colours of a many-sided interest?

If ever complaints are made that education is thought out and pursued as a whole only with passable mediocrity, we need but refer to those who, by their development of the idea of the destiny of man, have given us so little help towards drawing us out of the sorry mean between those views which, as it appears, have to be reconciled with each other. For in looking up to the height of our destiny, the individuality and the manifold earthly interests are generally forgotten, until we come to forget them altogether—and while morality is rocked to sleep in the belief in transcendental powers, the *true* powers and means which rule the world are at the disposal of the unbeliever.

To repair all at once what is wanting in the preparatory work is a problem which we dare not think of here! Suffice it if we are but successful in bringing the points in question more distinctly into view. Naturally, our chief business is to distinguish most carefully between the different chief concepts, *i.e.* many-sidedness, interest, character, morality—for on them must be directed all the labour which we propose to expend. During the analysis, the relationships of each to the others will perhaps adjust themselves. As to individuality however, it is evidently a psychological phenomenon; the examination of it therefore would belong to the second part of pedagogy already mentioned, which would have to be built on theoretical, while the present must be based on practical, conceptions. We cannot, however, here put individuality entirely on one side, or we should be constantly disturbed by the remembrance of it, and hindered from confidently concentrating our minds on the work of thinking out the main lines of the aim of education. Some steps therefore must here be taken to adjust individuality to character and many-sidedness; then the axioms and relationships arrived at can be mentally carried forward to the following books, and further progress made in bringing the objects of education into view from all sides, without losing the one in the other. Mere doctrines, however, can never take the place of personal practice.

V.   INDIVIDUALITY AND CHARACTER.

Each thing is differentiated, by its individuality, from others of the same species. The distinguishing characteristics are often called individual character, and thus in common language the two words, which we wish to define as opposites, are confounded with each other. But as soon as characters in a play, or the want of character in children, are spoken of, we immediately feel the word character is used in different senses. Mere individualities make a bad drama, and children have very marked individualities without possessing character. Children are wanting in that which *dramatis personæ* must possess, what above all goes to make up character in men as reasoning beings—that is WILL, and we mean will in the strict sense, which is far different from variations of temper or desire, for these are not *determined*, while the will on the contrary is. The *kind* of the determination constitutes the character.

Willing—determination—takes place in consciousness. Individuality, on the other hand, is unconscious. It is the mysterious root to which our psychological heredity (psychologische Ahndung) refers everything which, according to circumstances, comes out ever differently in human beings. The psychologist ultimately attributes character also to individuality, while the teacher of transcendental freedom, who has eyes only for the expressions of the already formed character, separates the intelligible from nature by an impassable gulf.[1]

---

[1]The following note, translated from Richter's edition of Herbart's works (*Anmerkung* 93), explains the theory of transcendental freedom, to which Herbart often alludes, and his reasons for rejecting it. "The reference is to Fichte's philoso-

Character then, almost inevitably expresses itself in opposition to individuality by conflict. For it is simple and steadfast; individuality, on contrary, continually sends forth from its depths other and new thoughts and desires. Even if its activity be conquered, it still enfeebles the execution of resolves through its manifold passivity and susceptibility.

This struggle is not confined to moral characters; every character knows it. For each individual in his own way seeks consistency. The ambitious man and the egoist complete themselves in victory over the *better* traits of individuality. The hero of vice and the hero of virtue, alike complete themselves in victory over self. In ridiculous contrast, weak individuals also exist, who, in order also to have a theory and a consistency, base their theory on the principle of not fighting but letting themselves slide. Truly a wearisome and a wonderful struggle out of light into darkness, out of consciousness into the unconscious. It is at least better to wage it sensibly than in a spirit of blind obstinacy.

VI.   INDIVIDUALITY AND MANY-SIDEDNESS.

If we had previously to separate things which appeared merged one in another, we have here to place in due order that which admits of arrangement.

---

phy, against which Herbart earnestly protested, because it accepted the theory of transcendental freedom. This theory was previously admitted by Kant, who assumed man has a two-fold character—an *empirical* determined by experience, intercourse, temperament, etc., and an *intelligible* (absolute capacity), which exists as a thing in itself transcendental, that is outside experience, time, and all chains of causation, and thus is not determinable, but determines only, and is at the same time the basis of that transcendental freedom. Still more sharply did Fichte define the concept. According to his whole teaching, the pure absolute Ego postulated that its activity was of endless duration, that it comprehended all that was real in itself, and, by means of absolutely unrestrained reflection on itself as a natural being, gained unlimited power over itself, and thereby acquired the capability of self-determination unconditionally and without exception, in conformity with the idea of independence. According to this it depends merely on a man's freedom whether he has placed himself on a higher instead of a lower level for 'only one resolution is necessary, and man is raised above all nature; the formation of another character if the present has become worthless, merely depends on his freedom." That from such a standpoint, the cultivation of morality—that is to say education which strives after this cultivation, would be negatived is apparent. Fichte perceived this himself and could only return to it by roundabout ways. For if morality depends on a free resolution without any external incentive, we can the less help any one to attain to it by external influence, since inward absolute freedom does not permit itself to be reached by external means. Herbart, therefore, was perfectly right in renouncing this freedom entirely, and in declaring its acceptance to be inconsistent with the aim of education."

Many-sidedness has neither sex, nor rank, nor age. With mental feelers everywhere, with ever-ready sensation, it suits men and girls, children and women; it is as you will, either courtier or citizen, it is at home in Athens and in London, in Paris and in Sparta. Aristophanes and Plato are its friends, though neither possesses it. Intolerance is in its eyes the only crime. It observes the gay, thinks the loftiest, loves the most beautiful, ridicules the distorted, and exercises itself in each. Nothing is new to it; but everything remains fresh. Custom, prejudice, aversion, and torpor disturb it not. Awaken Alcibiades, lead him through Europe, and you will see the many-sided man! In this one man, the only one as far as we know, individuality was many-sided.

In this sense, the man of character is not many-sided, because he does not *will* it. He *wills* not to be the medium for all the sensations which the moment sends, nor the friend of all who attach themselves to him, nor the tree whereon the fruits of all moods grow. He scorns to be the centre of contradictions. Indifference and strife are alike hateful to him. He maintains his sincerity and his earnestness.

Whether the many-sidedness of Alcibiades may or may not be reconcilable with individuality is a matter of indifference to the teacher, who cannot forego the culture of character. Deeper down the conception of many-sidedness as an attribute of the person will nevertheless be dissolved in ideas which may not harmonize with that picture.

But to individuality, which at times assumes airs, and makes demands, merely because it *is* individuality, we oppose the picture of many-sidedness, with whose demands it can compare its own.

We concede then that individuality may come into collision with many-sidedness; we do not forget that we declared war against it in the name of the latter, if it would not allow of proportioned many-sided interest. While we however, at once rejected dabbling in many things (Vielgeschäftigkeit), a large sphere yet remains for individuality in which to exercise its activity—to make choice of its vocation, and to acquire the thousand little habits and comforts, which so long as no more value is attached to them than they are worth, will do but little harm to the receptivity and mobility of the mind. The principle has been previously laid down, that the teacher should not make attempts which are beside the aim of education.

There are many individualities; the idea of many-sidedness is but one. The former is contained in the latter collectively as the part in the whole. And the part can be measured by the whole; it can also be enlarged to the whole. This has now to be accomplished by education.

But we must not picture this enlargement, as if to the already existent part other parts were to be gradually added. Many-sidedness in its entirety floats constantly before the teacher, but diminished and enlarged. His task is to increase the *quantity*, without changing the *outlines*, the proportion, the *form*. Only this work undertaken with the individual does always change his outline, as if from a certain centre point on an irregular angular body a sphere gradually grew, which was nevertheless incapable of ever covering over the extreme projections. The projections —the strength of individuality—may remain, so far as they do not spoil the character; through them the entire outline may take this or that form. It will not be difficult after the taste is formed, to unite with each of these a certain peculiar fitness. But the solid content of an interest equally enlarged on all sides, determines the store of the immediate intellectual life, which since it does not hang on one thread, cannot be destroyed by one stroke of fate, but can merely be diverted by circumstances. And since the moral order of life takes its direction from circumstances, a many-sided culture gives a priceless facility and pleasure in passing on to every new kind of activity and mode of life, that may at any time be the best. The more individuality is blended with many-sidedness, the more easily will the character assert its sway over the individual.

We have thus united what up to this point admits of union in the elements of the aim of education.

7.5 THE POSITIVE PHILOSOPHY*

by Auguste Comte

SOCIAL

The positive philosophy is the first that has ascertained the true point of view of social morality. The metaphysical philosophy sanctioned egotism; and the theological subordinated real life to an imaginary one; while the new philosophy takes social morality for the basis of its whole system. The two former systems were so little favourable to the rise of the purely disinterested affections, that they often led to a dogmatic denial of their existence; the one being addicted to scholastic subtleties, and the other to considerations of personal safety. No set of feelings can be fully developed otherwise than by special and permanent exercise; and especially if they are not naturally very prominent; and the moral sense,—the social degree of which is its completest manifestation,— could be only imperfectly instituted by the indirect and factitious culture of a preparatory stage. We have yet to witness the moral superiority of a philosophy which connects each of us with the whole of human existence, in all times and places. The restriction of our expectations to actual life must furnish new means of connecting our individual development with the universal progression, the growing regard to which will afford the only possible, and the utmost possible, satisfaction to our natural aspiration after eternity. For instance, the scrupulous respect for human life, which has always increased with our social progression, must strengthen more and more as the chimerical hope dies out which disparages the present life as merely accessory to the one in prospect. The philosophical spirit being only an extension of good sense, it is certain that it alone, in its spontaneous form, has for three centuries maintained any general agreement against the dogmatic disturbances occasioned or tolerated by the ancient philosophy, which would have overthrown the whole modern economy if popular wisdom had not restrained the social application of it. The effects are, at best, only too evident; the practical intervention of the old philosophy taking place only in cases of very marked disorder, such as must be always impending and ever renewed while the intellectual anarchy which generates it yet exists. By its various aptitudes, positive morality will tend more and more

---

*Reprinted from Auguste Comte, *The Positive Philosophy*, Volume 2, trans., Harriet Martineau (London: John Chapman, 1853), pages 554-561.

to exhibit the happiness of the individual as depending on the complete expansion of benevolent acts and sympathetic emotions towards the whole of our race; and even beyond our race, by a gradual extension to all sentient beings below us, in proportion to their animal rank and their social utility. The relative nature of the new philosophy will render it applicable, with equal facility and accuracy, to the exigencies of each case, individual or social, whereas we see how the absolute character of religious morality has deprived it of almost all force in cases which, arising after its institution, could not have been duly provided for. Till the full rational establishment of positive morality has taken place, it is the business of true philosophers, ever the precursors of their race, to confirm it in the estimation of the world by the sustained superiority of their own conduct, personal, domestic, and social; giving the strongest conceivable evidence of the possibility of developing, on human grounds alone, a sense of general morality complete enough to inspire an invincible repugnance to moral offence, and an irresistible impulse to steady practical devotedness.

POLITICAL ACTION

The political results of the positive philosophy have been so mixed up with the whole treatment of the future in this volume, and the near future has been so expressly exhibited in the twelfth chapter, that I need say little here under that head. I have only to glance at the growth and application of the division between the spiritual or theoretical organism and the temporal or practical, the beginning of which I have already sufficiently described.

DOUBLE GOVERNMENT

We have seen that Catholicism afforded the suggestion of a double government of this kind, and that the Catholic institution of it shared the discredit of the philosophy to which it was attached: and again, that the Greek Utopia of a Reign of Mind (well called by Mr. Mill a Pedantocracy), transmitted to the modern metaphysical philosophy, gained ground till its disturbing influence rendered it a fit subject for our judgment and sentence. The present state of things is that we have a deep and indestructible, though vague and imperfect, sense of the political requirements of existing civilization, which assigns a distinct province, in all affairs, to the material and the intellectual authority, the separation and co-ordination of which are reserved for the future. The Catholic division was instituted on the ground of a mystical opposition between heavenly and earthly interests, as is shown by the terms spiritual and temporal, and not at all from any sound intellectual and social appreciation, which was not then possible, nor is possible even yet; and when the terrestrial view prevailed over the celestial, the principle of separation was seriously endangered, from there being no longer any logical basis which could sustain it against the extravagances of the revolutionary spirit. The positive polity must therefore go back to the earliest period of the division, and re-establish it on evidence afforded by the whole human evolution; and, in its admission of the scientific and logical preponderance of the social point of view, it will not reject it in the case of morality, which must always allow its chief application, and in which everything must be referred, not to Man, but to Humanity. Moral laws, like the intellectual, are much more appreciable in the collective than in the individual case; and, though the individual nature is the type of the general, all human advancement is much more completely characterized in the general than in the individual case; and thus morality will always, on both grounds, be connected with polity. Their separation will arise from that distinction between theory and practice which is indispensable to the common destination of both. We may already sum up the ultimate conditions of positive polity by conceiving of its systematic wisdom as reconciling the opposing qualities of that spontaneous human wisdom successively manifested in antiquity and in the Middle Ages; for there was a social tendency involved in the ancient subordination of morality to policy, however carried to an extreme under polytheism; and the monotheistic system had the merit of asserting, though not very successfully, the legitimate independence, or rather, the superior dignity of morality. Antiquity alone offered a complete and homogeneous political system; and the Middle Ages exhibit an attempt to reconcile the opposite qualities of two heterogeneous systems, the one of which claimed supreme authority for theory, and the other for practice. Such a reconciliation will take place hereafter, on the ground of the systematic distinction between the claims of education and of action. We find something like an example of how this may be done,—theory originating practice, but never interfering with it except in a consultative way,—in the existing relations between art and science, the extension of which to the most important affairs, under the guidance of sound philosophy, contemplating the whole range of human relations. If the whole experience of modern progress has sanctioned the independence, amidst co-operation, of theory and practice, in the simplest cases, we must admit its imperative necessity, on analogous grounds, in the most complex. Thus far, in complex affairs, practical wisdom has shown itself far superior to theoretical; but this is because much of the proudest theory has been ill-established. However this evil may be diminished when social speculation becomes better founded, the general interest will always require the common preponderance of the practical or material authority, as long as it keeps within its proper limits, admitting the independence of the theoretical authority; and the necessity of including abstract indications among the elements of every concrete conclusion. No true statesman would think of disputing this, when once the philosophers had evinced the scientific character and the political aspect adapted to their social destination. It may be well however to present, in a summary way, the rational securities which will exist against any encroachment of moral upon political government, in order to meet the instinctive prejudices which still oppose the advent of what I have shown to be the first social condition of final regeneration.

In treating of the training for such an organization, I insisted on limiting it to the five nations of Western Europe, in order to secure its distinctness and originality from the confusion of modern speculative habits. But such a restriction must give way when we contemplate the final extension of the positive organism, first to the whole of the white race, and at length to the whole of mankind, as their preparation becomes complete. It was the theological philosophy which divided Western Europe into independent nationalities for five centuries past; and their interconnection, determined by their positive progression, can be systematized only by the process of total renovation. The European case must be much fitter than the national for manifesting the qualities of the spiritual constitution; and it will acquire new consistence and efficacy after each new extension of the positive organism, which will thus become more and more moral, and less and less political; the practical authority all the while preserving its active preponderance. By a necessary reaction, liberty will gain as much as order by this inevitable progression; for as intellectual and moral association becomes confirmed by extension, the temporal authority which is now necessary to keep the social system together will naturally relax as repression becomes less and less needed. As for the influence of human passions, which will arise under the new system as under every other, I have already spoken of them, so as to need only to say here that they will affect the early institution of the system more than its normal development. We have still to reap some of the bitter fruits of our intellectual and moral anarchy: and especially, in the quarrels between capitalists and labourers first, and afterwards in the unsettled rivalship between town and country. In short, whatever is now systematized must be destroyed; and whatever is not systematized, and therefore has vitality, must occasion collisions which we are not yet able accurately to foresee or adequately to restrain.

This will be the test of the positive philosophy, and at the same time the stimulus to its social ascendancy. With this troubled initiation, the worst will be over. The difficulties proper to the action of the new *régime*, the same in kind, will be far less in degree, and will disappear as the conditions of order and progress become more and more thoroughly reconciled. We have seen that the advent of the positive economy will have been owing to the affinity between philosophical tendencies and popular impulses: and if so, it is easy to see how that affinity must become the most powerful permanent support of the system. The same philosophy which asserts the intellectual supremacy of the general reason cannot but admit, without any danger of anarchy, the social supremacy of genuine popular needs, by establishing the universal sway of morality, governing at once scientific energies and political conclusions. And thus, after some passing troubles, occasioned by the unequal development of practical exigencies and theoretical satisfactions, the positive philosophy, in its political form, will necessarily lead up the human race to the social system which is most suitable to the nature of Man, and which will greatly surpass in unity, extension, and stability all that the past has ever produced.

THE ÆSTHETIC ACTION

One of the least anticipated results of this working out of opinions, morals, and institutions under the guidance of positive philosophy, is the development which must take place in the modes of expressing them. For five centuries, society has been seeking an æsthetic constitution correspondent to its civilization. In the time to come,—apart from all consideration of the genius that will arise, which is wholly out of the reach of anticipation,—we may see how Art must eminently fulfil its chief service, of charming and improving the humblest and the loftiest minds, elevating the one, and soothing the other. For this service it must gain much by being fitly incorporated with the social economy, from which it has hitherto been essentially excluded. Our philosophical speculation has shown us how favourable the human view and collective spirit must be to the rise and spread of æsthetic tastes; and our historical survey had before taught us, that a progressive social condition, marked and durable, is indispensable to the completeness of such a development. On both grounds, the future is full of promise. The public life and military existence of antiquity are exhausted; but the laborious and pacific activity proper to modern civilization is scarcely yet instituted, and has never yet been æsthetically regarded; so that modern art, like modern science and industry, is so far from being worn out, that it is as yet only half formed. The most original and popular species of modern art, which forms a preparation for that which is to ensue, has treated of private life, for want of material in public life. But public life will be such as will admit of idealization: for the sense of the good and the true cannot be actively conspicuous without eliciting a sense of the beautiful; and the action of the positive philosophy is in the highest degree favourable to all the three. The systematic regeneration of human conceptions must also furnish new philosophical means of æsthetic expansion, secure at once of a noble aim and a steady impulsion. There must certainly be an inexhaustible resource of poetic greatness in the positive conception of Man as the supreme head of the economy of Nature, which he modifies at will, in a spirit of boldness and freedom, within no other limits than those of natural law. This is yet an untouched wealth of idealization, as the action of Man upon Nature was hardly recognized as a subject of thought till art was declining from the exhaustion of the old philosophy. The marvellous wisdom of Nature has been sung, in imitation of the ancients, and with great occasional exaggeration; and the conquests of Man over nature, with science for his instrument, and sociality for his atmosphere, remains, promising much more interest and beauty than the representation of an economy in which he has no share, and in which magnitude was the original object of admiration, and material grandeur continues to be most dwelt upon. There is no anticipating what the popular enthusiasm will be when the representations of Art shall be in harmony with the noble instinct of human superiority, and with the collective rational convictions of the human mind. To the philosophical eye it is plain that the universal reorganization will assign to modern Art at once inexhaustible material in the spectacle of human power and achievement, and a noble social destination in illustrating and endearing the final economy of human life. What philosophy elaborates, Art will propagate and adapt for propagation, and will thus fulfil a higher social office than in its most glorious days of old.—I have here spoken of the first of the arts only,—of Poetry, which by its superior amplitude and generality has always superintended and led the development of them all: but the conditions which are favourable to one mode of expression are propitious to all, in their natural succession. While the positive spirit remained in its first phase, the mathematical, it was reproached for its anti-æsthetic tendency: but we now see how, when it is systematized from a sociological centre, it becomes the basis of an æsthetic organization no less indispensable than the intellectual and social renovation from which it is inseparable.

THE FIVE NATIONS.

The five elements of this great process will each bring their own special contribution to the new system, which will inseparably combine them all. France will bring a philosophical and political superiority; England, an earnest predilection for reality and utility; Germany, a natural aptitude for systematic generalization; Italy, its genius for art; and Spain, its familiar combined sense of personal dignity and universal brotherhood. By their natural co-operation, the positive philosophy will lead us on to a social condition the most conformable to human nature, in which our characteristic qualities will find their most perfect respective confirmation, their completest mutual harmony, and the freest expansion for each and all.

CHAPTER EIGHT

TECHNOLOGY AND EDUCATION

8.1   EDITORIAL   COMMENT

The impact of technology on the American culture and upon educational theory and practice has become a major issue of concern since World War II. As is usual on an issue of this kind, we have strong supporters as well as aggressive opponents. The most significant aspect of the controversy, however, would seem to be in how man (the teacher) uses the machine. As a refined tool it has great significance for our culture. As a weapon it may well be the instrument of our destruction.

The four selections on this topic represent significant cross currents of opinion. In his article "Technology and Education" Henry C. Ruark sees our advancing technology as contributing to more and better organization in all areas of social activity. Particular significance is found in the possibility of bridging the gap between the birth of an idea and its being put into practice. While the opportunity for progress is here, the future is still fuzzy.

The revolutionary nature of our age of automation is graphically portrayed by Donald Michael in his analysis "Cybernation: The Silent Conquest." The problems involved in the control of cybernation are held to be equally as significant as the advantages.

Present day mass communications come under severe criticism in the W. H. Ferry article "Masscomm as Guru." The social and cultural responsibilities of our mass communicative agencies are held to be the "most influential educational system any society has known." Probably the most disturbing implication of these activities is the tendency to minimize the importance of a human being.

To what extent is the theory underlying the use of the teaching machine behavioristic? And if the theory is basically behavioristic what results may be expected from its use? These are the fundamental questions confronting Professor Kneller in his discussion of "Automation and Learning Theory." While the objectives outlined by the advocates of the use of teaching machines are worthy and challenging, what, in the final analysis, may we expect from the general use of these instruments?

8.2 TECHNOLOGY AND EDUCATION*

by Henry C. Ruark, Jr.

Advancing technology is forcing better organization everywhere, and education is no exception. Probably at no other time has the American educational system undergone as agonizing a period as that in which we work; there is a continual clamor for change, a demand for action arising from one simple fact:

Education has been too slow to meet the changing demands of the modern world.

Three accelerating forces can be identified as major causes of the stresses and strains so easily observed:

1. *Rising birth rates, leading to rising enrollments.*
2. *Expanding knowledge in many fields, with its modifying effects on the curriculum.*
3. *Advancing technology and its influence on the instructional process.*

The effects of these three forces are inescapable facts of modern educational life. We can do little about the first. The others demand from us, first, professional efforts to understand what is happening, and second, action as educational leaders to make certain that the inevitable impact is made to serve well our long-held educational objectives.

In 1869, Thomas Henry Huxley spoke out on the scientific education of his day. He said:

> As industry attains higher status in its development, as its processes become more complicated and refined and competition more keen, the sciences are dragged in one by one, to take their full share of the fray; and he who can best avail himself of their help is the man who will come out uppermost in that struggle for existence. . . .

Huxley made his statement in the midst of the First Industrial Revolution, which was the product of inventive genius.

In 1960, Admiral Hyman Rickover spoke out on education. He said:

> Because we do not fully comprehend the changes brought about by the rise of totalitarianism and technological progress, we continue

*Reprinted from *Phi Delta Kappan*, Volume XLII, No. 9 (June, 1961), with permission of the publisher.

to think and act as if we were secure. . . . We forget that technology has wiped out distance as a factor in war.[1]

Rickover made his statement in the midst of the Second Industrial Revolution, which is the product of scientists and technicians. The admiral points out that we no longer have a real choice between policies of political isolation as against involvement in world affairs; neither do we have a real choice between policies of economic isolation as against involvement in world markets.

The admiral, characteristically, failed to point out that the technology which has brought these political and economic changes has also brought just as sweeping advances in communication, and has created potential changes in the instructional process which may well wipe out many present-day limitations on learning, including those he often cites in arguing that not every American should be afforded opportunity for self-development to whatever level he can attain. It is thus valid to say, perhaps, that we may no longer have a real choice between policies of the past in education as against involvement in the development demanded by the modern world.

It is generally conceded that there is a twenty-five to fifty year lag between initiation of an educational idea and its widespread acceptance in practice. What many persons, both in and out of education, fail to realize is that we are living in an era of fantastic change. This is a fact, one that we must understand and live with, but even constant repetition does not convince everyone.

This educational lag simply cannot be tolerated any longer. It cannot be tolerated because, like it or not, education has become our first line of defense. We neglect it at our peril, not only as a bulwark against atomic destruction, but also as our sole determining force to shape the world as we believe it must be shaped, if free men are to remain free to pursue the goals about which we dream.

New concepts of what constitutes education for competent citizenship today, new methods and materials of instruction, new demands for different and increased teaching skills are crowding in from every side.

Developments in communication have revealed great potentials for making the instructional process more effective and more efficient; among the many tasks demanded of us today, perhaps none is more urgent than assessing the role of new educational media in improving instruction.

---

[1]Hyman Rickover, "Your Child's Future Depends on Education," *Ladies Home Journal*, Oct., 1960, pp. 98-102.

Educators could not ignore these developments, even if they wished to do so. The child who comes to school today is not the same child who came to school yesterday. He is substantially, although subtly, different; the impact of change in the world, brought to him through his communication experiences, makes him so.

Today's student pays a price for his new knowledge. His experiences are to a large degree secondary and vicarious, rather than primary and direct; much of his new knowledge is neither profound, meaningful, nor accurate. Selectivity necessarily exercised by the media, imperfect absorption by the learner, and other factors too often lead to distortion and misunderstanding.[2] But education must build on the foundation laid by these communication experiences, and in the process correct and extend these learnings.

The instructional process is the heart of education, of course, and instructional materials can give shape and substance to the curriculum, control its content, and vitally affect the teaching-learning process. Reexamination of communications developments has greatly extended the meaning of the term "instructional materials." A few decades ago, the "older" medium—print—was supplemented by "audio-visual" materials such as motion pictures, filmstrips, slides, radio, and disc recordings. These materials appealed to both the visual and auditory senses and offered teachers a splendid means for enriching and accelerating the learning process. More recently, "newer" new media—audio and video tapes, language laboratories, educational television, and teaching machines—have revealed still other instructional potentialities.

Two Major Trends

As these media are used more and more widely, not only for enrichment and acceleration but also for basic instructional communication, two major trends are evident. One is toward mass instruction, wherein learning experience takes place in larger groups, utilizing many basic media of communication, with some emphasis on projected still and motion pictures or educational television. The second is toward individualized instruction—learning experiences on a "machine and me" basis—with heavy emphasis, even basic dependence, on automated devices such as the language laboratory and the teaching machine.

The impetus for these developments comes in large part from a currently strong interest in developing new curriculum materials in a number

---

[2]See Educational Policies Commission, *Mass Communication and Education*, The Commission, National Education Association, 1958, pp. 60-74.

of subject-matter fields, and an equally strong drive towards better utilization of staff and student time.

It is significant that major subject-area studies use the new instructional media to up-date subject matter. For instance, new instructional materials of many types are being prepared by the School Mathematics Study Group at Yale, the Biological Sciences Curriculum Study at the University of Colorado, the Wayne State University Modern Foreign Language Project, the Physical Sciences Study Committee at Massachusetts Institute of Technology, and the National Science Foundation.

THE 'PACKAGED COURSE'

A corollary development arising from this basic concern with curriculum and content is the "packaged course" concept, exemplified by series of films now available in physics, chemistry, biology, and mathematics. Some series are the result of film recordings from television classes based on the "master teacher" concept, bringing to mass audiences highly skilled presentations by a subject authority. Still other materials, designed to deal with attitudes and appreciations rather than skills and knowledge, are being produced to exploit the recognized powers of the motion picture in this field.

National interest in better utilization of staff and student time is reflected by the development and widespread use of "team teaching" and other new approaches. Decrying the "manpower waste" in the schools, the Fund for the Advancement of Education has embarked on many experiments in utilization of teacher and student time; most revolve around use of group instructional tools and materials. Thus we see the overhead projector and the motion picture used with groups of 250 or more, or the classroom use of televised instruction to bring the same program at the same or different times into classrooms in a whole school district, a whole state, or even a whole region. This approach is usually coupled with small-group and individual work for other aspects of learning.

It is evident that mass use of the newer instructional media reflects the basic concepts of mass production, the "newly traditional" answer in our Western world to all problems involving the same quantity-quality dilemma: "Standardize it, make it quickly, use machine tools, produce in huge quantity—and distribute widely."

But education deals with the most plastic of materials—the human individual. The same "machine tools" of educational technology which make possible this mass approach may also, it is now evident, create individualized instruction, in some cases self-instruction, and permit a very near approach to the time-honored Socratic or tutorial situation, involving each student in close contact with a patient and untiring teacher who draws out correct and carefully sequenced responses to skilled and probing questions. The teacher, of course, is really the person or persons who program the content material for whatever machine is used to present it.

This second trend, toward individualized instructional instrumentation (to adopt technologically-oriented language!) has been organized on an ascending scale of sophistication by Dr. James Finn: individual reading pacers and similar devices; individual viewing and listening equipment for existing slides, filmstrips, motion pictures and recordings; language laboratories of all types; specifically programed printed materials such as scrambled textbooks, programed texts, etc.; and true "teaching" machines of the Skinner and Pressey type.

TEACHING MACHINES EVERYWHERE BY 1964?

Programed material presented through automated devices and "teaching" machines represents a dramatic instructional innovation. It has been said that "the trouble with teaching machines is that they either sound like robots and scare everybody, or they sound so innocuous that nobody realizes they are revolutionary." But it has also been said that "the development of a successful machine that will teach a person the complex of interlocking symbolic and verbal knowledge which is the mark of an education is equivalent to a general theory of learning and teaching."[3] Dr. Eugene Galanter, author of this statement, predicted in 1960 that teaching machines would begin to come into general use in education within four years.[4]

The program is the heart of the machine technique; the machine serves only to control presentation of the program, to prevent students from cheating, and in some cases to record student learning rates and errors.

Today there are literally dozens of teaching machines of varying degrees of complexity and automation; most reflect either one or a combination of two basic approaches to the organization of learning materials into a program.

Whatever the program, it takes the form of either multiple choice responses or constructed responses. Very rarely are these two com-

---

[3]Eugene Galanter, "The Ideal Teacher," *Automatic Teaching*, Wiley, 1959, p. 1.
[4]Eugene Galanter, "The Mechanization of Teaching," *Bulletin of the National Association of Secondary School Principals*, April, 1960, p. 304.

bined, since each represents a different viewpoint of the learning process. In a multiple choice program, the learner chooses one of several responses. After he has committed himself, the machine reveals whether or not his choice was correct. If correct, he can go on to the next step; if not, he must choose another response until he discovers the correct one. In a constructed response, the learner writes or builds his response by manipulation of the machine. Again, he is immediately informed of correctness and can proceed only if his constructed response is accurate.

In both types of programs, cues, prompts, or hints can be used to further guide the learner. Proponents of the multiple-choice form (Pressey, Crowder) insist that some errors are natural and necessary; advocates of the constructed response (Skinner, et al.) try for "errorless" learning, with such small program steps ("frames") and liberal use of cues and prompts that the student is not allowed to make an error. The latter method is sometimes designated a "linear" program, since it moves the student straight ahead in a carefully guided line which is the same for all learners, except for rate of progress "down the line." The test of ability is not the degree to which a concept is understood but how quickly it has been grasped. For example, if such a program is truly valid and effective, while the average youngster is moving along in electronics and the slow learner is dealing with Newton's Laws, the gifted may be moving well into nuclear physics.

Branching off the main line onto a sidetrack and back again is possible with the multiple-choice approach. If a student's responses show that he is confused, he can be branched off through a succession of smaller and simpler steps until he demonstrates full and complete understanding, at which point he is brought back to the main line again. Or, if he demonstrates by rate and choice of responses that he has a background for certain learnings, he can be branched around a part of the main line program and moved ahead to more complex learnings.

Branching programs are sometimes called "contingent" programs, since the sequence of the program is contingent at all points upon the student's last response. Contingent or branching programing normally uses multiple choice responses which facilitate automatic scoring; place little emphasis upon step size or cueing; assume that a student should be allowed to make mistakes; and provide the potential of different remedial instruction for different types of errors.

Skinner and the 'Constructed Response'

Skinner at Harvard is adamant in contending that the constructed response is the only way to make sure the student is not merely identifying the most likely response, while advocates of multiple choice response and branching see advantages in a more natural and more flexible learning approach.

There is no definitive evidence to support one school of programing over the other at present. It appears likely, however, that in cases where there is strong internal logic in a subject, or where close adherence to a sequence is desirable for other reasons, Skinnerian linear programing offers real advantages. There are other learning objectives where it may be desirable to allow the learner to go his own way, so long as his performance meets acceptable standards; for instance, he can do so in areas where there are no unequivocally "right" answers, such as problem-solving situations in the social studies.

A third position on programing suggests that it should be linear where possible and branching where necessary, with assessment made of the learner's performance after a sequence of frames. At this point a judgment would be made, either by the machine or the student, to continue in a small-step linear program if the student has made many errors, or to branch ahead if he has made few errors.

Programs can be presented on paper as sheets or notebooks or as scrambled or programed texts; or on film, as motion pictures, filmstrips, microfilm, or slides. The paper forms, often less expensive, are usually expendable in use; film forms, although more expensive originally, can be used for many students and are adaptable to presentation of visual and auditory stimuli.

Research in the new media, stimulated by the tremendous upsurge in interest throughout the educational system and supported by large numbers of grants from foundations and from Title VII of the National Defense Education Act, is rapidly adding to our knowledge of specific capabilities, of differential applications, and of integration of these new materials and media. These significant new findings are being reported widely in the educational press and will be even more widely disseminated through federal and other channels. Added to the large body of experience and research already available to us, there seems little doubt that the result will be a broad response throughout our school system.

Another major factor is the support for new media of instruction specifically included by definition within the scope of special equipment and materials to be acquired by schools under Title III of the NDEA. Many states report a heavy emphasis on basic media resources in local district applications. For example, just before the passage of Title III the U.S. Office of Education reported just over sixty language laboratories in public schools; within the first two years of Title III programs the count shot up to well over 500 and has been growing larger ever since. One Western state estimates that at least 20 per cent of total expenditures under Title III are going into printed supplementary and basic audio-visual materials. Other states have reported similar experience.

POTENTIAL GREAT, BUT FUTURE FUZZY

There appears to be little doubt that these new media of communication are potentially powerful educational forces, that utilization of instructional technology both in the classroom and increasingly in the home is probably inevitable, and that education can be made more effective and efficient if these new tools of learning are widely and wisely used.

In a society increasingly characterized by technological advances, the shape of education in the coming years is certainly neither distinct nor fixed. Some persons who study current trends see tomorrow's classroom characterized by automated instructional methods; others have some reservations about mechanizing the instructional process.

NOT MERELY AIDS TO TEACHER

A significant point often overlooked is that the new media can no longer be regarded merely as *aids* to the teacher. Since they now store and disseminate subject matter in ways never achieved before, they are performing functions which were for a long time the exclusive domain of the teacher. The media can now illustrate, discuss, analyze, present content, form concepts, and build generalizations; they can even systematically prescribe areas for continued student inquiry.

These newly programed capabilities of the new media force a reformulation of the conventional role of the teacher in the classroom. Just as industry discovered that it could not attain present high production flows without major changes in the organization and employment of human effort, so will education require development of similar major changes before the true potentials of present-day and future technological devices can be achieved. The teacher will no longer be principally a communicator, presenting facts, constructing concepts, and guiding skill development; increasingly, the teacher will work with individual students on a tutorial basis, directing their learning and using machines for much presentation and routine exposition, pointing out further resources, and encouraging the student to accept increasingly higher levels of responsibility for his own educational growth.

Not everyone agrees with this view of things to come; some who are skeptical about the desirability of mechanizing parts of the instructional process, or question its value, call attention to the highly experimental nature of some of the newer devices and point to the almost total absence of learning theory undergirding use of these newer media. One author says that we seem to be witnessing a movement toward a learning theory based on an "automatic" model of man, and fears that modifications of educational goals and procedures may subvert "ultimate" or "external" values. Others decry the large financial investment and costs of maintaining new media, especially highly technical systems such as are required by various forms of television. Some fear that democratic values, such as the worth of the individual, may be lost amid the technological devices.

Still others are concerned that mechanization may bypass the essential elements of learning, such as readiness and motivation; that it may deny the student the social developments to be gained through contact with human instructors; and that it may lead to regimentation and a degree of curriculum rigidity such as we have never experienced.[5]

Those who advocate full use of the new educational media maintain that technology can offer the overworked classroom teacher relief from some routine, repetitive presentations of materials and that, since much of the information-dissemination part of teaching would be done by mechanical devices and teacher aides, the professional teacher would be released to serve as a sensitive guide for the learner. They maintain that the student would thus take greater responsibility for his own learning, and that the teacher would be freer to use her critical and creative talents to individualize instruction still further.

This Is the 'Systems Approach'

One author foresees still another development in classroom technology: a combination of the media for mass instruction with the media for individual instruction, to create a true "systems approach" in education. This demands thorough analysis and long-range planning; application of personnel, machines, and materials to the point of saturation of the instructional situation; and complex interplay of control and concentration of effort, on the basis of feedback of information from all stages of the process-flow within such an organized learning system. This would demand the application to education of the new "operational research" patterns which attempt to strip a problem down to its bare essentials, create a mathematical model of it, and then solve for the best answer. Methodologies from other sciences are also used in this type of analysis

---

[5]Gene C. Fusco, "Technology in the Classroom," *School Life,* March-May, 1960.

for planning purposes. As an example, the producer of a film series for a certain course and the manufacturer of a teaching machine might together develop a teaching machine program of multiple-choice response items, based on the material presented in the films. The films might be projected hourly on closed-circuit television, and students would work under program assignments with machines located in individual instruction spaces throughout the school building.[6]

Proponents of the application of the new media emphasize that no new technological break-through is needed to bring about the instructional transformation they envision; the present state of the communication arts makes the so-called "automated classroom" possible today.

Regardless of the enthusiastic hurrahs of proponents, or the equally vocal skepticism of the critics, it appears that instructional technology is here, and that it is here to stay. It also appears evident that no *one* of these technological developments will completely resolve our continuing quantity-quality dilemma. We will have to integrate and combine a variety of teaching-learning methods, materials, and devices to buttress our attack on educational problems as they exist, and we will probably need to provide for more effective individual counseling and guidance than ever before.

It would seem that the issues of classroom use of the new media will revolve around the same old problems of organization, staff, space, finance, and program with which we have become so painfully familiar.

Overseeing the media and machines in the classroom and controlling the flow of materials and programs will certainly require a growing body of specialists highly skilled in materials and resources. Such specialists will perhaps be based in an instructional materials center combining the facilities of the present school library and audio-visual services with the addition of small-group and individual learning spaces and the facilities demanded by local production of unique learning materials. They will be key personnel in a developing team of educators and subprofessional aides.

In many ways, the new media will demand more of the teacher than he has yet been asked to give. Finding out what a pupil's response to a stimulus actually is has never been an easy part of the teacher's task; and it will be even more difficult if the child spends any of his time learning from a technological device. The teacher will have to work more closely than ever before with the individual pupil to discover what effects the new methods are having on his attitudes and emotions.

Given the context of automated teaching, it becomes all the more

---

[6]James D. Finn, "Technology and the Instructional Process," *Audio-Visual Communication Review,* Vol. 8, No. 1, Winter, 1960.

vital for a teacher to discharge distinctly human responsibilities, too. If the values of a democratic society are to be preserved, the teacher must concentrate even more earnestly on responsibilities of developing the full potential of every child by stimulating his imagination, broadening his vision, stretching his powers to build his confidence, and helping him to appreciate the ideas of democracy.

NEW BUILDINGS ARE REQUIRED

The new instructional program probably cannot be effectively administered in conventional school buildings, and efforts to design them to accommodate the new media are already under way. Total flexibility of instructional spaces probably cannot be built in; expense may be too high, and acoustical difficulties may be too great. Above all, tomorrow's needs are impossible to foresee. On the other hand, the administrator cannot close his eyes to rapid changes in instructional technology and the modifications in instructional spaces that will be needed. It is obvious that some practical guidelines are badly needed, and they are being provided through various publications, one of the best being a Title VII research project recently completed under the direction of Dr. Amo De Bernardis of the Portland (Oregon) Public Schools.[7]

Financing is always a major concern in education, of course. It has been estimated that although a simple type of teaching machine can be built for $20, the production of the manuscript for a single program on that machine, say in arithmetic for one semester, will probably cost as much as $50,000. The installation of a sophisticated language laboratory can cost thousands of dollars, as can the purchase of just one among the many film series being offered. Costs of an in-service TV system range from several thousand dollars to more than $250,000. Clearly, instructional technology, although it will probably improve the instructional process, will certainly increase the operating costs of the schools.

But is cost to be the deciding factor? Many who advocate use of instructional technology in classroom teaching maintain that to use skilled teachers for the routine aspects of teaching, even though they can carry out the tasks for less than the machines will cost, is to waste precious human abilities and qualities. Educational technology promises to provide the teacher with greater opportunities to perform more creative functions, for more sensitively human ends. Can our society afford not to make the very best and most productive use of its greatest resource, its human materials?

---

[7]Amo De Bernardis, et al., *Planning Schools for New Media*. Division of Education, Portland State College, Portland, Ore., 1960.

COST IS NOT THE QUESTION

Perhaps the difficult question is *not* how much will the new media cost, but how we can best use them to upgrade the teaching-learning process through more significant learning experiences to such an extent that the cost factor becomes secondary.

After all, we are the nation which has traditionally faced the problems of providing the greatest educational opportunity for all to move towards the highest goals of which they are capable. Difficulties, costs, and dilemmas are not new to us.

We have left to the last a key question—that of programing and control. It is always poor programing, rather than the medium itself, which must bear the brunt of criticism in any discussion of the new media.

Teachers have had relatively wide latitude in selecting textbooks for a given subject field. Even if a text is not entirely satisfactory, creative teachers can supplement it with reference and resource books. In selecting audio-visual materials, teachers have been somewhat more restricted. High production costs and the limited market (until very recently) have made it difficult for a manufacturer to produce films, filmstrips, recordings, and the like at a low unit cost. The enormous cost and the centralization demanded in planning and designing materials for the new media inevitably raises the question of curriculum control. The preparation of motion pictures, TV programs, audio tapes, or teaching machine programs requires the services of highly specialized persons and the outlay of large sums of money. Such materials are revised only at great expense, and this barrier to flexibility has alarmed some persons who see a possibility of "freezing" the curriculum once an investment in these materials has been made by the local school district. Others point to the danger that a national curriculum might materialize; or that agencies not accountable to the public for their actions could produce standardized instructional materials in package form that could not easily be modified to meet the needs of local school districts. The same concern about the possible weakening of existing curriculum control always arises in connection with large television programs such as the state, regional, and airborne projects now underway.

It would appear that the answers to these problems are yet to be developed, but that the problems themselves vary only in degree and complexity from similar problems long ago faced in education. It would appear that we may expect somewhat similar solutions to be developed. One basic principle learned from experience with the new media does emerge: New media, just as other teaching materials, must be under the control of the teacher, who should select them for the unique contribution they can make to the teaching-learning situation as it exists in the classroom, for a particular group of learners. Basic principles underlying all good teaching and learning apply to the newer as well as the older instructional materials.

Administrators must first of all ensure that the purposes and goals of education in a democratic society will be protected and preserved; maximum development of each pupil must remain the basic goal of any instructional program; and the purposes of education as revealed in the instructional program; and the purposes of education as revealed in the instructional tools will be used and how they will be used.

I think we can agree that the influence of technology on education emphasizes the words of Whitehead, who said: "It is the business of the future to be dangerous."

Certainly technology is now making the future course of instruction capricious and hazardous. If we would be leaders for education, we must look forward, and not present what Herbert Muller has noted as "the curious spectacle of civilized man forever marching with his face turned backward—as no doubt the cave man looked back to the good old days, when men were free to roam, instead of being stuck in a damn hole in the ground."[8]

The good old days of education are gone, too. The days of the future will be what we make of them.

[8]Quoted in Finn, *op cit.*

8.3 CYBERNATION: THE SILENT CONQUEST*

by Donald N. Michael

Both optimists and pessimists often claim that automation is simply the latest stage in the evolution of technological means for removing the burdens of work. The assertion is misleading. There is a very good possibility that automation is so different in degree as to be a profound difference in kind, and that it will pose unique problems for society, challenging our basic values and the ways in which we express and enforce them.*

In order to understand what both the differences and the problems are and, even more, will be, we have to know something of the nature and use of automation and computers. There are two important classes of devices. One class, usually referred to when one speaks of "automation," is made up of devices that automatically perform sensing and motor tasks, replacing or improving on human capacities for performing these functions. The second class, usually referred to when one speaks of "computers," is composed of devices that perform, very rapidly, routine or complex logical and decision-making tasks, replacing or improving on human capacities for performing these functions.

Using these machines does not merely involve replacing men by having machines do tasks that men did before. It is, as John Diebold says, a way of "thinking as much as it is a way of doing. . . . It is no longer necessary to think in terms of individual machines, or even in terms of groups of machines; instead, for the first time, it is practical to look at an entire production or information-handling process as an integrated system and not as a series of individual steps."[1] For example, if the building trades were to be automated, it would not mean inventing machines to do the various tasks now done by men; rather, buildings

---

*Reprinted from *Cybernation: The Silent Conquest*, a report to the Center for the Study of Democratic Institutions (Santa Barbara, California: Center for the Study of Democratic Institutions, The Fund for the Republic Inc., 1962), pages 5-13, 40-46, with permission of author and publisher.
*This paper makes the following assumptions in looking on the next twenty years or so: *1)* international relations will derive from the same general conditions that pertain today; *2)* the weapons systems industries will continue to support a major share of our economy; *3)* major discoveries will be made and applied in other technologies, including psychology and medicine; *4)* trends in megalopolis living and in population growth will continue; *5)* no major shifts in underlying social attitudes and in public and private goals will take place.
[1]John Diebold, *Automation: Its Impact on Business and Labor,* National Planning Association, Planning Pamphlet No. 106, Washington, D. C., May, 1959, p. 3.

would be redesigned so that they could be built by machines. One might invent an automatic bricklayer, but it is more likely that housing would be designed so that bricks would not be laid. Automation of the electronics industry was not brought about through the invention of automatic means for wiring circuits but through the invention of essentially wireless—*i.e.*, printed—circuits (though today there are automatic circuit wirers as well).

The two classes of devices overlap. At one pole are the automatic producers of material objects and, at the other, the sophisticated analyzers and interpreters of complex data. In the middle zone are the mixed systems, in which computers control complicated processes, such as the operations of an oil refinery, on the basis of interpretations that they make of data automatically fed to them about the environment. Also in this middle zone are those routine, automatic, data-processing activities which provide men with the bases for controlling, or at least understanding, what is happening to a particular environment. Processing of social security data and making straightforward tabulations of census information are examples of these activities.*

Cybernated systems perform with a precision and a rapidity unmatched in humans. They also perform in ways that would be impractical or impossible for humans to duplicate. They can be built to detect and correct errors in their own performance and to indicate to men which of their components are producing the error. They can make judgments on the basis of instructions programmed into them. They can remember and search their memories for appropriate data, which either has been programmed into them along with their instructions or has been acquired in the process of manipulating new data. Thus, they can learn on the basis of past experience with their environment. They can receive information in more codes and sensory modes than men can. They are beginning to perceive and to recognize.

As a result of these characteristics, automation is being used to make and roll steel, mine coal, manufacture engine blocks, weave cloth, sort and grade everything from oranges to bank checks. More versatile automatic fabricators are becoming available, too:

---

*In order to eliminate the awkwardness of repeating the words "automation" and "computers" each time we wish to refer to both at the same time, and in order to avoid the semantic difficulties involved in using one term or the other to mean both ends of the continuum, we invent the term "cybernation" to refer to *both* automation and computers. The word is legitimate at least to the extent that it derives from "cybernetics," a term invented by Norbert Wiener to mean the processes of communication and control in man and machines. He derived it from the Greek word for "steersman." The theory and practice of cybernetics underlie all systematic design and application of automation and computers.

> *U.S. Industries announced . . . that it had developed what was termed the first general-purpose automation machine available to manufacturers as Standard 'off-the-shelf' hardware. . . . The new machine, called a TransfeRobot, sells for $2,500. . . . The Westclox Company of La Salle, Ill., has been using a TransfeRobot to oil clock assemblies as they pass on a conveyor belt. The machine oils eight precision bearings simultaneously in a second. At the Underwood Corporation typewriter plant in Hartford, the robot picks up, transfers and places a small typewriter component into a close-fitting nest for an automatic machine operation. In an automobile plant, the device feeds partly fabricated parts of a steering assembly to a trimming press and controls the press. The device consists basically of an arm and actuator that can be fitted with many types of fingers and jaws. All are controlled by a self-contained electronic brain.*[2]

At the other end of the continuum, computers are being used rather regularly to analyze market portfolios for brokers; compute the best combination of crops and livestock for given farm conditions; design and "fly" under typical and extreme conditions rockets and airplanes before they are built; design, in terms of costs and traffic-flow characteristics, the appropriate angles and grades for complex traffic interchanges; keep up-to-date inventory records and print new stock orders as automatically computed rates of sales and inventory status indicate. Computers have also been programmed to write mediocre TV dramas (by manipulating segments of the plot), write music, translate tolerably if not perfectly from one language to another, and simulate some logical brain processes (so that the machine goes about solving puzzles—and making mistakes in the process—in the ways people do). Also, computers are programmed to play elaborate "games" by themselves or in collaboration with human beings. Among other reasons, these games are played to understand and plan more efficiently for the conduct of wars and the procedures for industrial and business aggrandizement. Through such games, involving a vast number of variables, and contingencies within which these variables act and interact, the best or most likely solutions to complex problems are obtained.

The utility and the applicability of computers are being continually enhanced. For example, after a few hours of training, non-specialists can operate the smaller computers without the aid of programmers simply by plugging in pre-recorded instruction tapes that tell the com-

---

[2]"Multi-Purpose Automation Unit is Sold 'Off the Shelf,'" *New York Times*, June 23, 1961, p. 44.

puter how to do specific tasks. Instruction-tape libraries can supply pre-programmed computer directions for everything from finding the cube root of a number to designing a bridge. When the machine is through with one task, its circuits can be easily cleared so that a new set of pre-programmed instructions can be plugged in by its businessman operator.

But the capabilities of computers already extend well beyond even these applications. Much successful work has been done on computers that can program themselves. For example, they are beginning to operate the way man appears to when he is exploring ways of solving a novel problem. That is, they apply and then modify, as appropriate, previous experiences with and methods of solution for what appear to be related problems. Some of the machines show originality and unpredictability. To take one example from a recent paper of Norbert Wiener:

> *The present level of these learning machines is that they play a fair amateur game at chess but that in checkers they can show a marked superiority to the player who has programmed them after from 10 to 20 playing hours of working and indoctrination. They thus most definitely escape from the completely effective control of the man who has made them. Rigid as the repertory of factors may be which they are in a position to take into consideration, they do unquestionably—and so say those who have played with them— show originality, not merely in their tactics, which may be quite unforeseen, but even in the detailed weighting of their strategy.[3]*

Another example of a machine the behavior of which is not completely controllable or predictable is the Perceptron, designed by Dr. Frank Rosenblatt. This machine can learn to recognize what it has been before and to teach itself generalizations about what it recognizes. It can also learn to discriminate, and thereby to identify shapes similar to those it has seen before. Future versions will hear as well as see. It is not possible to predict the degree and quality of recognition that the machine will display as it is learning. It is designed to learn and discriminate in the same way that it is believed man may learn and discriminate; it has its own pace and style of learning, of refining its discriminations, and of making mistakes in the process.

It is no fantasy, then, to be concerned with the implications of the thinking machines. There is every reason to believe that within the next two decades machines will be available outside the laboratory that will

---

[3]Norbert Wiener, "Some Moral and Technical Consequences of Automation," *Science*, Vol. 131, No. 3410, May 6, 1960, p. 1356.

do a credible job of original thinking, certainly as good thinking as that expected of most middle-level people who are supposed to "use their minds." There is no basis for knowing where this process will stop, nor, as Wiener has pointed out, is there any comfort in the assertion that, since man built the machine, he will always be smarter or more capable than it is.

> *It may be seen that the result of a programming technique of [cybernation] is to remove from the mind of the designer and operator an effective understanding of many of the stages by which the machine comes to its conclusions and of what the real tactical intentions of many of its operations may be. This is highly relevant to the problem of our being able to foresee undesired consequences outside the frame of the strategy of the game while the machine is still in action and while intervention on our part may prevent the occurrence of these consequences. Here it is necessary to realize that human action is a feedback action. To avoid a disastrous consequence, it is not enough that some action on our part should be sufficient to change the course of the machine, because it is quite possible that we lack information on which to base consideration of such an action.*[4]

The capabilities and potentialities of these devices are unlimited. They contain extraordinary implications for the emancipation and enslavement of mankind.

The opportunities for man's enhancement through the benefits of cybernation are generally more evident and more expected, especially in view of our proclivity to equate technological advances with progress and happiness. In the words of the National Association of Manufacturers:

> *For the expanding, dynamic economy of America, the sky is indeed the limit. Now more than ever we must have confidence in America's capacity to grow. Guided by electronics, powered by atomic energy, geared to the smooth, effortless workings of automation, the magic carpet of our free economy heads for distant and undreamed horizons. Just going along for the ride will be the biggest thrill on earth!*[5]

But the somber and complex difficulties produced by cybernation, which already are beginning to plague some aspects of our society and economy, are only beginning to be recognized. Thus, although this

---

[4]*Ibid*, p. 1357.
[5]*Calling All Jobs*, National Association of Manufacturers, New York, October, 1957, p. 21.

paper will describe, first, the advantages of cybernation, which make its ever expanding application so compelling, it will, on the whole, emphasize the less obvious, sometimes acutely uncomfortable aspects of this development with which we must successfully contend if we are to enjoy the benefits of both cybernation and democracy.

THE ADVANTAGES OF CYBERNATION

In recent years deteriorating sales prospects, rising production costs, increased foreign competition, and lower profits have led business management to turn to our national talent for technological invention as the most plausible means of reducing costs and increasing productivity, whether the product is an engine block or tables of sales figures. And the government, faced with the need to process and understand rapidly increasing masses of numerical facts about the state of the nation and the world, is already using 524 computers and is the major customer for more of them.

What are the advantages of cybernated systems that make government and private enterprise turn to them to solve problems?

In the first place, in a competitive society a successfully cybernated organization often has economic advantages over a competitor using people instead of machines. As *U.S. News and World Report* says:

> *In one line of business after another, the trend is the same. Companies are spending millions of dollars to mechanize their operations, boost output and cut costs. . . . Says an official of a big electrical company: 'It is no longer a question of whether or not to automate, but rather it is how far to go and how fast to proceed. If you don't, your competition will.'* [6]

Not only must many organizations automate to compete, but the same principle probably holds for competing nations. We are by no means the only semi-cybernated society. Europe and Russia are well under way, and their machines and products compete with ours here and in the world market. The U.S.S.R. is making an all-out effort to cybernate as much of its planning-economic-industrial operation as it can.

In the second place, reducing the number of personnel in an organization reduces the magnitude of management's human relations tasks, whether these be coping with over-long coffee breaks, union negotiations, human errors, or indifference.

In the third place, cybernation permits much greater rationalization

---

[6]"When Machines Have Jobs—and Workers Do Not," *U.S. News and World Report*, Vol. 50, No. 6, February 6, 1961, p. 76.

of managerial activities. The computers can produce information about what is happening now, as well as continuously up-dated information about what will be the probable consequences of specific decisions based on present and extrapolated circumstances. The results are available in a multitude of detailed or simplified displays in the form of words, tables of figures, patterns of light, growth and decay curves, dial readings, etc. In many situations, built-in feedback monitors the developing situation and deals with routine changes, errors, and needs with little or no intervention by human beings. This frees management for attention to more basic duties. There is, for example,

> *. . . an automatic lathe . . . which gauges each part as it is produced and automatically resets the cutting tools to compensate for tool wear. In addition, when the cutting tools have been worn down to a certain predetermined limit, the machine automatically replaces them with sharp tools. The parts are automatically loaded onto the machine and are automatically unloaded as they are finished. These lathes can be operated for 5 to 8 hours without attention, except for an occasional check to make sure that parts are being delivered to the loading mechanism.[7]*

Another example, combining built-in feedback with a display capability, adds further illumination:

> *The Grayson-Robinson apparel chain, which has more than 100 stores throughout the country, receives print-punch tags daily from its stores and converts them to full-size punchcards. The complete merchandise and inventory control function is then handled on a computer. What styles are to be processed first are determined at the computer center. During any given week about 60 per cent of the sales data are received and summarized. On the following Monday morning the remaining 40 per cent of the sales data are received. The computer can then begin running style reports immediately after the tickets have been converted to cards. By this time the company can run up style reports by departments and price lines in order to obtain the necessary merchandising information. The entire reporting job is completed by Wednesday afternoon of each week, including reports on all inactive stockpiles.[8]*

---

[7]From a statement by Walter Reuther before the Subcommittee on Economic Stabilization of the Joint Committee on the Economic Report, U. S. Congress; *Automation and Technological Change,* 84th Congress, First Session, USGPO, 1955, p. 99.

[8]From statement of James A. Suffridge, President, Retail Clerks International Association before the Subcommittee on Automation and Energy Resources of the Joint Economic Committee, U. S. Congress; *New Views on Automation,* 86th Congress, Second Session, USGPO, 1960, p. 591.

Freeing management from petty distractions in these ways permits more precise and better substantiated decisions, whether they have to do with business strategy, government economic policy, equipment system planning, or military strategy and tactics. Thus, management in business or government can have much better control both over the system as it operates and over the introduction of changes into future operations Indeed, the changes themselves may be planned in conformity with, and guided by, a strategy that is derived from a computer analysis of the future environment.

In the fourth place, cybernation allows government and industry much greater freedom in locating their facilities efficiently in relation to the accessibility of raw products, markets, transportation, and needed (or cheaper) human and material resources. Distance is no longer a barrier to control and coordination. The computers that control automated processes need not be near the factories nor the data-processing computers near their sources of information or users if other considerations are more pressing. Widely dispersed installations can be coordinated and controlled from still another place, and the dispersed units can interact with each other and affect one another's performance as easily, in many cases, as if they were all in the same place.

In the fifth place, some degree of cybernation is necessary to meet the needs of our larger population and to maintain or increase the rate of growth of the Gross National Product. An estimated 80,000,000 persons will be added to our population in the next twenty years. Beyond increases in productivity per man hour to be expected from the projected 20 per cent growth in the labor force during this same period, productive growth will have to be provided by machines.

If the criteria are control, understanding, and profits, there are strong reasons why government and business should want to, and indeed would have to, expand cybernation as rapidly as they can. The versatility of computers and automation is becoming better understood all the time by those who use them, even though, as with the human brain, most present users are far from applying their full potential. Cheap and general purpose computers or modular components applicable to many types of automatic production and decision-making are now being manufactured. In good part, they are cheap because they themselves are produced by automated methods. Techniques for gathering the field data that serve as the "inputs" to the machines are being refined and themselves automated or semi-automated. For example, a large shoe distributor is planning to attach a pre-punched IBM card to each shoe box. When a sale is made, the card is returned to a central facility to guide inventory adjustment, reordering, and sales recording and analysis. Techniques for quickly implementing the "outputs" from the machines are also being invented. Methods are being developed for systematically establishing the precise kind and degree of cybernation required in specific situations as well as the changes needed in the rest of the institution or organization using cybernation.

. . . .

THE CONTROL OF CYBERNATION

Time and Planning

Time is crucial in any plan to cope with cybernation. Ways of ameliorating its adverse effects require thinking farther ahead than we ever do. In a society in the process of becoming cybernated, education and training for work as well as education and training for leisure must begin early in life. Shifts in behavior, attitudes, and aspirations take a long time to mature. It will be extraordinarily difficult to produce appropriate "culture-bearers," both parents and teachers, in sufficient numbers, distribution, and quality in the relatively brief time available. It is hard to see, for example, how Congress, composed in good part of older men acting from traditional perspectives and operating by seniority, could recognize soon enough and then legislate well enough to produce the fundamental shifts needed to meet the complexities of cybernation. It is hard to see how our style of pragmatic making-do and frantic crash programs can radically change in the next few years. This is especially hard to visualize when the whole cybernation situation is such that we find it impossible to determine the consequences of cybernation even in the medium long run. The differences expressed in the public statements of business and labor demonstrate that any reconciliation of interests will be a very long-range effort indeed. "Drastic" actions to forestall or eliminate the ill-effects of cybernation will not be taken in time unless we change our operating style drastically.

Education: Occupations and Attitudes

Among the many factors contributing to the stability of a social system are two intimately intertwined ones: the types of tasks that are performed; and the nature of the relationship between the attitudes of the members of the society toward these tasks and their opinions about the proper goals of the individual members of the society and the right ways of reaching them.

The long-range stability of the social system depends on a population of young people properly educated to enter the adult world of tasks and attitudes. Once, the pace of change was slow enough to permit a comfortable margin of compatibility between the adult world and the one children were trained to expect. This compatibility no longer exists. Now we have to ask: What should be the education of a population more and more enveloped in cybernation? What are the appropriate attitudes toward and training for participation in government, the use of leisure, standards of consumption, particular occupations?

Education must cope with the transitional period when the disruption among different socio-economic and occupational groups will be the greatest; and the later, relatively stable period, if it ever comes to exist, when most people would have adequate income and shorter working hours. The problem involves looking ahead five, ten, twenty years to see what are likely to be the occupational and social needs and attitudes of those future periods; planning the intellectual and social education of each age group in the numbers needed; motivating young people to seek certain types of jobs and to adopt the desirable and necessary attitudes; providing enough suitable teachers; being able to alter all of these as the actualities in society and technology indicate; and directing the pattern of cybernation so that it fits with the expected kinds and distribution of abilities and attitudes produced by home and school.

To what extent education and technology can be coordinated is not at all clear, if only because we do not know, even for today's world, the criteria for judging the consonance or dissonance in our educational, attitudinal, and occupational systems. We think that parts of the social system are badly out of phase with other parts and that, as a whole, the system is progressively less capable of coping with the problems it produces. But there is little consensus on the "causes" and even less on what can be done about them. All we have at present is the hope that most people can be educated for significant participation in such a world as we have foreseen here—we have no evidence that it can be done.

If we do not find the answers to these questions soon, we will have a population in the next ten to twenty years more and more out of touch with national and international realities, ever more the victims of insecurity on the one hand and ennui on the other, and more and more mismatched to the occupational needs of the day. If we fail to find the answers, we can bumble along, very probably heading into disaster, or we can restrict the extension of cybernation, permitting it only where necessary for the national interest. But judging the national interest and distinguishing it from private interests would confront us with most of the problems that have been outlined in this paper.

Perhaps time has already run out. Even if our style somehow should shift to long-range planning, it would not eliminate the inadequate training and inadequate values of much of our present adolescent and pre-adolescent population, as well as of those adults who will be displaced or remain unhired as a result of cybernation in the next decade. Only a partial solution exists in this case: Begin now a program of economic and social first aid for these people.

A Moratorium on Cybernation?

Can we control the effects of cybernation by making it illegal or unprofitable to develop cybernation technology? No, not without virtually stopping the development of almost all of new technology and a good part of the general development of scientific knowledge. The accumulation of knowledge in many areas of science depends on computers. To refine computers and make them more versatile requires research in almost every scientific area. It also requires the development of a technology, usually automated, to produce the articles needed to build new computers. As long as we choose to compete with other parts of the world, we shall have to develop new products and new means for producing them better. Cybernation is the only way to do it on a significant scale. As long as we choose to live in a world guided by science and its technology we have no choice but to encourage the development of cybernation. If we insist on this framework, the answers to coping with its effects must be found elsewhere than in a moratorium on its development.

Control: Public or Private?

There has always been tension between big industry, with its concern for profit and market control, and government, with its concern for the national interest. The tension has increased as big business has become so large as to be quasi-governmental in its influence and as government has had to turn to and even subsidize parts of business in order to meet parts of the national interest within a free-enterprise framework. Under these circumstances we can expect strong differences between government and business as to when and where it is socially legitimate to introduce automation.

Sufficient government control over who can cybernate, when, and where would not come easily. In the first place, decisions about control would have to be based on the intentions of local business and industry as well as on the national picture. For example, the effects on Congressional seating of shifts in populations as a result of cybernation-based industrial relocation would presumably enter the calculations. Longer-run consequences would have to be balanced against short-run profits or social dislocations. Implications for our military posture and for international trade would be significant. Moreover, it would be difficult for the government to make a case for control of private organizations on the basis of ambiguous estimates of the effects of automation on hiring policy. In any particular case, it becomes clear only well after the fact of cybernation whether increases or changes in production resulted in a corresponding increase in man-hours of work sufficient to compensate the economy for the jobs lost or the people unhired.

Finally, it must be kept in mind that the power of some of the largest unions is seriously threatened by automation. In a relatively short time they may not have the leverage they now have. Thus, a crucial counterbalance to the pressures from business may be absent when it is most needed. It is possible that the crisis that will arouse the government to exert control will not be evident until the blue-collar work force has been so eroded as to have weakened the unions irreparably.

Yet some sort of control is going to be necessary. There are, of course, the federal regulatory agencies. However, they have never been distinguished for applying their powers with the vigor sometimes allowed by their mandates, and there is no reason to suppose that their traditional weaknesses would suddenly disappear and that an agency created to cope with cybernation would be effective. Nor is there any reason to believe that an agency with the very wide-ranging powers that it would need would be approved before the crisis that it was supposed to avert was upon us.

In theory, control could be exercised by private enterprise. But in the unlikely case that competitors could see their mutual interests clearly enough to join forces, the very act of cooperative control would be incompatible with our anti-trust laws. Whether the government or some alter-government comprised of business, labor, and industry were to do the controlling, either group would have to undertake a degree of national planning and control thoroughly incompatible with the way in which we look upon the management of our economic and social system today.

AFTER THE TAKE-OVER

In twenty years, other things being equal, most of the routine blue-collar and white-collar tasks that can be done by cybernation will be. Our schools will probably be turning out a larger proportion of the population better educated than they are today, but most of our citizens will be unable to understand the cybernated world in which they live.

Perhaps they will understand the rudiments of calculus, biology, nuclear physics, and the humanities. But the research realm of scientists, the problems of government, and the interplay between them will be beyond the ken even of our college graduates. Besides, most people will have had to recognize that, when it comes to logic, the machines by and large can think better than they, for in that time reasonably good thinking computers should be operating on a large scale.

There will be a small, almost separate, society of people in rapport with the advanced computers. These cyberneticians will have established a relationship with their machines that cannot be shared with the average man any more than the average man today can understand the problems of molecular biology, nuclear physics, or neuropsychiatry. Indeed, many scholars will not have the capacity to share their knowledge or feeling about this new man-machine relationship. Those with the talent for the work probably will have to develop it from childhood and will be trained as intensively as the classical ballerina.

Some of the remaining population will be productively engaged in human-to-human or human-to-machine activities requiring judgment and a high level of intelligence and training. But the rest, whose innate intelligence or training is not of the highest, what will they do? We can foresee a nation with a large portion of its people doing, directly or indirectly, the endless public tasks that the welfare state needs and that the government will not allow to be cybernated because of the serious unemployment that would result. These people will work short hours, with much time for the pursuit of leisure activities.

Even with a college education, what will they do all their long lives, day after day, four-day week-end after week-end, vacation after vacation, in a more and more crowded world? (There is a population explosion to face in another ten to thirty years.) What will they believe in and aspire to as they work their shorter hours and, on the outside, pursue their "self-fulfilling" activities, whatever they may be? No one has ever seriously envisioned what characteristics these activities might have in order to be able to engross most men and women most of their adult lives. What will be the relationship of these people to government, to the "upper intellectuals," to the rest of the world, to themselves?

Obviously, attitudes toward work, play, and social responsibility will have changed greatly. Somehow we shall have had to cope emotionally with the vast gap in living standards that will then typify the difference between us and the have-not nations. We shall presumably have found some way to give meaning to the consumption of mass leisure. It would seem that a life oriented to private recreation might carry with it an attitude of relative indifference to public responsibility. This indifference, plus the centralization of authority, would seem to imply a governing élite and a popular acceptance of such an élite.

If this world is to exist as a coherent society, it will have to have its own "logic," so that it will make sense to its inhabitants. Today, for most of our population, our society makes sense, even though some other eyes hardly see us as logical in the formal sense of the word and the eyes of some of our own people look on us as a more or less pointless society. We make and solve our problems chiefly by other than mathematical-logical standards, and so must the cybernated generations. What these standards might be, we do not know. But if they are inadequate, the frustration and pointlessness that they produce may well evoke, in turn, a war of desperation—ostensibly against some external enemy but, in fact, a war to make the world safe for human beings by destroying most of society's sophisticated technological base. One thing is clear: if the new "logic" is to resolve the problems raised here, it will have to generate beliefs, behavior, and goals far different from those which we have held until now and which are driving us more and more inexorably into a contradictory world run by (and for?) ever more intelligent, ever more versatile slaves.

8.4 MASSCOMM AS GURU*

by W. H. Ferry

The topic of this paper is the social and cultural responsibilities of mass communications. My definitions are straightforward: "mass communications" means television, newspapers, mass-circulated paperbacks, radio, comic books, the great circulation magazines, and their accomplices and adjuncts: boards of directors, editors, public relations mechanics, advertisers, and writers. In including the last category I invoke the Nuremberg doctrine: great collective sins, as well as great collective achievements, are the products of individuals. Thus, the discussion must take in the scribblers and drudges of the trade as well as the Napoleons and Metternichs. "Responsibility" means the state of being responsible, that for which one is answerable—a duty or trust. "Social and cultural" signifies those areas of the common life apart from the political realm. I believe that the observations herein can be extended to the rest of the world, *mutatis mutandis,* even those portions as yet unexposed to the raptures of the TV soap opera, the gossip column, the dirty comic book.

At the outset I wish to stipulate that phrases like "notable exception" are salted through the following pages. I shall not attempt a weighing-up of mass communications, fair and balanced to the last gram. My thumb is firmly on one side of the scales. I shall be talking about macro-cause and macro-effect. I know about the occasional brilliant and illuminating broadcast, article, report, picture-essay, and I pay my respects to them herewith. They will be given no more attention in this paper. The acute sense of self-appreciation developed by mass communications tells us a great deal about them, for one thing. For another, it scarcely seems required to pay homage to an institution for doing what is expected of it.

I wish also to acknowledge that the common run of breaking news is probably as well reported these days as at any time. I am aware of the need of mass communications to make a living, its concern with "events," the impact of instantaneous electronic reporting. I know that mass communications are both cause and effect, acted upon by society as well as acting. There are titans in the field and I herewith salute them also. My comments are not directed at the conscientious and striving few but at the thoughtless and irresponsible many. I am not unsympa-

*Reprinted from W. H. Ferry, *Masscomm as Guru* a report to the Center for the Study of Democratic Institutions (Santa Barbara, California: Center for the Study of Democratic Institutions, The Fund for the Republic Inc., 1966), pages 9-19, with permission of the author and publisher.

thetic to the variety and intensity of the demands on mass communications, and I intend to add to them.

I shall use the word masscomm in the following pages, not because I like such ugly neologisms but to avoid the repetition of the equally dreary phrase mass communications.

A good many theories of the social and cultural responsibilities of masscomm have been elaborated over the years—by Walter Lippmann, Robert Hutchins, Father John Courtney Murray, the late Alexander Meiklejohn, by others. All of the theories are based chiefly on two grounds: the singular position accorded mass communications by the First Amendment, and the indispensability of criticism and guidance and fresh ideas to a democratic society.

The notion, of course, is that the people are sovereign, and need a clear stream of information and conflict of opinion to order the community. In 1947 a Commission on Freedom of the Press presented a Report which, in its five main requirements, provided a theory of responsibility. They are:

1. The press must give a truthful, comprehensive, and intelligent account of the day's events in a context which gives them meaning.
2. The press must provide a forum for the exchange of comment and criticism.
3. The press must project a representative picture of the constituent groups in the society.
4. The press must present and clarify the goals and values of the society.
5. The press must provide full access to the day's intelligence.

Though specifically addressed to newspapers, these requirements can readily be modified into a general theory applicable to the rest of mass communications. But that it is not commonly accepted is evidenced by the reception of the Report by the press. It was vilified, misrepresented, and ignored. The Commission's mild recommendation that a group of private citizens be organized to appraise the doings of the press and make statements from time to time on its misadventures and accomplishments met with rockets of denunciation. There was a great deal of identifying of the press with what its proprietors wanted to do, which seemed to them identical with their responsibilities. The Commission's Report also provided the occasion for a campaign of unrelieved self-admiration. Today's counterpart is television's crankiness toward critics and its relentless glorification of what it is already doing when it is suggested that it might improve its output.

So much for a commonly accepted theory of responsibility. I suspect that there are deep historical reasons for masscomm's non-acceptance of well-defined obligations. But I think the main reason is that masscomm is preoccupied with another responsibility, that of making money. Masscomm argues that it cannot fulfill social and cultural responsibilities by going broke. Fair enough; no one expects the extreme sacrifice. This is not really the issue. The issue is whether masscomm has made the pre-condition of profits the entire reason for its existence, and its only basic responsibility. This is a different general theory, so to speak, and seems to me to be close to the cuticle. The matter may be stated otherwise. The United States, for better or worse, is a money-seeking culture; masscomm is a money-seeker like any other corporation. Thus, it argues, it ought to be measured by the amount of money it makes, not by archaic ideas about responsibility to the community.

I propose that masscomm begin to take itself more seriously. The balance of this paper suggests that masscomm bears social and cultural responsibilities of much greater weight than it has been willing to shoulder. Whether such responsibilities can be undertaken by masscomm while still remaining solvent is the question. Perhaps we could find out if masscomm were to seek not to make more each year than the year before but to concentrate instead on looking to its fundamental obligations. I know that it is not especially rewarding to exhort particular men to reform themselves, and so these remarks must be considered less a collection of remonstrances to those now running masscomm than a general prayer that masscomm as an institution may rouse itself somehow to the performance of duties long and dangerously neglected.

Few spokesmen in masscomm would assert a doctrine of social and cultural non-responsibility. Nor would many of them deny that in some way and to some degree masscomm has shaped American institutions. Scott Buchanan says that the First Amendment is the source of all of the duties, privileges, and immunities of education, though the word itself does not occur in the Amendment, or, for that matter, anywhere else in the Constitution. Perhaps masscomm recognizes, whether unconsciously or no, that its wide warrant is obtained in the same place and that its task is essentially education. This, it will be perceived, is a one-word summary of the five requirements of the Commission on Freedom of the Press.

My view is that masscomm's social and cultural responsibilities are those of the largest and probably most influential educational system any society has known. The relation is teacher and taught. I do not suggest that masscomm is like a university. The differences are evident. Nor can one suggest that everything would be fine if masscomm merely modeled itself on the university, which itself is having grave difficulties these days about its proper functions.

And it might well be maintained that education would itself take on the irresponsible aspects of masscomm if it in turn depended on paying customers, free to come and go, buy or not buy, look or not look. But this is a heavily debatable proposition, and in any case my topic is masscomm, and not the machines of formal learning for the young.

Aristotle provides the point: "Men by nature desire to know." They do not cease desiring to know at 16 or 21 or 25. Learning proceeds throughout life, willy nilly. The means of learning change and become informal. What is learned changes. For most people masscomm provides the means of their continuing education, for good or ill; and masscomm's choice of topics and emphasis decides, for most people, what is learned. It is in these respects that I confer on masscomm the accolade and obligations of educator.

I cannot think of a nicer compliment than to call someone a teacher. But masscomm does not much care for the title. Perhaps that is because on every front it realizes that it must be given low marks as an educator. It does not fully inform, it mystifies as much as it clarifies, it seldom lifts up. The situation of American Negroes, for example, has been a disgrace from Reconstruction on, a running sore on the national body. It would be a festering canker to this day had the issue been left to masscomm. A few courageous Negroes and whites taught a public lesson in three years that was never in masscomm's curriculum, and the Negro now has at least a glimmering chance to break out of latter-day slavery. For generations two-thirds of our Negro population has lived in poverty or deprivation. Unemployment has been twice or more that of whites. Who knew these things?

It is commonly acknowledged now that the pot boiled over in Los Angeles in the summer of 1965 because of frustration and resentment and indignity stored up too long. How much were Californians told about the sputtering fuse? Even the best-intentioned of them were aware of little or nothing. Bishop Kennedy, the liberal and kindly Methodist leader of Southern California, apologized publicly for his ignorance after the Watts uproar. "I didn't know," he said, "that this was the way they lived."

Before Rosa Parks performed the momentous act of sitting in the wrong part of the Montgomery bus, what was the picture of the Negro nation presented to us by masscomm? Through its cloudy lens in the South we saw Negroes struggling patiently through courts to get their children into decent schools, indignant, perhaps even irritated, at the delays occasioned by the need to give the White South time to accommodate. Once in a while we picked up the odd bit of gossip in masscomm about the habitual injustice to Negroes in the criminal courts and their inability to vote in a good many places. According to masscomm, Southern Negroes were being treated well, in the Dixie version of that term, and were responding by forbearance and understanding. Mass communications portrayed a colored minority waking slowly to the possibility that it had some rights, even a few they had always known to be a white monopoly, and walking softly and patiently toward the Promised Land. Except for a troublemaking and querulous few, masscomm intimated, this minority was quite ready to forego voting, opportunity, schooling, dignity, until the white nation got used to the idea and became willing, piece by stubborn piece, to bestow these bounties.

The Northern portrait was even more illusory and vicious. Masscomm rejoiced that Jim Crow was not official doctrine in Detroit, Harlem, Chicago, Rochester, Philadelphia. Masscomm neglected to say it was standard practice. There was, to be sure, the occasional flare of trouble in these precincts, duly reported by masscomm and as duly attributed to Communists, Muslims, or chronic malcontents. Once again masscomm produced the wrong enemy. Inattentive authorities, greedy landlords, cybernation, bad education, all the complex causes of Negro misery that make up the real enemy, used to be mentioned by masscomm only once in a while. The favorite culprits of masscomm are, in the race situation as in all others, still Communists or agitators.

Masscomm assured us that Northern Negroes were aware of how much better off they were than their Dixie cousins. The white nation did not really need to be concerned about ghettoes, rats in bedrooms, the daily indignity of Negro life, because Negroes were used to them, grateful on the whole for the droppings from the white table. Above all, masscomm said, Negroes were accustomed to the thought that it would take generations of obeisance to white overlordship to win their way to equal justice and opportunity. If Northern Negroes were not entirely happy with their lot, they were not unhappy enough to say anything loud and impolite about it. The white nation needs a stereotype of the Negro, and masscomm was glad to provide the infamous caricature of him as gospel-hymning, crap-shooting, indolent, carefree, sex-powerful, and loving the squalor he lived in.

This, I think, is a not unfair outline of the general picture of the American Negro presented by mass communications in those pre-Parks, pre-SNCC, pre-riot years. It was not only a grossly unreal and ignorant picture—masscomm did not have Bishop Kennedy's excuse of not knowing—it betrayed irresponsibility toward millions of fellow citizens, and unconcern about a dirty condition by which the world would judge this country, even as South Africa is judged.

Masscomm felt free to ignore or misrepresent the real plight of the Negro North and South because it is white, rich, and privileged, because of sheer delinquency, and because masscomm believes its audience dislikes disagreeable realities. So, instead, it offered Potemkin villages and spun-sugar homilies about the success of the American Dream.

These are significant and not isolated instances of the failure of masscomm in the first task of education, to inform and clarify. This sedulous nonconcern for the rights and dignity of Negroes may be contrasted to the roaring that goes up whenever a question is raised that seems to infringe on masscomm's rights and dignity. Freedom of the press was stridently invoked not long ago to justify masscomm's desire to underpay newspaper boys. Its role as conscience of the community is played with passion when masscomm's institutional interests are involved. The conscience slumbers when the interests are those of the unlucky or helpless.

Masscomm's role as defender of the strong against the weak is illustrated by the current concern with poverty. Americans found out about poverty when two or three angry young men pulled back a blanket of ignorance and neglect and uncovered 40 million or so Americans living in degradation. The invisible poor discovered by Michael Harrington were invisible because masscomm didn't care. Masscomm was busy elsewhere, counting profits, celebrating the status quo, selling rubbish. That masscomm even missed a bet with its constituency is evidenced by the current popularity of the war on poverty.

Masscomm's delight in the shoddy, the tasteless, the mind-dulling, the useless, is well-established. It is a direct consequence of masscomm's allegiance to organized rapacity. Ethical qualms about the effects of dishonest commercials disappear like morning mist in the glow of a comfortable advertising contract. Equally well-established is masscomm's tendency toward submerging significant issues in a sea of pointlessness. Thus an important public situation will somehow be related, in a cause-and-effect manner, to a participant's fondness for bowties or popcorn or beards.

These practices are said by some to be an inevitable concomitant of affluence and literacy, unimportant, and to be viewed merely as bubbly sidewaters to the strong central currents of American life. I do not agree. These practices amount to a policy of trivialization, and trivialization comes close to the heart of the indictment. For it is the human being, and his importance, that are finally trivialized. Masscomm is not interested in the human being as the subject of ultimate concern, but in consumers as the object of never-ending blandishments.

The general theory of responsibility stated earlier does not require that masscomm treat only important public matters, and that it ignore the immense carnival of contemporary life, its sideshows and heroes, achievements and banalities. Offerings for sale, and entertainment, and diversion are a part, but they are not all. The general theory requires only that fundamental duties not be obscured or neglected in favor of the carnival, that all be kept in context and balance. It is the context and balance that are destroyed by the policy of trivialization.

The pristine vision of the First Amendment is that of an untrammeled press, somehow standing apart from government and society, reining in excesses, raising standards, asking irreverent questions, cutting down villains and villainy, praising the virtuous. It is to be the master warts-and-all portraitist of the American scene.

But masscomm does not portray what is there. It does not stand apart. It has signed up with the Yankees, so to speak—with the rich and powerful, with the government, with the successful and prestigious. Signing-up means joining the team, contracting to safeguard its interests and to help win its games. It would not be easy any longer for masscomm to find its own ground, to achieve the separateness that seems to me its first requirement. Now this pledge of allegiance is a familiar enough count in the true bill against masscomm. But the supporting data are not merely those usually presented—the grotesqueries of advertising, the unwillingness to print the story about the wife of the department store owner, the unending concern with the Beatles and Dick and Liz.

The prime consequence of signing up is the stupefaction and brutalizing of the nation. All the dirty garbage in our social and cultural order cannot be dropped at masscomm's door, to be sure. Neither must its capacities, enhanced daily by new techniques, be under-estimated—the growing capacity to inform and clarify but also to assault, caress, fuddle, bloat, and deaden the human sensorium. Thus I agree with the Rt. Hon. W. F. Deedes, M.P., who recently said of television, "It has within its power to decide what kind of people we become. Nothing less." I would only make the statement retroactive and extend it to the rest of masscomm.

It seems to me beyond argument that masscomm is a chief contributor, though not the only one, to the social and cultural malaise lying on us all. This is so because masscomm is a major beneficiary. It can make more money not meeting its responsibilities than by doing so. American culture is marked by the compulsive consumption of trash, and by the ennobling of practices such as intentional obsolescence. Masscomm enthusiastically endorses such activities. Our environment turns into a visual junkyard, our rivers stink, and masscomm declares that it is all regrettable but commerce must be served. Strangers might conclude from masscomm that we are conducting a civilization virtually without blemish, full of grinning families playing games in marzipan neighborhoods, with no problems or future except those of assuring ourselves more grins and fun.

Nor is it happenstance—to move to another example—that violence, delinquency, and crime have mounted as this country has increased its reliance on the weapons of universal terror. We cannot really expect that counsels of reconciliation and reason will prevail in our domestic affairs when we resort to war abroad with all the lethal paraphernalia provided by technology. I do not intend to go into our national policy in Vietnam and elsewhere; I wish only to note masscomm's posture with respect to these policies and events and the effect of this posture on the ethical standards of the country. Americans are killing and maiming and burning and torturing in Vietnam. We may even get into a nuclear war, an eventuality that masscomm appears to believe may some time be necessary, though of course unfortunate. These present and potential activities display no fundamental moral issues, according to masscomm. They are acclaimed as a great patriotic exercise. Masscomm, putative bastion of our liberty, does not protest as we turn into a garrison state. Far from inquiring seriously into the demoralizing results on the nation of dependence on militarism, terror, and overwhelming might, masscomm applauds. "My country right or wrong" is the advice most often given to us, in these dangerous days, by editorial writers. Quite apart from the question of peace and coexistence, which must be our ultimate destiny if it is not to be that of a cinder, the issue is what happens to a civilization when its darkest instincts are constantly being stimulated. I think that what happens is that a civilization turns sour, and becomes insensitive, and sanctions murder and torture, and forgets its moral obligation.

Let us consider for a moment the instructive lesson in moral outlook of Germany twenty-five years ago, if one may do so without implying that the United States is tottering on the brink of Nazism. The worst thing that Hitler did to his country was to brutalize it. He ruined the national conscience. With the glad assistance of a signed-up mass communications system, he debauched the minds of two generations. Parading the spectre of communism up and down his country, he turned paranoia into patriotism. The people were being made ready for the great orgy, always with masscomm as the indispensable instrument.

In what ways are the situations alike, in what ways different? There is the same enemy, communism. There is the same concentration of industrial-military might. There are the same dreadful paradoxes dressed in newspeak, for example, calling acts of war acts of peace. The invasion of other countries is justified by appeals to national honor and security. Hitler had a final solution and used it on six million human beings. We have a final solution ready if all else fails, nuclear war. The difference in scale is impressive. It took Hitler many years, many people, many pits, gallows, and ovens to achieve his final solution. With far fewer helping hands and in one-thousandth the time we can exterminate fifty times as many people.

I do not suggest that it is the duty of masscomm to agree either with my analysis of where we stand in the race between genocide and humanity, or with my remedies. Its obligation is far greater: to remain disengaged from the apparatus, to criticize its aims and its claims, to keep ethical issues in clear view, to let the citizenry know what is happening to them as they lean more and more on muscle and less and less on mind; and, above all, to stay out of the cheering section. The press was guaranteed its freedom almost two hundred years ago so that it could keep an unwinking eye on government. The irony today is the degree to which it has become the apparatus's main support. Whatever sanity is entering U.S. policies in the Far East is coming via teach-ins and demonstrations, not via masscomm. I believe that our chance of becoming involved in nuclear war is directly proportionate to the shared warmth of the masscomm-industrial-military-government axis. The heat is already intense.

Self-righteousness is a wonderfully effective emotion for brutalizing a nation, and there is no agent superior to masscomm for filling the reservoir of national self-righteousness. The apparatus, abetted by masscomm, needs to be able to call on two ingredients. First, great economic and military strength, preferably massive enough to be a source of embarrassment and guilt. These sensations cry out to be transmuted into something worthy, and masscomm obliges by making our overwhelming capacity for violence appear to be the gift of a far-seeing Providence. Thus we become the policeman of the world, with hosannas from masscomm for our manliness.

Second, we need an enemy—not just any old enemy, but one who is sinister, conspiring, terroristic, atheistic, power-hungry, monolithic, anti-human, and un-human. We possess this ingredient, too. How much this enemy is genuine historical development and how much a U.S. manufacture is something that history will have to decide. My view is that the enemy is in many respects a product of masscomm, especially in attributing to him those capabilities which make him seem so much smarter, stronger, and less human than Americans are. It seems to me an open question whether the apparatus and masscomm have gone to all the trouble of helping to fabricate such a terrible and terrifying enemy only to learn that somehow they have got hold of the wrong fellow. We are slowly beginning to see, despite masscomm, that nationalism and hunger are the true rascals. The chronic revolution that we shall all spend the rest of our lives enduring and trying to understand is no more a product of communism than a toothache is a product of the dentist's chair, or a neurosis the infliction of the psychoanalyst's couch.

But this is not what we learn from masscomm. Editors and publishers and broadcasters notoriously like uncomplicated views. Communism and the Communists are such satisfactory villain material too, stubborn, eccentric, close-mouthed, suspicious, that they can be used as excuses for any amount of immoral behavior. This is not to say that there are no genuine clashes of interest and principle, nor that Communists are particularly comfortable people to have around, either in the neighborhood or in the world. It is not to say either that masscomm in this country is alone guilty of enemy-fabricating, for we know its foreign counterparts are every bit as adept in the art. It is indeed one of the curiosities of our time that it is so hard to see much difference between controlled and uncontrolled masscomm in this respect. Both are vehicles—especially where the issues of war and peace are concerned—for ". . . all the smelly little orthodoxies now contending for our souls," as George Orwell pointed out.

We are here close to the crux of the matter. A signed-up system of masscomm is bound to present an unreal view of the world. This has consequences ranging from the merely mortifying to the possibly lethal. Thus we have, at the one side, got ourselves in the horrible box of identifying all "national liberation" movements with communism, thus raising the status of Communists and lowering our own. On the other side, the partial views of Communists as incorrigible adventurers and military expansionists may lead us into the final big war.

Here we encounter masscomm's first and last line of defense against irresponsibility: We give the customers what they want. We are, masscomm declares, stockbrokers of the national passions. Assuming as I do that masscomm's responsibility is primarily that of continuing liberal education, I do not take the defense seriously. Liberal education is education befitting a free man, and tending to make him more competent in the exercise of his responsibilities. Liberal education aims at improving the intelligence and sharpening perceptions of good and bad. There is no such thing as education, liberal or otherwise, based on the lowest common denominator, except the education of slaves and vassals.

Anyone acquainted with the literature of masscomm knows that the dispute about the validity of its appeal to democratic dogma is endless; the apologists for masscomm tirelessly intone the obligation to give the customer what he wants. The equating of audience ratings and circulation figures with political principles seems to me defective. But I do not propose to add much to this ancient rhubarb here, except to indicate a significant paradox. The democratic thesis is that of consent, participation, and improvement. Citizens agree to the basic structure and direction of the nation. They take part directly and indirectly in its governance, and have no choice except to do so. The commonwealth is supposed to move onward and upward as a result.

But if the customers decide what they want to see, hear, and read, and if the customers appear to want mainly piffle, what happens to their competence for self-government? What if the tendency of masscomm is to make difficult and in some cases impossible the conditions for self-government? In his book, *Not in the Public Interest*, David Williams says, "An informed public opinion is the essential element in a country which claims to be democratic." But what is needed is not only information about yesterday's Congress and traffic accidents, but information about those crucial developments and those significant shadows on the horizon now seldom finding reflection in masscomm. I acknowledge that the country is somehow limping onward, despite the failures of masscomm and other great national institutions. But "We're getting by" is not a satisfactory answer either, for the ultimate questions are whether self-government is really working or is being turned over to elites and machines; and whether the criterion of consistent improvement is being met.

There is a variation in masscomm's answer about giving the customer what he wants. Masscomm says that it does not create social emptiness and cultural chaos, but merely reports what it finds. Masscomm portrays itself as the demotic conduit of social intelligence. "Too bad," it says, "that so much sludge passes through the conduit." Also, the answer continues, it is not the fault of masscomm that people prefer fantasy to fact and—this is always asserted with great emphasis—it is not masscomm's problem but theirs if people prefer entertainment to clarification.

Masscomm's great delusion is self-delusion. It deludes itself that because other institutions, the educational apparatus and the family among them, also mould the community masscomm does not really have any decisive effect on social conditions and cultural development. This is why it can, in all innocence, look under every bed but its own in a search for the explanation of crime, vandalism, and race riots. This is why it accepts no institutional responsibility for the rape of rivers and forests, and for the bloodthirsty campaigns of the right wing.

Another virulent species of self-delusion is masscomm's stated conviction that it can meet the full range of its social and cultural responsibilities in spite of its attachment to the highly favored sectors of the community. It is like trying to bunt toward third while standing on your head. Masscomm is, to repeat, a fully paid-up member of the American palatinate, the confederation of the powerful and privileged. Its loyalty and interest run to institutions, not to people. This signifies the bankruptcy of the educational function, where people are the essence of the teacher-and-taught transaction. Self-delusion persuades masscomm that it is meeting its obligations when it is making money, and that its critics are wrong in some sort of ratio to the margin of profit.

The best one can conclude, and also the worst, is that masscomm does not know any better, and that it assumes it is doing as well as anyone has a right to expect in functioning as the viaticum of privilege.

I would moderate the severity of these remarks if some motion toward improvement could be discerned. I see little or none. After every social calamity—the race eruption, the escalation of crime, an American war against Asians—acres of print and hours of network time are allotted to explanation and analysis. For such performance, which becomes a little better as calamity becomes more frequent, we owe brief thanks. But masscomm has not yet learned the simple lesson that the time to deal with catastrophe is before it happens, and the companion lesson that in this respect it has very great responsibilities indeed.

In this anticipatory role its performance ranges from nil to silly. The uprising of the California students was a masscomm scandal. But the problem at Berkeley had been forming for years; President Clark Kerr described the causes in a celebrated book months before the event. From the earliest flickerings of trouble, masscomm misunderstood and misstated what was going on. Thus must gratitude for the good post mortem be balanced with condemnation for ante mortem bad performance.

It must be asked, therefore, where else one might look for the positive assumption of social and cultural responsibility, that is, for the shifting of taste and sensibility and the general welfare to higher levels. One would hope first that as more people are better educated, the result would be a general elevation. The rising trade in concerts, good books and records, museums, and discussion groups is adduced as a fair wind already blowing from this quarter.

One would hope for the continuation of demonstrations, which by now are accepted as the "free press" of the movement to win justice for Negroes, to banish impersonality from the university and the corporation, and to spread the word that peace, not violence, is the only possible destiny for a nuclear-knowing world.

One would hope for the calling of a Constitutional Convention to get out into the open the great tangle of eighteenth century ideals and twentieth century conditions which produces the fundamental perplexities of our time. A Constitutional Convention would have to appraise masscomm and determine its fitness to continue under present immunities and privileges.

One would hope, without any good reason for doing so, that there might be a wholesale reform in the great Corporate Community, with priorities changed, in the words of the Administration, from "the quantity of our goods [to the] quality of our lives."

Perhaps no more utopian than these suggestions is the notion that the managers of masscomm might themselves, in the light of the enormous and increasing difficulties confronting the country, undertake a regeneration. They are after all not malevolent, or less patriotic and concerned about the fate of the commonwealth than anyone else. They are stuck in a system from which they could, given massive will, unstick themselves.

Yet these therapies are probably too unreal or drastic to be considered, and we shall have mainly to look to government, the resort when all else fails. Alexander Meiklejohn, one of this country's mightiest educators, was perhaps the most devoted friend that masscomm has ever had. Throughout his ninety-odd years he battled relentlessly for an absolute reading of the First Amendment. Precisely because he was an educator he saw in an unfettered system of mass communications the means of carrying out the social and cultural responsibilities available to no other institution. He saw mass communications as the necessary companion to his dream of lifelong liberal education. But just before he died a few months ago Mr. Meiklejohn perceived that the theory was failing, or had failed. So he proposed that his cherished First Amendment be revised by adding the words:

"In view of the intellectual and cultural responsibilities laid upon the citizens of a free society by the political institutions of self-government, the Congress, acting in cooperation with the several states and with non-governmental organizations serving the same general purpose, shall have power to provide for the intellectual and cultural education of all of the citizens of the United States."

The adoption of such a revision would express an official commitment to fill the holes left by masscomm in the continuing education of citizens. It would clear the way (if indeed the way needs to be cleared) for the establishment by government of a public network. Masscomm needs competition, contrast, example; the citizen needs alternatives and visions of better possibilities in his education as an adult.

But I have no idea whether affirmative government of the kind foreshadowed in such suggestions would work. What is significant to me in

Mr. Meiklejohn's proposal is the inference that the private motors we have counted on to propel us constantly into a finer community are virtually out of gas.

It will be protested that I ask too much. The answer is that my demands are those made of liberal education wherever it is being conducted. It will be complained that all of the foregoing is a statement of personal predilections as to the proper course of society. I shall say that this is true, and grant further that I have a different opinion of Americans and their aspirations from masscomm's opinion of them. At the same time I assert that I have been expressing a general view.

I believe there is in this nation a rising awareness of the tendency toward demoralization of the common life; a growing appreciation that citizenship is more important than consumership; an increasing fear that the human being will be lost beneath the lumber of technology and bureaucracy; a quickening guilt about the friendless, the impoverished, the victims of wholesale injustice; a widening comprehension that getting richer is not synonymous with getting better; an impatience with half-truths and semi-realities. And I believe that I speak in some way for this forming consensus. If mass communications can catch a glimpse of this other yearning America, there is a chance, perhaps a very slight one, that they may yet share in the making of an active, moral democratic order, in the United States and the world.

8.5 AUTOMATION AND LEARNING THEORY[*]

by George F. Kneller

I

Most of the theory underlying the practice of automated teaching is behavioristic. B. F. Skinner's machines are designed in accordance with his special theory of behaviorism; they meet certain specifications derived from his understanding of how we learn, chief among which are: (1) The student must *compose his own response* rather than select it from a number of alternatives (as with Sidney Pressey). (2) There is an immediate feedback, made possible through immediate knowledge of results. (3) Responses to be learned are arranged in minimal steps. (4) Learning is shaped by reward, allegedly with a minimum of error and frustration involved.

Skinner says that his machine behaves "very much like a tutor," hence is a vast improvement over mass education and passive learning. He lists five parallels between his machine and a tutor: (1) There is constant teacher-learner interchange; the student is always alert and busy. (2) An item of knowledge must always be thoroughly learned before the learner can pass along to the next item. (3) The material presented is only that for which the learner is ready. (4) Techniques of hinting, prompting, suggesting are built into the machine, thus helping the student to come up with the right answer. (5) The machine, like a tutor, reinforces correct responses and shapes behavior.

Approved methodology has respectable roots in the history of learning theory, which may be etched somewhat as follows: (1) Learning should proceed from the known to the unknown. (2) All things should be taught in due succession and only one thing at a time. (3) Teaching should be simple and straight-forward, not complicated. (4) Proper order, position, and interconnection of subjects should be preserved. (5) An item of knowledge should not be abandoned before it is thoroughly understood. (6) Instruction should be adapted to the ability of the learner. (7) Children should learn by doing.

Advocates of automated teaching claim that, while most teachers ascribe to these principles, they do not in fact carry them out, for

[*]Reprinted from *Proceedings of the Sixteenth Annual Meeting of the Philosophy of Education Society* (1960), pages 62-68 with permission of the author and publisher.

reasons which the teaching machine can help to overcome. Professor John D. McNeil of the University of California tells us that, as a self-instructional device, the machine carries a systematically developed program which presents subject matter so carefully gauged to a learner's ability to conceptualize through the use of the Socratic method, which are appropriate to the individual's level of attainment. It extends one's ability to conceptualize through the use of the Socratic method, which requires that the learner make "progressive discriminations." It engages the learner in a continuous interchange with the experts who compose the instructional material. Since questions are carefully graded and since "stimulators" are used, such as clues to answers, the learner is encouraged to make responses which bring success. The device immediately rewards the learner when the response is correct. If the response is incorrect, it provides additional helpful information or presents the same problem in a different manner.

So much for background theory. At this point it is appropriate to ask some questions about the theory and whether the teaching machine actually implements it.

Skinner suggests, first of all, that learning via teaching machines is tantamount to "shaping" animal behavior because environmental conditions and scheduled reinforcement can be controlled. "Shaped behavior," he says, implies a "specific response to a specific stimulus." But one cannot help wondering just *what kind* of behavior is being shaped and controlled. If an animal is faced with a novel situation, with different colored knobs, let us say, put in different places, we know that it is unable to react intelligently to any of the knobs. Precisely because the animal does not learn the *concept* of "knob-pushing" it cannot transfer its training.

In this connection, Howard H. Kendler asserts that "the area of transfer of training has been minimized, if not ignored, by most researchers in the 'teaching machine' area." Admittedly Skinner emphasizes what he calls the "mediational process," which postulates that "In some situations behavior is not directly linked to environmental stimuli, but instead is mediated by implicit responses that function as cues for subsequent implicit or overt behavior." Nevertheless, as Kendler asserts, Skinner tends to ignore the problem of transfer. Take, for example, Skinner's remarks:

> Students may continue to be grouped in "grades" or "classes" but it will be possible for each to proceed at his own level, advancing as rapidly as he can. The other kind of "grade" will also change its meaning. . . . If machine instruction assures mastery at every stage, a grade will be useful only in showing *how far* a student has

gone. C might mean that he is halfway through a course. Given enough time he will be able to get an A. . . .

The difficulty here, however, is that performance does not necessarily mirror what and how much has been learned in the sense of being inwardly digested, and capable of being transferred to another learning experience. Learning accomplishment is reckoned to be additive in nature; items of knowledge are piled on top of each other.

It is customary for behaviorists to assert that learning is nothing more than changed behavior. It is a process of "connecting" and "conditioning." But, as Bayles tells us, learning is really a change in insights. It is not a mere response or set of responses to the world of knowledge but rather *what I take the world to be*, whereon I may *fashion* my knowledge and hence my *design for living*. Knowledge has to be *patterned*, not piled item on item. For transfer, this means that three items are involved: (1) The opportunity for transfer should exist in the learning situation itself or in the environment. (2) This opportunity must be actually seen or felt by the student as a personal acquisition. (3) The idea of purpose or goal must exist; that is, the student must be *disposed* to take advantage of the opportunity. It is precisely the element of purpose, of the need for a personal goal, that is lacking in connectionist-behaviorist theory. If, therefore, we want transfer, we have to teach for insights which are widely applicable or generalizable. Built into teaching machines should be the element of concept-formation as configurational; not simply as after-thought or as an extension of the teaching quality of the machine, as it is now, with items of knowledge in additive style considered primary. In fact, with their present orientation, the machines may well give us a false concept of knowledge, its demands, and its proper uses.

Professor McNeil claims that by "helping the participant become aware of the pattern that constitutes right responses, machines further intellectual development." This would seem to mean that intellectual development depends upon giving right responses to the right stimuli, and that correct responses lead inevitably to correct concepts. But whether actual understanding takes place is all the more doubtful because we cannot be sure of what an individual can *do* with a concept once he has acquired it. As Robert M. Gagné of Princeton [now of Univ. of Calif. at Berkeley—ed.] says:

> The question of "understanding" is not one of how predictably a concept (or verbal response) can be supplied to varying stimulus situations. It is rather one of whether the student can *use* the concept in solving problems, perhaps even novel ones, and in the various forms of behavior that go under the name "thinking."

Studies on concept utilization by Kelleher, Kendler, and d'Amato show that, even if a particular concept is learned, it does not mean that it will be transferred only in one way. Transfer may indeed occur, but not necessarily the kind desired. If there is no guarantee that an understanding will have the right carry-over, how can real "intellectual development" take place?

Self-instructional devices, we read, "extend one's ability to conceptualize through the use of the Socratic procedure, which requires that the learner make progressive discriminations." Here one is compelled to wonder about the actual sources of genuine conceptualization. A concept, says Gagné, is "a (thought) process that intervenes between the stimulus situation and the pattern of responses which is observed." We may deal with a concept only when the responses that occur are "not situation-bound." Gagné cites two fundamental differences between behaviors shaped by instrumental conditioning and those by conceptualizations: (1) Shaping an instrumental response is a matter of connecting the response with a specific "discriminative stimulus," the shaping of behavior taking place via "specificity of stimulus control." On the other hand, conceptually mediated behavior shows a very great generality with respect to stimuli and results in "generalizability to new stimulus situations." (2) The shaped response is tied to a more or less immediately preceding stimulus; whereas concepts display the possibility of a delay, or an internal process, which is carried forward in time until triggered by another stimulus.

All this would indicate that a teaching program in arithmetic, for example, does not result merely in a set of responses like "9" to the stimulus situation "4 plus 5," but rather in the acquisition of a concept like "add," which can control *all* the great variety of specific responses used in handling whole numbers, decimals, and fractions. In spelling, what we need to develop is the ability to spell new words, not just the words that the student has learned. In both cases, a student is able, by the concepts he has understood, to solve a problem which he has not seen before and spell a word he has not learned.

Some awareness of the impasse, on the part of behaviorists, is demonstrated by Evan R. Keislar, who states that, in order to promote generalization within a broad class of items, "the learner should acquire a variety of verbal responses." These responses, through intraverbal associations such as verbal principles, definitions, or characteristics, may help evoke appropriate responses to new items later on. If this can be accomplished, Keislar says, automated teaching will result in "more than 'mere recognition' of the right answer."

In Kendler's opinion, however, transfer does not merely mean how responses can function as cues. Rather, it is "how simple verbal responses develop into abstract ones and these in turn result in still higher abstractions." The questions we should be working on are: (1) How does the cue function of abstractions change as level of abstraction increases? (2) How do different responses merge together to produce novel forms of intellectual behavior? As of now, we are still not clear about the mediational processes that generate novel behavior.

Resumé. It would therefore appear that principles involved in the transfer of training need to be examined far more carefully than commentators on teaching machines have done to date, and a better conception of the psychology of transfer and of symbolic processes must be achieved if we are going to do full justice to teaching machines. Progressive discrimination may, indeed, take place under automated teaching. But it is not a characteristic element of concept formation. Rather, it represents only a correct specific response to a specific situation. Conceptual learning involves "generalizability," which is its most striking characteristic and is the chief agent for facilitating the transfer of training.

III

I pass along to other doubtful claims. Skinner says, "The effect (of the machine) is surprisingly like that of a tutor," in that there is "constant interchange between the program and the student." However, it would appear that the *quality* of this interchange is so different as to destroy the analogy completely. A tutor may draw on his entire personality to change, modify, stimulate, goad, blame, praise, ridicule, encourage a student wherever needed. Students also work for teachers simply because they like them. How well will they like the machine? Skinner continues: "Like a good tutor, the machine insists that a given point be thoroughly understood before the student moves on." Understood, maybe, but how? Will it be personally appropriated? Will the student assimilate it? Will he be allowed to reject it? If so, How?

Both Skinner and McNeil state that, "Mistakes, if made, result in no social disapproval or ridicule from others." Certainly, there are advantages to be gained in working apart from the group. But, in a class of 30 students all of whom are working individually with a machine, the performance of each of them will eventually become known to others in the class, and social interaction will simply be delayed. Even so, social disapproval is something that the pupil had better get used to early in life. And, if mistakes can be made without social disapproval, they might either tend to lead to social irresponsibility or logically result in some sort of self-flagellation, which would be just as unfortunate.

I suggest, however, that the statement is vulnerable enough without my assaulting it further.

The teaching machine is supposed to remove drudgery from teaching. I am not so sure there is very much *genuine* drudgery in teaching as an act in itself. Commonly, drudgery is related to drill, to teaching straight content, to correcting papers. I am not prepared to admit that either drill or teaching straight content, or grading papers is something that should be handed over to a machine, unless I could be certain that the machine would actually do the job better; not better in the sense of more efficiently, but better in *all* aspects related to the comprehensive job of teaching. Teaching, like love, is a many-splendored thing; and true teaching, like true love, never runs smooth. Drill and content-inculcation and correcting papers are an essential and not an accidental part of the total job of teaching. As Thomas F. Gilbert says, "A good teacher is a more complicated, flexible 'teaching machine' than you could possibly build. If you can't get a good program into him, you will never get one into a mechanical gadget!"

For me, however, the greatest question of all relates to the kind of knowledge that is to be taught and tested for. In the programming of what passes for knowledge we shall have to be very careful indeed, for no more valid information can be derived from a set of data than is already inherent in the data. Although the *method* of producing information or knowledge in the student may be efficient and time-saving (the student showing up brilliantly when tested), the facts contained in the test will only reflect the accuracy of the content originally programmed into the machine.

It would also appear that, the moment we program material, we perforce tend to make statements and establish content in far too precise a manner. Answers must be positivistic and oriented exclusively toward objective, empirical data. I am not sure that the world of knowledge today is prepared to be so cold and precise. And, even if such precision were possible, the tendency of the machine would be to impress upon our students many a false notion regarding the nature of knowledge. I am not saying that the machine would actually do this. I am saying that we shall have to be very careful lest, in the interest of clean-cut content teaching or testing, machines leave false impressions about the proper nature of knowledge and of conceptualization.

I am also concerned about values. The more visionary of our experts on teaching machines predict that we shall also be able to teach and test for values, as, indeed, we are actually teaching logic by way of machines. But this can only mean that we have, or shall have, *norms* of values. Just how specific are value norms, or even value alternatives, in American democratic education? If they exist, they lie on a very elementary level of comprehension and are hardly subject to the kind of precise, objective discrimination that would be necessary for advanced programming. Other technologists presage the day when educational diagnoses can take place, much as with a motor car engine. But this would imply that we have in education a sort of mechanistic situation that can be scientifically or technologically analyzed and determined, or that education itself is largely a science capable of exact measurement, when the fact of the matter is that education itself really has very little that is accurately measurable or scientific about it.

Now all this does not mean that teaching machines should not be used. Rather it indicates that claims as to their efficacy and potentiality must always be guarded. It may very well be that machines can help us specify our values more clearly without necessarily assuming they must be normative. They may help us on our way toward finding more scientific data in order to yield a more objective assessment of the tasks of education. In short, machines may compel us to concentrate more on factor analysis in any field that is to be programmed, in order to reduce unnecessary or obstructive variability. And finally, the mathematical prowess of computers is such as to sort out many complex, quantitative arrangements that may keep the human mind from getting on with the central problem to be examined.

Indeed, the *teaching machine is here to stay*. We cannot separate education from automation any more than we can separate education from the impact of any other social force. It is a product of our day and age. And all this is as it should be, for education must not follow the laws of the Medes and the Persians and the Spartans, which never changed. On the contrary, we know from both biology and history that failure to adapt is the surest cause of defeat and extinction. Adjust or perish! Modern automation in teaching is the direct outcome of a new age in the advancement of human civilization, an age of science and technology. To state that education can remain a thing apart from this new age is to ask it to commit spiritual suicide.

But, for all I have said pro and con, the machines, I predict, will have hard going, not because of skepticism or hostility on the part of either public or teachers, but mostly because we shall probably never be able to keep them in constant repair. In the usual classroom I have rarely seen an audio-visual program work without a hitch, and faulty showings are frequently interrupted by loud guffaws, applause, and chuckles from students whose goals and values are at some divergence from those of the mechanical teacher. No. If history teaches us anything, the machines will fail because they will not always work. They will constantly need repair. Students will constantly try to beat the machine or throw it out of gear. We shall either have to have a corps of engineers always at hand or make engineers and technicians out of school teachers. And how many of them are mechanically-minded? Instead of having more time to spend on more important phases of education than mere drilling, our teachers will in turn have to apply themselves to repairing the machines, greasing them, adjusting their parts, policing students who are using them, locking them up for the night, covering them with cloths to keep off the dust, providing the business office with periodical inventories of all the machines and equipment and tools and gadgets in their possession. Thus the machines may fall under their own physical demands!

One final word of consolation to those who still fear complete mechanization: I heard tell the other day of a teacher who had just spent two hours visiting an IBM exhibition of automatic machines and on his way down the elevator an attractive woman screamed. It appears that a young man had pinched her. The teacher could not help but shout aloud in glee: "Thank heaven there are some things left that still have the personal touch!" If there is no one left on earth otherwise to guarantee this sacred fact, rest assured that the philosophers will gladly fulfill their duty!

CHAPTER NINE

PROFESSIONALIZATION
OF TEACHING

9.1 EDITORIAL COMMENT

The problem of professionalizing teaching has been with us for more than a century, and, while much progress has been made in this direction, the issue is still very much confused. The readings for this chapter have been selected with the idea of pointing to the significance of professionalizing teaching as well as helping to clarify the areas of controversy.

Dr. Willard Spalding's major concern in his "Some Thoughts About the Education of Teachers" is to make it quite clear that teaching as a profession is very much more than a matter of methodology on how to teach a subject. Teaching as a professional activity calls for a liberal education, skills in methods of instruction, a basic social philosophy, a community of mind, and a body of professional content to which the activity is related.

The fact that there has been a long recognized distinction between the knowing of a subject and the responsibility of teaching an individual is spelled out with meaningful significance in the James Carter essay on "An Institution to Prepare Teachers." Knowing that this essay was first published in 1825 causes one to reflect on why so little progress has been made in the intervening period on the resolution of this issue.

The article by Dr. Jerome Bruner on "The Functions of Teaching" adds much to the clarification of our thinking on the psychological aspects of the problem. Bruner stresses the leadership role and responsibility of the teacher as well as the continuing need for a more adequate theory of teaching.

In contrast with the point of view of the psychologist on teaching we have that of an educational philosopher in the article by Professor Harry Broudy on "Criteria for the Professional Preparation of Teachers." Points of greatest significance stressed by Dr. Broudy are (1) the teacher as a person; (2) the teacher as a member of a profession; and (3) the teacher as specialist. Justification for the teacher as a specialist can be found only in relation to his larger professional responsibility.

9.2 SOME THOUGHTS ABOUT THE EDUCATION OF TEACHERS*

by Willard B. Spalding

Over more years than I like to count, but each of which I recall with far more joy than grief, I have been engaged in activities involving teachers, teacher education, and teaching. Out of many rewarding interactions with others similarly engaged and out of much reading stimulated by these relationships I have accumulated an agglomerate of ideas about the education of teachers. I shall not try to relate each idea to other ideas, for to do so would force me to develop a structural framework which might reveal contradictions and inconsistencies which I now ignorantly enjoy. However, so that you may trace my progress through my remarks and have some realization of when I may complete them, I will divide them into four main parts: (1) educating teachers to teach; (2) educating teachers to become professionals; (3) educating teachers to share in the governance of schools; and (4) educating teachers to participate in public decisions about schools. In each part, I will describe some problems and suggest some solutions.

EDUCATING TEACHERS TO TEACH

When I first began to teach, texts and courses in methods explained what teachers should do and how they should do it. Explanation, demonstrations, assigning lessons, conducting recitations, drilling pupils were important acts of teachers. Like the maestro of a great orchestra, the skillful teacher led his pupils through the lesson, reaching a climactic crescendo when all did what was expected of them.

Early in my teaching experience I became aware of an heretical movement in methodology, stemming out of John Dewey's thinking, but coming to my first attention through the writings of Kilpatrick and Rugg. After receiving the new gospel, I joined the Progressive Education Association and participated enthusiastically in its conferences. Purpose, motivation, pupil-planning, projects, units, and evaluation now were important terms in teaching.

Some educators within this heretical movement formalized teaching into patterns and rituals, often known as plans, which were publicized

*Reprinted from *The Educational Forum*, Volume XXIX, No. 3 (March, 1965), pages 265-273, with permission of the author and Kappa Delta Pi, an Honor Society in Education, owner of the copyright.

far more widely than they were used; there is even some doubt about the extent to which the Dalton Plan was used in Dalton. Some rituals, like unit instruction, were used far more widely than they were understood.

Both the early proposals discussed at meetings of the Progressive Education Association and the formalized patterns developed elsewhere were derived both from learning theory and from beliefs about the roles of schools in a democratic society. As a consequence, the aims of instruction were supposed to be stated in terms of observable behaviors of pupils appropriate to a democratic society. Tests were seen more as diagnostic instruments than as measures of the degree of success in teaching. Grades like A, B, C, D, E were dropped in favor of descriptive phrases.

But teachers, on the whole, remained in control of classrooms. Master teachers continued to lead their pupils through approved behaviors: teacher-pupil planning, purposing, and so on. Group conformity characterized the pupils' planned searches for knowledge. Teachers rewarded pupils by using descriptive phrases as they had previously used grades.

Emphases upon methodology were seen by some scholars as lessening emphasis upon academic content to be learned. And there was more than a modicum of truth in the charge that stating the aims of teaching in terms of behavior of students omitted the objective of imparting knowledge of academic subjects. Progressive education, which had largely forgotten Dewey's original concern for mastery of content, became an opprobrious term used vehemently in the *argumenta ad homines* which characterized conflicts between "educationists" and "academicians." Out of the melees came a variety of polemic books, but among the polemics no classics appeared.

What did emerge was a scholarly concern about the content to be learned in various academic disciplines. Groups of academicians, often with some educationists attached, studied new and old knowledge in mathematics, biology, and physical science. Once decisions were made about "new" content to be taught, questions about how to teach it were inevitable. "Experiments" were conducted; methods were chosen or invented. Terms such as awareness of relationships, discovery, generalization, and learning how to learn became important. Bruner and others rediscovered John Dewey's theories, claiming them as their own. Teachers now developed skills by which they were able to lead their classes in approved ways to get expected results.

During all of these years, most theories of method were developed from theories of learning, with some attention to content and to the social context of the school. Teachers were not attentive to these theories but were continuing to be concerned about what they should do to produce expected results. They were simple-minded enough to believe that the best methods consisted of what teachers should do. In my early years, I was convinced that they were indeed simple minded; now, in my later years, I am equally convinced that their simplicity was wisdom. True, students are expected to learn in schools, so theories of method must have some positive relations with theories of learning. And since pupils are expected to learn subjects, theories of method must have some positive relations with theories of content. Nevertheless, theories of method can and should be derived from and explained by what teachers do when they do their best.

Currently, scholars in many papers of the world are studying the acts of teachers, with a variety of findings, some of which are not entirely consistent with others. Widespread intensive study of teaching in order to develop and add to theories of teaching is the most heartening current aspects of the field of educating teachers to teach. Enough results have been published to provide substance to pre-service, internship, and in-service courses in how to teach, each of which I will now describe.

A pre-service course in how to teach—and as I see it only one such course is needed—can combine current findings about methods of teaching with opportunities to observe professional teachers and with opportunities to practice teaching. Both observation and practice should be followed by classroom consideration of the extent to which theory was exemplified in the acts of teaching. The practice of teaching under these circumstances can be for relative brief periods at intermittent times. The course should aim at producing the level of competency required to begin work as an intern.

The years of internship can prepare students to begin the long years of professional work. As I see it, upon completion of undergraduate education—four years leading to a bachelor's degree—each beginning teacher would receive an intern's certificate entitling him to teach only under the general supervision of a college and of a professional teacher. He would receive a regular five-year certificate when his level of performance was adequate for continuing work as a beginning professional. During internship, colleges and school districts can join to provide continuing instruction and demonstration. Interns would be paid for half-time work and would study about half-time: the time to be spent at work and at study would be modified to meet varying circumstances. Intern teachers would continue to develop personal arts of teaching as they perfected their knowledge of theories of teaching under the guidance of professional teachers and of college faculty.

Pre-service and internship education of teachers to teach must include as much opportunity as possible to acquire knowledge of subjects taught, and especially of the two central elements in these subjects, their internal structures of relationships and their methods of scholarship.

Learning theory, as I see it, should be taught to a different end in pre-service from that in the internship years. Undergraduates need to learn how to learn, to acquire attitudes and abilities which will enable them to intentionally acquire new methods and new content as knowledge of each advances. A pre-service course in learning theory could provide a basis for learning how to learn. During internship students need to know how people learn when subject to teaching; a second course in learning theory could be directed toward this end.

Educating Teachers to Become Professionals

My first attendance at a teacher's convention was at Worcester, Mass. in the fall of 1925. In those days one could recognize such a convention by the simple device of crouching low in the rear of the hall and seeing the women's hats silhouetted against the proscenium. Teachers dress better today, and their conventions have also improved. Yet at this first meeting I heard Edwin Markham lecture on how to read poetry and William Burnham talk about normal human behavior; both men knew what they were talking about, and knew how to convey their knowledge to me.

The year 1925 provided my first experience with a superintendent who was determined to have a 100% professional faculty. By paying dues to the county, state, and national education associations one became professional. It was not until several years later, when we had both moved to other posts, that I learned that my partial non-conformity had been in vain—he had paid my dues to the county association and so had been able to report 100 per cent membership.

Over the years, professions have been studied thoroughly by scholars of a variety of disciplines. While all the answers about what is the nature of a "profession" are not yet in, enough are available to guide the education of teachers to become professionals.

First, a profession has a lore which is stated in technical language. The professional lore of the teaching profession is made up of theories and methods of teaching, of the history of teaching and of schools, of theories of content to be taught, of philosophies of teaching and of schools, in short of all that a professional teacher must know. Some of our lore is of high quality, some calls for improvement, in some areas it is almost non-existent. I could speak at considerable length, for example, on the need for greater knowledge of the heroes who exemplify the profession of teaching at its best.

In our use of technical language, we fall further below what is best. Teachers, especially those who are professors of education, should be proud of their use of the technical language of the profession of teaching. For far too many years we have been shamed by and ashamed of pedagese. Yet, a profession cannot become strong when would-be practitioners are careless in their choices of words to describe what they do and when they do not invent new terms to denote new practices. As we develop our technical language, call it pedagese if you will, let us do so with skill and with pride.

Second, each member of a profession is expected to act ethically and to expect other members to do the same. Professional action can protect the public from unethical practices. Without such action a beautifully written code has little value.

Third, the prerogatives of a profession which is composed for the most part of employed bureaucrats must be stated clearly and defended vigorously. Since most persons who hold positions in the higher levels of the bureaucratic hierarchy were once teachers, there are special problems in maintaining teachers' prerogatives against subtle pressures from principals, supervisors, and superintendents. The problems are further complicated when those in higher echelons seek to create the impression that they are still members of the profession of teaching when, in fact, they have entered the profession of educational administration.

Fourth, a profession becomes organized with four purposes in mind: (1) to improve the economic condition of its members, (2) to bring the profession's strength to bear upon development of public policy in areas of professional concern, (3) to improve the quality of its members performance, (4) to protect the public from practitioners who are not professionals or who are professionally unethical. The profession of teaching has been more effective in its efforts to achieve the first and second purposes than in efforts to achieve the latter two.

Pre-service education of teachers to become professionals requires not only critical examination of professions in general and of the profession of teaching in particular, but it also requires the development of students' commitment to becoming professionals. Here I do not advocate a special course; I prefer to see content about professions included in courses already suggested. Models of professional teachers can influence students substantially. Teachers whom students observe or who guide practice teaching can provide strong influences. College faculty can also be models of professional behavior.

But the most effective education to become professional will take place during internship as interns work with professional teachers, talk with them in many informal situations, and begin to participate in professional organizations. The college and the school district will develop instruction and experiences which will produce professionals.

Educating Teachers to Share in the Governance of Schools

On my first job, I taught five subjects, one of which I had never studied in college, and served as principal of a school with six teachers, enrolling pupils in grades 1-11. The superintendent told me what to do; I told the teachers what to do; and the school ran smoothly.

As I continued as principal and later as superintendent, I became adept at inspectorial supervision: sitting in the rear of the classroom; noting what the teacher did; leaving a carbon copy of my notes with the teacher; and returning later for a conference about what had gone on. For much of this time I was enrolled as a graduate student in summer sessions and was acquiring an understanding of and a commitment to progressive education at its best. So my notes contained comments about pupil-teacher planning, developing pupils' motivation to learn, a permissive atmosphere in the classroom, and other activities which I believed to be desirable and which I expected teachers to do.

Over the years I had developed some skill in conducting conferences to discuss my comments, and teachers generally felt free to disagree with them, to explain where I had missed something important, and to communicate fully about what they were trying to do. Some of the professionals among them questioned whether or not my behaviors in supervision were consistent with the behaviors which I expected of teachers.

At about this time I enrolled in a graduate course taught by Alfred Simpson in which he emphasized the participatory process in developing educational policy—a process in which laymen and professionals together examined local school systems and developed policy to guide their improvement. A basic principle of this process still seems sound to me, namely, that those who are intimately affected by policies should share in the development of these policies.

Eventually I attempted to combine what I then knew about teaching and learning and what I was learning about the participatory process in a chapter of the forty-fifth *Yearbook of the National Society for the Study of Education*. I expected it to be provocative and controversial, instead it was generally ignored. I still like most of it.

My experiences as Dean of the College of Education at the University of Illinois made me become increasingly aware of my need to acquire new roles in educational administration. For the first time, I was working with a faculty each of whom knew more about what he was teaching or studying than I did. I became convinced that an educational administrator working with a faculty of competent professionals should be subject to their advice but not to their commands. Advice should be available when an educational administrator (1) selects, retains, and promotes the most competent professionals he can find; (2) plans to secure for them working conditions and resources which will enable them to perform at their best levels of quality; (3) develops a structure of governance which will strengthen faculty influence upon the development of institutional policy; and (4) considers ways to encourage individuals to do the best that they can in whatever ways their professional judgment tells them are best.

I believe that educational administrators in public school systems will acquire these four roles, and that the speed with which this happens will be directly related to the growth of professionalism among teachers. When teachers become professionals, supervision will disappear; administration will become, and should become, a professional service to a professional faculty.

To a substantial degree, educating teachers to teach and to become professionals establishes a firm base for educating them to share in the governance of schools. For unless they know more about teaching and about what to teach than do administrators, they will be told what to do and how to do it. And unless they exhibit continuous self-improvement, administrators will organize them in in-service programs to this end. When teachers are perceived as lacking knowledge and skill and as satisfied with the quality of their teaching, they are often also perceived as unready to share fully in the governance of schools.

But further education is needed. Pre-service education can include formal instruction with related field work in the processes by which individual schools and school districts are governed, with special attention to the roles of the faculty. Internship can include observation and guided participation in the governance of the school and the school district where the intern is employed, with subsequent consideration in seminars of what takes place. Throughout a teacher's professional life, his professional organization should continue his education to share in the governance of schools.

Educating Teachers to Participate in Public Decisions about Schools

When describing the participatory process, I stated the principle that those intimately affected by a policy should share in the development of the policy. The participatory process and the principle underlying it deserve continuing use. However, the roles of the professional teacher and of the professional organization of teachers deserve further examination, especially since they can be learned in pre-service education, in internship, and in professional life.

Recently, in conversations with editors of magazines in various fields of education, I have pointed out that over the years most intelligent writers have changed their points of view about professional problems and their solutions as new evidence and new experiences led them to new conclusions. However, they continue to be embarrassed by accurate quotations of ideas which they now repudiate. I have suggested a new department entitled "I Recant," in which a writer would review his past publications and repudiate points of view which no longer present his perceptions of the truth. If any magazine establishes such a department, I will be eager to use it. Even the titles of two of my early articles embarrass me: "The Great American Public Does Not Want Good Schools" and "Teacher Organizations are Poor Stuff." Neither statement is true today.

One of the major reasons why people want good schools is because teacher organizations have helped them become aware of how good schools can be. Throughout the nation in bond elections and tax elections teacher organizations have participated vigorously and effectively in educating the public about quality and cost in public education.

Yet the task is not done nor will it ever be done, for each school must continue to adapt to expanding knowledge about what is taught and about how to teach it or it will lower its level of quality. Organizations of professional teachers need continuing programs through which the public learns about adaptations needed to maintain or achieve quality in public education.

Each program must be designed so that adaptations which are clearly the prerogatives of professionals are set apart from those which are clearly in the public domain. Obviously there will be some middle ground for debate over who should decide what. But as this debate continues, the middle ground will become as clearly delimited as are the prerogatives on both sides of it. And it will be substantially smaller than it is today.

Professional organizations should act vigorously to keep choices of methods out of both the public domain and the area of debate. Methods of teaching are among the unique behaviors which set teaching apart from other professions. A teacher's *choice of method* is subject to criticism from fellow professionals who possess more lore; his *results* are subject to criticism by the public. If Johnny can't read, his parents have every right to complain. When they do complain and if their complaints are correct, professional organizations should be ready to help Johnny's teacher improve his choices of methods. At the same time they should oppose vigorously any attempt by the public to impose a choice of method.

Another role of professional organization of teachers in influencing the development of policy about public schools is that of developing and supporting specific positions in respect to current issues affecting the development of quality in public education. Does *de facto* segregation affect quality in public education? If so, what does the profession of teaching propose to do about it? Does urban sprawl affect quality in public education? If so, what does the profession of teaching propose to do about it?

I could go on through a long list of issues. In respect to each I would ask the same two questions, for they imply the same two procedures: First, research to discover whether or not there will be adverse, favorable, or no effects upon the quality of public education; second, the development of proposals for action by the organized profession of teaching.

Finally, a professional organization should study its practices in influencing decisions about public education to insure that they involve and are supported by most of its membership and that they are appropriate to the profession of teaching.

Pre-service education of teachers to participate in public decisions about schools can include study of past and current issues; observation of professional organizations at work in local districts, in the state, and in the nation; and active participation wherever possible. Experiences in ringing doorbells to get out the vote, in distributing pamphlets, in speaking to various groups can be made available to students.

During internship, when opportunities for involvement in professional organizations increase, interns should be expected to participate under the guidance of the professionals with whom they work. And after internship, professional organizations should continue to educate their members to discharge effectively their professional responsibility to participate in public decisions about schools.

CONCLUDING REMARKS

Throughout my comments, I have talked about the education of teachers as if the structure of growth which I advocate were actually in use. I conclude my remarks by describing this structure briefly. It consists of three levels or stages in the development of professional teachers: pre-service education, internship, and professional.

The first level, pre-service education, ends with the receipt of a bachelor's degree and of a certificate to practice as an intern. In it there is a modicum of professional study, a major in academic work. It is designed to prepare students to serve successfully as interns. While primarily the responsibility of a college, it will involve cooperative interaction with schools and with the profession.

The second level, internship, ends with the receipt of a regular certificate to teach and may also yield a master's degree. In it there is part-time employment (not more than half-time) with a professional seminar in which interns, master professional teachers, and college faculty consider how to improve the interns' performance. Interns will continue academic study. Internship will be a joint responsibility of colleges and school districts, and will include active cooperation with the profession.

The professional level will persist for a teacher's working life. Here the professional organization is solely responsible, but it will cooperate actively with colleges and school districts.

9.3   AN INSTITUTION TO PREPARE TEACHERS[*]

by James G. Carter

The following outline constitutes Essay VI. of Essays on Popular Education, published by Mr. Carter in the Boston Patriot, with the signature of Franklin, in the winter of 1824–25. The series was commenced on the 17th of December, 1824; and the essay containing the outline was published on the 10th and 15th of February, 1825.

It will do but little good for the Legislature of the State to make large appropriations directly for the support of schools, till a judicious expenditure of them can be insured. And in order to this, we must have skillful teachers at hand. It will do but little good to class the children till we have instructors properly prepared to take charge of the classes. It will do absolutely no good to constitute an independent tribunal to decide on the qualifications of teachers, while they have not had the opportunities necessary for coming up to the proper standard. And it will do no good to overlook and report upon their success, when we know beforehand that they have not the means of success. It would be beginning wrong, too, to build houses and to tell your young and inexperienced instructors to teach this or to teach that subject, however desirable a knowledge of such subjects might be, while it is obvious that they cannot know how, properly, to teach any subject. The *science of teaching* —for it must be made a science—is first, in the order of nature, to be inculcated. And it is to this point that the public attention must first be turned, to effect any essential improvement.

And here let me remark upon a distinction in the qualifications of teachers, which has never been practically made; though it seems astonishing that it has so long escaped notice. I allude to the distinction between the possession of knowledge, and the ability to communicate it to other minds. When we are looking for a teacher, we inquire how much he *knows*, not how much he can *communicate;* as if the latter qualification were of no consequence to us. Now it seems to me that parents and children, to say the least, are as much interested in the latter qualification of their instructor as in the former.

Though a teacher cannot communicate more knowledge than he possesses, yet he may possess much, and still be able to impart but little. And the knowledge of Sir Isaac Newton could be of but trifling use to

*Reprinted from James G. Carter, *Normal Schools and Other Institutions, Agencies, and Means Designed for the Professional Education of Teachers* (Hartford, Connecticut: Case Tiffany and Company, 1851), pages 75-83.

323

a school, while it was locked up safely in the head of a country school-master. So far as the object of a school or of instruction, therefore, is the acquisition of knowledge, novel as the opinion may seem, it does appear to me that both parents and pupils are even more interested in the part of their teacher's knowledge which they will be likely to get, than in the part which they certainly cannot get.

One great object in the education of teachers which it is so desirable on every account to attain, is to establish an intelligible language of communication between the instructor and his pupil, and enable the former to open his head and his heart, and infuse into the other some of the thoughts and feelings which lie hid there. *Instructors and pupils do not understand each other.* They do not speak the same language. They may use the same words; but this can hardly be called the same language, while they attach to them such very different meanings. We must either, by some magic or supernatural power, bring children at once to comprehend all our abstract and difficult terms, or our teachers must unlearn themselves, and come down to the comprehension of children. One of these alternatives is only difficult, while the other is impossible.

The direct, careful preparation of instructors for the profession of teaching, must surmount this difficulty; and I doubt if there be any other way in which it can be surmounted. When instructors understand their profession, that is, in a word, when they understand the philosophy of the infant mind, what powers are earliest developed, and what studies are best adapted to their development, then it will be time to lay out and subdivide their work into an energetic system of public instruction. Till this step toward a reform, which is preliminary in its very nature, be taken, every other measure must be adopted in the dark; and, there-fore, be liable to fail utterly of its intended result. Houses, and funds, and books are all, indeed, important; but they are only the means of enabling the minds of the teachers to act upon the minds of the pupils. And they must, inevitably, fail of their happiest effects, till the minds of the teachers have been prepared to act upon those of their pupils to the greatest advantage.

If, then, the first step toward a reform in our system of popular education be the scientific preparation of teachers for the free schools, our next inquiry becomes, How can we soonest and most perfectly achieve an object on every account so desirable? The ready and obvious answer is, establish an institution for the very purpose. To my mind, this seems to be the only measure which will insure to the public the attainment of the object. It will be called a new project. Be it so. The concession does not prove that the project is a bad one, or a visionary, or an impracticable one. Our ancestors ventured to do what the world had never done before, in so perfect a manner, when they established the free schools. Let us also do what they have never so well done yet, and establish an institution for the exclusive purpose of preparing instructors for them. This is only a second part, a development or consummation of the plan of our fathers. They foresaw the effect of universal intelligence upon national virtue and happiness; and they projected the means of securing to themselves and to us universal education. They wisely did a new thing under the sun. It has proved to be a good thing. We now enjoy the results of their labors, and we are sensible of the enjoyment. Their posterity have praised them, loudly praised them, for the wisdom of their efforts. Let us, then, with hints from them, project and accomplish another new thing, and confer as great a blessing on those who may come after us. Let us finish the work of our fathers, in regard to popular education, and give to it its full effect. Let us double, for we easily may, the happy influences of an institution which has already attracted so much notice from every part of our country, and drawn after it so many imitations, and send it, thus improved, down to posterity for their admiration.

If a seminary for the purpose of educating teachers scientifically be essential in order to give the greatest efficacy to our system of popular education, then, in the progress of the discussion, the three following questions arise in the order in which they are stated. By whom should the proposed institution be established? What would be its leading features? And what would be some of the peculiar advantages to the public which would result from it? To answer these several questions at length would require a book; while I have, at present, only leisure to prepare one or two newspaper essays. A few hints, therefore, upon the above three topics are all that I dare profess to give, and more than I fear I can give, either to my own satisfaction or that of those readers who may have become interested in the subject.

The institution, from its peculiar purpose, must necessarily be both literary and scientific in its character. And although, with its design constantly in view, we could not reasonably expect it to add, directly, much to the stock of what is now called literature, or to enlarge much the boundaries of what is now called science, yet, from the very nature of the subject to which it would be devoted, and upon which it would be employed, it must in its progress create a kind of literature of its own, and open a new science somewhat peculiar to itself—the science of the development of the infant mind, and the science of communicating knowledge from one mind to another while in a different stage of maturity. The tendency of the inquiries which must be carried on, and the discoveries which would be constantly made, in a seminary for this new purpose, would be to give efficacy to the pursuits of other literary and scientific institutions. Its influence, therefore, though indirect, would be not the less powerful upon the cause of literature and the sciences generally. These remarks may seem to anticipate another part of my subject; but they are introduced here to show that a seminary for the education of teachers would stand, at least, on as favorable a footing in relation to the public, as other literary and scientific institutions. It seems now to be believed that the Legislature of the State are the rightful proprietors of all public institutions for the diffusion of knowledge. And if they are of any, they certainly ought to be of one for such a purpose. Because there are none in which the public would be more deeply interested. There are none which would tend so much to diffuse knowledge among the whole mass of the people. And this, as has been before remarked, is a solemn duty enjoined upon our government by the constitution under which they are organized, and from which they derive their authority. Besides, it is the first impulse of every government, operating as quickly and steadily as instinct, to provide for its own preservation. And it seems to be conceded on all hands, by the friends as well as the enemies of freedom, that a government like our own can only exist among a people generally enlightened; the only question as to the permanency of free institutions being, whether it be possible to make and to keep the whole population of a nation so well educated as the existence of such institutions supposes and requires.

Our government, therefore, is urged by every motive which the constitution can enjoin or self-preservation suggest, to see to it that knowledge is generally diffused among the people. Upon this subject of popular education, a *free* government must be *arbitrary;* for its existence depends upon it. The more ignorant and degraded people are, the less do they feel the want of instruction, and the less will they seek it. And these are the classes of a community which always increase the fastest up to the very point, where the means of subsistence fail. So that if any one class of men, however small, be suffered as a body to remain in ignorance, and to allow their families to grow up without instruction, they will increase in a greater ratio, compared with their numbers, than the more enlightened classes, till they have a preponderance of physical power. And when this preponderance becomes overwhelming, what hinders a revolution and an arbitrary government, by which the mind of a few can control the physical strength of the many?

If this reasoning be correct, a free government must look to it betimes, that popular ignorance does not gain upon them. If it does, there is a thistle in the vineyard of the republic, which will grow and spread itself in every direction, till it cannot be eradicated. The ignorant must be allured to learn by every motive which can be offered to them. And if they will not thus be allured, they must be taken by the strong arm of government and brought out, willing or unwilling, and made to learn, at least, enough to make them peaceable and good citizens. It would be well, indeed, if the possibility could be held out to all of successfully aspiring to responsible stations in society. A faint hope is better than despair. And though only one chance in a thousand be favorable, even that is worth something to stimulate the young to greater efforts, to become worthy of distinction. The few who, under all the disadvantages which adverse circumstances impose, can find their way by untired perseverance to places of trust and influence in the republic, serve to give identity of feeling, of purpose, and pursuit to the whole. They harmonize and bind together all those different and distant classes of the community, between which fretful jealousies naturally subsist.

These are hints, only, at an argument, perhaps unintelligible ones, to establish the principle, that free governments are the proprietors of all literary and scientific institutions, so far as they have the tendency to diffuse knowledge generally among the people. The free schools of Massachusetts, as the most efficient means of accomplishing that object, should therefore be the property and the peculiar care of government. An argument will, at once, be drawn from these principles why they should assume the direction of the schools, so far as to insure to the people over whom they are appointed to preside, competent teachers of them. And as this is the main purpose of the proposed institution, the reasoning seems to be conclusive why they should be its proprietor, or, at least, its patron and protector.

An institution for the education of teachers, as has been before intimated, would form a part, and a very important part, of the free-school system. It would be, moreover, precisely that portion of the system which should be under the direction of the State, whether the others are or not. Because we should thus secure at once, a uniform, intelligent, and independent tribunal for decisions on the qualifications of teachers. Because we should thus relieve the clergy of an invidious task, and insure to the public competent teachers, if such could be found or prepared. An institution for this purpose would become, by its influence on society, and particularly on the young, an engine to sway the public sentiment, the public morals, and the public religion, more powerful than any other in the possession of government. It should, therefore, be responsible immediately to them. And they should carefully overlook it, and prevent its being perverted to other purposes, directly or indirectly, than those for which it is designed. It should be emphatically the State's institution. And its results would soon make it the State's favorite and pride, among other literary and scientific institutions. The Legislature of the State should, therefore, establish and build it up, without waiting for individuals, at great private sacrifices, to accomplish the work. Such would be the influence of an institution for the education of teachers; and such is the growing conviction of the strength of early associations and habits, that it cannot be long before the work will be begun in some form. If it be not undertaken by the public and for public purposes, it will be undertaken by individuals for private purposes.

The people of Massachusetts are able and willing, yea, more than willing, they are anxious to do something more for popular education, for the diffusion of knowledge generally. The only questions with them are how and where can means be applied to the purpose to the greatest advantage. It may safely be submitted, by the friends of the free schools, to a republican people and their republican government, which institutions on comparison most deserve the public bounty; those whose advantages can be enjoyed but by a few, or those which are open to the whole population; those which have for their main objects good that is remote, or those whose happy influences are left at once, through the whole community. Which institutions deserve the first consideration, and the most anxious attention of a popular government, those which will place a few scholars and philologists upon a level with the Germans in a knowledge of Greek accents, or those which will put our whole people upon the level of enlightened men in their practical knowledge of common things? These objects may all be important to us. But the former will be provided for by individuals; the latter are the peculiar care of government.

The next question, mentioned above, as arising in the progress of this discussion, was, what would be the leading features of an institution for the education of teachers. If the institution were to be founded by the State, upon a large scale, the following parts would seem to be obviously essential. 1. An appropriate library, with a philosophical apparatus. 2. A principal and assistant professor in the different departments. 3. A school for children of different ages, embracing both those desiring a general education, and those designed particularly for teachers. 4. A Board of Commissioners, or an enlightened body of men representing the interests and the wishes of the public.

1. A library should of course be selected with particular reference to the objects of the institution. It would naturally and necessarily contain the approved authors on the science of education in its widest sense. It would embrace works of acknowledged merit in the various branches of literature and science intimately connected with education; such as

anatomy and physiology, the philosophy of the human mind and heart, and the philosophy of language.

Physical education forms a very essential part of the subject, and should be thoroughly understood. This branch includes the development of all the organs of the body. And works upon the physiology of children should be added to the library. Books on gymnastics, containing directions for particular exercises adapted to the development of the several organs, belong to the library of the accomplished instructor, as well as to that of the surgeon. Indeed, if the former properly use them, they will enable him to give a firmness to the parts of the body which may, perhaps, supersede the necessity of the interference of the latter to set them right in manhood.

The philosophy of the infant mind must be understood by the instructor before much progress can be made in the science of education; for a principal branch of the science consists in forming the mind. And the skill of the teacher in this department is chiefly to be seen in his judicious adaptation of means to the development of the intellectual faculties. Every book, therefore, which would aid in an analysis of the youthful mind, should be placed in the library of the proposed institution.

The human heart, the philosophy of its passions and its affections, must be studied by those who expect to influence those passions, and form those affections. This branch of the subject includes the government of children, especially in the earliest stages of their discipline. The success of the teacher here depends upon the good judgment with which he arranges and presents to his pupils the motives that will soonest move them, and most permanently influence their actions. The mistaken or wicked principles of parents and instructors, in this department of education, have, no doubt, perverted the dispositions of many hopeful children. If successful experience has been recorded, it should be brought to the assistance of those who must otherwise act without experience.

Lastly, the study of the philosophy of language would be essential to the scientific teacher. The term language is not here understood to mean a class of words called Greek, or another class of words called Latin, or even that class of words which we call English. It means something more general, and something which can hardly be defined. It embraces all the means we use to excite in the minds of others the ideas which we have already in our own minds. These, whatever they are, are included in the general definition of language. This is a great desideratum in our systems of education. We do not possess a language by which we can produce *precisely* the idea in a pupil which we have in our own mind, and which we wish to excite in his. And impatient and precipitate teachers quite often quarrel with their pupils, because they do not arrive at the same conclusions with themselves, when, if they could but look into their minds, they would find that the ideas with which they begin to reason, or which enter into their processes of reasoning, are altogether different. Every book or fact, therefore, which would do any thing to supply this desideratum, or enable the teacher better to understand precisely the idea which he excites in the mind of his pupils, should be collected in the instructor's library.

2. The institution should have its principal and its assistant professors. The government and instruction of a seminary for the education of teachers would be among the most responsible situations which could be assigned to men in literary or scientific pursuits. As many of the objects of the institution would be new, so the duties of its instructors would also be new. No commanding minds have gone before precisely in the proposed course, and struck out a path which others may easily follow. There are no *rules* laid down for the direction of those who will not think upon, or who cannot understand the subject. Men must, therefore, be brought to the task who have the ability to observe accurately and to discriminate nicely. They must also collect the results of what experience they can from books and from others, in order to enable themselves to form some general principles for the direction of their pupils, who will go abroad to carry their improvements to others. It is not supposed for a moment that all who may receive instruction at the proposed institution with the intention of becoming teachers, will necessarily be made thereby adept in the science, any more than it is believed that all who happen to reside four years within the walls of a college are necessarily made expert in the mysteries of syllogism and the calculus. But having seen correct general principles of education successfully reduced to practice, they may, at least, become *artists* in the profession, and be able to teach pretty well upon a system, the philosophy of which they cannot thoroughly comprehend.

3. A school of children and youth of different ages and pursuing different branches of study would form an essential part of the institution. In the early stages of the education of children, the discipline should consist almost wholly of such exercises as serve to develop the different faculties and strengthen all the powers of the mind. And in the subsequent education of youth, when the discipline comes to consist partly in the development of the mind, and partly in the communication of knowledge, the course of instruction would be the same, whether the pupil were destined to be a teacher or not. The objects of the institution do not, therefore, become peculiar till after the pupil has acquired a certain degree of freedom and strength of mind; nor till after he has made the acquisition

of the requisite amount of knowledge for the profession of teacher. Though a pupil would necessarily inbibe a good deal of clearness and method in his intellectual exercises by submitting the direction of them to a skillful instructor, the study of the science of teaching cannot properly begin till he changes relations with those about him; and, instead of following a course prescribed by another, and exhibiting the powers of his own mind without an effort to take cognizance of them, he assumes to look down upon humbler minds, to direct their movements, and to detect and classify the phenomena of their subtle workings.

After the young candidate for an instructor, therefore, has acquired sufficient knowledge for directing those exercises and teaching those branches which he wishes to profess, he must then begin his labors under the scrutinizing eyes of one who will note his mistakes of government and faults of instruction, and correct them. The experienced and skillful professor of the science will observe how the mind of the young teacher acts upon that of the learner. He will see how far and how perfectly they understand each other, and which is at fault if they do not understand each other at all. If the more inexperienced teacher should attempt to force upon the mind of a child an idea or a process of reasoning for which it was not in a proper state, he would be checked at once, and told of his fault; and thus, perhaps, the pupil would be spared a disgust for a particular study, or an aversion to all study. As our earliest experience would in this manner be under the direction of those wiser than ourselves, it would the more easily be classed under general principles for our direction afterward. This part of the necessary course in an institution for the education of teachers might be much aided by lectures. Children exhibit such and such intellectual phenomena; the scientific professor of education can explain those phenomena, and tell from what they arise. If they are favorable, he can direct how they are to be encouraged and turned to account in the development and formation of the mind. If they are unfavorable, he can explain by what means they are to be overcome or corrected. Seeing intellectual results, he can trace them, even through complicated circumstances, to their causes: or, knowing the causes and circumstances, he can predict the result that will follow them. Thus every day's experience would be carefully examined, and made to limit or extend the comprehension of the general principles of the science. Is there any other process or method than this to arrive at a philosophical system of education? If any occurs to other minds, it is to be hoped that the public may soon have the benefit of it.

4. The fourth branch, which I mentioned above as constituting an important part of an institution for the education of teachers, was a Board of Commissioners. Although they would, probably, have but little to do

with the immediate government and instruction of the institution, they would be valuable to it by representing the wishes of the community, and by bringing it more perfectly in contact with the public interests. Besides, it must occur to every one, that in the general management of such an establishment, many of the transactions would require characters and talents very different from those that would, generally, be found in the principal or professors. Men might easily be found who would lecture to admiration, and yet be wholly incompetent to assume the general direction of the establishment. The professors, too, would always want assistance and authority in determining what acquisitions should be required for admission into the institution, and what proficiency should be deemed essential in the candidates before leaving it to assume the business of teaching. Upon what principles shall the school be collected? How shall the privilege of attending as new learners in the science of education be settled upon applications from different parts of the State or country? These and many similar questions would render a body of men, distinct from the professor, important to the institution. Many decisions, too, must necessarily be made, affecting individual and private interests. This would be an invidious duty, and the instructors should be relieved from it as far as possible. It is confidently believed that the peculiar advantages to be enjoyed at such an institution by children and youth generally, as well as by those designed for teachers, would command a price sufficient to defray nearly the whole expenses of the establishment. If not so, then might not each town send one or more young men to the institution to be properly educated for instructors, and require them in return to teach their public schools to liquidate the expense? All these means, however, are subjects for future consideration, and are to be devised after the utility of the institution has been demonstrated.

The peculiar advantages of an institution for the education of teachers would be far too numerous and too important to be either embraced or enforced in the space which remains for this topic. A few, therefore, of the most obvious ones are all that can here be alluded to. One advantage, and a very certain one, would be to raise the character of teachers generally; and consequently, in the same degree, the character of the schools which they teach. Let us pause, for a moment, to consider to what an extent we are interested in every thing which affects our system of public instruction; and hence derive a motive, before we pass on, to enforce attention to every suggestion for improvement in it.

There were in the district of Massachusetts, according to the census of 1820, five hundred and twenty-three thousand one hundred and fifty-nine souls. Of this number, two hundred and forty-one thousand seven hundred and eleven were under the age of eighteen years. The numbers have since been much augmented. If the population has increased only as fast since the last census as it did between the census of 1810 and that of 1820, there are now, in round numbers, about two hundred and fifty thousand children and youth in Massachusetts under the age of eighteen years. This, it will be perceived, amounts to almost one-half of the whole number of souls. If we take from the older those between the ages of eighteen and twenty-one, and add them to the younger part of the population, we shall find at least half, and probably more than half of the whole, under twenty-one years.

These are all flexible subjects of education, in its most comprehensive sense; though they are not all within the influence of that part of it which can be easily controlled by legislation, or indeed by any means except by an enlightened public opinion. A few of this great number have left the schools and all direct means of education, and entered upon the active business of life. And a portion of the younger part of them are yet subjects only for domestic education. But after these deductions from the two extremes, it will not be extravagant to state, that one-third of the whole population are of a suitable age, have opportunity, and do actually attend school some portion of the year. In Massachusetts we have not the means of knowing accurately the numbers of children and youth who attend our schools; because we have no system of returns to any public authority, by which such facts can be ascertained. But I am confirmed in the belief that the above is not an extravagant estimate, by two circumstances. One of them is, several towns have been carefully examined, and this is about the proportion of the population found in their schools. And the other is, official documents and acknowledged authorities from the neighboring State of Connecticut informs us that one-third of the population attend their free schools a part of the year. And probably the same would be found to be true of New York, as well as of the remainder of the New England States.

These are statistical facts. Others may reason upon them and draw what conclusions they can, about immigration, the future prospects of New England, her comparative influence in the Union, and the facilities she affords for a *manufacturing district*. They have been introduced here because they suggest motives stronger than any others, to enforce attention to our means of popular education. One-third of our whole population are now at that period of life when their principles and characters are rapidly forming. Habits, both moral and intellectual, are taking their direction, and acquiring the strength of age. In all this, the schools must have a deep influence. Both the degree and the kind of influence are, to a certain extent, within our control, and consequently depend upon our efforts. In twenty years, and surely twenty years are not beyond the ken of a tolerably clear-sighted politician, this part of our population will succeed to most of the responsible places and relations of their fathers. They must receive all that we have to leave for them. They must take our names, and attach to them honor or infamy. They must possess our fortunes, to preserve or disperse them. And they must inherit our free institutions, to improve, pervert, or destroy them. Here, then, are the strongest political motives, as well as paternal affection, urging upon us attention to all the means of forming correctly the characters of those who are to receive from us our choicest blessings. And what means within our control can be devised more efficient for this purpose, than those primary seminaries for instruction, where the mass of the people must receive several years of their education? Find, if they are to be found, or create, if they are not now to be found, a class of teachers *well skilled* in their profession, and put them into all our free schools. What an effect would soon be produced in their condition! And what a renovating influence these same schools would soon have upon the character of the whole people who have access to them!

But these are general advantages of a good class of teachers. I promised to speak of the peculiar advantages of the proposed institution to produce them. The library, collected with particular reference to the objects of the institution, would contain the *facts* of the science of education scattered along in the history of the world. Facts are the materials of philosophy. And we cannot philosophize, safely, till we have an extensive stock before us. The library would naturally collect, not only those phenomena relating to the subjects which have already been observed, but also the records of those which must be daily passing before our eyes. Books connected with and collateral to the science will be as important to the purposes of the institution as those professedly written upon the subject. And frequently they will be found to be much more so. Because the former contain the facts and the phenomena, while the latter have only an author's reasoning and conclusions upon them. And the authors who have written upon education, with very few exceptions, have reasoned speciously, but from very limited and imperfect inductions. So that their conclusions, though they may be correct, as far as they had the necessary means of making them so, are liable to fail, totally, when reduced to practice under circumstances a little different from those from which the principles have been formed. We want more experience before we begin to reason at large and to draw sweeping conclusions on the subject. And our library would be chiefly valuable as containing that experience, or the results of it, accurately and authentically recorded.

But the conclusions of writers on the subject, though received and repeated by every body, are not binding and beyond question, till we know that the facts from which they reasoned are *all* which can affect the principles that they deduce from them. And to believe that the experience of two thousand years, embracing the present age, which is so full of phenomena of all kinds, has not added something to our means of a copious and safe induction to principles of education, requires a stretch of credulity with which my mind is not gifted. It will be safer, as a general rule, to assume that they teach us what to avoid, rather than what to imitate.

When we have collected the means of reasoning correctly, which books can afford, and added to them the living materials of philosophy, which will be constantly exhibited in the school which is to form a part of the institution, we are to place all these before instructors of discriminating minds, who are able and willing to *observe* as well as to reason. We are, then, to turn the public attention toward them in good earnest, and let them see that something is expected from them. There is a moral certainty, under such circumstances, that the expectation will be gratified. When the public attention is turned toward any subject, all the ardent and discriminating minds act in concert. And like the rays of the sun converged to a point by a lens, they act with an intensity which must produce an effect.

It would be a natural result of the proposed institution to organize the teachers into a more distinct profession, and to raise the general standard of their intellectual attainments. It would therefore concentrate and give energy and direction to exertions and inquiries, which are now comparatively wasted for want of such direction. No one, indeed, can now foresee, precisely, what effect would be produced upon our systems of education and principles of instruction by subjecting them to such an ordeal. To foretell the improvements that would be made, would be to make them, and supersede the necessity of an institution for the purpose. Though the necessity would still remain for some similar means to propagate them among the people. But if our principles of education, and particularly our principles of government and instruction, are not already perfect, we may confidently expect improvements, though we may not know, precisely, in what they will consist.

Many persons knew twenty years ago that steam was expansive. But who foresaw the degree to which its expansion could be raised, or the purposes to which it could be applied? Public attention was turned to the subject in earnest, and we now see vessels moving in every direction by its power. It was known long since that light wood would float, and water run down hill. But who foresaw, twenty years ago, the present state of our internal improvement by means of canals? Public attention and powerful minds were directed to the subject, and we now see boats ascending and descending our mountains, and traversing our continent in every direction. Those who were before almost our antipodes, have now, by the facilities of communication, become our neighbors. The most intrepid prophet would hardly have dared, even ten years ago, to predict the present state of our manufactories. This has all been done, because it could be done, and many minds were turned to the subject, and resolved that it should be done. All these are in many respects analogous cases, and go to show that we do not always know how near to us important improvements are; and that it is only necessary to direct the public attention to a subject in order to insure some inventions in it.

A great variety of other peculiar advantages to the public, it occurs to me, must arise from an institution for the education of teachers. But I have confined myself to those only which seemed to be the most striking and important. All others will be found to be involved, in a great degree, or wholly, in those which I have stated. And although to enumerate them might add some new motives for attention to the subject, they could not strengthen much the argument in favor of an institution somewhat like that which has been above described. I must now take my leave of the subject for the present; my only regrets being that I have not had ability to do more justice to the several topics which I have discussed, nor time to do more justice to my own views of them.

9.4   THE FUNCTIONS OF TEACHING*

by Jerome S. Bruner

I should like to beg of you that you grant me the privilege of innocence. It is not my intention of passing in review the various theories
that now exist concerning the proper function of teaching, then to weigh
and evaluate these in the interest of a synthesis. I do not have the requisite learning for such a venture. Nor is it what really I want to do. My
intent, rather, is to examine the nature of the processes involved in
communicating knowledge and, in a certain measure, to examine the
structure of knowledge as we have come to understand it in the past
decade, and in the light of these two considerations, to examine what the
unique position of teaching and teachers might be. My warrant for asking this privilege of innocence is not very strong, for though I have
taught for fifteen years and been taught still longer, that gives me no
more warrant to speak than I would have if the subject were the nature
of prose, and I have been speaking prose longer than I have either
taught or been taught. The remainder of my warrant rests upon the fact
that I have busied myself for more than a decade with the nature of
the knowing process—cognition as it is called in the catalogues. But
what my efforts have yielded is the firm conviction that while we know
a certain amount about learning and about thinking, we know precious
little about teaching and its functions. So I shall use this opportunity to
examine the shape of the gaps. I hope I fare as well as Lord Russell
who long ago gave a lecture at Harvard on the philosophical implications
of quantum theory and relativity when these implications were even less
well understood than they are today. When his exposition was completed,
Alfred North Whitehead, who was chairing the meeting, congratulated
Lord Russell by saluting him for not having obscured the great darkness
of the subject.

Sparing the Learner the More Dangerous
Consequences of Learning

Let me begin by proposing that the first function of the teacher and
teaching is to spare the learner the more dangerous consequences of
learning. That is to say, the existence of the teacher makes possible the
commission of error without irreversible harm occurring. Let me put it

*Reprinted from *Rhode Island College Journal*, Volume I, No. 2 (March, 1960),
pages 35-42, with permission of the author and publisher.

in terms of food gathering behavior and the learning involved therein. A hungry young organism is out gathering food and he sees something that might be either a mushroom or a toadstool. The most direct way of finding out which it is would be to pick the object from its stalk and eat it. If it is a mushroom, the child will live to pick another day. If it is not, he has removed himself irreversibly from the arena of learning. The teacher enters by playing the role of vicar for consequences, and his existence makes feasible the committing of error. In short, the teacher states in one way or another that eating this particular thing will kill you or not kill you as the case may be. It follows from this, does it not, that one of the first functions of teaching is to make possible the presence of error, and, as we shall see shortly, to make error possible in an instructive way. The consequences of error, then should always be less grave when there is teaching present than when learning is direct and unmediated by a teacher. This is an obvious point, but it is not a trivial one and it may easily be forgotten.

INSTRUCTIVE ERROR

I used the expression "instructive error," and we must now look at what such an error amounts to. To be instructive, an error must have the effect of reducing the range of alternative errorful acts that the learner will perform in comparable situations later. To use the language of commonsense rather than information theory, this means that the learner must have some sense of what it was about his act that was in error so that he may be spared committing one like it again. What is most interesting about errors is that they have a logical structure, some of them quite interesting and others quite trivial. The trivial errors are errors such as those we make in spelling—failures to observe convention. Teaching spelling as a set of rote conventions turns out, in consequence, to be rather a dull enterprise. So, too, learning spelling. Yet on closer inspection it turns out that spelling is somthing more than a set of simple rote conventions—something more than that the vocalic /sla/ can be written as SLEIGH or SLAY, with a somewhat different arbitrary meaning in each case. In fact, the sequential letter structure of all Western languages is a beautiful pattern of transitional probabilities that make possible the construction of nonsense words with a high degree of approximation to the language—so high in fact that the words are not in the dictionary only by chance. VERNALIT, MOSSIANT, POKERSON, APHYSTER, RICANING, ANTHROPAND—all of these are words we have constructed to obey the transitional rules of English orthography. We know from the work of William Hull that one can effect real improvements in the spelling of real words by teaching children to practice recognizing brief exposures of such nonsense words as these and writing down the letters that they see—indeed, doing this without ever encountering the same pseudo-word twice. In short, we can even convert the errors of convention into something more interestingly generic—where an error can be interpreted as something not that violates an arbitrary convention concerning the spelling of a word, but something that violates a general rule about how things are put together.

But this is a bit of a diversion. The real point about instructive error and the logical structure that underlies it is that when there is a teacher present, it should be possible to utilize the error to increase its instructiveness, to make the error understandable. In most cases this consists of making clear the distinction between signal and noise, or essence and accident as it used to be called in the classical philosophy. In the case of the mushroom-toadstool example, it consists of calling attention to the fact that the toadstool in contrast to a mushroom has certain distinctive features of size and shape and color and habitat. In the case of our spelling example, it consists of pointing out that a given way of spelling does or does not violate a rule of transitional probability in English—does or does not regardless of whether the particular spelling used constitutes a word correctly or incorrectly. In short, if we can say that teaching makes possible the commission of error, it also serves the function of an analyzer, as the physicist would say—it analyzes the essential from the non-essential, and thereby elucidates error.

MACHINES PROGRAMMED FOR ARTIFICIAL INTELLIGENCE

Before we turn to a third function of teaching, let me comment briefly on one universal feature of all minds and of all instruments that simulate mind—machines programmed for artificial intelligence. It is a feature worthy of being mentioned over and over again. They all are characterized by a limited span of attention or immediate memory as it is sometimes called. That is to say, we can hold in mind simultaneously only a certain number of independent items, hold them in mind and manipulate or transform them. The estimate for human beings is that about seven unrelated items can be held in mind, and that much beyond this there is interference between the items and a notable drop in their manipulability. This limited span is not something to lament, and it is not something on whose expansion you can reasonably hope to work. Brute memory training is a rather unrewarding form of exercise for it yields only the realization that not much can be done about it—not much in the sense of expanding the simple span. The only reasonable thing that you can do is to see that, as my colleague George Miller puts it, the seven slots are filled with gold rather than dross. Let me explain this by an example.

Turning dross into gold consists of recoding materials into a form such that one can not only hold more in mind, but hold it in mind in a way such that one can regenerate information. Let me duly inform you, for example, that a certain free falling body dropped a distance of 144 units in 3 seconds, 256 units in 4 seconds, had reached a distance of 1600 units at 10 seconds, and at 13 seconds was observed at a distance of 2704 units from its point of origin. This is pretty dull stuff, and fortunately we know that you will have forgotten it in a few minutes. In the form presented it just about chokes up your channel capacity, as span is sometimes called by communications engineers. If you teach well, you will have had your students scurrying for a recoding by now, one that will permit easy holding in mind and ready manipulation—in this case the manipulation that results in adequate interpolation and extrapolation: "Where was the object at 5 seconds, where was it at a minute?" Or, "Is this happening on earth or on the moon?" Some of you have already recognized that the numbers are readily recodable in terms of the formula for falling bodies in the earth's gravitational field with a constant of gravitation of about 32, the formula being as ancient as Galileo. You can hold it in mind and leave enough room to hold in mind simultaneously a correction formula to take account of atmospheric densities. The two formulae taken in conjunction will permit you to regenerate any and all information you need about distances fallen on any planet in any atmospheric field, and if you do a little more recoding, you may rediscover some more laws of nature.

TEACHING CAN NEVER BE JUST THE
PRESENTATION OF MATERIAL

My digression, intricate in detail though it was, has an overwhelmingly important point to be drawn from it about the nature of teaching. It is that teaching can never be just the presentation of material, material about some subject. It cannot be that unless you have no respect for nor knowledge about the nature of the human span. For it is the proper function of the teacher to present information in such a way and in terms of such a structure that the learner can get maximum regenerative travel from the material to which he has been exposed. This immediately brings up the rewardingly complicated issue of how one presents different kinds of material in order to honor properly this particular function of teaching. What materials should be presented to the learner at different stages, and in what order and pattern? We have experts who are charged with the task of devising subject-matter curricula, and I do not mean to belittle the importance of what they do. Usually they are highly knowledgeable about children and what they can absorb, and likely as not they have had such direct experience in dealing with children in the process of learning particular subjects. Almost never, however, are they the great creative minds in the substantive fields for which they are designing a curriculum. And here I wish to make a debatable point. It is that the structure of a field and therefore the order of approach to it is best understood by the person who has the deepest understanding of the field—he is the one who best knows what things are worth struggling to understand and when. If we are to do an adequate job of presenting models or structures in terms of which facts and data can be recorded for better retention and subsequent use, the great men in the substantive fields will have to work with the expert on the process of child learning to devise curricula that are comprehensible and worth comprehending. It is far from clear, for example, that the particulars of primary arithmetic are worth teaching first in view of the fact that they are such a special case of more general mathematics which, once grasped, provides a simple basis for deriving ordinary arithmetic. The difficulty with ordinary arithmetic is that it is so special—however useful it may be in toting up the cost of milk and barley—that it is hard to generalize.

To me, one of the happy signs of our times is that precisely what I am urging is now taking place—alas, only in the sciences, however. The Physical Sciences Study Committee at M. I. T., under the direction of such distinguished physicists as Jerrold Zacharias and Francis Friedman are devising courses in high school physics; comparable projects are in progress at Yale and Illinois in mathematics; at Colorado in biology; and the National Academy of Sciences is now instituting a special study group to investigate the way to regularize on a long-term basis such enterprises across the whole spectrum of the sciences and other branches of learning. It is still too early to say much about the project save that the guiding principle will be to bring together the efforts of three kinds of people: men of the deepest learning in the substantive fields to be taught; students of the principles and techniques of the communication of knowledge such as psychologists, information theorists, specialists in the theory of display, etc.; and finally, experts in the learning capacities of children with experience in the reality of teaching in school settings.

ADDITIONAL FUNCTIONS OF TEACHING

Let me turn now to some additional functions of teaching. I should like to consider next something that is as paradoxical as it is simple. It has to do with the protected nature of the learning situation where school teaching occurs. When we learn in the process of doing, *in situ*, there is little separation between the act of learning and doing something with what we have learned. Teaching has the effect of separating the two, learning and doing. This is partly a function of the fact that the teacher is present properly to cushion the consequences of learning which removes learning from its usual context. It is partly due, too, to the fact that the teacher, in order to set forth the structure of a subject matter, must remove the learning from the context of action so that various alternative ways of looking at material may be considered. It is a necessary *antimony*, this distinction between reflection and action. Yet it has a danger. The danger is that that learning may become passive and benchbound, that the learner (as I have put it elsewhere) does not make the leap over the boundary between learning and thinking. By thinking I mean the operation of utilizing information to go beyond that which has been given to that which might be likely. Any operation that involves going beyond the information given is what constitutes the link between the isolated learning of the teaching situation to the requirement of action based upon what has been learned. It is such internalized action—these operations of going beyond—that constitutes the condition for getting travel out of what has been learned. Let me spell out this matter a little.

REVERSIBILITY

Mental growth from childhood to adolescence and then to adulthood consists, according to Piaget and others, of internalizing action, rendering it into symbolic form, and then endowing it with what has been called reversibility. The last point is of huge importance, reversibility. Overt action once learned tends not to have this property. Having learned to write words from left to right, for example, we are not thereby enabled to trace out the same words from right to left. Cognitive or mental operations, on the other hand, are notably reversible. In simplest form, we imagine that we have eaten something, and we can then immediately imagine the reverse of not having eaten it, considering the two simultaneously if necessary. In more formal terms, reversibility in the case of mathematical operations consists of being able to add two quantities together and then to reverse them back to their original form by subtraction. It is the internal means whereby we are enabled to scan alternatives, to work without being irreversibly committed to action.

Now the only way in which I know of to assure that operations are performed on what has been learned—that thinking occurs—is to shift emphasis from time to time from the intake side to the output side, to *make* learners do something with what they have learned. Indeed, the learning process geared together with good teaching can combine the two. The simplest version of this is to make the student predict or extrapolate to new facts before they are told to him so that the new information has the effect of confirming or infirming the cognitive operations in terms of which he is using his already mastered knowledge. The story is told of the great English historian Trevelyan that on the occasions when he had gone home to his study without the source materials that he needed for the next sections of his work, he would often reconstruct by prediction what must have happened. Needless to say, he would be quite uncannily correct on all matters save the inessentials— names, dates, and places. I do not mean to say that names, dates, and places are unimportant. Rather, what is centrally important is what happens. So perhaps students ought to have the kinds of historical textbooks in which the next chapter can be sealed up and the student tested on his ability to foretell what would be in it before reading it. I could not be more serious. Is it not the function of historical intuition that it presumes to aid one in a sense of what our own times mean? Would it not be a modest start in the development of such intuition to ask a student who has just completed a "unit" on the age of discovery to try some predictions about the age of colonization?

Once I did see a teacher specifically encourage a class to organize and use minimal information to draw a maximum number of inferences and it impressed me deeply. The teacher modeled his technique, I suppose, on the tried method of the storyteller. He presented the beginnings of the Whiskey Rebellion and said to his pupils, much in the manner of Ellery Queen speaking to his readers, "You now have enough to reconstruct the rest of the story. Let's see if we can do it." He was urging them to cross the barrier from learning into thinking. It is unhappily true that this is a rare exception in our schools.

RESEARCH EXPERIMENT AT HARVARD

I do have one experiment to report that provides encouragement, one that was devised and carried out by the research group with which I am associated at Harvard in collaboration with teachers in the fifth grade of a good public school. It is on the unpromising topic of the geography of the North Central States and is currently in progress so that I cannot give all of the results. We hit upon the happy idea of presenting this chunk of geography not as a set of knowns, but as a set of unknowns. One class was presented blank maps, containing only tracings of the rivers and lakes of the area as well as simple notation of the natural resources. The students were asked as a first exercise to indicate where the principal cities would be located, where the railroads, and where the main highways. Books and maps were not permitted and "looking up the facts" was cast in a sinful light. Upon completing this exercise, a class discussion was begun in which the children attempted to justify why the major city would be here, a large city there, a railroad on this line, etc.

The discussion was a hot one. After an hour, and much pleading, permission was given to consult the rolled-up wall map. I will never forget one young student, as he pointed his finger at the foot of Lake Michigan, shouting "Yipee, *Chicago* is at the end of the pointing-down lake." And another replying, "Well, OK: but Chicago's no good for the rivers and it should be here where there *is* a big city (St. Louis)." These children were thinking, and learning was an instrument for checking and improving the process. To at least a half dozen children in the class it is not a matter of indifference that no big city is to be found at the junction of Lake Huron, Lake Michigan, and Lake Ontario. They were slightly shaken up transportation theorists when the facts were in.

The children in the conventional class got their facts all right, sitting down, benchbound. And that was that. We will see in six months which group remembers more. But whichever does, one thing I will predict. One group learned geography as a set of rational acts of induction—that cities spring up where there is water, where there are natural resources, where there are things to be processed and shipped. The other group learned passively that there were arbitrary cities at arbitrary places by arbitrary bodies of water and arbitrary sources of supply. One learned geography as a form of activity. The other stored some names and positions as a passive form of registration.

If I have made it appear up to this point that teaching has to do principally with the task of rendering the world less dangerously consequential, more economical to handle cognitively, and more predictable, I have left out one important feature of the teaching task. It has to do with the degree to which the adult teacher is in a more advantageous position than the child to recognize and communicate a sense of the alternative plights into which man can fall. In a somewhat more formal context a moment ago, I remarked in passing that the teacher, by delaying the necessity for external action and emphasizing reversible internal operations, gave the child a sense of alternatives. With respect to the life of a society, there are similarly alternative models upon which one can pattern oneself. These are frequently called the myths of a society, and myth in this sense does not mean untruth. Penelope as a faithful wife is not an untruth by virtue of being a fiction, nor is Emma Bovary in the plight of *la femme incomprise* faced with the grievous problems of love and adultery. Hercules is not just a story, but a symbolizing of aspirations for omnicompetence and infinite wiles. If one grasps the symbolism of Perseus slaying the hateful Medusa, guiding the telling thrust by her reflection in his polished shield rather than by looking upon her directly and being turned to stone, then one has grasped the metaphoric meaning of the law and wherein one becomes the victim of evil attacked directly—the protection of the mediating shield.

The enduring body of a culture's literature is a storehouse of myths that symbolize and condense the myriad forms of the rather limited range of plights that characterize the life of a people. The great student of myth and legend, Joseph Campbell, remarks that there has been a breakdown in what he calls the "mythologically instructed community," the community that shares a set of instructive myths about life and its alternative ways. In contrast to the classic times of Greece, we are indeed without a unified corpus of myth. In its place have arisen the forms of modern literature, notably the novel, and in the literature of the last century and a half one finds traced not so much externalized myth as what might better be called a record of voyages into the interior. It is by knowledge of those voyages that one comes to a sense of the alternative forms of coping or fleeing, one gains a knowledge of life beyond what one might immediately encompass in direct experience however long one lives.

And how does this relate to the function of teaching? I should like to propose that the teacher of literature has a function akin to the teacher of empirical subjects such as science and history. Where the latter attempts somehow to provide a model, indeed alternative models of the *external* world one encounters, it seems to me that it is the function of the teacher of literature to use the corpus of novels and drama to elucidate the *internal* world and its alternative expressions. And indeed, much of what I said earlier about learning and thinking might well hold here. What better exercise for the development of a tragic sense—without which there can be no sense of comparison—than to have to make an attempt at writing the last act of *Hamlet* having read the others that preceded it. Or if not writing the last act anew, at least considering the various ways in which it might come out and why.

CRITERIA FOR JUDGING THE ADEQUACY OF A
THEORY OF TEACHING

Consider now a more general matter that may have the effect of binding together what I have said thus far about the functions of teaching. It would appear, upon reading the literature on the subject in a sketchy way, that there is a certain lack of adequate theory in the field of teaching. Rest easy, I do not propose to set forth a theory of teaching at short notice! Rather, I would like to consider what might be taken to be adequate criteria for judging whether a theory of teaching is adequate, whether it condenses and provides a means for generating new ideas. And let me say that when I use the word theory, I have in mind a very useful thing.

I should begin by commenting that theory is often misunderstood. It is in effect a heuristic or guide that gets you from where you happen to find yourself to where it is that you want to be—particularly so when we are dealing as now with a theory of practice, and all theory is that, once one tries to operate with it. It should be self-evident, should it not, that a theory-in-use has an objective: you wish to build a faster sloop or predict eclipses of the moon or to educate a child in some particular way. Characteristically, a theory-in-use is derived from a more general model or theory about the nature of things that has prediction as its aim. The construction of sloops is a good case in point, for it is guided by theoretical understanding of principles of aerodynamics, hydrodynamics, and the doctrine of the parallelogram of forces. In order to use such knowledge, you have to have in mind what it is that you want to accomplish—whether you want a rough weather boat, one that can operate in shoal water, whether the objective is a spacious hold, and so on. So it goes with the theory of education. Before you can use theoretical formulations concerning the learning process, the nature of child development, and the structure of knowledge in substantive fields you must be clear what you want to use the knowledge for. I have very strongly the impression that one of the grave sources of confusion in the field of education is that educational theorists have difficulty using available knowledge not so much because the knowledge is shaky, but because they do not know what they want to use it for. In short, we are not clear in our image of what constitutes an educated person— the place that we want to get with a learner starting from here. Nor do I think that our confusion is all an affliction. At least it guarantees a certain pluralism in our approach to young people and saves us from the temptation to squeeze everybody into the same mold.

Minimum Objectives in Fashioning a Theory of Teaching

But there is a limit to proclaiming the virtues of our confusions. I would like to bring my remarks to a close by suggesting some of the minimum objectives that seem to me to be worthwhile in fashioning a theory of teaching.

The first of them should be that the educated person should be one who has internalized a sense of the instructiveness of error. This means in effect that he knows how to try out his ideas with the aid of advice and that error does not stand for defeat. If teaching has succeeded, then fear of error should have been made to subside. In essence, this implies that the individual is better enabled to try out his ideas and to determine whether they are useful or not. It is a simple objective, but it is an exceedingly important one.

A second objective has to do with what some of my colleagues on the Cognition Project at Harvard refer to as "recoding push." Good teaching should have the effect of leading a person to condense and transform what he has encountered into a form that honors the deeper general structure of whatever he has experienced. He, the learner, must have learned ways of respecting his limited cognitive capacities by rendering the welter of material to which he is exposed into something more manageable and he must first recognize when things have become unmanageable. This holds as much for daily life where the "he said, she said, I said" approach to understanding what goes on between oneself and others often blocks deeper understanding, as it holds for any other aspect of life—such as reading the newspaper or attempting to understand technical problems in one's business or profession.

A third objective is that the learner end his formal exposure to teaching well equipped with a set of models or condensations of the nature of the world with which he must cope—the physical world, the biological, the social. Here I have in mind that the task of communicating substantive knowledge is as paramount in fact as we sometimes make out in giving it lip service. I do not think that we will make the desired progress along this front until we reexamine freshly and critically the structure of the knowledge that is to be communicated, and in this endeavor I sense that a revolution is about to take place which will have the effect of bringing the man of learning back into working contact with the teacher.

Finally, it seems to me, the well educated learner should have acquired a sense of the varieties of the human condition—and now I am speaking less of social studies and more of human intuition. So long as the schools feel the need to avoid controversial materials in their teaching of literature—and make no mistake about it, the artistically gripping presentation of human lives is likely to be controversial in the school setting, even if it is becoming less so in that startling medium called television—so long as there is the need to avoid the controversial, we will be tempted to teach pablum rather than plight. I have seen a social studies book in which the passionately fixated Christopher Columbus was presented as a nice kid with a brother Bart amiably going about the task of convincing people that an ocean crossing would be interesting. Its readability figure was superbly low, but it was a lie against the passion to explore. The justification was that it related the experience of Columbus to the experience of the sixth grader. And we in an age in which artificial moons have become a part of common sense!

These are minimum objectives, and obviously there are many more—like making the student aware of the nature of the government under which he lives and what his prerogatives are thereunder. I do not mean to belittle these objectives. The ones I have suggested, if achieved, can only make the achievement of the others more worthwhile.

I have said nothing about the ideal of personal adjustment in education, for it is not within the purview of this essay. I do know that an overburden of personal problems, creating the ground for neurotic processes, can be the prime enemy of the type of vigorously open mind that I have been urging we take as an objective in our teaching efforts. But it is not my impression that good teaching of genuinely worthwhile subject matter has ever had the effect of creating neurosis. What I would suggest is that we pursue our teaching with the utmost vigor while at the same time combatting the kinds of forces in the home, the school, and the society at large that produce crippling effects on the learner. It will not avail us much, will it, if we produce the well adjusted child whose principal virtue is that he is not disturbed. The task is to produce students who, by virtue of the teaching they have received, are able to go beyond what they have been taught to the formulation of their own identity and individuality.

9.5 CRITERIA FOR THE PROFESSIONAL PREPARATION OF TEACHERS*

by Harry S. Broudy

In the Platonic dialogue *Protagoras*, Socrates spoke as follows:

> Now I observe that whenever we are met together in the assembly, and the matter in hand relates to building, the builders are summoned as advisors; when the question is one of shipbuilding, then the shipbuilders; and the like of other arts which they think capable of being taught and learned. . . . When, however, the question is an affair of state, then everybody is free to have a say— carpenter, tinker, cobbler, sailor, passenger; rich and poor, high and low . . . and no one reproaches him, as in the former case, with not having learned, and having no teacher, and yet giving advice. . . .

Whereupon Protagoras, the famous Sophist, set him straight by observing that everybody—parents, police, and the public in general— teaches virtue; hence, no specialists are needed. However, he admitted modestly that some persons could do it so much better than the general run of mankind that, like himself, they made a profession of it.

This colloquy is not an unfitting setting for the current serious and sometimes bitter controversy about teaching and the preparation of teachers, for it suggests the sense in which we are all teachers of a sort and the sense in which teaching can be what the Greeks called *techné* (an art based on knowledge), or what we would call a profession, in which case not everyone is a teacher but only those who cultivate the special knowledge and skill on which it is based. Above all, it raises the question as to whether or not there is such knowledge.[1] Sooner or later one must ask whether the expertness needed for teaching can be picked up from one's own experience as a pupil, by apprenticeship with a master teacher, or by application of common sense; or whether there is a special body of knowledge and skill that has to be mastered through formal study. Accordingly, the identification of the kinds of knowledge and skill used in teaching is a task that cannot be postponed indefinitely, if the controversy is to be resolved rationally.

*Reprinted from *The Journal of Teacher Education*, Volume XVI, No. 4 (December, 1965), with permission of the author and publisher.
[1]The perennial nature of the problem is illustrated by an article, "Is There a Science Education?" written by Josiah Royce for *Educational Review* in 1891. He did not think that there was.

But where is one to begin? Perhaps with the formula for the good teacher. Because every instance of teaching is the resultant of more variables than we can identify, and because the values of these variables remain indeterminate, the thousands of hours and millions of dollars spent on trying to identify the traits of a good or successful teacher have given employment and even careers to worthy educational researchers, but not much else. Any generalization about the good or bad teacher will elicit a counter-example from any half dozen people who are in a mood to reminisce about their school days. Mr. Conant's efforts in this direction are no exception. One would be hard put to form an image of what a good teacher would be like from the welter of prescriptions given for producing one.

At this stage of our knowledge about teaching and learning, the approach has to be much more modest than that of the controlled experiment or the massive questionnaire: it is to examine the roles that a person who teaches is expected to play as he or she carries out the tasks normally assigned to the position. What knowledge and what skill are presupposed by these roles?

THE TEACHER AS A PERSON

The first and most consistent role that a teacher plays is that of a human being, a person. This platitude lies at the root of some of the bitterest aspects of the controversy, not because anyone denies that teachers are human, but because to be a human being is thought to involve the kind of schooling that has been called liberal or general. The generally accepted belief that a teacher needs a liberal education more than, let us say, a plumber or a barber is based on the confusion of two notions. One is that the teacher will need it in order to give instruction in some of the content contained in the liberal studies, e.g., history or literature. The other notion is that the teacher, like Quintilian's orator, ought to be a good person skilled in speaking (teaching). I shall in all charity remain silent on the claim that the liberal arts, as usually taught in the university, are liberal in any but a catalogue sense of the term. The professors of these subjects are as specialized and as proud of their specialism as is the engineering faculty or that of law. On the modern campus there is only one culture, the professional culture, and the rules for promotion and scholarly distinction are about the same regardless of department. Hence liberality in the Aristotelian sense of the term, education for the sake of cultivating the person, is a rare commodity indeed, although naïve undergraduates are rioting around, allegedly because they still yearn for it.

But even if the liberal arts could make men human—and taught in a liberal spirit they might—there is, I repeat, no compelling reason for teachers being made more human than anyone else. This argument will, no doubt, leave many unconvinced. It will be urged that the teacher affects the lives of children as engineers and plumbers do not. Presumably this means that teachers shape character and therefore should themselves exemplify ideal character; and that this, in turn, calls for more liberal education than the general public needs. But the most that can be made of this dubious argument is that if a society does not provide general education for all its citizens, it ought at least to insist on it for its prospective teachers. However, once the requirement is couched in terms of what a person needs to play the role of teacher, it becomes part of professional education. Thus, at one time, public school teachers were expected to refrain from using profanity, alcohol, and tobacco; and air line hostesses are expected to be gracious and attractive. For them, temperance and charm are professional requirements; that they are also desirable for all human beings is another matter.

This distinction is more than a quibble. We can achieve institutional peace only if the professional faculty has complete authority over professional needs and the general faculty is in complete charge of what all men, simply because they are men, ought to know. The conflicts between these faculties result when there is an attempt to skimp on the development of teachers as persons or persons as teachers.

Unfortunately, teacher education has a long history of skimping, and we are still watching the strange spectacle of men willing to spend so little on what they say they value so much. To recruit large numbers of public school teachers, we skimped on their liberal education. The best among them made up in a pedagogical devotion what they lacked in learning. Today we are urged to meet the teacher shortage and raise the quality of teachers by skimping on their professional training. The gradual lengthening of the teacher preparation curriculum was an attempt to draw public school teachers into the liberally educated classes, and the fight will not be won until they are all drawn from such classes and then trained in thoroughly professional schools.

If it is granted that the teacher is first of all a person, is there any special type of person he ought to be? If so, we have never been able to decide what it is. In a recently published volume, a colleague and I wrote essays on Socrates, Protagoras, Isocrates, Quintilian, Alcuin, Abelard, Ascham, the Jesuits, Comenius, Pestalozzi, Froebel, Herbart, and Kilpatrick as exemplars of teaching method.[2] If anyone can find any

---

[2]Broudy, H. S., and Palmer, John R. *Exemplars of Teaching Method.* Chicago, Ill.: Rand McNally & Co., 1965.

important set of common traits in their personalities, we would like to know about it.

Moreover, if a peculiar personality pattern is essential to teaching, can it be produced, or is one born with it? If inborn, it is a function of teacher selection rather than of teacher preparation; if produced, it would be helpful to know how it is done. Surely the college years are too late for producing basic personality changes.

Our inability to find a general formula for the good teacher (although we can spot this or that good teacher) has been used to deny that there is knowledge from which teacher preparation can design its curriculum and to allege that it must rely on the wisdom of the elders, such wisdom being the special gift of the master teachers who can spot the good and bad teacher prospects during their apprenticeship. Yet lack of a personality formula has not caused medicine or law to throw their professional curricula on the mercy of the wisdom of the elders.

Our lack of knowledge about the personality formula merely means that we must look in another direction for professional criteria, viz., to the requirements of the roles played by the teacher as (1) a member of the educational profession and (2) as a specialist in that profession.

The Teacher as a Member of the Educational Profession

A profession rests heavily on a body of systematized knowledge organized in terms of distinctive problems of practice. The word "knowledge" distinguishes it from a craft; the word "practice," from pure research. So defined, the term "professional" does not apply to plumbers, physicists, biologists, or historians, but it does apply to the sanitary engineers and to teachers of physics, biology, and history.

Education as a professional field of study, therefore, has to have distinctive problems of practice and resources of knowledge that can be used to deal with these problems. Such problems arise out of the need to formulate and justify educational policy, to design and justify curriculum designs, to formulate and justify schemes of organization and support, and to formulate and justify strategies of teaching and learning. They are distinctive of education and define the domain of professional training in the field of education.

The knowledge about these problems falls into two major types: the foundational and the specialized. The first is needed by all workers in the educational field regardless of their role in the educational system. This would include college presidents and professors as well as public school administrators and kindergarten teachers. Each of the four problem areas can and needs to be studied in its historical, psychological, philosophical, and social contexts, because these are the major contexts in which educational institutions operate and in which the problems peculiar to them occur. There are, no doubt, other relevant contexts, but these four are indispensable to an understanding of what the whole educational enterprise is all about. These problems, studied in these contexts, make up the sixteen basic topics in the foundations of education.

There is, or need be, nothing vague or fuzzy or repetitive in foundational courses, but they do presuppose that the student will have had the basic courses in history, philosophy, psychology, and the social sciences as part of his *general* education. Since colleges of education cannot assume this will be the case, they should insist on them as prerequisites for admission to foundational courses. When the student is not properly prepared, there is a great danger that the foundation course will be turned into a watered-down version of the parent discipline or into wordy discussions of life in general, education in general, and society in general; in short, a general bull session conducted for credit.

Foundational courses also suffer from a tacit promise and expectation that they will help the teacher directly in the daily tasks of the classroom —keeping unruly children quiet or placating a neurotic principal. Unfortunately, foundational knowledge cannot be *applied* directly to problems of practice any more than physics can be applied to fix an ailing motor car. Foundational knowledge, and indeed all general education, is used interpretively as precise but large-scale cognitive maps on which problems are plotted but not solved. For the solving of problems, i.e., for the applicative use of knowledge, theory has to be supplemented by technology, and only the specialist (who has both) uses knowledge applicatively. Being mistaken in the uses to which foundational knowledge is put, one can be understandably wrong in judging it useless.

The cognitive map wrought by the foundational course does for the professional life what general education is expected to do for human life as a whole. Professional cognitive maps are constructed on projections furnished by their distinctive domains of practice; life cognitive maps are fashioned on projections derived from the domains of the intellectual disciplines. Neither sort of map is useless, but without appropriate technologies, it cannot be used applicatively. Yet, in the absence of adequate interpretive maps, one is at a loss to know what an appropriate technology would be and where it might be found.

THE TEACHER AS SPECIALIST

Because of the constantly swelling school population, teaching has undergone the usual division of labor and has developed numerous specialties. What, then, are the types of knowledge needed by the teacher as an instructor, as a specialist in teaching?

1. *Foundations of the specialty.* The very same logic that justifies general education for all men and foundational work for all professional workers in education justifies the study of one's specialty in its historical development, its psychological relationships, its philosophical presuppositions and implications, its societal contexts and import. For example, the teaching of mathematics has a history dating back at least to Plato; it has problems of motivation and presentation that are psychological as well as sociological; its current place in the curriculum is dictated by our military and economic anxieties, and its relation to other types of knowledge and to the good life are problems of the highest philosophical order which are far from being clearly understood even now.

One does not expect such study—in course form or some other form —to be given in the mathematics department (because it so rarely is offered there), but it would be odd indeed if a school turning out specialists in the teaching of mathematics would not provide this orientation to the specialty. I have no doubt that organization and development of material for such studies can be an interdisciplinary venture,[3] but the primary responsibility is on the professional faculty.

2. *Professional Content.* We come now to an ingredient in teacher preparation which has borne far too much of the weight of the controversy, viz., subject matter. There are two uses of the knowledge of a subject that are relevant to the teaching of it. "Repertory content" is the name I would give to that part of the subject matter, say of English or history or mathematics, that will be presented to the tutee. Thus the play *Hamlet*, the binomial theorem, and the Whiskey Rebellion are samples of repertory content. These will be presented to the tutee; he will be persuaded to respond to them, modify his response in the direction sought by the teacher, undergo tests upon them, etc.; in short, to study them.

What does one have to know about *Hamlet* or English literature or English history or the drama or Middle English in order to teach *Hamlet* to high school students? Here is the sort of question that scholars in English literature might very well help to define and perhaps solve. That a knowledge about the changes in the language, for example, is invaluable for the teacher is not in question. It gives him the freedom of

---

[3]Often such materials come into being when a doctoral student with an historical training and interest in mathematical education chooses to do a dissertation in the history of education. Such monographic literature in time becomes an item on the reading list of advanced students in mathematical education, and later still abstracts from it begin to appear in textbooks on the teaching of mathematics which, in turn, are used in courses given to prospective mathematics teachers.

maneuver in the teaching of *Hamlet* without which the class bogs down in the footnotes or, what is worse, resorts to highly simplified texts without any footnotes at all. The question concerns rather the packaging of materials from philosophy, English history, drama, and the other relevant fields so that they become functional for the teacher in teaching but are not necessarily taught to the pupils. This might be called the pedagogical content of a subject.

The standard response of the subject matter scholars to the problem of professional content has taken the form of prescribing courses or sequences of courses in the various subject fields. This standard response, however admirable as a counsel of perfection, is not the answer to the question; it is a somewhat cavalier evasion of it. The proper answer to the question entails viewing the problem from the professional end of the telescope. Courses and programs in the liberal arts college are rightly organized for scholarship in the standard disciplines or for general education and not for the professional use of them. In the latter, materials are organized around the problems of practice, and this difference makes all the difference. Once we acknowledge the hegemony of the liberal arts college over general education, it may be possible for the various professional schools (law, medicine, engineering) to enlist their fruitful collaboration in selecting and packaging those elements within their disciplines that are relevant and necessary for the professional part of the curriculum.

The distinction between repertory and interpretive (pedagogical) content is important because the relative amounts of each needed by the teacher vary with the level at which the subject is being taught. There is a logic of subject matter and of teaching that saves the judgments as to how much of each is needed from being completely *ad hoc* or arbitrary. There are questions that arise in a high school class in Shakespeare that cannot be answered or discussed without knowledge of language morphology, or history, or history of the theatre, or the character of the English court. This is the knowledge the teacher uses for eliciting and evaluating pupil response, although he may never utter it to the pupils. But the questions that arise in a college class in Shakespeare may not coincide with those in the high school and certainly would not with those that pop up in an elementary school version of the same play. Pedagogical content in one situation may be repertory content in another

To the detriment of the whole enterprise of teacher preparation, educationists have not been and even today are not clear on the role of subject matter in instruction. There is no agreement as to whether the pupil ought to learn some specific content from some standard discipline, a method of thinking, an attitude of being critical about life in general, or the knack of getting along with his fellows. Usually schoolmen vow to work for all of them. In such a confusion, even with the best of intentions, it is difficult to decide just what competence the teacher should have and just what knowledge or training would provide it. For it is one thing to train teachers to teach *Hamlet;* quite another to teach good citizenship by the use of *Hamlet.*

3. The next dimension of specialized study is the *technological.* The difference between foundational and specialized study in a professional field is that in the latter one learns how to apply knowledge in concrete cases. As noted before, this requires not only knowledge but also a technology in which the generalizations are transformed into procedures and devices. For example, the knowledge about isotopes cannot be used in medicine without a special technology for introducing them into the body and observing their effects. We have developed three types of instruction in professional education (in all professions) to accomplish this: laboratory exercises, clinical experience, and internship.

The laboratory exercise is intended to concretize theory and to test it—for the pupil, not for the discipline. For example, one of the standard tasks in schoolkeeping is the grouping of pupils for instruction. There are a number of principles in terms of which one might group a class of thirty pupils: homogeneous grouping, age grouping, interest grouping, stratified grouping. A laboratory exercise to illustrate these principles might ask the student to group thirty pupils whose scores on a number of tests are made available to him. The justification of the grouping in terms of the principles involved constitutes the basic learnings of the exercise. In the preparation of teachers, laboratory experience can be provided by demonstrations with live pupils, through simulated situations on video tape or film, or through curriculum materials laboratories, audiovisual aid laboratories, etc.

Whatever the form of the laboratory exercise, it is important to note that the laboratory task is never more than an abstracted and often schematized sample of a whole class of real tasks. The demonstration, the made-up grouping task, the make-believe test—all of these should conform to the schemata of some theory and be designed to illuminate and illustrate it.

Clinical experience, on the contrary, involves real individual cases chosen for their significance as exemplars. In the clinic, we select for instructional purposes the classic case of the slow learner or the discipline problem. Clinical instruction is ideally carried on by a master teacher who is also a good theoretician with a small group of advanced students who have studied theory but have little or no practice aside from laboratory exercises in various courses. The master involves the students in the diagnosis of a particular real problem, the prescription, and the prognosis, and then goes ahead and treats the case himself, presumably in a masterly way. His treatment is a model against which the discussants check their thinking. Real school classrooms are neither good laboratories nor clinics.

Internship is working on a real task under a minimum of supervision and needs, I believe, no extended discussion. Teaching internship has to be carried on in a real classroom. It does, however, need to be distinguished from the laboratory and clinical phases of technical training with which it is almost always confused.

Mr. Conant and the Ford Foundation have founded their schemes of teacher preparation on the centrality of practice teaching. This strategy reflects the conviction that teaching is fundamentally no more than a set of skills acquired by apprenticeship, preferably with a master teacher; but what is perhaps even more important, direct experience in a real classroom is depended upon to give the three kinds of learning that we have distinguished as laboratory, clinical, and internship. This is a clumsy strategy, to say the least. The internship idea is sound if the laboratory, clinical, and theoretical work has already been done at the primary training institution. It is not sound when used as a substitute for the other dimensions of professional training, and this is what many of the five-year programs of teacher training can be suspected of trying to do. Practice teaching or student teaching is a tremendous drain on instructional space and manpower—a drain that could be slackened if the laboratory work could be done elsewhere than in the training classroom. With the possibilities opened up by the new developments in video tape recording and simulated training systems, real classrooms could be used for educative internship, in the manner of our best teaching hospitals.

4. *Research.* A professional field of study would not be worthy of that designation if it were not growing by systematic methods of inquiry. If no genuine scholarly research in the problems of education is possible, or if it is not taking place, then education cannot qualify as a professional field of study, and its claim to professional status in the university or in the social order is fraudulent. A professional practitioner, therefore, may be a producer and certainly ought to be a consumer of research. The methods of research, its canons, its status, and its prosperity are of concern to him; he tries to keep up with it. Research is therefore included in his professional training.

The import of the discussion is that the professional training of teachers is structurally no different from the professional training of engineers, physicians, and lawyers. In a fully developed program of professional training, the foundational dimensions, the general theory, the specialized technology, the specialized instrumentation and research methodology are provided through a variety of instructional means: courses, lectures, readings, laboratory work, clinical experience, and internship. Every move to omit or to minimize any one of these dimensions can therefore be construed as an attack on the professional maturity or status of teaching.

The attacks on teacher-training programs have tried to deprofessionalize teaching in the public schools in several ways. First, by equating the foundational knowledge with general education. Thus it has been argued that a good course in philosophy makes a course in the philosophy of education unnecessary, or that there is no history of education but only history. Second, it has been argued that specialized study in a given subject matter field will take care of the special content of a subject needed for teaching. This results from ignoring the difference between repertory and interpretive-pedagogical content. Third, there is the effort to regard all technical work in teacher training as tricks of the trade to be picked up by apprenticeship in something called student teaching. This results from ignoring or not understanding the differences among laboratory, clinical, and internship experiences in the specialized training of the professional.

One can criticize a program of teacher training for not being adequate in this or that dimension, and this sort of criticism most of our programs probably deserve. Or one can charge that there simply is not enough knowledge to warrant a professional program at all, and that a mildly intellectualized craft training is all that is required. This is the real and basic issue, and it can be decided only by examining the knowledge available.

Those who would deny that such a body of knowledge exists, or could exist, or that the roles of the teacher demand it are invited to dispute the analysis or examine the shelves of any university library. Instead of such rational argument, we find casually tossed-off remarks to the effect that the study of education is not a discipline, or that it is a pseudo-discipline, or that, whatever it is, it can be dispensed with in the training of teachers.

Let me reiterate therefore that no claim is made for education as a discipline with a homogenous subject matter such as mathematics or physics or geology. But then no professional field of study is a discipline in this sense. On the contrary, every professional field of study draws on a number of parent disciplines for the knowledge relevant to the problems of practice which are peculiar to itself and which delimit it from other professions. This does not exclude the study of education from the family of intellectual pursuits any more than it excludes engineering, medicine, or law.

That the field of study we call professional education is far from being systematized, and that not all of its dimensions have been equally developed, is only too true. For example, the recent discovery of a non-licensed physician practicing away at a great and prosperous rate in Detroit despite the lack of a medical degree or graduation from a medical school did not incite anyone to brand medical education as unnecessary, nor have we heard proposals that a much shortened master of healing degree be substituted for the long period of medical training now required. The field of medical study is too well developed to be attacked in this way.

Yet, as our opening remarks on the Socratic question indicate, the writing and thinking about education have as long a history as those about medicine and law. That a field should attract so steadily the attention of some of our best minds and yet be no more than a craft to be learned by apprenticeship seems remarkable indeed.

That public school instruction can be manned by bright and devoted amateurs is the illusion which misguides many of the critics of teacher preparation. If the admirable goals of elitist schooling are to be realized for all educable youth, it will take a much more sophisticated curriculum and teaching corps than five hard subjects taught by a handful of bright liberal arts graduates. Can we get enough of these bright graduates to become genuine professionals? Do we have a field of study worthy of their abilities and their time? Can we utilize their gifts in dealing with general education for the masses, including the masses so culturally deformed that ordinary instructional measures seem impotent? In the face of the overwhelming deluge of numbers, amateurs coming from the "good" colleges will be about as helpful as caviar in a famine.

Education at all levels is moving into mass production, as it was bound to do in a culture dominated by large-scale machine industry now reaching its logical apogee in automation. As this happens, all the blessings and dangers of mass production can be expected to confront education, as they have industry and politics. The salvation of our society will depend on the ability of education to exploit the blessings of technology in behalf of what makes life worthwhile, viz., the possibility of high-grade individual experience in something called "the good life." That solving these problems will require less than a generation of professional educators trained and educated in fully developed professional schools, I find it impossible to believe. Socrates, it turns out, asked the right question, and history has brought us to the point when we can no longer postpone the answer.

CHAPTER TEN

CRITIQUE OF EDUCATION IN THE UNITED STATES

10.1 EDITORIAL COMMENT

It is from the give and take of ideas that progress has been achieved in our educational efforts. The fact that there is much ferment over the quality of public schools in the United States can be taken as a good omen for the future. This is not to say that all of the criticism of the profession of teaching is constructive or well informed, but rather to emphasize the need for mutual respect for differences of opinion where no single pattern of objectivity is possible.

In the essay of Alfred North Whitehead on "Requisites for Social Progress" we have the solid opinion of a great scholar on the limitations of our present educational effort. Note that he is convinced that we pay far too much attention to intellectual analysis and the acquirement of "formularised information." Emphasis is placed on the need to "draw out habits of aesthetic apprehension," for the "habit of art is the habit of enjoying vivid values." The dangers of our present situation are real but the possibilities for progress are still with us.

Many professional educators have expressed strong negative opinions on the ideas of Robert M. Hutchins; yet, no one has provided more challenging thought and deeper educational concern over the limitations of present educational practices. In his "A Conversation on Education" Dr. Hutchins sees our educational efforts dominated far too much by money interests and giving far too little concern for the roles of art and of intellect in the educational enterprise. The lack of respect for the mind is the "single, grave, overwhelming defect in the American character."

In searching for a clear well-balanced but concise treatment of "Existentialism, Phenomenology, and the Philosophy of Education" the paper of Dr. L. F. Troutner seemed to best fit the needs of our critique. Existentialism, while vitally significant as a movement in modern thought, is held to be grounded in the false assumption that man is a rational animal. Introduction of the method of phenomenology is thought to have genuine possibilities for improvement in our educative efforts.

As a final reading it seemed appropriate to concern ourselves with "the logical implications of philosophic theory for educational theory and practice." In this respect Dr. Joe Burnett raises a very interesting and provocative question. "Do formal philosophies have logical implications for educational theory and practice?" The analysis of the question leads to the conclusion that there is educational value in such an approach, but that there is very little of worth in such efforts if the derived general philosophy "is not framed or modified in the light of the most definable, tested statements concerning empirical practice."

10.2   REQUISITES FOR SOCIAL PROGRESS*

by Alfred North Whitehead

Wisdom is the fruit of a balanced development. It is this balanced growth of individuality which it should be the aim of education to secure. The most useful discoveries for the immediate future would concern the furtherance of this aim without detriment to the necessary intellectual professionalism.

My own criticism of our traditional educational methods is that they are far too much occupied with intellectual analysis, and with the acquirement of formularised information. What I mean is, that we neglect to strengthen habits of concrete appreciation of the individual facts in their full interplay of emergent values, and that we merely emphasise abstract formulations which ignore this aspect of the interplay of diverse values.

In every country the problem of the balance of the general and specialist education is under consideration. I cannot speak with first-hand knowledge of any country but my own. I know that there, among practical educationalists, there is considerable dissatisfaction with the existing practice. Also, the adaptation of the whole system to the needs of a democratic community is very far from being solved. I do not think that the secret of the solution lies in terms of the antithesis between thoroughness in special knowledge and general knowledge of a slighter character. The make-weight which balances the thoroughness of the specialist intellectual training should be of a radically different kind from purely intellectual analytical knowledge. At present our education combines a thorough study of a few abstractions, with a slighter study of a larger number of abstractions. We are too exclusively bookish in our scholastic routine. The general training should aim at eliciting our concrete apprehensions, and should satisfy the itch of youth to be doing something. There should be some analysis even here, but only just enough to illustrate the ways of thinking in diverse spheres. In the Garden of Eden Adam saw the animals before he named them: in the traditional system, children named the animals before they saw them.

There is no easy single solution of the practical difficulties of education. We can, however, guide ourselves by a certain simplicity in its general theory. The student should concentrate within a limited field. Such concentration should include all practical and intellectual acquire-

---

*Reprinted from Alfred North Whitehead, *Science and the Modern World* (New York: The Macmillan Company, 1925; copyright renewed 1953 by Evelyn Whitehead), pages 284-295, with permission of the publisher.

ments requisite for that concentration. This is the ordinary procedure; and, in respect to it, I should be inclined even to increase the facilities for concentration rather than to diminish them. With the concentration there are associated certain subsidiary studies, such as languages for science. Such a scheme of professional training should be directed to a clear end congenial to the student. It is not necessary to elaborate the qualifications of these statements. Such a training must, of course, have the width requisite for its end. But its design should not be complicated by the consideration of other ends. This professional training can only touch one side of education. Its centre of gravity lies in the intellect, and its chief tool is the printed book. The centre of gravity of the other side of training should lie in intuition without an analytical divorce from the total environment. Its object is immediate apprehension with the minimum of eviscerating analysis. The type of generality, which above all is wanted, is the appreciation of variety of value. I mean an aesthetic growth. There is something between the gross specialised values of the mere practical man, and the thin specialised values of the mere scholar. Both types have missed something; and if you add together the two sets of values, you do not obtain the missing elements. What is wanted is an appreciation of the infinite variety of vivid values achieved by an organism in its proper environment. When you understand all about the sun and all about the atmosphere and all about the rotation of the earth, you may still miss the radiance of the sunset. There is no substitute for the direct perception of the concrete achievement of a thing in its actuality. We want concrete fact with a high light thrown on what is relevant to its preciousness.

What I mean is art and aesthetic education. It is, however, art in such a general sense of the term that I hardly like to call it by that name. Art is a special example. What we want is to draw out habits of aesthetic apprehension. According to the metaphysical doctrine which I have been developing, to do so is to increase the depth of individuality. The analysis of reality indicates the two factors, activity emerging into individualised aesthetic value. Also the emergent value is the measure of the individualisation of the activity. We must foster the creative initiative towards the maintenance of objective values. You will not obtain the apprehension without the initiative, or the initiative without the apprehension. As soon as you get towards the concrete, you cannot exclude action. Sensitiveness without impulse spells decadence, and impulse without sensitiveness spells brutality. I am using the word 'sensitiveness' in its most general signification, so as to include apprehension of what lies beyond oneself; that is to say, sensitiveness to all the facts of the case. Thus 'art' in the general sense which I require is any selection by which the concrete facts are so arranged as to elicit attention to particular values which are realisable by them. For example, the mere disposing of the human body and the eyesight so as to get a good view of a sunset is a simple form of artistic selection. The habit of art is the habit of enjoying vivid values.

But, in this sense, art concerns more than sunsets. A factory, with its machinery, its community of operatives, its social service to the general population, its dependence upon organising and designing genius, its potentialities as a source of wealth to the holders of its stock is an organism exhibiting a variety of vivid values. What we want to train is the habit of apprehending such an organism in its completeness. It is very arguable that the science of political economy, as studied in its first period after the death of Adam Smith (1790), did more harm than good. It destroyed many economic fallacies, and taught how to think about the economic revolution then in progress. But it riveted on men a certain set of abstractions which were disastrous in their influence on modern mentality. It de-humanised industry. This is only one example of a general danger inherent in modern science. Its methodological procedure is exclusive and intolerant, and rightly so. It fixes attention on a definite group of abstractions, neglects everything else, and elicits every scrap of information and theory which is relevant to what it has retained. This method is triumphant, provided that the abstractions are judicious. But, however triumphant, the triumph is within limits. The neglect of these limits leads to disastrous oversights. The anti-rationalism of science is partly justified, as a preservation of its useful methodology; it is partly mere irrational prejudice. Modern professionalism is the training of minds to conform to the methodology. The historical revolt of the seventeenth century, and the earlier reaction towards naturalism, were examples of transcending the abstractions which fascinated educated society in the Middle Ages. These early ages had an ideal of rationalism, but they failed in its pursuit. For they neglected to note that the methodology of reasoning requires the limitations involved in the abstract. Accordingly, the true rationalism must always transcend itself by recurrence to the concrete in search of inspiration. A self-satisfied rationalism is in effect a form of anti-rationalism. It means an arbitrary halt at a particular set of abstractions. This was the case with science.

There are two principles inherent in the very nature of things, recurring in some particular embodiments whatever field we explore—the spirit of change, and the spirit of conservation. There can be nothing real without both. Mere change without conservation is a passage from nothing to nothing. Its final integration yields mere transient non-entity. Mere conservation without change cannot conserve. For after all, there is a flux of circumstance, and the freshness of being evaporates under mere repetition. The character of existent reality is composed of organisms enduring through the flux of things. The low type of organisms have achieved a self-identity dominating their whole physical life. Electrons, molecules, crystals, belong to this type. They exhibit a massive and complete sameness. In the higher types, where life appears, there is greater complexity. Thus, though there is a complex, enduring pattern, it has retreated into deeper recesses of the total fact. In a sense, the self-identity of a human being is more abstract than that of a crystal. It is the life of the spirit. It relates rather to the individualisation of the creative activity; so that the changing circumstances received from the environment are differentiated from the living personality, and are thought of as forming its perceived field. In truth, the field of perception and the perceiving mind are abstractions which, in the concrete, combine into the successive bodily events. The psychological field, as restricted to sense-objects and passing emotions, is the minor permanence, barely rescued from the nonentity of mere change; and the mind is the major permanence, permeating that complete field, whose endurance is the living soul. But the soul would wither without fertilisation from its transient experiences. The secret of the higher organisms lies in their two grades of permanences. By this means the freshness of the environment is absorbed into the permanence of the soul. The changing environment is no longer, by reason of its variety, an enemy to the endurance of the organism. The pattern of the higher organism has retreated into the recesses of the individualised activity. It has become a uniform way of dealing with circumstances; and this way is only strengthened by having a proper variety of circumstances to deal with.

This fertilisation of the soul is the reason for the necessity of art. A static value, however serious and important, becomes unendurable by its appalling monotony of endurance. The soul cries aloud for release into change. It suffers the agonies of claustrophobia. The transitions of humour, wit, irreverence, play, sleep, and—above all—of art are necessary for it. Great art is the arrangement of the environment so as to provide for the soul vivid, but transient, values. Human beings require something which absorbs them for a time, something out of the routine which they can stare at. But you cannot subdivide life, except in the abstract analysis of thought. Accordingly, the great art is more than a transient refreshment. It is something which adds to the permanent richness of the soul's self-attainment. It justifies itself both by its immediate enjoyment, and also by its discipline of the inmost being. Its discipline is not distinct from enjoyment, but by reason of it. It transforms the soul into the permanent realisation of values extending beyond its former self. This element of transition in art is shown by the restlessness exhibited in its history. An epoch gets saturated by the masterpieces of any one style. Something new must be discovered. The human being wanders on. Yet there is a balance in things. Mere change before the attainment of adequacy of achievement, either in quality or output, is destructive of greatness. But the importance of a living art, which moves on and yet leaves its permanent mark, can hardly be exaggerated.

In regard to the aesthetic needs of civilised society the reactions of science have so far been unfortunate. Its materialistic basis has directed attention to *things* as opposed to *values*. The antithesis is a false one, if taken in a concrete sense. But it is valid at the abstract level of ordinary thought. This misplaced emphasis coalesced with the abstractions of political economy, which are in fact the abstractions in terms of which commercial affairs are carried on. Thus all thought concerned with social organisation expressed itself in terms of material things and of capital. Ultimate values were excluded. They were politely bowed to, and then handed over to the clergy to be kept for Sundays. A creed of competitive business morality was evolved, in some respects curiously high; but entirely devoid of consideration for the value of human life. The workmen were conceived as mere hands, drawn from the pool of labour. To God's question, men gave the answer of Cain—'Am I my brother's keeper?'; and they incurred Cain's guilt. This was the atmosphere in which the industrial revolution was accomplished in England, and to a large extent elsewhere. The internal history of England during the last half century has been an endeavour slowly and painfully to undo the evils wrought in the first stage of the new epoch. It may be that civilisation will never recover from the bad climate which enveloped the introduction of machinery. This climate pervaded the whole commercial system of the progressive northern European races. It was partly the result of aesthetic errors of Protestantism and partly the result of scientific materialism, and partly the result of the natural greed of mankind, and partly the result of the abstractions of political economy. An illustration of my point is to be found in Macaulay's Essay criticising Southey's *Colloquies on Society*. It was written in 1830. Now Macaulay was a very favourable example of men living at that date, or at any date. He had genius; he was kind-hearted, honourable, and a reformer. This is the extract:—'We are told, that our age has invented atrocities beyond the imagination of our fathers; that society has been brought into a state compared with which extermination would be a blessing; and all because the dwellings of cotton-spinners are naked and rectangular. Mr. Southey has found out a way he tells us, in which the effects of manufactures and agriculture may be compared. And what is this way? To stand on a hill, to look at a cottage and a factory, and to see which is the prettier.'

Southey seems to have said many silly things in his book; but, so far as this extract is concerned, he could make a good case for himself if he returned to earth after the lapse of nearly a century. The evils of the early industrial system are now a commonplace of knowledge. The point which I am insisting on is the stone-blind eye with which even the best men of that time regarded the importance of aesthetics in a nation's life. I do not believe that we have as yet nearly achieved the right estimate. A contributory cause, of substantial efficacy to produce this disastrous error, was the scientific creed that matter in motion is the one concrete reality in nature; so that aesthetic values form an adventitious, irrelevant addition.

There is another side to this picture of the possibilities of decadence. At the present moment a discussion is raging as to the future of civilisation in the novel circumstances of rapid scientific and technological advance. The evils of the future have been diagnosed in various ways, the loss of religious faith, the malignant use of material power, the degradation attending a differential birth rate favouring the lower types of humanity, the suppression of aesthetic creativeness. Without doubt, these are all evils, dangerous and threatening. But they are not new. From the dawn of history, mankind has always been losing its religious faith, has always suffered from the malignant use of material power, has always suffered from the infertility of its best intellectual types, has always witnessed the periodical decadence of art. In the reign of the Egyptian king, Tutankhamen, there was raging a desperate religious struggle between Modernists and Fundamentalists; the cave pictures exhibit a phase of delicate aesthetic achievement as superseded by a period of comparative vulgarity; the religious leaders, the great thinkers, the great poets and authors, the whole clerical caste in the Middle Ages, have been notably infertile; finally, if we attend to what actually has happened in the past, and disregard romantic visions of democracies, aristocracies, kings, generals, armies, and merchants, material power has generally been wielded with blindness, obstinacy and selfishness, often with brutal malignancy. And yet, mankind has progressed. Even if you take a tiny oasis of peculiar excellence, the type of modern man who would have most chance of happiness in ancient Greece at its best period is probably (as now) an average professional heavy-weight boxer, and not an average Greek scholar from Oxford or Germany. Indeed, the main use of the Oxford scholar would have been his capability of writing an ode in glorification of the boxer. Nothing does more harm in unnerving men for their duties in the present, than the attention devoted to the points of excellence in the past as compared with the average failure of the present day.

But, after all, there have been real periods of decadence; and at the present time, as at other epochs, society is decaying, and there is need for preservative action. Professionals are not new to the world. But in the past, professionals have formed unprogressive castes. The point is that professionalism has now been mated with progress. The world is now faced with a self-evolving system, which it cannot stop. There are dangers and advantages in this situation. It is obvious that the gain in material power affords opportunity for social betterment. If mankind can rise to the occasion, there lies in front a golden age of beneficent creativeness. But material power in itself is ethically neutral. It can equally well work in the wrong direction. The problem is not how to produce great men, but how to produce great societies. The great society will put up the men for the occasions. The materialistic philosophy emphasised the given quantity of material, and thence derivatively the given nature of the environment. It thus operated most unfortunately upon the social conscience of mankind. For it directed almost exclusive attention to the aspect of struggle for existence in a fixed environment. To a large extent the environment is fixed, and to this extent there is a struggle for existence. It is folly to look at the universe through rose-tinted spectacles. We must admit the struggle. The question is, who is to be eliminated. In so far as we are educators, we have to have clear ideas upon that point; for it settles the type to be produced and the practical ethics to be inculcated.

10.3   A CONVERSATION ON EDUCATION*

by Robert M. Hutchins

*What in your opinion
is the ideal education?*

Ideal education is the one that develops intellectual power. I arrive at this conclusion by a process of elimination. Educational institutions are the only institutions that can develop intellectual power. The ideal education is not an *ad hoc* education, not an education directed to immediate needs; it is not a specialized education, or a pre-professional education; it is not a utilitarian education. It is an education calculated to develop the mind.

There may be many ways, all equally good, of developing the mind. I have old-fashioned prejudices in favor of the three R's and the liberal arts, in favor of trying to understand the greatest works that the human race has produced. I believe that these are the permanent necessities, the intellectual tools that are needed to understand the ideas and the ideals of our world. This does not exclude later specialization or later professional education; but I insist that without the intellectual techniques needed to understand ideas, and without at least an acquaintance with the major ideas that have animated mankind since the dawn of history, no man may call himself educated.

*How much truth
is there in the charge
that education
can be dangerous?*

Education can be dangerous. It is very difficult to make it not dangerous. In fact, it is almost impossible. The only way that you can prevent education from being dangerous is to try to develop an educational system in which the pupil is exposed to no ideas whatever. We are working hard on this, but fortunately we seem unlikely to succeed, at any rate in the immediate future. I think there is some possibility that the rulers of the oligarchy in Russia may come to regret the exposure of their total population to as high a degree of education as they are now exposing them to.

*Reprinted from *A Conversation on Education*, A Report to the Center for the Study of Democratic Institutions (Santa Barbara, California: Center for the Study of Democratic Institutions, The Fund for the Republic Inc., 1963), with permission of the author and publisher.

370

Do you feel there is any danger
of thought control or political control
in our schools if federal aid
to education is increased?

The answer to this question is no. I am *for* federal aid to education. I am *for* federal aid to parochial schools. I am *for* federal aid to anybody who will do a sound educational job. The demand for education is such that all who offer it are now tax-exempt. The next step will be to recognize that since they are assisting in the performance of a public task, they may receive public help.

It is unjust to deprive the people of one state of education simply because they live in a locality that is poorer than another. We are either one country or we are not. If we are one, we had better see to it that everybody in it gets a decent education if we can because we can't tell when he is going to be living next door to us! Fifty per cent of the families in America have moved within the last five years. A good part of the state of Mississippi has moved in next door to where I used to live in Chicago. Think of where the population of Los Angeles has come from. Since we know that everybody in this country is on the move, we can't tell whose education or what state's education we may suffer from—or profit by—in our own community.

On the question of thought control, one of the great American delusions is that money automatically carries with it the control of an educational program. It is true that money may do that. But it is only true in countries that allow it to happen. The Minister of Education of the Netherlands has the power under the law of appointing all the professors in the universities of Holland. I asked him once why he didn't exercise this power. Why didn't he appoint a teacher that the professors at the University of Leyden wouldn't like and then see what would happen? He answered, "My government would fall." In other words, the people of Holland are perfectly willing to let him have the authority as long as he doesn't use it. They recognize that there may be an emergency under which it would be useful for him to have the power. But as long as there is no emergency, as long as the universities are doing their job the way the people want them to do it, the faculties have complete control of the universities in Holland despite the fact that all the money comes from the state.

Seventy-five per cent of the money for Oxford and Cambridge comes from the public treasury. No Englishman supposes for a moment that any representative of the government can in any way affect the teaching, the study, or the research program of those universities.

The reason for the American delusion is that American education developed *ad hoc*. The Puritans said that they dreaded to leave an illiterate ministry to the churches when their present ministers should lie in the dust, and so they founded Harvard. They founded schools in Massachusetts Bay because the ministers had to have congregations that could read. The Morrill Act of 1862 gave 30,000 acres of federal land for every seat to which a state was entitled in Congress. For the establishment of what? Institutions to study the practical arts and improve the condition of our people. Half of these institutions were incorporated into state universities, thus introducing a type of curriculum hitherto unknown in the Western world.

So the situation in this country is one in which the educational system has always been somebody doing something to somebody else, and the one who puts up the money to get it done is considered to be entitled to see that it *is* done. But this is a wholly erroneous conception of education. If education is seen as achieving its best results under a system that permits those who are dedicating their lives to it to determine policy, and if this is understood by the people, the fact that the government of the United States rather than, say, the government of California may be controlling the educational system will be wholly immaterial. As for me, I would rather trust the government of the United States than, for example, the government of Illinois any day.

What is the relationship, if any,
between education and the artist,
especially the literary artist,
in our society?

I believe that art is a way of looking at the world, a way of making it intelligible, a way of understanding it—a most important way of looking at it and understanding it. I think that art is didactic, but it is not and should not be expressly didactic. A poet who started out to write a didactic poem would write a bad one. A literary artist who started out to write a text-book might write a good text-book but he would not be a good literary artist.

The object of the artist is to say what he sees, and the problem of all creative work is how to get outside your culture so that you can see it. The program at Oxford University known as Ancient Greats would be incomprehensible to us because we have been brought up on the idea of *ad hoc* education. We think that if the problem is, let us say, how to make young people moral, the way to do it is to have elementary, intermediate, and advanced courses in morality.

The proconsuls of the British Empire in the nineteenth century went out with an educational equipment consisting of a thorough mastery of the language, history, and philosophy of Greece and Rome—two civilizations that were dead. It was through the study of these two high civilizations that these men, two thousand years after Greece and Rome had died, were able to get outside their own civilization, outside their own structure of government, outside their own history, and mark out the lines that their empire should follow.

And so it is with the artist. His contribution is in seeing something that the rest of us cannot see and helping us to see it. The contribution of the artist is critical, therefore, rather than didactic. And perhaps this is one of the differences between socialist realism, as we see it in Russia, and the kind of art that is developing elsewhere in the West. Socialist realism is the slave or servant of the official dogma. The best of the art in the rest of the world is not propaganda but, rather, another way of seeing our society so that we can understand and judge it.

Do you think our university degrees
reflect the learning,
the quality of education,
that comparable degrees do in Europe?

No. Ordinary Americans arriving at age 22 are about where the ordinary European is at the age of 18 or 19. Liberal education is almost totally absent in this country. In the Middle West the high school is the place where the band practices. The freshman and sophomore years in college are a repetition of high school courses. The junior and senior years are periods of specialization, and in this country specialization is a process by which one narrows the field of vision. The usual definition of a specialist is a man who knows more and more about less and less; the American definition of a specialist is a man who knows less and less about less and less.

There is one odd fact which I will cite as consolation; that is, if American students have not learned very much, at least they have not been drained of their vitality. They have not been over-examined. They have not been over-taught. They have not, God knows, been over-worked! The result is that they arrive at age 22 in a state of freshness and exuberance quite unknown among European students of the same age. A European student has been so pursued by his parents and his teachers as he has gone from one competition to another competition to another competition, from scholarship to scholarship to scholarship, that by the time he reaches 22 he is totally exhausted.

American students at the age of 22 exhibit on entrance to graduate or professional school the most remarkable powers of recuperation. I have seen "big-men-on-campus" at Yale, who never did a stroke of work from the time they were born until the time they graduated from Yale College, blossom into geniuses in the law school. This is important. But it is important, you will notice, only for those who go on. For those who leave college at the age of 22 and go to work, all we can say is that they have had, we hope, an interesting social experience.

To be fair, there are some promising signs in education. It has been said that we have not had the three R's in America, we had the six R's: Remedial Reading, Remedial 'Riting, and Remedial 'Rithmetic. But there is no doubt that under the National Defense Education Act remedial arithmetic, as least, is soon going to be a thing of the past, and a new level of mathematical and scientific achievement will be reached. A blow has also been struck against the lockstep in American education. There are hundreds of high schools and six hundred colleges that now cooperate to put the student where he belongs in terms of his ability to do the work instead of in terms of his period of incarceration.

At Harvard a fifth of the freshman class was admitted without completing the formal requirements of the secondary school. This is unprecedented. Programmed learning, the so-called teaching machines (which are not teaching machines at all), may make an important contribution because they will require a complete re-analysis of the course of study. If they succeed, it will mean that each individual in a group will proceed at his own pace. The class as such would disappear. And the principal handicap to progress within the group will be removed.

> *What effect*
> *do you think*
> *the American educational system*
> *has on the American character?*

The educational system does not, I think, have quite the influence on the formation of character that is commonly supposed. The family is the place in which moral training is given. And Aristotle is as correct today as he was two thousand years ago when he said that those may be given sound moral instruction in the educational system who have been morally well disposed at home. The responsibility of the family and the church for moral instruction is greater than that of the educational system. Or shall I put it this way: The influence of the educational system on the moral character of the young is less than that of the family and less than that which the church could have.

If I had to try to compare the influence on the American character of, let us say, the University of Chicago with that of, let us say, Henry R. Luce, I would say that Mr. Luce had from two to twenty-five times as much influence as the University of Chicago. I might even say that Mr. Luce and his magazines have more effect on the American character than the whole educational system put together. It is not, however, necessary for me to go that far in order to make the point. If you take all the radio and television stations of this country, if you take the newspapers and the magazines and roll them up together, and ask yourself what the influence of these institutions is upon the American character as opposed to the educational system, I think you would admit that the mass media have carried the field.

But let us not be invidious. The educational system has steadily deteriorated; the mass media have steadily deteriorated. Since we cannot assume that they have no influence, we must assume that they have a bad influence. This is the assumption that I make. The educational system has turned into a program of accommodating the young until we are ready to have them go to work. The object of American education is to get everybody into school and keep them there as long as possible. Since they are there and must stay there, they have to do something. What they do is to learn what Dr. James B. Conant calls "marketable skills," to the acquisition of which he thinks 85 per cent of our school children are destined. This is in spite of the fact that Dr. Conant knows perfectly well that by the time they graduate the skills will be unmarketable. Either the skill will not be in demand at all, or it will be in demand at an entirely different level. This means that the pupil who spends his time acquiring a marketable skill will have nothing to market.

If I were to try to locate a single, grave, overwhelming defect in the American character, it is lack of respect for the mind. There is no particular reason why we should have this respect as far as the practical operation of our lives is concerned. In 1776 Adam Smith said that the best investment a man could make in the colonies was to marry a widow with four children. There was so much work to do that anybody could get rich in no time. The aim of the whole industrial system is to reduce all operations down to the level where they can be performed by a twelve-year-old child, and demand very little of his attention at that. This was so in the nineteenth century: Horatio Alger didn't need a mind. And in 1948, a psychologist at Connecticut College, speaking before the American Association on Mental Deficiency, showed that the average male moron makes $3.50 per week more than a normal male worker; and the female moron makes more than a normal female industrial worker. So what is the advantage of not being a moron?

Another evidence of our lack of respect for the mind is the way in which we make a virtue out of a boy's working his way through college. When I was young, if you didn't work your way through college, you were a sissy, you were a sponger on your family. It never occurred to anybody that working your way through college was an anti-educational program. Education was not regarded as intrinsically of value. The value lay in the rugged, self-sustaining experience of working. I worked eight hours a day in a factory when I was in college. I would have been far better off at home. But I wasn't supposed to learn anything in college anyway. I was supposed to have the great character-building experience of working my way through. When you consider that the Scots for generations have been clubbing together to send their boys to the best public schools, to the best universities, with all expenses paid, because they understand the intellectual value of the educational experience, the American attitude seems fantastic.

When Herbert von Bismarck was following his father into the secretary's office of the Vatican and the secretary let the Prince von Bismarck in but wouldn't let Herbert in, Herbert Bismarck pounded the door. The secretary said, "What's the matter?" He said, "I am Count Herbert von Bismarck." And the papal secretary said, "That explains but does not justify your conduct." I have offered explanation of the American lack of respect for the mind, but I cannot justify it. And I do not believe that this explanation will stand up much longer. It seems to me imperative to develop the intellectual power of this country if we propose to cope with the problems that we see on every hand.

What sort of problems
are you thinking about?

I will give you just one. It is estimated that over the next ten years thousands of new jobs a week will be required to meet the employment needs of the population, regardless of automation. If you count in the people who are going to be replaced by automation, the number of new jobs that will be needed reaches astronomical proportions. It is freely predicted that automation will get rid not merely of handworkers but also of middle management. (Sears, Roebuck, for example, has 2,000 people at the middle-management level.) It is estimated that in 1970 50 per cent of the boys graduating from high school will not be able to find work.

This is a new situation. Our founding fathers believed that the twin curses of mankind were indolence and the love of money. The way to overcome the first was to appeal to the second. But what is going to happen in a workless, wantless, diseaseless, and, if we are to survive at all, a warless world?

It is suggested that machines are going to do all the work and can produce everything we need. In 1959 we consumed 8,000 kilograms of coal or its equivalent per capita in this country as compared to 8 in Ethiopia, and something like 3,800 in Russia. And the energy gradient is steadily rising. Calculations have been made of the energy put forth by slaves in previous days. According to these calculations every man, woman, and child in the United States now has eighty-five slaves. There is no question that if we operated our farms and our factories at full capacity we could feed the world.

What are we going to do with our goods? What are we going to do with ourselves? We are not going to find out by that simple method of trial and error which was satisfactory in the days when we were filling out the frontiers and building up the industrial system behind the walls afforded us by two oceans. The problem of world organization, for example, is central, and anybody who thinks that we are going simply to stumble into the right formulation of a world organization is out of his mind.

In sum, the great immediate task in this country is the development of intellectual power.

> *Your pessimism bordering on despair*
> *is partially justified.*
> *However, the very fact that technology*
> *rests on major scientific competence*
> *deserves recognition, does it not?*

I agree with the statement. Anything I have said that sounds derogatory of natural science has been misinterpreted. I am a great supporter of natural science, as the record at the University of Chicago will show; and St. John's College, with which I was connected, is the only college in the United States that requires every student to have four years in the laboratory. I believe that science is an indispensable part of liberal education.

I think that C. P. Snow, with his view of two separate, disconnected cultures—science on the one hand and the humanities on the other—is utterly mistaken. The notion that there *are* two cultures, or that anybody who is seriously interested in education is seriously in favor of two cultures, is absurd. Everybody who is interested in liberal education, everybody who is interested in trying to help young people understand the world in which they are going to live, must recognize that science is a necessary part of their education.

This has nothing to do with what I am not despairing but concerned about, which is the role of technology in our lives. Let it be admitted that technology is a human product and ought to be subject to human control. But how do you do this when the whole civilization in which we live is becoming more and more technological and where, more and more, technology is taking us over without our even knowing it? This is the problem.

Do you think it likely
that the American people
will permit themselves to be taxed
so that an adequate public school
system may be developed?

Yes. But one must add that there is something to be said for those who do not believe in increasing the cost of education. Nobody really knows what an adequate system of education in the United States would cost, because the expenditures on education in the United States are of the most heterogeneous character. Take a town like Eau Claire in Wisconsin. It has a new, two-million-dollar high school which is the pride and joy of the community. Of course the present inhabitants and their grandchildren are going to be in debt for years paying for it. According to the study I made of it when I was there, exactly one-half of this building is devoted to educational purposes. The rest of it is gymnasium, "natatorium"—they don't call it a swimming pool—shops, and so on. And the salaries of the teachers are less than half what they ought to be. As a matter of fact, 50 per cent of the teachers of Eau Claire ought not to be there because the subjects they teach ought not to be taught.

Take the American university system. Let us say that a university should be a center of independent thought. Let us say that nobody should be admitted to a university unless he is capable of independent thought. Let us say, further, that nobody should teach in a university unless he has demonstrated the same capability. Then let us ask, how many students in American universities have demonstrated the capacity for independent thought? How many professors have demonstrated this capacity? How many courses require thought of any kind? If we were to eliminate the students, the professors, and the courses that do not require thought, who knows what our budget would be?

Direct education, education in how to do this, how to solve this, how to get there, is almost always a delusion. What is wanted from education is not a miscellaneous rag-bag of remedies or helpful hints for current situations, because the one thing you know is that those situations are not going to remain current. If you try to give helpful hints to healthy housewives aged 14, by the time they are 22 we may all be living in tents.

The job of education is to train the mind to cope with new situations and new complications, to develop critical judgments of new problems as they present themselves for solution.

> *Since we agree that the*
> *public educational system is far from*
> *vigorous in its demands upon the mind*
> *of the student, what can the parent who*
> *really desires an education for his children*
> *do for them? Private schools are few.*
> *Parochial schools—but we wish a separation*
> *of church and state in education.*
> *Parental supplements—*
> *please don't mention the PTA.*
> *How can one decide?*

The best test of where *not* to send your children is a school's requirements for physical education. If they are extensive, you should take your child somewhere else at once. There is a general view in California that the object of education is to keep the young outdoors. Well, we should take advantage of our natural endowments. But I think this has been carried to excessive lengths.

What can one do? What can any individual do in this bureaucratic culture? The sources of power are mysterious and remote. We don't even know how to find the people who are really making the decisions, and if we are lucky enough to identify the office, we would undoubtedly be told that the man who had made the decision was out of town. There is probably no way of breaking through the barriers with which people who have vested interests in certain operations protect themselves from public interference.

Anyone who watched, as I did, the Los Angeles Board of Education during the heroic struggle that culminated in the prohibition of all references to UNESCO in the schools of Los Angeles will recognize why it often seems almost hopeless to try to fight against the forces that are preventing education from arising in this country. But, as it happens, this is an interesting example. Something *did* happen in Los Angeles. It took a little while, but they carried the business of anti-education in the educational system just a little too far, and the anti-UNESCO people finally lost out.

So I think that the only thing it is possible to do in a democratic country on any subject is to keep talking and to seize every opportunity to talk. I recently ran across a letter from Thomas Jefferson to John Adams. Jefferson, at the age of 70, wrote to John Adams, aged 78. Jefferson said, more or less in these words, "I state my difference with you not because I wish to begin a controversy when we are both too old to change opinions arrived at over a long life of experience and reflection. I state my difference with you only because I believe that we ought before we die to explain ourselves to one another."

This in a sentence or two is the aim of a democratic society. It is not necessary that we should agree. But it is necessary that we should explain ourselves to one another.

Ernest Barker put it this way, "The object of democracy is to engage all the people in the effective discussion of their public affairs." I grant that the next step is almost an act of faith. That is, one has to say, "I have faith that if there is effective discussion on the part of all the people in their public affairs, their public affairs will improve."

This act of faith I am willing to make.

I believe a life without theory has come to an end in the United States. A search for principles has begun. We have been absent-minded. Now at last we have to apply our minds. We have to think. And the task of revitalizing the American creed and creatively reinterpreting it and making it once more the light and hope of the world is primarily an intellectual task.

10.4 EXISTENTIALISM, PHENOMENOLOGY, AND THE PHILOSOPHY OF EDUCATION*

by L. F. Troutner

For a twenty-minute paper, "Existentialism, Phenomenology, and the Philosophy of Education" admittedly represents quite a mouthful. To guard against choking as well as to aid in the digestion, at the outset I am going to outline the argument of this short essay.

Among other things the existentialist thinkers have pointed up for the whole world to see the irreducible uniqueness of each individual existent. Not, let me hasten to add, an individual unique and solitary viewed in opposition to society, but rather an individual-intending-his-world, i.e. a unique individual existent as "being-in-the-world." In so doing they have also laid bare one of the special problems which is endemic to philosophy itself, viz., how can one connect the philosophical enterprise of "thinking about man" with existent man in all his uniqueness and particularity. This special problem involves not only general philosophy but, even more so, the philosophy of education, i.e., if one assumes it is important to connect "thinking about the *education* of man" with the unique "existence of each individual man." The methods of rationalism and empiricism have tended to conceal this problem. The method of phenomenology, on the other hand, though maybe not resolving it will at least reveal the problem which is always the first step in any eventual resolution. At the same time the introduction of phenomenology to education will keep our eyes and energies focused on the *site* of education, i.e., the *Lebenswelt* of each individual existent. Hence, the three big bites: Existentialism, Phenomenology, and the Philosophy of Education.

One of the most insightful definitions of existentialism comes from the pen of Ronald Grimsely, the Welsh philosopher. He defines it as "*a fresh attempt to connect thinking about man with the 'existence' of man as something unique and personal and perhaps irreducible to non-human terms.*"[1] So described it represents an attempt to bridge the gap between thinking about "lived reality" and the "reality lived." It represents an attempt to bridge the gap between intellectualizing about life and life as lived. Whether or not this is possible is still open to question; but

---

*Reprinted from *Proceedings of the Twentieth Annual Meeting of the Philosophy of Education Society* (1964), pages 118-124, with permission of the author and publisher.
[1]Ronald Grimsley, *Existentialist Thought*, Cardiff: University of Wales Press, 1955, p. 5. (Italics is mine.)

in spite of some very formidable difficulties, the existential thinker is attempting to effect a meaningful union between philosophizing about existence and existence itself.

As Grimsley's definition suggests, all existential thinkers are faced with a peculiar problem when they attempt to formulate a "philosophy of existence." This problem stems directly from the basic incompatibility between "existence" and "philosophy" as most philosophers traditionally use the words. Existence is immediate, concrete, self-conscious, and radically subjective. According to M. Lalande's *Vocabularie de Philosophie*, "existence" must be understood "in the strong, concrete sense of living or lived reality, in opposition to abstractions and theories."[2] Philosophy, on the other hand, is usually thought of in terms of conceptualization and theorizing which involves a certain detachment. The existentialist is committed to the concrete particularity of existence, of which he himself forms a part, and consequently he finds it very difficult to separate himself from the object of his thought. All existential thinkers wrestle with this problem of the expression of existence, or, more precisely, the problem of "personal or 'non-objective' thinking and its expression."

How can we connect thinking about man conceptually with the concrete existence of man? How can we philosophize about the immediate experience of existence which is so personal and particular without changing it into something other than existence? The existential thinker finds himself in a dilemma similar to St. Augustine's who, when asked: "What is time?" answered; "If nobody asks me, I know; but if I wished to explain it to one who should ask me, I do not know."[3] In any case there is a sense in which the very act of conceptualizing existence makes of it something other than existence. The existentialist thinkers are split down the middle as to the possibility of such a conceptualization.

From one perspective immediate experience does seem to be ineffable. William Earle, one of the foremost American existential commentators, argues, and quite convincingly, the impossibility of conceptualizing the immediate experience of existence. Since conceptualization is inherently categorical and/or essential, and since existence must perforce refer to my existence, i.e. "the life whose meaning I am seeking is the life I am now living,"[4] a conception of existence constitutes a contradiction in terms. Much of the thought of the founding fathers of existentialism

---

[2]As quoted in *Ibid.*, p. 3.
[3]As quoted in Rollo May (ed.), *Existence—A New Dimension in Psychiatry and Psychology*, New York: Basic Books, Inc., 1958, p. 68.
[4]William Earle, "The Concept of Existence," *The Journal of Philosophy*, LVII (No. 23, November 10, 1960): 742.

leads one to the apparent impossibility of structuring a "philosophy of existence." Both Kierkegaard and Nietzsche advocated a type of "thinking existence" rather than "thinking about existence," a "passionate thinking" rather than "thinking about passion."

This "*existential* attitude," as Tillich describes it, dominates the thought of Kierkegaard, Nietzsche, and Marcel. In other existential thinkers, however, the *philosophical expression* of this attitude, which they consider possible, dominates. In other words there are those who believe that the structure of existence possesses certain essential traits and that it can be done by using the method of phenomenology and, at the same time, subordinating existence to the larger category of Being.

But what does all this have to do with education? Actually the outcome of this "special problem" is not so important to education as what it points to. Regardless of what position you take on this issue, the result is the same as far as its impact upon education. All existential thinkers are pointing up the absolute particularity of each individual existent as being-in-the-world. If you claim that it is impossible to conceptualize immediate experience, you are at the same time saying that the existence of each individual is so unique that it is impossible to generalize about it. If, on the other hand, you take the opposite position that existence can be described in general concepts, you still end up accentuating the absolute singularity of elements of existence, viz., alienation, anxiety, temporality, project, etc., when actualized in a particular existent allow for such manifold variations that the result is a unique patterning in each instance. The configuration of my "alienation-anxiety-temporality-project," for example, is unique—and so is yours.

At the same time the existential thinker accentuates the uniqueness of each individual existent he is also pointing up the difficulty of connecting "thinking about" the *education* of man with "man the existent." From a slightly different vantage point the problem which plagues the formulation of a "philosophy of existence" is the very same problem which is involved in any attempt to construct a philosophy of education —education here being used in its more generic sense. There is no particular problem in connecting concepts with other concepts, or generalizations with other generalizations. After all, that's what philosophers and educational philosophers do all the time—Hegel being one of the best examples. But to connect concepts about the education of man, concepts like knowledge, value, and the nature of man with man in his concrete existence is quite another matter.

It is relatively easy to connect thinking about the education of man with existent man when man is defined as a "rational animal" or as a "psycho-biological satisfaction-seeking, problem-solving organism." It is relatively easy to connect thinking about the education of man with existent man when man is viewed empirically as a natural object or epistemologically as a knowing subject. *But note this fact.* Existent man is not a rational animal. In his own unique particularity he is much more than, in fact he is radically different from, a rational animal or a problem-solving organism. He is also much more than and radically different from an empirical object or an epistemological subject. Here we are not attempting to connect thinking about the education of man with existent man, but rather we are taking the easy way out. We are merely connecting one set of abstractions with another that is somehow vaguely *supposed to represent* existent man. The existentialist has laid bare this supposition for what it is—a misrepresentation of fact. Here we see language being separated from its referent, and, much as Marx suggests, taking on a life of its own. As Husserl recommends, we must "get back to the facts themselves!" the facts here meaning the phenomenon as it reveals itself. We must return to a "radical empiricism" which is concerned with "the fullness of experience in its total concrete, existential density."[5]

How can one begin to connect thinking about the education of man with existent man? This is not an easy task, as the existentialist will testify. But one thing is quite certain. If past performances mean anything, we cannot make this strategic juncture by using the methods of rationalism or empiricism. We have yet to see the fact of my existence in all of its immediate particularity successfully incorporated into any strictly rationalistic or empirical philosophical formulation. To make this strategic juncture the method of phenomenology is needed.

The phenomenological method is a descriptive method, and the type of philosophy that it suggests can be called a radical empiricism. It differs in many ways from traditional empiricism. For example, it refuses to accept unclarified and unfounded metaphysical assumptions like the latent body-mind dualism with its consequent view of "the subject as a passive receptor of discrete, atomic, impressions from the outside world" that is found in the British variety of empiricism and the additional assumption that the subject of experience is itself nothing but another object among objects that is so characteristic of the American-Deweyan variety of empiricism. Husserl's challenge to make of philosophy a rigorous science of experience does not refer to a simple and uncritical scientific naturalism, but rather "to a presuppositionless philosophy which will reach what is absolutely primary and most fundamental in experi-

---

[5]Pierre Thevenaz, *What is Phenomenology?* Chicago: Quadrangle Books, Inc., 1962, p. 28

ence." Phenomenology goes to the fundamental structure of conscious experience. "It does not concentrate exclusively on either the object of experience or on the subject of experience, but on the point of contact where being and consciousness meet."[6]

The science of "Pure Phenomenology" developed by Edmund Husserl claims to "be nothing beyond a Theory of Essential Being (essences) developed within a medium of pure intuition."[7] Basic to such a formidable claim is the belief that "universal essences" do exist, not in a separate realm as in Plato, but as constituted in experience. "The truth is that everyone sees ideas, 'essences,' and sees them, so to speak, continuously; they work with them when they think and they also pass judgments about them. But, from their theoretical 'standpoint,' people explain them away."[8] To Husserl, that there is something meant in the world of experience. Two people could say the same sentence, but to each the meaning might be different. But this only points to the fact that there is an ideal essence or meaning involved because they both could have meant the same thing.

The battle cry of Phenomenology is "back to the things themselves." The "things" to which a return is demanded are "phenomena"—but with a very special meaning. Husserl adopted the Greek usage of the word "phenomenon" which means "that which displays itself." It signifies something which presents or "exhibits" itself to the experiment. The purpose of the phenomenologist is to describe this phenomenon as it is, "as it reveals itself." And that which shall be revealed will be its general structure, its "essence" or meaning. But it will reveal itself to us only if we do not attempt to coerce it into one of our ready-made conceptual strait-jackets, only if we bracket out all theoretical "thinking models." This bracketing is necessary in order to free our experiential content from any muddying. We want to see these "ideas" or essences pure and unadulterated so our description will also be pure.

It is here being suggested that there is no valid reason why the same method cannot be applied to the phenomenon of education. Before one can "see" education phenomenologically, however, one must bracket out all unnecessary abstractions and all artificially conceived educational models and slogans which tend to conceal rather than reveal the reality which they are supposed to represent. Approaching education in this way

---

[6]Much of this description of phenomenology as a radical empiricism was gleaned from James Edie's excellent introduction of *What Is Phenomenology?* pp. 13-37.
[7]Edmund Husserl, *Ideas: General Introduction to Pure Phenomenology*, New York: Macmillan, 1952, p. 192.
[8]As quoted in John Passmore, *A Hundred Years of Philosophy*, London: Gerald Duckworth and Company, 1957, p. 190.

we can cut through the jungle of educational theorizing and get at the basic structure of the reality under question. It means bracketing out those educational thinking models that use "rational animals," "problem-solving organism," or "epistemological subjects" in their design. It means undercutting such concepts as "subject-object," "knowledge," "values," "curriculum," etc., and intuiting the essence of education. The addition of such an approach, it is believed, will make several substantial contributions to education.

(1) In being forced to slough off all educational thinking models preparatory to a phenomenological examination of education, the educator and especially the philosopher of education will become aware of the fact that he has been seeing education through a thinking model, and that his design generally allowed him to see only that portion of reality under investigation which can be accommodated by the design.

The revealing of assumptions hitherto held unconsciously always represents a net gain. There can be little doubt that thinking models such as the scientific, biological, or rationalistic designs can be useful tools to man, but implicit within their use lurks a real danger. With use follows familiarity, and soon, unknowingly, man fails to distinguish between his thinking models and his thinking self. He becomes his model, at which point the model starts to use the man rather than the man using the model. The agency for preception becomes the design, not the designer. The design working through the man selects and filters out the appropriate facts. Hence, imperceptibly, control passes from the conscious thinking self to the unconscious thinking model.

(2) The phenomenological approach to education will in contrast illuminate the empirical perspective of education for what it is: a method of objectifying and measuring some part or aspect of education in terms of some previously considered hypothetical construction. It will further reveal that the hypothesis in only a *representation* of an *aspect* of education, not education as it reveals itself in its basic structure.

It is impossible to measure the phenomenon as it is, the essence of the thing in *totality*. But one can measure a *part* of a thing by developing a theoretical formulation about it and then measuring it in terms of the theory. Instead of being receptive to the being of things as they are, in this case education, man has invested his objective representation of the real with being. This "scientific" attitude results in our becoming very busy with the scraps and pieces of information about education provided for us by the empirical method instead of being concerned with "seeing" education in its totality. .This may in part account for the fact that it is only the academically interested and the administrator, not the teacher, who is the closest to education. Any bearing such studies may have on education depends upon the hypothesis, validity of research design, the reliability and validity of the statistics used, the assumptions of the researcher, his community and culture *plus* a valid logical relationship, which often amounts to an ontological leap, between the findings and the *site* of education. It is small wonder that the teacher in the classroom has little use for the results of educational research. It is impossible to research the basic structure of education which has been reformulated into a representation of that which is.

(3) The introduction of phenomenology to education will also serve to point out the gulf between rational thought and education as it is revealed. Ever since Plato's Forms it somehow seems natural for the reason of western man to lift itself into aery abstractions and to forget about the earth, man, and being. In modern philosophy, especially since Descartes, man has figured largely as a thinking epistemological subject —"As an intellect that registers sense-data, makes propositions, reasons, and seeks the certainty of intellectual knowledge, but not as the man underneath all this, who is born, suffers and dies."[9] The existentialist is protesting against just such abstractness born of rationalism. In its stead they are attempting to bring the entire man complete with such unpleasantries as death, anxiety, guilt, fear and trembling, boredom, and despair into philosophy.

A logical, coherent, rational system of thought is a beautiful spectacle to behold, but, like Hegel's magnificent edifice, the individual existent in his lived reality cannot be accommodated in this type of building. It is all well and good to define man as a rational animal, but the human existent knows that much of him is not animal and not rational. It is all well and good to say that truth is a conformity of the thought of the subject with the external object, but this is all noise and empty symbolization unless truth is rooted in existence. The great weakness of the rational approach to education is that the thought tends to be cut off from the *site* of education which is the human existent.

(4) The final contribution of the phenomenological approach to education, as this author sees it, is attendant upon the results of such an examination. How would the basic meaning of education be described phenomenologically? How does its essential structure reveal itself to consciousness? Let us assume an intuitive inquiry is made and that one of the findings is that the *site* of education is the *Lebenswelt*, that particular "world view" of each individual existent. Under these circumstances the presence of a phenomenological approach to education in

---

[9]William Barrett, *Irrational Man—A Study in Existential Philosophy*, Garden City, New York: Doubleday & Co., Inc., 1958, p. 245.

the philosophy of education classification and at the same time it will constantly point a finger at the fact that much of empirical and rational education never touches the site of education. In other words the acceptance of a phenomenological approach to education will have the salutary effect of keeping the eyes of the educator focused on the ballgame rather than on a lot of statistics, hypotheses, and theories about the condition of the playing field, the average attendance, the gross gate, how much money is made on concessions, card stunts, etc. It will also help to restore some balance to our perspective of education. No longer will it be possible to reduce education to something like a machine which is used by societies to transmit their "culture." No longer will it be possible to think of education solely in terms of its multiplying dimensions and aspects such as finance, administration, pupil personnel services, teaching, counseling, etc. Education is more than the sum of its many dimensions. When it is reduced to its absolute minimum—that "something" without which it is nothing—we "see" education as that mysterious development that occurs in the private *Lebenswelt* of each individual existent, a world view which is unique in each case.

Although the existential thinker does not concern himself with the subject of formal education, *existentialism and education do meet on the primordial, preconceptual level of the immediate experience of Existence,* in the *Lebenswelt* of each individual. The introduction of the method of phenomenology into educational thinking will serve as an ever constant reminder of the significance and import of this strategic juncture where thinking about the education of man and the existence of man meet.

10.5 SOME OBSERVATIONS ON THE LOGICAL IMPLICATIONS OF PHILOSOPHIC THEORY FOR EDUCATIONAL THEORY AND PRACTICE*

by Joe R. Burnett

This paper poses answers to two questions. The first question is: "Do formal philosophies have logical implications for educational theory and practice?" The answer given is Yes, and it is an answer which will be justified by defining "logical implication" in a way consistent with ordinary philosophic usage. That way is had by conceiving logical implication in what will be termed a "situational"[1] manner, as opposed to what will be called "lay" and "formal" manners.

The second question is a mundane one, but one to which educational philosophers have seldom given specific consideration. It is: "What do educational philosophers do when they effectively develop the logical implications of a given formal philosophy for educational theory and practice?" Needless to say, the brevity of this paper precludes a thorough consideration of this question. But several things are mentioned which seem either necessary or, if not necessary, highly helpful to the effective use of formal philosophies.

I

Returning to the first question: *Do* formal philosophies have logical implications for educational theory and practice?

There can be distinguished three conceptions of "logical implication" in use today, and two of these conceptions would lead one to answer the question in a negative manner. These two conceptions will be called the "lay" and the "formal" views of logical implication.

The lay view mistakenly assumes that formal philosophies are, *in and of themselves*, rich with implications for specific cases of practice. In philosophy today this is taken to be the position of pre-Kantian rationalism and the method of learning which Bacon described as contentious—

*Reprinted from *Proceedings of the Fourteenth Annual Meeting of the Philosophy of Education Society* (1958), pages 51-57, with permission of the author and publisher.
[1]The "situational" position taken in this paper has been most fully developed by pragmatists in their theory of instrumental logic; but, since the position is not unique to pragmatism, the somewhat neutral term "situational" has been utilized in order to label the general position.

the position that from certain given first principles one could, merely by logical extension of those principles, derive statements about individual matters of fact not previously known. Today also, there are people who think that the lay view is characteristic of educational philosophizing. For instance, Sidney Hook remarks that "There is a great deal of nonsense talked about philosophy of education. This is particularly true of claims that a metaphysical epistemological position has logical implications for educational theory and practice."[2]

The lay view is nonsense because a general philosophic theory or system ordinarily specifies nothing about an individual matter of fact until the fact has been denoted and a statement concerning it "connected"[3] with the general philosophic theory. In short, on the basis on a general philosophic theory alone, one cannot logically deduce statements about a particular event or fact in the space-time matrix. It takes something more than the possession of general theory. It takes ability to formulate and connect statements concerning particular matters of fact with the general theory in a way which permits of valid process.

The second view, the formal view, is concerned with logical implication primarily as it functions internally to a given theoretical system. It is the position which stresses what Charles W. Morris speaks of as the "ultimate separation of valid form from empirical denotation."[4] Philosophers who emphasize this notion of logical implication tend to identify their concern with questions of valid form, and not directly with questions of empirical denotation and material truth.

Educational philosophers have noted the relevance and correctness of this view,[5] but they have gone right on, as many of us will continue to do in our lecturing and writing, utilizing formal philosophies in order to deduce descriptions and directives for empirical practice. But this mode

---

[2]Sidney Hook, "The Scope of Philosophy of Education," *Harvard Educational Review*, Vol. 26, No. 2 (Spring), 1956, p. 145.
[3]The notion of "connection" is not fully developed herein. For some examples of what is meant, in the context of popular discourse, see John Wisdom's article on "God," reprinted from *Proceedings of the Aristotelian Society*, 1944, in *Philosophy and Psycho-Analysis* (Oxford: Basil Blackwell, 1953), pp. 149-168. For a general discussion of related concepts, see Carl G. Hemple, "Fundamentals of Concept Formation in Empirical Science," *International Encyclopedia of United Science*, Vol. II, No. 7 (Chicago: University of Chicago Press, 1952), Chapter Two.
[4]Charles W. Morris, "The Relation of Formal to Instrumental Logic," *Essays in Philosophy*, T. V. Smith and W. K. Wright (eds.) (Chicago: Open Court Publishing Company, 1929), p. 255.
[5]See, for instances, the positions of Edward H. Reisner, "Philosophy and Science in the Western World: A Historical Overview," p. 32, and Mortimer J. Adler, "In Defense of the Philosophy of Education," pp. 230-235, *The Forty-First Yearbook: Part I, Philosophies of Education*, Nelson B. Henry (ed.) (Chicago: National Society for the Study of Education, 1942).

of proceeding is largely "out of order" in the formal view. Indeed, to some people it appears as downright absurdity.

For what appears to be an instance, attention is called to Professor Hook's criticism of a statement made by Professor Harry Broudy. Professor Broudy remarked that, among other methods, ". . . (a) common method of building a philosophy of education is to derive it from some philosophic position such as Idealism, Realism, Thomism, Pragmatism, or Existentialism. This approach asks the question: What does a given position imply for education?"[6] Professor Hook stated that "To encourage philosophers as Mr. Broudy does 'to derive (a philosophy of education) from some philosophic position such as Idealism, Realism, Thomism, Pragmatism, or Existentialism,' is to encourage them to perpetrate garrulous absurdities."[7]

This seems to be an instance in which a person using the "formal" conception looks with alarm at one of the traditionally accepted modes of procedure in educational philosophy. Let it be said that Professor Hook is correct in his criticism, *if* it is Professor Broudy's contention that deductive elaboration of philosophic positions for either theory or practice in education need concern itself *only* with philosophic systems *per se*.

Reading Professor Broudy's comments in context suggests that this was not his contention.[8] In any event, Professor Broudy need not have meant that, because a third conception of logical implication can justify the manner in which he thinks people can build philosophies of education. The third conception is the "situational" one.

On this conception people do not come to theory as an isolated entity in a world-vacuum: they come to it with experiences and views about facts and values. The character of the human organism is *not* such that relations between general propositions and system of general propositions are absolutely compartmentalized in the course of experience. This view does not at all contradict the formal one; nor does it deny the high worth of the formal view for some problems.

Basically and briefly, the situational view holds that the individual who confronts general theory is often possessed of a body of knowledges and values. When those values and knowledges are given a symbolic

---

[6]Harry S. Broudy, "How Philosophical Can Philosophy of Education Be?" *The Journal of Philosophy*, Vol. LII, No. 22 (Oct. 27, 1955), p. 617.
[7]Sidney Hook, *op. cit.*, p. 148.
[8]In addition to the remark quoted above, Professor Broudy notes that "Logically it may even be impossible to make anything more than plausible guesses because educational theory takes into account existential factors that have the brutishness of particulars *and do not necessarily follow from any principle*." (My italics.) Harry Broudy, *loc. cit.*

expression which can be connected for the effecting of logical process with theory, the possibility of logical derivation of further symbolic formulations becomes obvious.

Most people do the major part of their "connecting" without being aware of it: they are unaware that they bring anything to a general theory or proposition which allows the derivation of other propositions. If one were to ask a group of college students what implications the statement "All men are mortal" contains *within itself*, the students would in all probability say that it contains the implication that "I am mortal," "We are mortal," or, for the rare student who has had logic, "Socrates is mortal!" The question is illicit (since it assumes that there is an implication of the statement when taken alone); but the point is that the students probably would not realize that they had to supply and connect a second statement (e.g., "I am a man," "We are men," "Socrates is a man.") in order to get an implication.

If one assumes that the context and impetus for use of general theory are present, it is obvious that the consideration of theory *qua* theory, as in the formal view, is not at issue. Because they have worked in such a situation, educational philosophers are found pre-disposed to that assumption. Perhaps they are a little too much pre-disposed to the position that people should not ever approach theory as divorced from the context of empirical affairs, in which case there is a consequent loss of concern for purely formal analysis. And purely formal analysis is of vital importance.

II

On the basis of such an argument, one can say that the most general statements of metaphysics and epistemology do have implications for specific practices *if, and only if*, there is established a connection between them and statements of empirical practice which permits a valid process. There is, to be sure, still some reason to question the empirical usefulness of connections between metaphysical (say) tenets and descriptions of specific empirical events. The point here is merely that the connections can be made, and inference can proceed apace.

But a more important problem awaits. We need account for the fact that some connections of general theory with descriptions of specific practice are manifestly *better* connections than others. For instance, it is obvious that some of Dewey's pragmatism with conceptions of practice are patent misinterpretations of Dewey, practice, or both. Other connections apparently lead to complete adequacy. The question: Is *any* connection of a general theory and a description of specific empirical practice equally correct merely on the basis that a connection is established which admits of valid inference?

We can probably agree that the answer is No. We are as familiar with the poor usage of educational and philosophic theory in recent times as Shakespeare was with the fact that the Devil was one of those who could most often cite Scriptures in his own justification.

I will discuss only a few of the ways, and those but briefly, which appear to be highly relevant or necessary in the "correct" connection between theory and statements concerning empirical events. At the same time, it should be noted that it may be impossible to specify the sufficient conditions for adequate or "correct" connection—this for the reason that there seems to be something involved in the connection of theory to practice which is closely akin to the "inductive leap." The connection process appears to be more of an imaginative or psychological "art" than a strict, logical process. Having said these things, the discussion can turn to some of the things philosophers of education do which appear highly relevant to the effective application of formal philosophies to educational theory and practice.

First, and most obvious, a thorough acquaintance, depth- and breadthwise, with the general system being utilized is necessary. Even if a general philosophic system is never completely systematic, its general tenor and meaning can be fully understood only by grasping its conceptions in their interrelations, as well as with respect to their isolated characters. For instance, much damage has been done to the efficacy of Dewey's thought simply because some educators and laymen were satisfied to take a portion of his thought as entirely representative of the whole of it.

Second, it is especially important for educational philosophy that inquiry into theoretical systems be extended into the practical and "popular" writings of the people who formulate the theoretical systems. This is because the popular writings (and sometimes, of course, the formal philosophic writings) often contain the philosopher's conceptions of empirical situations which he himself takes to illustrate or sanction his general theory. In the practical or popular writings one finds not merely the "Master's" system, but his conception of how the system should be used in specific situations. Specifically, one finds highly suggestive examples. These examples are, of course, *mere* examples: they may even reveal themselves as being other than consonant with the Master's general theory. But they are often a source of suggestions which, if one is well-grounded in theory, indicate extensions of the theory's application and connection to practice that otherwise would not be had. Examples of this sort do not lay down *the* tantamount to affirmation that he who would be a good pragmatist (say) would be admonished simply or merely to "Believe on Dewey and His example!" Yet, for him who would be a good pragmatist, the admonition does have "something to it."

It is on the basis of their having fulfilled these two conditions that one can begin to explain why some of the most defensible and valuable contributions to certain philosophies have come from the followers of those movements, as well as from their initiators. Kant had the idea when he suggested that our ideal with Plato was that of coming to a better understanding of Plato than Plato had of himself!

Third, those educational philosophers who are acquainted with the generally accepted standards of theorizing are in a position to be critical in the study of a given philosophy itself. Such a critical perspective allows them to evaluate a philosophy in many aspects of its internal character, independently of its direct employment or relevance in empirical affairs. For instance, to be able to apply criteria of internal consistency, parsimony, and "fertility" and "primitiveness" of basic concepts is to be able to judge relatively well the likely worth of any philosophy which is a candidate for application to empirical practice.[9]

The fourth point. Our connections of theory and empirical practice are more likely to be consonant or correct when there is precise understanding of the data and conclusions of the tested theories of the sciences. This and a fifth point can be developed conjointly. The fifth point is that the most adequate connections are apt to be found with educational philosophies which are themselves generalized from tested conceptions of experience. Educational philosophy needs pay attention to the conditions for formulating theory which is based upon assertions concerning educational practice which are scientifically verified. Philosophy of education in the past seems to have held a sort of "trickle down" theory concerning the manner by which descriptions and directions for practice must be obtained; tacitly maintaining, that is, that the results of deductive elaboration which were deductively elaborated (trickled down) from formal philosophies would be all that would be needed for adequate description and prescription concerning educational practice. There is a lot to that position, since many philosophers in the grand manner of philosophy have been scientists or else highly cognizant of the theories of the sciences. But the trickle-down theory is hardly of worth if employed with respect to the ancient philosophers, unless corrections are made with respect to their scientific inadequacies. Consequently, the view or theory must be balanced by one which recognizes

─────────────

[9]It is obvious that philosophies are here being discussed as though they followed the pattern of the pure sciences in their theoretical structure. It is not easy to see that all of them do; but most of the traditionally "great" philosophic systems can be so treated.

that very little of worth is likely to be capable of derivation from a general philosophy if that philosophy itself is not framed or modified in the light of the most defensible, tested statements concerning empirical practice. Of course, there is no *necessary* reason why a theory generalized out of warranted or tested assertions about practice *must* be better than one formulated largely *a priori*. But it can be argued that the likelihood is that it will be better, if only because the concepts will have greater specificity of meaning when connected with statements regarding specific instances of empirical fact.

III

In summary, the view presented here is that:

First, one can utilize formal philosophy, including metaphysics and epistemology, in order to derive logical implications for educational theory and practice;

Second, this can be done by conceiving "logical implication" in a manner herein termed "situational," while for purposes other than those spoken of herein the "formal" conception of logical implication is adequate and necessary;

Third, central to the "situational" view is the problem of "connecting," which appears to be a non-logical (not illogical), imaginative process;

Fourth, there are conditions, but probably not sufficient ones, which can be specified for making connections with a general philosophic theory in order that effectiveness in applying the theory is increased—for example, the five conditions of (i) full knowledge of the philosophic theory being utilized; (ii) knowledge of the connections, if any, made by the formulator(s) of the general philosophic theory; (iii) knowledge and use of the tested theories of the sciences for understanding empirical reality; and (v) use of philosophic theory, when possible, which is generalized out of the tested conceptions of the sciences. (A sixth condition was stated which was not listed separately; *viz.*, that the symbolic formulations which are connected with philosophic theories utilize terminology which allows valid inference.)

Index

397